and the trials he endured. He warns of impending wolves in sheep's clothing, urging the elders to shepherd the flock with vigilance. Paul's primary focus is on the ethical principles that should guide the church. In fact, the speech is not merely a collection of ethical precepts; it is also a reflection of Paul's own life. He exemplifies the virtues he preaches, demonstrating the power of faith in action. His unwavering commitment to the gospel, his willingness to suffer for his beliefs, and his compassionate care for others inspire and challenge his listeners.

The ethical message of the Miletus speech is timeless. The speech's focus on Christological motivation underscores the centrality of faith and love in Christian life. Dr. Kizhakkeyil believes the Miletus speech speaks to the heart of every Christian, regardless of time or place. Paul's words remind us of the importance of living a life that is both righteous and compassionate. They challenge us to be stewards of the gifts we have been given, to use our resources wisely. It offers a timeless guide for Christians seeking to live a life that is pleasing to God and beneficial to others. By examining the speech's ethical emphases, we can gain a deeper understanding of Paul's teachings and the enduring principles that should guide our own lives.

Assisi Saldanha, C.Ss.R.
Biblist and Scripture Professor at St. Alphonsus Seminary, Bangalore and
St. Peter's Pontifical Institute, Bangalore

Wisdom Research Series - 9

Paul's Ethical Emphases in the Miletus Speech

A Theological Analysis of Acts 20:32–35

James Kizhakkeyil

Christian World Imprints

Wisdom Research Series: Dr. Thomas Karimundackal (Editor)
Papal Seminary, Pune (tomksj@gmail.com)

First Published in 2025 by

Christian World Imprints
Christian Publishing & Books from India
A-71 Group, Wazirpur Industrial Area
Delhi-110052
cwidelhi2017@gmail.com
www.ChristianWorldImprints.com
Phone: +91 11 41526079

ISBN: 978-93-6065-491-7

Printed in India.

Contents

Acknowledgements xi
Preface xiii
Abbreviations xv
General Introduction xxi
Delimitation xxii
Presuppositions xxii
Status Quaestionis xxiv
Originality of the Study and Statement of Arguments xxvi
Method of Research xxvii
Structure of this Book xxviii

Part 1: Preparing to Interpret the Ethical Emphases in Acts 20:32–35 1

Chapter 1: The Ethical Emphases of Ancient Farewell Speeches: 3
A Contextual Study 3
1.1. The Importance of a Contextual Study 3
1.2. The Greco-Roman Context of Speeches 5
1.2.1. The Classical Oratory 5
1.2.2. Rhetorical Speeches 6
1.2.2.1. Parts of a Rhetorical Speech 7
1.2.2.2. *Pathos* and *Ethos* in Rhetorical Persuasion 8
1.2.2.3. The Genres of Greco-Roman Rhetorical Speeches 8
1.2.2.3.1. Forensic Speeches 9
1.2.2.3.2. Epideictic Speeches 10
1.2.2.3.3. Deliberative Speeches 11
1.2.3. Genres and Ethics 12
1.2.4. Ethics in Greco-Roman Farewell Speeches 13
1.2.4.1. Homer, Illiad 6 14

1.2.4.2. Xenophon, Cyrus 8.7.6–28 15
1.2.4.3. Plato, Phaedo 15
1.2.4.4. Josephus, Jewish Antiquities. 12.6.3 (Mattathias) 15
1.2.4.5. Plutarch, Otho 15 16
1.2.4.6. Diogenes Laertius, Epicurus 10.16–18 17
1.3. Old Testament Background of Farewell Speeches 17
1.3.1. 1 Samuel 12:1–25 20
1.3.2. Tobit 14:3–11 21
1.3.3. Genesis 47:29–49:33 23
1.3.4. Deuteronomy 31–33 24
1.3.5. Joshua 23 24
1.3.6. 1 Kings 2:1–10 25
1.3.7. 1 Mac 2:49–70 26
1.4. Drawing a Comparison between Miletus Speech and Ancient Speeches 27
1.4.1. Xenophon 8.7.6–28 (Cyrus' Farewell Speech) and Miletus Speech 27
1.4.2. Homer, Illiad 6 (Hector's Farewell Speech to Andromache) and Miletus Speech 28
1.4.3. Samuel's Farewell Speech and Miletus Speech 28
1.4.4. Tobit's Farewell Speech and Miletus Speech 29
1.5. Concluding Remarks 30

Chapter 2: An Overview of the Pauline Speeches in Acts 31
2.1. Preliminary Observations 31
2.2. Some Important Features of Pauline Speeches in Acts 32
2.3. The Function of Pauline Speeches within the Narrative of Acts 35
2.3.1. An Overview of the Major Pauline Speeches 36
2.3.2. The Apologetic Function of Pauline Speeches 40
2.3.3. The Deliberative Function of the Pauline Speeches 43
2.4. The Miletus Speech of Paul within the Pauline Speeches 44
2.4.1. The Narrative Context of the Miletus Speech 44
2.4.2. The Nature of the Miletus Speech 44
2.4.3. The Ethical Character of the Miletus Speech 45

Part 2: The Ethical Emphases of the Miletus Speech: An Investigation into Acts 20:32–35 49

Chapter 3: Grace: A Gift Fundamental to Ethical Life 51
3.1. Preliminary Analysis of 20:32 51

3.2. The χάρις Motif 54
3.2.1. χάρις in Luke-Acts 57
3.2.2. χάρις in Paul 58
3.3. Grace as Power 60
3.3.1. Grace as Power in Luke-Acts 61
3.3.2. Grace as Power in the Pauline Letters 62
3.4. The "Operative Grace" 63
3.5. Grace: Affinity of Luke and Paul 64
3.6. Grace: The Requisite for Ethics and Morality 66

Chapter 4: Acts 20:33: Ethics of "Pure Intention" 69
4.1. Preliminary Observations of 20:33 69
4.1.1. The Objects of Greed in 20:33 71
4.2. Meaning and Attestation of "Greed" in the Scripture 72
4.2.1. ἐπιθυμία/, ἐπιθυμέω—Meaning 72
4.2.2. Usage of ἐπιθυμία/, ἐπιθυμέω in the LXX and Its Equivalent in the Hebrew Bible 73
4.2.3. The Use of ἐπιθυμία / ἐπιθυμέω in the NT 74
4.3. The Dangers of ἐπιθυμία / πλεονεξία in Luke-Acts 74
4.3.1. Greed Illustrated: Parables on Greed 75
4.3.2. Greed Condemned: Anecdotes on Greed 77
4.4. Condemnation of ἐπιθυμία / πλεονεξία in Paul 79
4.4.1. Rom 7:7: οὐκ ἐπιθυμήσεις 79
4.4.1.1. Old Testament Background for οὐκ ἐπιθυμήσεις in Paul 80
4.5. Desire: Action or Intention? 85

Chapter 5: Acts 20:34: Ethics of Manual Labor 87
5.1. Initial Comments on 20:34 88
5.2. Work in General: Scriptural Evidences 89
5.3. Scriptural Foundation for the Labor Ethics of Paul 91
5.3.1. Biblical Notion and Precepts 91
5.3.1.1. Torah, Historical, and Prophetical Books 91
5.3.1.2. Wisdom Books 93
5.3.1.2.1. Book of Proverbs 94
5.3.1.2.2. Book of Qohelet 94
5.3.1.2.3. Book of Sirach 94
5.3.2. The Example and Teachings of Jesus 94
5.3.3. Greco-Roman Influence 95
5.3.4. Jewish Practice and Family Upbringing 97

5.4. "I Worked with My Own Hands": The Work Ethics of Paul 98
5.4.1. New Testament Attestation Regarding Paul's Manual Work 98
5.4.1.1. First Corinthians 4:12 98
5.4.1.2. First Corinthians 9 99
5.4.1.3. Second Corinthians 11:23, 27 100
5.4.1.4. First Thessalonians 2:9 100
5.4.1.5. Acts 18:3 101
5.4.2. Pauline Teaching Regarding Manual Work 102
5.4.2.1. Ephesians 4:28 102
5.4.2.2. First Thessalonians 4:11–12 103
5.4.2.3. Second Thessalonians 3:6–13 104
5.4.3. "To Support Myself and My Companions": Primary Goal of Paul's Work 105

Chapter 6: Acts 20:35 A: Paul as an Ethical Model 109
6.1. "In All this I Have Given You an Example" (v. 35a): Preliminary Notes 110
6.2. The Use of Examples and its Importance in the Greco-Roman World 110
6.2.1. The Power of Examples in Ethical Exhortation 111
6.3. Goal of the Use of Examples in the Scriptures 112
6.3.1. In the LXX 112
6.3.2. In the New Testament 113
6.4. Paul and the Ethics of Imitation 114
6.4.1. Ancients' Concept of Imitation 114
6.4.2. The Concept of Imitation According to Paul 115
6.4.2.1. Paul as a τύπος 116
6.4.2.2. μιμέομαι and μιμητής in Paul and Pauline Traditions 116
6.4.2.2.1. "For You Became Imitators of the Churches of God": 1 Thessalonians 2:14 118
6.4.2.2.2. "Join in Imitating Me": Philippians 3:17 120
6.4.2.2.3. "I Urge You, then, Be Imitators of 121
Me": 1 Cor 4:16 121
6.4.2.2.4. "Become as I Am": Gal 4:12 122
6.4.2.2.5. "Be Imitators of God": Eph 5:1 122
6.4.3. Christological Dimension of Imitation 123

6.5. Paul as a Model of Charity: The Collection for Jerusalem 123
6.5.1. The Ethics of the Jerusalem Collection 124
6.5.1.1. The Manner of the Collection 125
6.5.1.2. Interpretative Views on the Collection 126
6.5.1.3. Pauline Terms for the Collection 127
6.5.1.3.1. κοινωνία 127
6.5.1.3.2. χάρις 128
6.5.1.3.3. λογεία, and εὐλογία 129
6.5.1.3.4. διακονία 129
6.5.1.3.5. ἐλεημοσύνη 129
6.5.1.4. Purpose of the Collection 129
6.5.1.4.1. Ethical and Moral 130
6.5.1.4.1.1. An Act of Christian Charity 130
6.5.1.4.2. Reciprocal 131
6.5.1.4.3. Communitarian 132
6.6. Paul as a Model for the Second-Generation Christians 133

Chapter 7: Acts 20:35: Ethics of Giving 137
7.1. Introductory Comments on Acts 20:35 137
7.1.1. The Use of δεῖ in Acts 20:35 138
7.2. The Climactic Maxim (20:35b) as a Fitting Aphorism 140
7.2.1. Ancients' Use of Maxims and Acts 20:35 140
7.2.2. Purpose and Implications of the Use of the Maxim in 20:35 143
7.3. Giving: An Important Lucan Theme 145
7.3.1. Background for ἀντιλαμβάνομαι τῶν ἀσθενούντων and the Motif of Giving 146
7.3.1.1. Greco-Roman Background 146
7.3.1.2. LXX Background 148
7.3.1.2.1. Torah Stipulations 149
7.3.1.2.2. Prophetic Exhortations 151
7.3.1.2.3. Wisdom Books 151
7.3.2. ἀντιλαμβάνεσθαι τῶν ἀσθενούντων and the Giving Motif in the Lucan Writings 152
7.3.2.1. Giving Motif in the Lucan Writings 152
7.3.2.1.1. Giving Motif in the Gospel of Luke 152
7.3.2.1.1.1. In Chapters 1–9 152

7.3.2.1.1.2. In the "Central Section" 154
7.3.2.1.1.3. Jesus Ministry in Jerusalem 158
7.3.2.1.2. Motif of Giving in Acts 159
7.4. Ethics of Giving in the Pauline Writings 160
7.5. From Ethical Concern to Moral Obligation 164

Part 3: Theological Ethics, Ethical Concerns, and Prospects of Acts 20:32–35 167

Chapter 8: Interplay of Theology and Ethics in the Miletus Speech 169
8.1. The Purpose of the Miletus Speech 169
8.1.1. Transfer of Authority and Mission through Commissioning 169
8.1.2. To Highlight the Importance of Paul 172
8.1.3. To Provide a Pastoral Testament and Testimony 176
8.1.4. Apology for Paul 178
8.1.5. Deliberative Purpose 179
8.2. Normative Function of the Figure of Paul 182
8.3. Lucan Paul's Imperative as a Moral Duty 184
8.4. Ethics of Poverty and Riches 185

Chapter 9: Ethical Vision and Implications of Acts 20:32–35 189
9.1. Let Grace be the Guiding Force 189
9.2. Leaders Must Have Pure Intentions 191
9.3. A Call to Generous Giving 192
9.4. A Call to Christian Responsibility 202
9.5. Imitation of Jesus and the Saints 204
9.6. Uphold the Dignity of all Labor and Laborers 205
9.6.1. Importance and Dignity of Manual Labor 206
9.6.2. Dignity of Laborers 207

General Conclusion 213
Bibliography 219

Acknowledgements

This book, a revised and edited version of my Doctoral Dissertation submitted to the Pontifical University of St. Thomas Aquinas (PUST), popularly known as *Angelicum*, is a testament to the grace I have received from God and the invaluable support of numerous individuals.

I am profoundly grateful to Prof. Massimo de Santis, my thesis mentor, for his friendly guidance, invaluable suggestions, wholehearted support, and scholarly insights. His contributions have been instrumental, and I thank him deeply.

I extend my heartfelt thanks to all the professors and staff at PUST and PBI for their support throughout my academic journey.

I also wish to acknowledge those who directly or indirectly contributed to the successful completion of this book. I owe a special debt of gratitude to Cardinal Joseph Tobin, then Superior General of the C.Ss.R., for sponsoring my stay in Rome during my Licentiate studies at Biblicum. I am also deeply grateful to the Roman Province, whose sponsorship made my doctoral studies possible. I am also grateful to the current and former Provincials of the Liguori Province, as well as all my confreres and friends worldwide, for their interest in my work and studies.

A special thank you to Fr. Assisi Saldanha C.Ss.R., who, despite his busy schedule, took the time to review the draft of this book and offered valuable suggestions.

Lastly, I am grateful for the love and support of my relatives and friends. I fondly remember my beloved mother, Mary, who was called to eternal rest midway through the writing of this book. To her, who imparted to me the greatest moral lessons of life, I dedicate this book.

James Kizhakkeyil, C.Ss.R.

Acknowledgements

Preface

One of the decisions of the 25th General Chapter (2016) of the Congregation of the Most Holy Redeemer (C.Ss.R), of which I am a member, is to treat moral theology as a priority and a common apostolate of the Congregation. This decision of the Chapter inspired me to research on a passage from the Bible that is closely related to moral science. Moreover, current Biblical studies engage increasingly in determining and specifying ethical or moral values both overt and hidden in a Biblical text.

Everything that Luke wanted to communicate to the Ephesian elders is realized through the figure of Paul, the speaker and the main protagonist of Luke's story in Acts 20:18–35. This thesis attempts to uncover the theological, ethical, and moral emphases and visions of Paul's speech delivered at Miletus. In addition, it will also elucidate the close theological and ethical ties Luke shared with Paul. Nevertheless, the main thrust of the thesis concerns the ethical paraenesis of Lucan Paul.

By the grace of God the writing of this book was smooth, although there were moments of difficulties and quandary especially at those junctures when Biblical texts had to be specifically related to and seen through the spectrum of ethics and morality. For this reason, there are limitations to this book as I had to omit a detailed study of certain points related to moral theology. Nevertheless, I believe the book achieves its aim, which is that of giving due emphasis to an ethical and moral reading of a Biblical text.

Abbreviations

AB	Anchor Bible Commentary
ABD	*Anchor Bible Dictionary*
AcOr	*Acta Orientalia*
AJutT	Acta Jutlandica Theologisk Serie
ALGHJ	Arbeiten zur Literatur und Geschichte des Hellenistischen Judentums
ANF	*The Ante-Nicene Fathers*
ANTC	Abington New Testament Commentaries
AYBC	Anchor Yale Bible Commentaries
BAFCS	*The Book of Acts in its First Century Setting*
BCE	Before the Common Era
BDAG	Bauer, W., F. W. Danker, W. F. Arndt, and F. W. Gingrich, *A Greek-English Lexicon of the New Testament and Other Early Christian Literature.* 3rd ed. Chicago, 2000.
BDB	F. Brown, S. R. Driver, and C. A. Briggs, *A Hebrew and English Lexicon of the Old Testament*, Oxford, 1952
BDF	F. W. Blass, A. Debrunner, *A Greek Grammar of the New Testament and Other Early Christian Literature*, translated and revised R. W. Funk, Chicago, 1961
BECNT	Baker Exegetical Commentary on the New Testament
BEThL	Bibliotheca Ephemeridum Theologicarum Lovaniensium
Bib	*Biblica*
BiBh	*Bible Bhashyam*
BT(N)	Bibliothèque Théologique (Neuchatel)
CBQ	*Catholic Biblical Quarterly*
CBR	*Currents in Biblical Research*
CCC	Catechism of the Catholic Church
CE	Common Era
Cf.	*Confere* (compare)

Ch. / Chs.	Chapter / Chapters
CRINT	Compendia Rerum Iudaicarum ad Novum Testamentum
CUA	Catholic University of America
DMT	*Dictionary of Moral Theology*
DNTD	Das Neue Testament Deutsch
DOTHB	*Dictionary of Old Testament. Historical Books*
DOTP	*Dictionary of Old Testament. Pentateuch*
DOTWPW	*Dictionary of Old Testament. Wisdom, Poetry, and Writings*
DPL	*Dictionary of Paul and His Letters*
DR	*Downside Review*
EBS	Ecumenical Biblical Studies
EDNT	Exegetical Dictionary of the New Testament
EHS.T	Europäische Hochschulschriften.Theologie
EJ	*Encyclopedia Judaica*
Enc.	*Encyclopedia*
Eng.	England
ET	*Expository Time*
Exp	*Expositor, The*
Frg.	Fragment
Fs.	*Festschrift* (in honor of)
GS	*Gaudium et Spes*
GTA	Göttingen Theologische Arbeiten
Herm.	Hermeneia
HTR	*Harvard Theological Review*
HUCA	*Hebrew Union College Annual*
HUTh	Hermeneutische Untersuchungen zur Theologie
ICC	International Critical Commentary
IntB	Interpreter's Bible, The
Interp.	*Interpretation*
Interp.	Interpretation, Resources for the Use of Scripture in the Church
Interpr.	Interpretation. A Bible Commentary for Teaching and Preaching
ITS	*Indian Theological Studies*
IVPNTC	InterVarsity Press New Testament Commentary
JAOS	*Journal of American Oriental Society*
JBL	*Journal of Biblical Literature*
JSJ	*Journal for the Study of Judaism*
JSNT	*Journal for the Study of the New Testament*
JSNTS	Journal for the Study of the New Testament Supplement Series
JSOTS	Journal for the Study of the Old Testament Supplement Series

JSPL	*Journal for the Study of Paul and his Letters*
KEK	Kritisch-Exegetischer Komentar uber das Neue Testament
KJV	King James Version of the English Bible
LABC	Life Application Bible Commentary
LCL	Loeb Classical Library
LE	*Laborem Exercens*
LeDiv	Lectio Divina
LG	*Lumen Gentium*
LNTS	Library of New Testament Studies
LTE	Library of Theological Ethics
LXX	Septuagint (= Greek)
Mish.	Mishnah
Aboth	Aboth
Ḳidd.	Ḳiddushin
MissTod	*Mission Today*
MM	*Mater et Magistra*
ms(s)	*manuscriptum* (manuscript[s])
MT	Masoretic Text
NAC	The New American Commentary
NAS	The New American Standard Bible, 1977
Neot	*Neotestamentica*
NIB	*New Interpreters Bible, The*
NIBC	The New International Bible Commentary
NICOT	The New International Commentary on the Old Testament
NICNT	The New International Commentary on the New Testament
NJB	The New Jerusalem Bible, 1985
NPNF	*Nicene and Post Nicene Fathers*
NRSV	New Revised Standard Version, (of the Holy Bible)
NT	*Novum Testamentum*
NTD	Das Neue Testament Deutsch
NTS	*New Testament Studies*
NTSup	Novum Testamentum Supplements
PIB	Pontificio Istituto Biblico
PNTC	Pillar New Testament Commentary
PP	*Populorum Progressio*
PSV	Parola Spirito e Vita
PUST	Pontifical University of St. Thomas Aquinas
QA	*Quadragesimo Anno*
RCS	Religion and Culture Series
RivBib	*Rivista Biblica*
RN	*Rerum Novarum*
RTM	*Rivista di Teologia Morale*

SANT	Studien Zum Alten und Neuen Testament
SBL	Society of Biblical Literature
SBLBMI	Society of Biblical Literature The Bible and Its Modern Interpreters
SBLDS	Society of Biblical Literature Dissertation Series
SBLMS	Society of Biblical Literature Monograph Series
SBLSP	Society of Biblical Literature Seminar Papers
SBLSPS	Society of Biblical Literature Seminar Papers Series
SBLSymS	Society of Biblical Literature Symposium Series
SBT	Studies in Biblical Theology
SCA	Studies in Christian Antiquity
SNT	Studien zum Neuen Testament
SNTU	Studien zum Neuen Testament und seiner Umwelt
SNTSMS	Society for New Testament Studies Monograph Series
ST	Studies in Theology (series)
ST	*Summa Theologica*
SUNT	Studien zur Umwelt des Neuen Testaments
SVTP	Studia in Veteri Testamenti Psuedephigrapha
TDNT	Kittel, G. and Friedrich, G., ed., *Theological Dictionary of the New Testament*, vols. 1–10, Grand Rapids: 1964–76 (English version of *TWNT*)
Test.	Testament
Test. Iss.	Testament of Issachar, The
Test. Jos	Testament of Joseph, The
Test. Jud.	Testament of Judah, The
TynB	*Tyndale Bulletin*
WBC	The Word Biblical Commentary
WUNT	Wissenschaftliche Untersuchungen zum Neuen Testament
ZNW	Zeitschrift fur die Neutestamentliche Wissenschaft

Ancient Greco-Roman Authors and Writings

Ap. Rhod.	Appollonius Rhodius
Arist.	Aristotle
NE	*Nicomachean Ethics*
Pol.	*Politica*
Rh.	*Rhetoric*
Rh. ad Ale.	*Rhetorica ad Alexandrum*
Rh. ad Her.	*Rhetorica ad Herennium*
Cic.	Cicero
De Inv.	De Inventione
De Off.	De Officiis
De Or.	De Oratore

Or.	Orationes
Part. Or.	Partitiones Oratoriae
Rh. ad Her.	Rhetorica ad Herennium
Tusc. Dis.	Tusculanae Disputationes
Clem.	Clement
Controv.	*Controversiae*
Dem.	Demosthenes
Demo.	Democritus
Did.	*Didache*
Dio Cass.	Dio Cassius
Dio Chry.	Dio Chrysostom
De Phil	De Philosophia
Eub.	Euboicus
Or.	Orationes
Diod.	Diodorus Siculus
Diog. Laer.	Diogenes Laertius
Epic.	Epicurus
Dion.	Dionysius of Halicarnassus
Ant. Rom.	Antiquitates Romanae
Isa.	Isaeus
Epict.	Epictetus
Diatr.	*Diatribe*
Gall. W.	*Gallic War*, The
Hermog.	Hermogenes of Tarsus
Progymn.	*Progymnasmata*
Herod.	Herodotus
Hist.	The Histories
Hom.	Homer
Il.	Illiad
Isoc.	Isocrates
Anti.	*Antidosis*
Evag.	Evagoras
Nic.	Nicocles
Jos.	Josephus
Ant.	Antiquities of the Jews
War	The Jewish War
Luc.	Lucian
Somn.	Somnium sive Vita Luciani
Tox.	Toxaris
Lys.	Lysias
Mus. Ruf.	Musonius Rufus
Frg.	Fragments

Plato

Gorg.	*Gorgias*
Rep.	*Republic*
Phaed.	Phaedrus
Pliny Ep.	The Epistles of Pliny
Plut.	Plutarch
Alex.	Alexander
Dem.	Demosthenes
De vit. aer. al.	De vitando aere alieno
Mor.	Moralia
Per.	Pericles
Ps. Isoc.	Pseudo Isocrates
Demo.	Demonicus
Quint.	Quintilian
Inst.	Institutio Oratoria
Rh. Alex.	Rhetorica ad Alexandrum
Sen.	Seneca
Ep.	Epistulae
Sen. Y.	Seneca the Younger
Ep. Lucil.	Epistulae Morales ad Lucilium
De Benef.	De Beneficiis
Tac.	Tacitus
Ann.	*Annals*
Hist.	*Historiae*
Thuc.	Thucydides
Xen.	Xenophon
Cyr.	*Cyropaedia*
Oec.	*Oeconomicus*

General Introduction

A few decades ago Willem C. van Unnik stated that Luke-Acts is one of the great storm centers of New Testament scholarship.[1] The truth of van Unnik's statement has been verified by recent research on Luke-Acts which is on the cutting-edge of Biblical theology and exegesis. These studies demonstrate that Luke-Acts are both fascinating and relevant for the modern world. They enable Biblical scholars to extract more from the NT texts and to demonstrate their relevance for today's Christians. It could be said that the Lucan materials are the most relevant and challenging work ever written. Their social orientation makes them particularly significant to both the religious and the secular world.

One of the vastly researched topics in Acts is the speeches given by various characters like Peter, Stephen, Paul, and others. In a recent study Marion L. Soards has identified thirty-six speeches in the Book of Acts delivered by various individuals.[2] Although all speeches contain some ethical elements, the Miletus speech conveys the most ethical message of all. This speech can be considered as the most important segment of Acts since it is presented at the climactic point of Paul's public ministry in Ephesus.[3] It would be a colossal task to uncover and elaborate all the theological and ethical elements in the speech; consequently we limit this study only to its final four verses. Nevertheless, other important ethical considerations of the speech may be indicated or explained in the course of this study as the context requires.

---

[1] Willem C. van Unnik, "Luke-Acts, a Storm Center in Contemporary Scholarship," in *Studies in Luke-Acts*, Leander E. Keck and J. Louis Martyn, ed. (London: SPCK, 1968), 16.

[2] Marion L. Soards, *The Speeches in Acts: Their Content, Context, and Concerns* (Louisville, KY: John Knox, 1994), 21–22. Soards' numbering is exaggerated, as he included even brief instructions or exhortations given by individuals in the list of speeches.

[3] Craig S. Keener, *Acts: An Exegetical Commentary*, vol. 3, *15:1–23:35* (Grand Rapids: Baker Academics, 2014), 2946. More on this idea will be presented in a later chapter.

Delimitation

The selection of the final four verses of the speech (20:32–35) for this thesis requires some explanation. One can easily observe that the Miletus speech proper begins at v. 18b and ends at v. 35. The phrases, "ὡς δὲ παρεγένοντο πρὸς αὐτὸν εἶπεν αὐτοῖς" at 18a and "καὶ ταῦτα εἰπὼν" at v. 36, demarcate vv. 18b–35 as a segment, which we call the Miletus speech. This speech may be broadly divided into three segments referring to the past (18b–21), present (22–28, 32–35), and future (29–31).[4] In all three segments one can notice various ethical elements, but the final verses appear to be highly ethical in content. The distinguishing feature of these verses is that they are exhortations given on various subjects.

There are three criteria for the selection of these verses. The first criterion is based on philology. καὶ τὰ νῦν at v. 32 begins a new thought. On the basis of what has been said up to this point, the listeners are entrusted to the grace of God so that they model their behavior and conduct themselves as persons of grace after the manner of the speaker himself and their supreme model, Jesus Christ. Second, the exhortations given here are inherently linked with the 'word of His grace.' In other words, grace is the *sine qua non* for the performance of any ethical act, especially supporting the weak, by labor and generous giving. And third, the preceding verses (29–31) are an exhortation to future vigilance against "fierce wolves,"[5] but the *tempus* changes into the present in v. 32. "Now" they are being instructed and commissioned for a greater task. All that they have to attend to is emphatically presented in vv. 32–35. Therefore, we take vv. 32–35 as a specifically ethical segment.

Presuppositions

Before we proceed, certain terms and concepts need clarification. The present study presupposes the author of the Gospel of Luke (or the Third Gospel) and Acts of the Apostles (henceforth referred to as "Acts") to be "Luke the physician," a travelling companion of Paul as mentioned in Col 4:14; 2 Tim 4:11; and Philm 1:24. It is not my intention to reexamine the identity of the author of Luke-Acts, since it has long been accepted that Luke is indeed the author of both the Third Gospel and Acts. Therefore, following Henry

[4] A threefold division of the speech was already suggested by Ernst Hänchen. See *The Acts of the Apostles: A Commentary* (Oxford: Basil Blackwell, 1971), 526. There is no consensus among scholars on the division of the speech. For example, Jan Lambrecht takes vv. 28–35 as exhortations and warnings to the elders in "Paul's Farewell Address at Miletus: Acts 20:17–38," in *Les Actes des Apôtres: Traditions, rédaction, théologie*, Gembloux–Duculot, J. ed. (Leuven University Press, Year unknown), 316. Keener treats vv. 28–32 as warnings to guard the flock. See *Acts*, 3:3029 ff.

[5] All the translated words, phrases, and verses of the Bible appear in this thesis are from the NRSV unless otherwise stated.

J. Cadbury,[6] whenever mention is made together of the Gospel of Luke and Acts, I use the term "Luke-Acts."

Second, it is our presumption that Acts is an apologetic historiography. There have been attempts to view it as a "travel narrative,"[7] or a "novel,"[8] or a "biography,"[9] or "epic"[10] of some leading figures in the early church. The reasons for and against situating Acts in any of the above genres are often compelling. But to view Acts as an apologetic historiography, a "Gospel of the disciples," written with specific theological motives, is more reasonable.[11] Moreover, Acts is closer in style and content to Hellenistic Jewish histories, which were mostly apologetic, than to extant Greco-Roman histories.[12]

Third, we presuppose that Acts was composed after the formulation of the Gospel of Luke. Though some scholars have argued an early date for

---

[6] *The Making of Luke-Acts* (London: Macmillan, 1927), 8.

[7] For example, Wilfred L. Knox, *Acts of the Apostles* (Cambridge: University Press, 1948) suggested Acts' genre as travel narrative.

[8] E.g., Richard I. Pervo, *Profit with Delight: The Literary Genre of the Acts of the Apostles* (Philadelphia, PA: Fortress Press, 1987); and Susan M. Praeder, "Luke-Acts and the Ancient Novel," in *SBL Seminar Papers 1981* (Chico, CA: Scholars Press, 1981), 169–292 compare Acts with ancient novels.

[9] E.g., Richard Burridge, *What are the Gospels? A Comparison with Greco-Roman Biography* (Grand Rapids: Eerdmans, 2004); and G. H. R. Horsley, "Speeches and Dialogues in Acts," *NTS* 32.4 (1986), 613.

[10] E.g., Marianne P. Bonz, *The Past as Legacy: Luke Acts and Ancient Epic* (Minneapolis: Fortress Press, 200); and Dennis R. MacDonald, *Does the New Testament Imitate Homer?: Four Cases from the Acts of the Apostles* (New Haven: Yale University, 2003).

[11] Keener studied the genre of Acts and concludes that Acts fits best in the genre of apologetic historiography. See Craig S. Keener, *Acts: An Exegetical Commentary*, vol. 1, *Introduction and 1:1–2:47* (Grand Rapids: Baker Academics, 2012), 51. For a detailed presentation of Acts as a work of ancient historiography see pp. 90–115. He also mentions various authors who attribute to Acts different genres such as novel, epic, travel narrative, "acts," etc. For a detailed presentation of various genres, see pp. 53–89. In addition to Keener authors such as Thomas E. Phillips and Gregory E. Sterling view Acts as apologetic historiography. See Thomas E. Phillips "The Genre of Acts: Moving towards a Consensus?" *CBR* 4 (2006), 365–96; and Gregory E. Sterling, *Historiography and Self-Definition: Josephus, Luke-Acts and Apologetic Historiography*, NTSup 64 (Leiden: Brill, 1992).

[12] Examples of Greco-Roman Histories are Herodotus, Thucydides, Xenophon, Polybius, Dionysius of Halicarnassus. See Oswald Padilla, *The Speeches of Outsiders in Acts: Poetics, Theology, and Historiography* (Cambridge: University Press, 2008), 3.

Acts,[13] the majority consider it as a post 70 CE work and as a sequel to the Gospel.[14]

Fourth, it is our supposition that the letters attributed to Paul come in two groups: one written by Paul himself (proto-Pauline letters) and the others by Christian disciples who are familiar with Paul and Pauline traditions (deutero-Pauline/sub-Pauline letters). Acts is the only non-epistolary book that transmits elements of the Pauline tradition. Thus, in this thesis we will be referring repeatedly to proto-Pauline and deutero-Pauline materials/traditions.

Status Quaestionis

Though numerous scholars have written extensively on the speeches in Acts, to my knowledge none has produced a scholarly work elaborating the ethical emphases and moral significance of the Miletus speech. The works of Jaques Dupont, *Le Discourse de Milet: Testament Pastoral de Saint Paul (Actes 20:18–36);*[15] Hans J. Michel, *Die Abschiedsrede des Paulus an die Kirche: Apg 20:17–38: Motivgeschichte und Theologische Bedeutung,*[16] and Steve Walton, *Leadership and Lifestyle: The Portrait of Paul in the Miletus Speech and 1 Thessalonians*[17] are monographs which attempt to understand and explain the Miletus speech from different angles. But the ethical elements of the speech have not been a main concern for these authors. In addition to the above-mentioned scholars, Ernst Hänchen,[18] Jan Lambrecht,[19] Thomas M.

[13] E.g., E. R. Goodenough, "Perspective of Acts," in *Studies in Luke-Acts: Essays in Honor of Paul Schubert,* Leander E. Keck and J. Louis Martyn, ed. (London: SPCK, 1968), 58; Frederick F. Bruce, *The Acts of the Apostles: The Greek Text with Introduction and Commentary* (London: Tyndale Press, 1951), 10–14; Colin J. Hemer, *The Book of Acts in the Setting of Hellenistic History,* WUNT 49 (Tübingen: Mohr Siebeck, 1989), 365–410.

[14] E.g., Ben Witherington, *The Acts of the Apostles: A Socio-Rhetorical Commentary* (Grand Rapids: Eerdmans, 1998), 61. He also suggests that Luke's priority was to make the Gospel reaching Rome, the hub of the empire, see p. 807. Scholars like Adolf Von Harnack (*The Acts of the Apostles,* J. R. Wilkinson, trans., London: Williams & Norgate, 1909, pp. 290–97), and Keener, 1:400–401 proposes a post 70 date for Acts. For a survey on various dating of Acts see Richard I. Pervo, *Dating Acts: Between the Evangelists and the Apologists* (Santa Rosa, CA: Polebridge Press, 2006), 359–63.

[15] LeDiv 32 (Paris: Cerf, 1962).

[16] SANT 35 (München: Kösel Verlag, 1973).

[17] SNTSMS 108 (Cambridge: University Press, 2000).

[18] *The Acts of the Apostles: A Commentary.*

[19] "Paul's Farewell Address at Miletus: Acts 20:17–38."

Budesheim,[20] Duane F. Watson[21] Collin J. Hemer,[22] Charles K. Barrett,[23] Evald Lövestam,[24] Marion L. Soards,[25] Ben Witherington,[26] Beverly R. Gaventa,[27] Craig S. Keener[28] and others[29] have contributed different perspectives to the study of the speech. We will be returning to these authors at various junctures of this thesis. The exhortatory character of the speech, especially of vv. 32–35, has been detected by many scholars such as Charles. K. Barrett, Hans Conzelman,[30] Joseph A. Fitzmyer,[31] Ben Witherington, Robert C. Tannehill,[32] Charles H. Talbert,[33] Darrell L. Bock,[34] C. S. Keener and others. Within the exhortatory framework, the ethical thrust of the passage has been particularly noted by Lambrecht,[35] Hemer,[36] William J. Larkin,[37] and Keener.[38] Since none of these scholars has engaged exclusively in a study of the ethical or moral

---

[20] "Paul's Abschiedsrede in the Acts of the Apostles," *HTR* 69 (1976), 9–30.

[21] "Paul's Speech to the Ephesian Elders (Acts 20:17–38): Epideictic Rhetoric of Farewell," in *Persuasive Artistry: Studies in New Testament Rhetoric in Honor of George A. Kennedy*, Duane F. Watson, ed., JSNTS 50 (Sheffield: Academic Press, 1991), 184–208.

[22] "The Speeches of Acts: I. The Ephesian Elders at Miletus," *TynB* 40.1 (1989), 77–85.

[23] "Paul's Address to the Ephesian Elders," in *God's Christ and His People: Studies in Honor of Nils Alstrup Dahl*, Jacob Jervell and Wayne A. Meeks, ed. (Oslo; Bergen-Tromsö: Universitetforlaget, 1977), 107–21.

[24] "Paul's Address at Miletus," *ST* 41 (1987), 1–10.

[25] *The Speeches in Acts.*

[26] *The Acts of the Apostles,* 610–27.

[27] "Theology and Ecclesiology in the Miletus Speech: Reflections on Content and Context," *NTS* 50 (2004), 36–52.

[28] *Acts*, 3:2992–3067.

[29] Keener refers on a number of occasions to T. C. Alexander's PhD thesis "Paul's Final Exhortation to the Elders from Ephesus: The Rhetoric of Acts 20:17–38" (Emory University, 1990). I could not access the dissertation to view the contribution he has made.

[30] *Die Apostelgeschichte* (Tübingen: Mohr Siebeck, 1972).

[31] *The Acts of the Apostles: A New Translation with Introduction and Commentary* (New York: Doubleday, 1998).

[32] Robert C. Tannehill, *The Narrative Unity of Luke-Acts: A Literary Interpretation,* vol. 2, *The Acts of the Apostles* (Philadelphia, PA: Fortress Press, 1986).

[33] Charles H. Talbert, *Reading Acts: A Literary and Theological Commentary on the Acts of the Apostles* (New York: Crossroad, 1997).

[34] *Acts*, BECNT (Grand Rapids: Baker Academics, 2007).

[35] Lambrecht, "Paul's Farewell Address," 316.

[36] According to Hemer ("The Speeches of Acts," 81) this speech is exhortatory. It is the only speech in Acts that has a strong moral tone.

[37] William J. Larkin, *Acts*, IVPNTCS (Downers Grove: InterVarsity Press, 1995), 297, 299.

[38] Keener, Acts, 3:2995.

aspects of the speech, their investigations of other non-ethical details do not necessarily require comments.

Originality of the Study and Statement of Arguments

As narrated in Acts, towards the end of the third missionary journey of Paul, Luke makes Paul to deliver the Miletus speech. Since it was customary at that period for orators to deliver speeches and for writers to include speeches in their works, Luke follows a similar strategy. Acts is replete with speeches that served the same purpose which the contemporary orators and writers achieved through them. Therefore, speeches in Acts are to be evaluated generally against their Greco-Roman and Jewish counterparts; so also, the Miletus speech. As this is the only speech in Acts delivered to an exclusively Christian audience, it must be studied in comparison with other major speeches of Acts. Compared to other material and speeches in Acts, the Miletus speech is similar to the Pauline Letters (including the deutero-Pauline Letters) in its theological and paraenetic character. Thus, this thesis will provide a brief study of "Paulinism"[39] in Acts to provide a closer understanding of the theological and/or ethical discussions in the final verses of the speech. The major contribution of this thesis will be its examination of the use and function of Acts 20:32–35 as ethical exhortations of Lucan Paul. It will demonstrate how they fit into the overall theology of Luke and Paul and what they demand from present-day Christians and Christian leaders.

As noted above, a number of scholars have pointed out in passing the exhortatory, ethical, and moral character of the speech, especially of Acts 20:32–35. To my knowledge, however, to date the ethical emphases of these verses have not been a subject of in-depth scrutiny. Towards the end of the farewell discourse, Paul exhorts the elders of Ephesus to imitate his own example of labor and charity and to be faithful to the words of Jesus. This involves a program of supporting "the weak." I will argue that, in line with the socio-theological concerns expressed by Luke, Paul's personal example and his exhortations given here are intended to instill a social concern, thus contributing greatly to social ethics, particularly to Christian ethics of labor and giving.

At this point, I must make reference to three crucial works: a book edited by Charles E. Curran and Richard A. McCormick[40] and two monographs, one by Richard. B. Hays[41] and another by Elizabeth Schüssler

[39] The word "Paulinism" refers to the theological ideas of Paul found in Acts.

[40] See The Use of Scripture in Moral Theology (New York: Paulist Press, 1984).

[41] See *The Moral Vision of the New Testament: Community, Cross, New Creation. A Contemporary Introduction to New Testament Ethics* (San Francisco: Harper San Francisco, 1996).

Fiorenza.[42] The first book contains studies by various authors concerning the importance of Scripture in the realm of ethics and morality. They show that among its various functions, sacred scripture serves as a textbook of ethics and morality for Christians. Though it is true that the Bible is much more than a moral or ethical textbook, all Christian ethical discussions begin from the Bible. Moreover, many books of the Bible (or segments of it) are ethical throughout and offer values or suggest courses of action. Accordingly, we will examine what values or courses of action the Miletus speech sets before the reader of Acts. Richard Hays in his book suggests four tasks of the NT ethics[43] of which the hermeneutic and pragmatic tasks are crucial and directly related to ethical praxis.[44] Finally, Fiorenza suggests that, instead of viewing scripture only as an external authority, or historico-critically or symbolically, an awareness of the public-political responsibility of Biblical scholarship is necessary to understand it as communicative praxis.[45] This paradigm inaugurates a "rhetorical-ethical turn" in hermeneutics. In essence, it involves a "communicative practice of values, interests and visions." Our investigation of the selected passage will be based on this "rhetorical-ethical turn" in hermeneutics which has become a springboard for modern communicative praxis. In a Christian context, ethics is the prerogative, since it is only by living Christian values that one is truly Christian; all else is secondary. For that reason, we will determine which values, interests, and visions Lucan Paul communicated through the Miletus speech.

Method of Research

The approach to this study is synchronic and theological-ethical. It is synchronic inasmuch as it analyses the text as it has been transmitted to us and it takes into account those themes, structures, and words that have an exegetical importance. It is theological-ethical since, by applying hermeneutics, we seek to grasp the meaning of the text through verbal and thematic investigations, and then interpret its theological and ethical implications. The impact of the Bible on countless readers throughout the centuries is known to the world. Its interpretation has crucial theological and ethical implications. For instance, Daniel Patte[46] proposed the use of ethics in Biblical interpretation as a means of moving beyond objectivist

[42] *Rhetoric and Ethic: The Politics of Biblical Studies* (Minneapolis: Fortress Press, 1999).

[43] See *The Moral Vision*, 3–7.

[44] Hays mentions five representative hermeneutical strategies: Christian realism of Reinhold Niebuhr, Karl Barth's obedience to the command of God, John Howard Yoder's following the way of Jesus, character shaped by tradition of Stanley Hauerwas, and Fiorenza's feminist critical hermeneutic of liberation.

[45] Fiorenza, *Rhetoric and Ethic*, 18.

[46] See *Ethics of Biblical Interpretation: A Reevaluation* (Louisville, KY: John Knox, 1995).

scholarship that is so focused on factual and methodological purity that it cannot hear the voices of others, such as women, minorities, or religious conservatives. Therefore, it is necessary to employ an ethical selectivity in Biblical interpretation.

Structure of this Book

This book is divided into three parts. Part One will prepare and orient the reader toward the interpretation of the ethical emphases in the Miletus speech. Here we will examine important background literature which could have been known to Luke and may have served as source-materials for him. In addition, an introduction to the Pauline speeches will be provided in this section. Part Two will examine the ethical emphases of the text in question by means of a detailed theological and ethical investigation. Part Three will attempt to identify the theological and ethical content of the speech and of 20:32–35 in the context of the ethical vision of Lucan Paul. This will be followed by a general conclusion.

Part 1

Preparing to Interpret the Ethical Emphases in Acts 20:32–35

Chapter 1

The Ethical Emphases of Ancient Farewell Speeches
A Contextual Study

This chapter is an attempt to place the Miletus speech in its ancient context. In this study I examine few specimens of farewell speeches[1] found in the Greco-Roman and Jewish writings[2] to determine the ethical emphasis found in them in view of deciphering similar emphasis present in the Miletus speech.

1.1. The Importance of a Contextual Study

How legitimate and important is it to approach the ethical emphases of the Miletus speech in terms of the Greco-Roman and ancient Jewish writings? First, it can help us to recognize Luke's "historiographic matrix." Since the NT lies on the cusp between Jewish and Greek culture and that the life and

---

[1] A "speech" is a formal address or discourse delivered to an audience. A "farewell speech" is an address in the first-person voice reportedly given by someone shortly before his or her death. Typically, the speaker refers to his old age or imminent death and exhorts the hearers to live along certain lines in the future. However, a person might leave special instructions before his departure not necessarily indicating imminent death. Miletus speech obviously falls in this latter category. The speakers are usually leaders of such great historical prominence that the speeches tend to mark momentous turning points in life. See William W. Klein, Craig L. Blomberg, and Robert L. Hubbard, *Introduction to Biblical Interpretation* (Nashville: Thomas Nelson, 1993), 335.

[2] By Jewish writings I mean Biblical, Deutero-Canonical, and Intertestamental Jewish literature. Later, in this chapter, two specimens of farewell speeches (from LXX) will be briefly studied as Luke seems to be more indebted and at home to LXX than to the MT. One sample from the intertestamental writings also will be examined because of its ethical thrust and its influence on the NT.

religious traditions it depicts are Jewish[3] it is not accidental that many NT writers reveal their knowledge and influence of ancient rhetoric and culture. Pauline letters and Acts particularly reveal the influence ancient rhetoric and culture had on these works.[4] Martin Dibelius was one of the first to suggest studying the speeches in Acts in its ancient context. In the OT too we notice a proper historiography, composed artistically with certain line of thought and theological motives. In these books we do find (farewell) speeches (incorporated into historiography) that serve a literary purpose.[5] Since Acts is a book of history, its author was influenced by the ancient historians, and consequently the speeches in the Acts must be studied in the light of the works of these authors.[6]

Secondly, there are rhetorical speeches made with ethical emphases found in the Greco-Roman and Jewish literature. The Miletus speech contains ethical exhortations similar to many speeches delivered by the ancients. Examination of such rhetorical practice "involves recognizing Luke's persuasive narrative strategies, an approach helpful for discerning the message he endeavored to communicate."[7] Hence, the study of Miletus speech in its literary and cultural milieu must be seriously taken into account.

And finally, it provides a valid clue to the theological and ethical framework of Luke and helps to clarify, in particular, the theology and purpose of the Miletus speech in Acts. It was common for the departing ancients to deliver farewell speeches often in a paraenetic tone. If the Miletus speech is composed in the style of these speeches, then it must also have borrowed and be transmitting certain values and perspectives included in them. A comparison between Miletus speech and ancient farewell speeches allows us to discover how much Luke was influenced by and familiar with these works. Thus, any effort to study the Miletus speech to find literary and

---

[3] See George A. Kennedy, *New Testament Interpretation through Rhetorical Criticism* (Chapel Hill: The University of North Carolina Press, 1984), 8.

[4] Paul, who's letters (including the Deutero-Pauline letters) amount to 28% of the NT, comes across as at home in Greek idiom and rhetoric of his time and in the conventions of Greek epistle, and when addressing Greeks he is able to make reference to classical literature (Acts 17:28; 1Cor 15:33; Tit 1:12). See Kennedy, *New Testament Interpretation*, 10. In the same way Luke is not ignorant of the Greco-Roman and Biblical style and rhetoric and this is most evident in Acts. Apparently, Luke and other New Testament writers Paul, James, Peter, and the Gospel writers were thus at home in Greek and Biblical rhetoric.

[5] A convincing argument on the necessity to evaluate the theology and purpose of the Miletus speech in terms of the Jewish farewell speeches is offered by John Kurichianil. See "The Speeches in the Acts and the Old Testament," *ITS* 17.2 (1980), 181–86.

[6] Martin Dibelius, *Studies in the Acts of the Apostles*, Heinrich Greeven, ed. (London: SCM, 1973), 138–85. Dibelius downplays the role of the OT influence in the speeches of Acts.

[7] Keener, *Acts*, 1:26.

thematic parallels from the Greco-Roman and Jewish literatures is always justified.

Before we proceed to examine few specimens of farewell speeches, we will place the farewell speeches in their broader Greco-Roman and Jewish context since these literatures reflect the socio-cultural practices and conventions of that period.

1.2. The Greco-Roman Context of Speeches

1.2.1. The Classical Oratory

This contextual study requires an evaluation of the Greco-Roman rhetorical speeches[8] to which NT speeches are more or less analogous. A full-blown oratory developed in ancient Greece.[9] The establishment of democracy in Greece was the principal reason for the blooming of oratory there.[10] The political system, for example, operated through the direct speech of the citizens.[11] This demanded proper training of citizens in oratory.[12] The

---

[8] Edward Schiappa presents the origin of rhetoric in Greece and how it developed in various spheres and groups. His "reconstruction" of the origins of rhetorical theory invites a different approach to the origins and classification of different types of rhetoric of classical period. See *The Beginnings of Rhetorical Theory in Classical Greece* (New Haven: Yale University Press, 1999). However, Kennedy's various texts, *The Art of Persuasion in Greece* (New Jersey: Princeton University Press, 1963); *The Art of Rhetoric in the Roman World 300 BC–AD 300* (New Jersey: Princeton University Press, 1972); and *New Testament Interpretation through Rhetorical Criticism* are considered to be standard reference works in English on Greco-Roman rhetoric. This chapter finds and quotes much information from Kennedy's works.

[9] According to the tradition preserved in many ancient writers the art of rhetoric was invented in the second quarter of the fifth century BCE in Syracuse in Sicily. It was thought by later writers that rhetoric was brought to Athens by the famous sophist Gorgias, who came on an embassy from Leontini to request Athenian help in 427 (Diod. 12.53.1–5) and that it developed there as part of the sophistic movement. Sophistry was a practical kind of philosophy which taught the techniques of life, of which rhetoric was clearly one, and which in the case of some thinkers deepened into a more complete system of knowledge. See Kennedy, *Art of Persuasion*, 26. William W. Hallo demonstrates the existence of rhetoric among the Sumerians, Akkadians, and Israelites much before the classical rhetoric. See "The Birth of Rhetoric," in *Rhetoric before and beyond the Greeks*, Carol S. Lipson and Roberta A. Binkley, ed. (Albany: State University of New York Press, 2004), 25–46.

[10] From the fifth century BCE onwards, democracy became the standard form of Government there. On evolution and nature of democracy in Greece see Kurt A. Raaflaub, "Democracy," in *A Companion to the Classical Greek World*, Konrad H. Kinzl, ed. (Malden: Blackwell, 2006), 386–415.

[11] Kennedy, *Art of Persuasion*, 4. The Greek word for a speech is λόγος.

[12] Kennedy observes that boys had already learned to read and write, had learned some arithmetic, and in Greece had had musical and gymnastic training when at about the age of fourteen, they were sent to school of the rhetorician for theoretical instruction in public speaking and for practical exercises. They might continue the latter for the rest of their lives.

system of democracy naturally involves electing representatives for various offices. The elected members were not only politicians, but also judges, legislators, and rulers. The people exercised its supreme authority through three main institutions each fulfilling a different function: the Popular Courts (διακαστήρια), the Council of Five Hundred (βούλή), and the Assembly (ἐκκλησία).[13]

Justice was administered by the popular law courts. Cases were brought in by individuals and the defendant was obliged to plead his case in person.[14] This required tremendous skill in rhetorical speeches. The party that persuaded the jurors would win the case. It was the duty of the orator to argue for the client to get a positive verdict.[15] The documented attic orations reveal that judicial speeches outweigh other types.[16]

1.2.2. Rhetorical Speeches

All the speeches made by the ancients were rhetorical speeches. According to Aristotle, the origin of rhetoric was attributed to the need to be able to argue one's case effectively in a law court[17] where an artistically developed and uninterrupted speech was possible and even necessary.[18]

Other than judicial speeches there were speeches of praise or blame, of exhortation or dissuasion at various occasions such as funerals, national festivals, and military gathering etc. All these speeches were rhetorical and thus emerged as a phenomenon within the socio-political life of the classical Greece.

See, Kennedy, *Art of Persuasion*, 7. Quintilian describes every stage of the upbringing and education of boys of his time, see, Quint. *Inst.*, books 1 and 2.

[13] Christina Pepe, The Genres of Rhetorical Speeches in Greek and Roman Antiquity (Leiden: Brill, 2013), 9.

[14] Nonetheless, one could either request the assistance of a "synegoros" (συνήγορος) who is a relative or friend of the defendant, or call in for an expert the "logograph" (λογογράφος) who aided the defendant by instructing the art of rhetoric or even composing an entire speech to be learned by-heart and reproduced before the court. See Kennedy, *Art of Persuasion*, 127; Pepe, *Rhetorical Speeches*, 10.

[15] Even if a defendant seemed guilty he could be acquitted if he mentioned valiant deeds by ancestors and proved that he had served the city well (Lys. 30.1). Demosthenes 44.8 says that "generosity and justice" sometimes triumph over the laws. More on this can be found in "Law and Rhetoric: Community Justice in Athenian Courts," by Robert W. Wallace in *A Companion to the Classical Greek World*, K. H. Kinzl, ed. (Malden: Blackwell, 2006), 416–31, see especially p. 417.

[16] The three classical types of speeches are forensic, deliberative, and epideictic. The nature of these speeches will be explained in a while.

[17] Pepe, *Rhetorical Speeches*, 11.

[18] Kennedy, *Art of Rhetoric*, 8. For an elaborated presentation of the same see Pernot, *Rhetoric in Antiquity*, 24–56.

Kennedy classifies rhetoric into 'primary' and 'secondary.' 'Primary' rhetoric is the art of persuasive public speaking as part of social and civic life, and 'secondary' rhetoric is the use of the techniques of primary rhetoric in literature whose main focus is not public speech.[19] This division of Kennedy is very useful for the modern approaches to rhetoric, and today we are almost exclusively concerned with the 'secondary' rhetoric since these materials are amply available to us.

1.2.2.1. Parts of a Rhetorical Speech

A speaker should possess the faculties of invention, arrangement, style, memory, and delivery.[20] Invention (*inventio* which is also called the *stasis* or *status*) comes first and is the subject matter, which then relates to the finding out of the question at issue, and the appropriate arguments to use in proof or refutation.[21] The enthymeme and the example used in invention are fundamental in argumentative structures which underlie the construction of rhetorical reasoning.[22] Enthymeme is 'a proposition with a reason.'[23] For Aristotle, enthymeme, example, and amplification are forms which are common to all discourses.

The second part of rhetoric is arrangement (táxiς, *dispositio*). Arrangement means the organization of a speech into parts which are: 1) *prooemium* (prooímion, in Latin *exordium*) or introduction; 2) narration (diήghsiς, in Latin *narratio*) the exposition of the background and factual details; 3) proof (pístiς, in Latin *probatio*); 4) epilogue or conclusion (έpílogoς, in Latin *peroratio*).

The third part of rhetoric is style (λέξις, in Latin *elocutio*).[24] It involves four virtues of correctness, clarity, ornamentation, and propriety. The fourth part of rhetoric is memory (μνήμη, in Latin *memoria*). It usually identifies

---

[19] See also Philip E. Satterthwaite, "Acts against the Background of Classical Rhetoric," in *The Book of Acts in Its Ancient Literary Setting* (Bruce W. Winter and Andrew D. Clark, ed., vol. 1 of the *BAFCS*, Bruce W. Winter, ed.; Grand Rapids: Eerdmans, 1993), pp. 337–79, see especially p. 338.

[20] Arist. Rh. ad Her. 1.2.3. Cicero later describes the five parts of oratory or five tasks of an orator as invention, arrangement, style, memory and delivery. See Cic. Or. 21.69. Kennedy identifies the Lysianic structure as direct evidence, proof or refutation by probability, and proof by character.

[21] The qualities of a speaker presented here are from Kennedy, *Art of Persuasion*, 10–12.

[22] Pepe, *Rhetorical Speeches*, 180. For the relationship between enthymeme and example, see Arist. *Rh.* 1356a38–1356b6. Chapters 20–26 of Book 2 deal with example and enthymeme.

[23] Quint. *Inst.* 5.10.1–2. An example of enthymeme in Arist. *Rh.* 1394b is "There is no man who is really free, for he is the slave of either wealth or fortune." The first verse 'there is no man who is really free' is a maxim but taken with the next verse it is an enthymeme.

[24] 'A speech has two parts,' wrote Aristotle, moving from *lexis* to *taxis*, 'you must state your case, and you must prove it.' Arist. *Rh.* 1414a 30.

words or topics with physical objects and seeks to imagine these against a well-known background. The fifth part of rhetoric is delivery (ὑπόκρισις, in Latin *actio*). This involves rules for the control of the voice, gestures, and stance.[25]

1.2.2.2. *Pathos* and *Ethos* in Rhetorical Persuasion

The technicalities of speeches have less to do with our present study. However, *pathos* and *ethos* and the three genres of speeches, which I elaborate below, do contribute to this study in determining especially the genre, purpose, and theology of the Miletus speech.

In a speech *pathos* and *ethos* are closely related.[26] *Pathos* is defined as 'creating a certain disposition in the audience.'[27] It is persuasion through emotional appeal.[28] On the other hand, *Ethos* is a means of persuasion in speech that creates a moral character.[29] One effect of *ethos* is to produce a feeling of goodwill in the audience towards the speaker so that the projection of the appropriate character achieves more subtly the effects sought by explicit appeals for a favorable hearing.[30] It will be explicated later how *pathos* and *ethos* applied in the Miletus speech.

1.2.2.3. The Genres of Greco-Roman Rhetorical Speeches

I briefly examine here the genres of rhetorical speeches, determination of which helps to uncover the emphases of a work and thus the intent of the author. This can later help to verify the genre of Miletus speech and to bring to light the emphases and the intent of Luke.

According to Aristotle the kinds of rhetoric are three in number. Aristotle speaks of a δικανικόν, an ἐπιδεικτικόν and a συμβουλευτικόν γένος[31] corresponding to the three kinds of hearers:[32] forensic (also known as

---

[25] *Partitiones oratoriae* by Cicero, *Rhetorica ad Herennium* attributed to him and the writing of Dionysius of Halicarnassus contain much of the traditional theories of rhetoric. In Quintilian's *Institutiones Oratoriae* rhetorical theory finds its most complete expression.

[26] For means of *pathos* and *ethos* used in persuasion, see Christopher Carey, "Rhetorical Means of Persuasion," in *Persuasion: Greek Rhetoric in Action*, Ian Worthington, ed. (London: Routledge, 1994), 26–45.

[27] Arist. *Rh.* 1356a; 1377b.

[28] See for example, Gorg. *Helen*, 9–10; Quint. *Inst.* 3.1.12; Plato, *Phaed.* 267c; Arist. *Rh.* 1404a.

[29] Arist. *Rh.* 1377b.

[30] See Carey, "Rhetorical Means of Persuasion," 35.

[31] Arist. *Rh.* 1358b3.

[32] Arist. *Rh.* 1358a22.

judicial or dicanic); epideictic (also called demonstrative); and deliberative (or symbouleutic).[33]

1.2.2.3.1. Forensic Speeches

The first (chronologically) and the most widely used genre was forensic because the majority of Greek speeches were written to be delivered in courts of law.[34] The forensic kind is either accusatory or defensive; for litigants must necessarily either accuse or defend.[35] In forensic speeches the basic argument involves the question of truth or justice.[36] The time appropriate for forensic speeches is past; for it is always in reference to things done that one party accuses and the other defends.[37] The end of the forensic speaker is the just or the unjust.[38] From what we know about the judicial practices in Athens, initially most legal cases were heard either before single magistrates or before the Areopagus. Subsequently in place of the magistrates and Areopagus large popular juries called dicastery (δικαστήρια) were chosen.[39] The presentation of the case, though not initially, was by the litigants themselves, each in a single set speech with sometimes a single opportunity for rebuttal. This imposed on each litigant, and potentially on each Athenian citizen, a need to be an effective public speaker, to be able to organize a long speech and deliver it clearly and effectively.[40]

---

[33] Arist. *Rh.* 1358b3.

[34] Kennedy, *Art of Persuasion*, 152.

[35] Arist. *Rh.* 1358b3.

[36] Kennedy, *NT Interpretation*, 20.

[37] Arist. *Rh.* 1358b4.

[38] Arist. *Rh.* 1358b5.

[39] A body of 6000 was used as a pool from which individual panels of 201 or more juror were chosen by lot for each case. These juries had complete jurisdiction to determine both law and fact, and the presiding official was simply a chairman with no power of control or instruction. Such juries affected greatly the nature of trials. See these observations in Kennedy, *Art of Persuasion*, 27–28.

[40] Practically every person in Greece in connection with some judicial matters was expected to make a speech in the court. In order to win over the jury with convincing presentation with emotional plea, presumably a litigant or prospective litigant would call upon a speechwriter, a logographer, and furnish him with information about the case. The latter worked this up into a speech, perhaps consulting the litigant along the way, and perhaps, but not necessarily, interviewing witnesses. See Kennedy, *Art of Persuasion*, 127. Could a litigant ask several writers to submit speeches and then choose between them? Did writers offer unsolicited speeches to litigants? According to Kennedy neither seems likely. Did the general public know who had written a speech at the time of delivery? Usually the skill of the opponent himself is attacked and the whole convention of ghostwriting carefully masked. See Kennedy, *Art of Persuasion*, 128. According to Thucydides Antiphon was the man most able to help anyone who consulted him about a case in the courts or the assembly; he is a complete legal advisor, not just a speech writer. Thuc. 8.68.1.

1.2.2.3.2. Epideictic Speeches

The epideictic[41] kind has for its subject praise or blame.[42] The time appropriate for epideictic speeches is present, for it is the existing condition of things that all those who praise or blame have in view. It is not uncommon, however, for epideictic speakers to avail themselves of other times, of the past by way of recalling it, or of the future by way of anticipating it.[43] The end of those who praise or blame is the honorable and disgraceful.[44] Epideictic originally referred to demonstrations of merit or faults, but comes to include all oratory which is not deliberative or judicial.[45] They are addressed to spectators, who are concerned with the ability of the speaker. The most distinguished manifestations of epideictic are funeral and festival orations, encomium, and invective which are all concerned with praise or blame.

(a) Funeral Speeches: "funeral speech" (ἐπιτάφιος λόγος) had both a civic and official character. This was delivered during a funeral ceremony in Athens to honor the victims of war. It consists usually of praise, exhortation, consolation and lamentation, the last element being absent in some instances.[46] The most interesting rhetorical feature of such speeches is the highly formulaic quality which they achieved almost immediately. It was a kind of religious rite.[47]

(b) Festival Speeches:[48] There were speeches delivered on the occasion of the Panhellenic festivals organized for example at Olympia and Delphi.[49] These speeches consist normally of praise of the god associated with the festival, praise of the city in which the festival is held, praise of the context itself and of the crown

---

[41] More generally these speeches are classed as ἐπιδειξεις, or demonstrations, and the genre is called epideictic.

[42] Arist. *Rh.* 1358b3.

[43] Arist. *Rh.* 1358b4.

[44] Arist. *Rh.* 1358b5.

[45] Kennedy, *Art of Persuasion*, 10.

[46] Pepe, *Rhetorical Speeches*, 12–15. The usual structure of funeral oration was threefold: praise, lament, and consolation. See also Kennedy, *Art of Persuasion*, 155.

[47] Kennedy, *Art of Persuasion*, 154. Examples of funeral orations are Plut. *Per.* 8.6; Dionysius' introduction to the essay on Demosthenes, but preserved at second hand by Syrianus. According to Kennedy one of the most interesting studies of funeral oratory is the dialogue of Plato called the *Menexenus*. The historical references in the speech are anachronistic. Moreover, why should Plato, the most illustrious opponent of rhetoric, take the trouble to compose a good funeral oration? See *Art of Persuasion*, 158.

[48] Panegyric is the technical name for a festival speech.

[49] Pepe, *Rhetorical Speeches*, 18.

awarded, and finally, praise of the king or officials in charge.[50] Examples of famous festival speeches are the *Olympiacus* of Gorgias, *Panegyricus* of Isocrates, the *Olympiacus* of Lysias, and the *Panegyricus Traiani* of Pliny the Younger.

(c) Encomia: An encomium is a speech of praise either of some person or place. The Encomium offers a valuable perspective on how people were typically perceived in the ancient world and what was thought essential or important about them.[51] Gorgias' *Helen* is a very famous Greek encomium. Lucian's many works such as *Demosthenes, Demonax, The Fly*, etc. are encomia. The Gospels and the Acts could be viewed as encomia of Jesus and the apostles.

1.2.2.3.3. Deliberative Speeches

Aristotle was the first to use συμβουλευτικός to refer to a particular type of discourse. The action of συμβουλεύειν presupposes deliberation as its outcome, "its function is concerned with the sort of things we debate."[52] The deliberative kind is either hortatory or dissuasive; for advice given both privately and publicly either exhorts or dissuades. The essence of the γένος συμβουλευτικόν is inscribed in its very name: it is a speech which gives advice, orients behavior and has value insofar as it leads to taking a decision.[53] The time appropriate for deliberative kind is future; for the speaker, whether he exhorts or dissuades, always advises about things to come. Since the function of this genre is exhortation or dissuasion, we shall see in a later chapter how it is closely related to the genre of the Miletus speech.

Those who give συμβουλή are the orators who give it to private individual or to an audience.[54] Deliberation consists in carrying out possible means for achieving the end, foreseeing their efficacy and choosing the easiest and best.[55] Aristotle claims that a wise man is able to best deliberate.[56]

---

[50] Kennedy, *Art of Persuasion*, 167.

[51] Jerome H. Neyrey, "Josephus' *Vita* and the Encomium: A Native Model of Personality," *JSJ* 25 (1994), 179–80.

[52] Pepe, *Rhetorical Speeches*, 160. Aristotle says that deliberative oratory is concerned with the useful and the harmful; its subjects are five in number: finance, war, defense, commerce, legislation. See Kennedy, *Art of Persuasion*, 118. For a fuller treatment of this genre see Arist. *Rh.* 1357a–1359a; Quint. 3.8.1–70.

[53] Pepe, *Rhetorical Speeches*, 165.

[54] Arist. *Rh. Ale.* 1421b17–19.

[55] Arist. *NE* III2b17ff.

[56] For Aristotle the virtue associated with this genre is wisdom. See Arist. *Rh.* 1366b20–21; also, Pepe, *Rhetorical Speeches*, 165.

While expression of emotions is necessary in deliberative speeches, what really carries weight in such speeches is the authority of the speaker.[57]

(a) Military Speeches: Military speeches are examples of this genre. There were speeches of exhortation delivered on the occasion of military expeditions and the audience (ἐκκλησία) in this instance was constituted by the army members. It was customary for generals to deliver impassioned and sophisticated addresses to this body; and the generals were themselves politicians and accomplished orators. The general would address his troops on the eve of battle, in a crucial moment for the fate of the army, delivering a speech of exhortation (παρακλητικός).[58] Military exhortations began to feature regularly in the fifth century historiography especially that of Thucydides.[59]

From what we have described so far in this section it is evident that all the species of speeches have a considerable ethical orientation. But this is more evident in deliberative speeches as the objects of deliberation are "good." There seems always a balance between ethics and rhetoric, in the sense that rhetoric mostly aims at ethics.[60] Few observations below will explore the ethical orientation of genres.

1.2.3. Genres and Ethics

Our examination of the genres so far reveals that no genre is deficient of values. In fact each genre is comprised of moral values, the end set before it is a good, for the deliberative genre "advantageous/harmful," for the judicial "just / unjust," and for the epideictic "honorable/disgraceful."[61] It is commonly understood that history was written in antiquity with a consciously didactic or moral purpose, often stressed by the writer in his preface, and sometimes reiterated throughout the work. The highest conception of the historian's task is that he is pledged to the truth, and that the truth is 'useful.'[62]

In what way epideictic relates to ethics? Both Plato and Aristotle relate epideictic to ethics, considering praise to be the correct response to virtue, blame to vice. The 'objects of praise and blame,' are 'virtue and vice, the noble and the base;' the highest form of virtue consisting in being useful to other people.[63] Any heroic activity, where a man has neglected his own

---

[57] Quint. *Inst.* 3.8.12.

[58] Pepe, *Rhetorical Speeches*, 17.

[59] See other examples in Hom. *Il.* 4.239; 8.172–77; 238–41.

[60] Although this is not the mind of Plato.

[61] Arist. *Rh.* 1358b20 ff; Cic. *Topics* 91.

[62] Hemer, *The Book of Acts*, 79.

[63] Arist. *Rh.* 1366a23–1366b5.

interest to do what was honorable,[64] must be praised. Aristotle ascribes a pragmatic or persuasive function to epideictic, which can arouse the listeners to emulation.[65]

Plato and Isocrates give epideictic a social function, reinforcing the norms of public morality.[66] Roman writers Quintilian and Cicero devote much space to epideictic that shows its importance to Roman oratory.[67] In Cicero's *De Oratore*, the orator is seen as excelling all others in his power to encourage men to virtue or reclaim them from vice through *vituperare* and *laudare*.[68] Epideictic, for Cicero, is of great importance to inculcating ethics in the individual as in the state.

Like the epideictic, the deliberative genre also contains ethics; for the goal of deliberative genre is to persuade or dissuade the audience. The use of persuasive speech is to lead to decisions.[69] Since exhortation is the object of deliberative speeches, such speeches are necessarily ethical. A speaker exhorts about the useful or the harmful and about good or bad. Such speeches aim the best for the public in the future. Many of the Greco-Roman and Jewish farewell speeches are deliberative and sometimes contain elements of epideictic. And finally the forensic genre basically deals with just or unjust. Even though the topic of this genre concerns just or unjust, the end of the genre is not necessarily a matter of ethics.

1.2.4. Ethics in Greco-Roman Farewell Speeches

Almost all philosophical, historical and rhetorical books contain elements of ethics and morality. Historians' agendas were several and one of them was their moral and ethical agenda employed in their writings.[70] Ethics became popularized and penetrated many levels of society.[71] Evidence for this is

---

[64] Aristotle praises Achilles because he championed his fallen friend Patroclus though he knew that this meant death and to die thus was the nobler thing for him to do; the expedient was to live on. See Arist. *Rh.* 1359a.

[65] Brian Vickers, *In Defense of Rhetoric* (Oxford: Clarendon Press, 1988), 55.

[66] Vickers, *In Defense of Rhetoric*, 55.

[67] Vickers, *In Defense of Rhetoric*, 58. See also Quint. *Inst.* 3.7.1–28 particularly 3.7.10–14 and Cic. *De Or.*

[68] Cic. *De Or.* 2.9.35.

[69] Arist. *Rh.* 1391b8.

[70] For example, works written by or attributed to Aristotle such as *Nicomachean Ethics*, *Eudemian Ethics*, *Magna Moralia* and *Virtues and vices*. Plutarch's *Moralia* is another example of this genre. The theme of the *NE* is how men should live and of the *Moralia* is various ethical and moral considerations.

[71] Philosophers were invited to deliver discourses on moral topics in the salons of the wealthy; some of them spoke, when invited, to gatherings in the forum or such places as the public baths; and others were attached to the homes of persons of means or joined the retinues of governmental

found in many sources and documented speeches delivered to the masses.[72] Moreover, abundant speeches were made by the ancients at various occasions. Many of these speeches are ethical/moral in character.[73] Among the immense ethical documents and speeches one encounters a number of farewell speeches. These are speeches delivered to disciples or individuals prior to the death of a leader or philosopher which usually have an ethical nature. We sketch a few of these specimens in order to survey the ethical emphases found in them which will help us to outline the ethical nature of Miletus speech. In any case, no detailed evaluation of these speeches seems within the scope of this book.

1.2.4.1. Homer, Illiad 6

Hector decided to leave the battlefield and return to Troy to "tell the elders who speak counsel and our wives to pray to the gods" (*Il.* 6.113–15). He told Hecuba, his mother, to "gather together the older women" at the temple of Athena to pray that the goddess "may have mercy" (*Il.* 6.269–76). He then went to the home of Paris and Helen to shame his brother into returning to battle. Helen asked Hector to linger, but he was eager to leave: "I will go home to see my own family, my beloved wife and infant son. For I do not know if ever again I shall return to them or if the gods will subdue me at the hands of the Achaeans" (*Il.* 6.365–68).

After these words, Hector rushed to join the fight. Andromache, however, ran to meet him bringing their son Astyanax with her. Hector's farewell thus took place at the gate of the city. Andromache pleaded him not to fight: "Come now, take pity and stay here on the wall, lest you make your son an orphan and your wife a widow." Hector's response is very dramatically presented.[74] For our benefit I will briefly present the final exhortations found in the speech.

> Dear wife, why so desperate? Why so much grief for me? No man will hurl me down to death, against my fate. And fate? No one alive has ever escaped it, neither brave man nor coward, I tell you—it's born with us the day that we are born. So please go home and tend to your own tasks, the distaff and the loom, and keep the women working

---

officials. …… Some Stoics, but especially Cynics, preached in the market places and on street corners, where they urged all who passed by to listen to them as they spoke of virtue. See Abraham J. Malherbe, *Moral Exhortation: A Greco-Roman Sourcebook* (Philadelphia, PA: Westminster Press, 1986), 13.

[72] Malherbe, *Moral Exhortation*, 13.

[73] Themistocles is said to have delivered a speech in which throughout he contrasted what was better and lesser elements in human nature. See Herod. *Hist.* 8.83.

[74] See especially *Il.* 6.441–50, 454–55, 459–502.

> hard as well. As for the fighting, men will see to that, all who were born in Troy but I most of all.[75]

1.2.4.2. Xenophon, Cyrus 8.7.6–28

Xenophon wrote a biography of Cyrus, the great Persian King, which gives a glimpse of his character. Before the end of his days he called his sons, friends, and Persian magistrates and when they all had come, Cyrus delivered a farewell speech. The speech of Cyrus clearly indicates the end of his days (*Cyrus* 8.7.6). Cyrus' speech has antecedent history (*Cyrus* 8.6.6–8) and makes reference to the efforts or services of him by which his friends were made happy (*Cyrus* 8.7.7–8). His speech includes the transition to the present and future concern (*Cyrus* 8.7.9). More importantly, ethical advices such as respect for everyone, friendship and faithfulness, love of brother, immortality of the soul, and fear of gods are listed in Cyrus' speech (*Cyrus* 8.7.10–26). And finally, the instruction of Cyrus gets support from the history of the past (*Cyrus* 8.7.24).

1.2.4.3. Plato, Phaedo

Phaedo has its scene the prison of Socrates. Socrates gives a final example and teaching by correcting his friends who urge him to put off the poison.[76] He even instructs Crito to offer a cock to Asclepius (in thanksgiving for his death). The following statement made by William S. Kurz indicates the ethical emphases it gives. "The genre highlighted the speaker's impending death, care of those remaining, regulation of discipleship, thanks to the gods, an accounting for his life, consolation to an inner circle of followers, didactic speeches, and political and philosophical testaments."[77] Moreover, it distinguishes between right and wrong actions; it treats, though not in a profound way, reward and punishments, justice, truth, courage, temperance, and other moral virtues.

1.2.4.4. Josephus, Jewish Antiquities. 12.6.3 (Mattathias)

This exhortatory farewell speech of Mattathias is quite different from the one we encounter in the first Book of the Maccabees. The speech reveals the apologetic and exhortatory orientation of the author. When Mattathias had ruled one year, and was fallen into disease, called for his sons, and set them round about him, and said:

---

[75] *Il.* 6.490–93.

[76] Plato, *Phaedo* 116d–117a.

[77] William S. Kurz, "Luke 22:14–38 and Greco-Roman and Biblical Farewell Addresses," *JBL* 104.2 (1985), 254.

O my sons, I am going the way of all the earth; and I recommend to you my resolution, and beseech you not to be negligent in keeping it, but to be mindful of the desires of him who begot you, and brought you up, and to preserve the customs of your country, and to recover your ancient form of government, which is in danger of being overturned, and not to be carried away with those that, either by their own inclination, or out of necessity, betray it, but to become such sons as are worthy of me; to be above all force and necessity, and so to dispose your souls, as to be ready, when it shall be necessary, to die for your laws; as sensible of this, by just reasoning, that if God see that you are so disposed he will not overlook you, but will have a great value for your virtue, and will restore to you again what you have lost, and will return to you that freedom in which you shall live quietly, and enjoy your own customs. Your bodies are mortal, and subject to fate; but they receive a sort of immortality, by the remembrance of what actions they have done. And I would have you so in love with this immortality, that you may pursue after glory, and that, when you have undergone the greatest difficulties, you may not scruple, for such things, to lose your lives. I exhort you, especially, to agree one with another; and in what excellency any one of you exceeds another, to yield to him so far, and by that means to reap the advantage of every one's own virtues. Do you then esteem Simon as your father, because he is a man of extraordinary prudence, and be governed by him in what counsels he gives you. Take Maccabeus for the general of your army, because of his courage and strength, for he will avenge your nation, and will bring vengeance on your enemies. Admit among you the righteous and religious and augment their power.

1.2.4.5. Plutarch, Otho 15

Before committing suicide[78] Otho gave the following speech:

> This day, my fellow-soldiers, I deem more blessed than that on which you first made me emperor, since I see you so devoted to me and am judged worthy of so high honor at your hands. But do not rob me of a great blessedness – that of dying nobly in behalf of fellow-citizens so many and so good. If I was worthy to be Roman emperor, I ought to give my life freely for my country. ……and we sin against our country whether we conquer or are conquered. For the victor's gain is our country's loss. Believe me when I insist that I can die more honorably than I can reign. For I do not see how my victory can be of so great advantage to the Romans as my offering up my life to secure

[78] The Greco-Roman ancients considered suicide as a noble act than to be killed by another. They also valued the immolation of the self for a noble cause, like for the nation.

peace and concord, and to prevent Italy from beholding such a day again.

1.2.4.6. Diogenes Laertius, Epicurus 10.16–18

The farewell speech itself is not a significant one, but the account about Epicurus' heroic acts nearly before his death displays the ethical thrust of the story. As per the will of Epicurus, he left the house, garden, and some funds to trustees of the school he founded. Remaining funds were left to honor his deceased family and to celebrate his birthday annually and his memory monthly. His slaves were freed and made arrangements for the marriage of the daughter of Metrodorus.[79] Hermippus relates that Epicurus entered a bronze bath of lukewarm water and asked for unmixed wine, which he swallowed, and then, having bidden his friends remember his doctrines, breathed his last. Here is something of my own about him: "Farewell, my friends; the truths I taught hold fast."

In the above specimens, I have tried to display instances of Greco-Roman farewell speeches which reveal the ethical character of those presented. At this point, I will not compare any of these speeches with the Miletus speech; it will be done later, if needed, in each individual case to discover possible affinity between them. In the following section I will expound samples of important farewell speeches extant in the LXX in order to outline the ethical emphases found in them.

1.3. Old Testament Background of Farewell Speeches

In the Old Testament,[80] reports of farewell speeches ('testaments'[81]) are generally part of a larger editorial composition which reports the final

---

[79] Dio. Laer. *Epic.* 10.16–22.

[80] In this study I will use the LXX as the primary source document and therefore samples of Biblical farewell speeches may also include illustrations from Deutero-Canonical Books of the OT. Moreover, Luke demonstrates knowledge and influence of the LXX; his influence of the Hebrew Bible (MT) is not very evident. See Kurz, "Luke 22:14–38," 256–57. Studies on the different aspects of the subject have been undertaken by various scholars. Soards for example shows the LXX influence on the speeches of Acts, see *Speeches in Acts*, pp. 143–57. See also Gert J. Steyn, *Septuagint Quotations in the Context of Petrine and Pauline Speeches of the Acta Apostolorum* (Kampen: Kok Pharos, 1995); Gregory E. Sterling, "Luke as a Reader of the LXX," in *Biblical Interpretation in Early Christian Gospels: Vol 3; The Gospel of Luke*, Thomas R. Hatina, ed., LNTS 376 (New York: T&T Clark, 2010), 161–79.

[81] The Biblical 'farewell speeches' and 'testaments' are synonymous terms since the functions of both are practically the same. Also seen in John J. Collins, "Testaments," in *Jewish Writings of the Second Temple Period: Apocrypha, Pseudepigrapha, Qumran Sectarian Writings, Philo, Josephus*, Michael E. Stone, ed., CRINT 2.2 (Assen: Van Gorcum, 1984), 325; William S. Kurz, *Farewell Address in the New Testament* (Collegeville: Liturgical Press, 1990), 19. The word 'Testament' is more a Pseudepigraphic since the word is almost always associated

acts and death of an important person.[82] According to Klaus Baltzer, these farewell reports were born from 'covenant formulary' (*bundesformular*). He writes: "Literally the farewell speech comprises the elements of a covenant formulary."[83]

Harm Hollander does not agree with Baltzer. He argues that the 'testament' is a genre of its own, and certainly not a development of the *Bundesformular*. It is not juridical at all, and the 'testament' can quite easily do without the actual term covenant (διαθήκη).[84]

While both these arguments have some elements of truth, it is difficult to determine the precise *sitz im leben* of farewell speeches. However, Hollander's argument that "the 'testament' is a genre of its own" seems to be more convincing and the *sitz im leben* of the origins of 'testaments' and / or farewell speeches seems to be ancient wisdom.[85] The wisdom of the older person was valued and passed on to his sons or students. The expression "my sons" found in 'testaments,' attests to its affiliation with Wisdom Literature. The farewell situation adds solemnity. Before leaving his sons or students, the father or teacher recalls to them the main elements of his life and teaching. The lessons of the past are preserved for the next generation.[86] Even those narratives and predictions found in the 'testaments' are a vehicle for wisdom instructions. There is little reason to give a farewell address at the end of someone's life if not aimed at giving instructions. A major function of farewell addresses is therefore paraenetic.

In the MT often the farewell accounts use the word (צָוָה), command, in the sense of giving final testamentary orders (Gen 49:29; 1 Kgs 2:1).[87] Such

---

with these types of writings, for example the Testament of Moses, the Testament of the Twelve Patriarchs, and the Testament of Abraham.

[82] Burke O. Long, *1 Kings with and Introduction to Historical Literature* (Grand Rapids: Eerdmans, 1984), 43.

[83] Klaus Baltzer, *The Covenant Formulary in Old Testament, Jewish, and Early Christian Writings* (Philadelphia, PA: Fortress Press, 1971), 137.

[84] Hollander, *Joseph as an Ethical Model*, 6.

[85] See Eckhard von Nordheim, *Die Lehre Der Alten. 1. Das Testament als Literaturgattung im Judentum der Hellenistisch Römischen Zeit*, ALGHJ 13 (Leiden: Brill, 1980), 234–42; also Kurz, "Luke 22:14–38," 264. However, wisdom instructions do not contain specific deathbed setting. The moral exhortation typical of wisdom is only one element of the 'testaments,' and often other elements such as narratives and predictions have an upper hand. See Collins, "Testaments," 330.

[86] von Nordheim, *Die Lehre Der Alten*, 233, see also pp. 234–42. The ideas of Nordheim are borrowed by Kurz, "Luke 22:14–38," 264.

[87] Long, *1 Kings*, 43.

speeches are not to be dismissed as pious fraud.[88] The last words of a parent facing death were viewed as of primary importance. Death was believed to be a time when God granted prophetic knowledge and visions of the other world to the righteous.[89] Final speeches were seen as authoritative because no person would be expected to tell an untruth at the hour of death/judgment, nor would the dying person fail to give children both goods and truth (or warning). They must have been commonly delivered when a national leader, or a family or tribal head, conscious of impending death, would pass on his final words and bequeath his last possessions to heirs and successors.[90]

Johannes Munck has identified four motifs that characterize Jewish Testaments/farewell speeches though all these are not always found together. (1) Calling together of family to instruct them; (2) delivery of exhortations; (3) telling of stories about oneself, in some instances, as an example to follow or to guard against; and (4) possibly also a communication of some prophecies about the destiny of the people.[91]

Observations regarding farewell speeches in the OT reveal that they have a strong ethical thrust. Eckhard Von Nordheim states that if there is no ethical instruction (*Verhaltensanweisung*) there is no farewell speech;[92] ethics is primary.

In the LXX, like in the Hebrew Bible,[93] farewell speeches are attributed only to famous individuals and they are theologically and historically important. The specimens we examine below reveal the ethical emphases they

---

[88] Robert G. Boling, *Joshua: A New Translation with Notes and Commentary*, AB 6 (Garden City, NY: Doubleday, 1982), 526.

[89] In the Miletus speech Paul foretells what will happen to him in the future in 20:23 & 25. Information received from the other world as well as ethical teaching and distribution of inheritance are typical of 'testaments.' See Anitra B. Kolenkow, "The Literary Genre "Tesament,"" in *Early Judaism and Its Modern Interpreters*, Robert A. Kraft and George W. E. Nickelsburg, ed., SBLBMI 2 (Atlanta: Scholars Press, 1986), 259.

[90] Long, *1 Kings*, 45. Long further states that farewell speeches were made to convey the last wishes and exhortations of a person nearing death. They mean to bring to a close an epoch, a life, a period of history, and to cite a definitive theological perspective on such an era; usually they also look ahead to further episodes in the canon. See p. 45.

[91] Johannes Munck, "Discours d'adieu dans le Nouveau Testament et dans la Littérature Biblique," in *Aux Sources de la Tradition Chrétienne: Mélanges Offerts à M. Maurice Goguel à l'occasion de son soixante-dixième Anniversaire*, BT(N) (Neuchatel: Delachaux & Niestle, 1950), 159. See also the motifs of a farewell speech gathered by Ethelbert Stauffer, *Die Theologie des Neuen Testaments* (Genf: Oikumene, 1945), 321–24; Hans-Joachim Michel identifies 13 motifs. See *Die Abschiedsrede des Paulus an die Kirche: Apg 20:17–38: Motivgeschichte und Theologische Bedeutung*, SANT 35 (München: Kösel Verlag, 1973), 48–54.

[92] Nordheim, *Die Lehre Der Alten*, 233.

[93] The main difference between the LXX and Hebrew farewell speeches is numerical, i.e., LXX contains additional books, hence more farewell speeches.

give in exhortatory manner. The first two speeches in the list (the speeches of Samuel and Tobit) get bigger treatment because the first has been identified as sharing many elements in common with the Miletus speech, and the latter has exhortations parallel to the Miletus speech.

1.3.1. 1 Samuel 12:1–25

1 Samuel 12:1–25 is given the category of a "farewell speech" (of Samuel) though many factors are seen to take away from it the quality of a "farewell speech."[94] The subsequent narrative indicates that Samuel continued to exercise his ministry even after this event.[95] Moreover, no prophet successor to Samuel is announced anywhere in the speech.[96] However, this can certainly be considered as a farewell speech for the following reasons. (a) An indication about the old age of Samuel (1 Sam 12:2) in the narrative does press primarily for the need to see it as a farewell speech. (b) Samuel himself in the speech vaguely indicates the termination of his ministry (1 Sam 12:2b). Though he continued to exercise his ministry even after delivering this speech, the time-frame he did it was very short and the bulk of his ministry was performed before the speech had been made. Samuel continues as a prophet, and will again play an important role as king-maker, "for there is a greater king than Saul still to be anointed." Samuel "will no longer be the center of interest in the narrative."[97] (c) It was necessary for the author of Samuel to insert this key speech at a crucial point of history when the people had already decided for a temporal king to rule over them. Now that they have a king, who will act as the successor to Samuel, he will lead the people (1 Sam 12:2). Other elements typical to farewell speeches found in the speech such as addressing a gathering (1 Sam 12:1), historical summary (1 Sam 12:3–12), prophetic view of the future (1 Sam 12:14–17, 25), and exhortations to good behavior of the speaker (1 Sam 12:20–25) make it by far a farewell speech.

Moving to the speech proper, there is no time or place given. Possibly it was delivered at Ramah, the hometown of Samuel and the place where the people first requested a king.[98] Samuel begins the speech by justifying his own conduct with regard to the matters between him and the people

---

[94] The reasons for not considering it a farewell speech are found in Bruce C. Birch, "The First and Second Books of Samuel: Introduction, Commentary, and Reflections," *NIB* 2:1060.

[95] Samuel twice rejects Saul (1 Sam 13 and 15); anoints David as successor of Saul (1 Sam 16) and gives protection to David when he flees from Saul (1 Sam 19:18–24).

[96] Even in the farewell speech of Joshua, no mention is made of a successor.

[97] P. Kyle McCarter, *I Samuel: A New Translation with Introduction and Commentary*, AB 8 (Garden City, NY: Doubleday, 1980), 221.

[98] David T. Tsumura, *The First Book of Samuel*, NICOT (Grand Rapids: Eerdmans, 2007), 317.

rather than between God and his people or his servant king (v. 3).[99] Here, most probably, they are testifying to Samuel's integrity as a judge, not as a prophet, in contrast to his sons who took bribes and perverted justice (8:3).[100]

Samuel's speech becomes clearly ethical when he confesses that he has not defrauded or oppressed anyone or taken a bribe from anyone (v. 3).[101] He boldly professes that he has not taken from anyone an ox or a donkey. Ox and donkey are among the larger cattle.[102] These terms are used to assess one's possession. The expression 'taken a bribe' reminds us of the evil conduct of Samuel's sons (8:3) rather than the right of the king (8:11). Samuel contrasts himself with his sons rather than with the king.[103] The prophet then provides a historical summary (12:3–12) which is unique to many farewell speeches.

The intercessory (12:17–18, 23) and exhortatory (12:20–25) role of the prophet appear in the speech. In connection with our thesis, I look for ethical accents in the speech rather than the intercessory role of the prophet. Samuel exhorts the people to love, serve and fear the Lord shunning all useless things. The earlier history of Israel points to the fact that they were always going after other gods. Therefore, 'shun all useless things' is, most probably, a reference to keep off from all apostasy. He wants a total commitment of the heart (vv. 20 and 24). Samuel in the end makes known to the people, in pure deuteronomistic style, the retribution of the Lord. Acting faithfully deserves blessings as in the past, and any contrary behavior, either from the part of the people or the king, will invite total destruction (v. 25).

1.3.2. Tobit 14:3–11

The Book of Tobit belongs to the LXX canon and it seems that the book has been influenced by the Book of Deuteronomy; its influence is particularly visible in the final speech of Tobit[104] (Tob 14:3–11). The book draws insights from Deuteronomy to elaborate how a virtuous life should be; in this sense, it is very ethical in every aspect. In the book Tobit is the hero who becomes

---

[99] Tsumura, *The First Book of Samuel*, 315.

[100] Tsumura, 315.

[101] Keith Bodner, *1 Samuel: A Narrative Commentary* (Sheffield: Phoenix Press, 2008), 109.

[102] Compare with "oxen and donkeys and flocks" in Gen 32:5; Ex 22:4, 9.

[103] Tsumura, *The First Book of Samuel*, 318.

[104] For a list of items that runs parallel between Deuteronomy and Tobit 14:3–11 see Carey A. Moore, *Tobit: A New Translation with Introduction and Commentary*, AB 40A (New York: Doubleday, 1996), 294–95. Also useful here is the work of Alexander A. Di Lella, "The Deuteronomic Background of the Farewell Discourse in Tobit 14:3–11," *CBQ* 41 (1979), 380–81.

a model for his people Israel.[105] The book graphically portrays relationships in family life and in community. Moreover, the book has an overriding social orientation. Tobit himself is a paradigm of virtue regarding almsgiving and righteousness. In 1:16–17; 2:2; 4:5–19; 14:3–11 he is either an example or exhorts others to inculcate certain virtues. The words δικαιοσύνη (righteousness) and ἐλεημοσύνη (almsgiving) mentioned at the beginning of the book (1:3) as characteristic virtues of Jewish piety appear again at the end of the book (14:8–11) forming an inclusion. What is more striking is the example and exhortation to almsgiving that appears throughout the book (1:16; 4:7, 10–11; 7:7; 12:8–9; 14:2).

From these introductory comments it can be concluded that the ethical exhortations in the farewell speech of Tobit are a summary of the whole teaching of the book in general. The book, in the beginning, presents Tobit as a man of truth, righteousness, and charity and these themes are elaborated in the book through vivid personal examples and exhortations. The exhortations in the Book of Tobit revolve around God, oneself and neighbor. It is primarily to do what is pleasing in God's sight and to remember and praise God. Secondly it is to make every effort at righteous behavior and finally to assist one's neighbors by deeds of almsgiving (ἐλεημοσύνη).[106] The instructive mode of the book continues throughout and the instructions are stereotypical.[107]

The farewell speech of Tobit is more akin to the Jewish Testaments[108] than to the Biblical farewell speeches because of its strong ethical accents and the use of stereotypical phrases such as "my son" or "my children." Tobit exhorts his son to trust the word of God spoken through the Prophets (vv. 4–5).[109] He also predicts what will become of the people and the Temple (vv. 6–7). Verses 8–11 are ethical in which Tobit instructs his son and grandchildren in righteous living.[110]

---

[105] Irene Nowell, "The Book of Tobit: Introduction, Commentary, and Reflections," *NIB* 3:1061. Alexander Di Lella says that Tobit is the paragon of virtues. See "A Study of Tobit 14:10 and its Intertextual Parallels," *CBQ* 71 (2009), 504.

[106] Francis M. Macatangay, *The Wisdom Instructions in the Book of Tobit* (Berlin: De Gruyter, 2011), 112.

[107] For example, see the ethical themes found in Tob 12:8–9 they are truth, almsgiving, and righteousness. What is clear in the text is that "almsgiving saves one from death," and it "purifies all sin." Almsgiving will grant full and satisfying life to those who engage in it. It is a good (ἀγαθός) gift before God.

[108] A sample of Jewish Testament will be briefly studied below.

[109] Nowell, *The Book of Tobit*, 1069.

[110] Similar instructions were previously given to his son (4:3–21 and 12:1–10). One of the striking features of these instructions is that it only includes those virtues of which his own

Almsgiving is one of the chief theological teachings of the book.[111] If a person transgresses the commands of the Lord and commits sin, his deeds of charity will pay off and purge him of his sins. He will enjoy life with God and the blessings such life bestows.[112] In this context the story of Ahiqar[113] in the mouth of Tobit further enhances the author's purpose of dramatizing the theology of almsgiving.[114] In simple terms, the reader must understand that God will reward almsgiving. In the speech, through the wisdom instructions, Tobit affirms a prominent concept of the Book of Deuteronomy: theory of retribution.

1.3.3. Genesis 47:29–49:33

This farewell speech is delivered by Jacob before his sons and grandchildren. This is the first farewell speech documented in the Bible. The speech indicates the last wishes of a dying individual as paramount. In the Genesis account there is a charge with regard to his burial (47:29–31; 49:29–33); the blessing of Joseph and his two sons linking with an antecedent history (ch. 48); Jacob's oracles[115] on the future of all the tribes (49:1–28). In the twofold instructions given to Joseph regarding his burial indicates his faith in God and that his ultimate hope is the promise of God.[116] The story of Jacob is dominated by his quest for blessing. Now at the end of his life that quest is completed since he has received more than what he expected. He reflects on the fulfillment of the promises.[117] Jacob recalls the rise of the patriarchal tribes and points to the future of each of them by transposing the story to the Exodus narrative.[118]

---

life has been an example: Truth, righteousness, almsgiving (1:3), and mindfulness of God and prayer (3:2–6; 5:17; 11:14–15; 13:1–18). Consult Nowell, *The Book of Tobit*, 1069.

[111] Di Lella, "A Study of Tobit 14:10," 497.

[112] Understandably, the cultic form of atonement is downplayed. See Macatangay, *The Wisdom Instructions*, 107. In fact, the farewell speech amplifies the theme of "almsgiving" (vv. 8–11). As noted above, this virtue creates an inclusion (1:3; 14:9) that frames the book.

[113] The story of Ahiqar is found in the fifth century BCE Elephantine Aramaic work, which most likely is of Assyrian origin. The story narrates how Ahiqar, who has no children, adopts Nadin (in G^{II} of the Book of Tobit this name appears as Nadab) his nephew and educates him to succeed him in the court of the Assyrian King Esarhaddon (681–669 BCE). Nadin, being so ungrateful, cunningly plots to kill Ahiqar, but the plan fails and Nadin is put behind bars and eventually dies there. On the other hand, Ahiqar is reinstated in his former office. See, Di Lella, "A Study of Tobit 14:10," 498.

[114] Di Lella, 504.

[115] Genesis 49, the oracle of Jacob is in the form of a 'testament' and in fact called the 'Testament of Jacob' in some manuscripts. See, Collins, "Testaments," 330.

[116] See also Gordon J. Wenham, *Genesis 16–50*, WBC 2 (Dallas: Word Books, 1994), 452.

[117] Wenham, *Genesis 16–50*, 492.

[118] Trent C. Butler, *Joshua*: *13–24*, WBC 7b, 2nd ed. (Grand Rapids: Zondervan, 2014), 268.

At first glance the speech does not seem to give any specific ethical charge, nevertheless the ethicality of the speech can be detected in the many values and concerns implicit in the speech. God always keeps his promises, so man must also. God's blessing is upon those who love and trust Him, yet, sometimes even in the midst of man's unfaithfulness God is ever faithful to his promise. God's blessings received gratuitously must be imparted gratuitously to others, especially to one's family and clan.

1.3.4. Deuteronomy 31–33

The entire Book of Deuteronomy can be seen as a farewell speech of Moses,[119] nonetheless, chapters 31–33 demonstrate the traits of a typical farewell speech. The speech is a near preparation of Israel for life without the presence of the unique leader.[120] Though the speech gets disrupted at 31:7 and 9, but resumes at 33:1, pronouncing his blessings on each of the tribes, the disrupted blocks should also be seen as an integral part of the farewell speech. One such block (32:1–43) 'sings a lawsuit (בִּיר) against his people, including a negative narration of their history.'[121]

The exhortations found in the speech, in fact, are reminiscent of the teaching of Deuteronomy. They are concerning obedience, observance of the law, apostasy, and the powerful presence of the Lord amidst them. The content of the farewell speech leads to a call to obedience in face of divine judgment to come.[122] In the speech Moses exhorts Joshua and the people. He says to Joshua, "Be strong and be courageous" (31:6). The words are repeated in 31:7; 31:23. The recurring words of encouragement itself is a lesson. To avoid all temptation from the nation's gods, Israel must avoid all contact with the nations. Israel is to serve only Yahweh, an injunction that is found throughout the Bible, especially in Deuteronomy (Deut 4:19, 28; 6:13; 7:4, 16; 8:19; 10:12, 20; 11:13, 16; 12:2, 30; 13:5, 7, 14; 17:3; 28:14, 36, 47, 64; 30:17; 31:20).

1.3.5. Joshua 23

The penultimate chapter of the Book of Joshua uses a farewell speech of the protagonist of the story "to summarize the literary section and form a bridge to the next major section of the literary piece."[123] This speech by Joshua is

---

[119] Walter Harrelson, "The Significance of "Last Words" for Intertestamental Ethics," in *Essays in Old Testament Ethics*, James L. Crenshaw and John T. Willis, ed. (New York: KTAV, 1974), 206.

[120] Ronald E. Clements, "The Book of Deuteronomy: Introduction, Commentary, and Reflections," *NIB* 2:515.

[121] Butler, *Joshua*, 276.

[122] Butler, 276.

[123] Butler, 268.

addressed to all Israel since it does not mention a successor unlike in many other farewell speeches. The burden for future success is placed strictly on the congregation. Joshua speaks from the perspective of faith in Yahweh, praising all Yahweh's fighting for Israel, before turning to speak of the future and the dangers it hold for a disobedient Israel.[124]

The following features seen in the speech make it highly exhortatory and ethical. According to R. G. Boling the commandment and the treaty-teaching encompass all that is necessary for right and abundant living.[125] In the first half of the speech (vv. 3–10) the Suzerain's promise and the reality of the treaty blessings are seen to have been operative alongside Israel's loyalty throughout the lifetime of Joshua.[126] The instruction 'be firm' in v. 6 reminds of the obligation, whereas the prohibition in v. 7 call to mind a covenant proviso (Ex 20:5; Deut 5:9). The basic principle to love the Lord your God gets restated in v. 11. Loyal love is the demand of Yahweh. It is not just a "robotic obedience," but a total commitment and desire to please God by serving. Three emphases can be clearly seen in the speech: Obedience of Torah; Love of Yahweh; and mingling with Pagans (which will make them idolaters). Any disobedience, apostasy, and unfaithfulness will cause them perish. The speech, in short, is purely in deuteronomistic style.

1.3.6. 1 Kings 2:1–10

This sample brings before the reader the farewell speech of David to his son Solomon.[127] He is asked to be courageous and show himself a man (v. 2). This charge is similar to the charge Moses gave to Joshua in Deuteronomy 31. Solomon is further charged, in deuteronomistic terms,[128] to be faithful to the legacy of Moses.[129] Being obedient and faithful to the Lord is primary that will make Solomon prosper. David then instructs Solomon to take revenge on Joab who acted wickedly. The speech also instructs Solomon to deal mercifully with the sons of Barzillai (v. 7), but to punish Shimei. David does want Solomon to be an agent of retribution in dealing with Joab and Shimei but it should be in wisdom.[130] The speech, amidst other instructions, is aimed at subtly provoking the anger of Solomon against Joab and Shimei in a retributive way.

---

[124] Butler, 268.

[125] Boling, *Joshua*, 509.

[126] Boling, 522.

[127] 1 Chr 28 and 29 can be treated as the farewell speech of David.

[128] These terms found in v. 3 are "statutes" (חֻקָּה), "commandments" (מִצְוָה), "ordinances" (מִשְׁפָּט), and "testimonies" (עֵדוּת).

[129] Choon-Leong Seow, "The First and Second Books of Kings," *NIB* 3:26.

[130] The author does not specify what this wisdom is.

1.3.7. 1 Mac 2:49–70

The farewell speech of Mattathias in the LXX, like many other Biblical farewell speeches, is replete with deuteronomistic terms. The opening words of the speaker, in pictorial words—arrogance and scorn have now become strong; it is the time of ruin and furious anger—peep into the historical context of the reign of Antiochus Epiphanes IV, the Seleucid King, who introduced pagan cult in Jerusalem. The opponents are wretched, godless, and evil. Israelites under the leadership of Mattathias opposed vehemently the foreign rule. The fight against the enemy must go on even after the death of their leader. So Mattathias before his death called his sons and exhorted them to be zealous for the law even to the point of death.

The speech narrates a historical summary (vv. 51–60) as usually do other farewell speeches. It is curious to note that there is no mention of the great figures like Isaac, Jacob, and Moses in the list of the worthies. The insertion of the uncommon names of Phinehas[131] and Caleb is purposeful as the former demonstrated great zeal and received the covenant of everlasting priesthood (v. 54)[132] while the latter, as the name signifies,[133] was faithful in testifying in the assembly (v. 56).[134] In addition, the reference of Elijah and Daniel was important for the author because the former was victorious against idol worship, and the latter overcame the commands to worship idols.[135] The author of the book deliberately chose these names since the mention of the qualities of these characters was important for him to exhort the people in their specific historical context where the virtues of zeal and faithfulness, more than any other, were especially required to fight against the profanation of their religion and other abominable practices of the king.

In vv. 61–64 there are words of exhortations such as "observe" (ἐννοέω), "do not fear" (μὴ φοβέομαι), "act like a man" (ἀνδρίζομαι), and "be courageous" (ἰσχύω) which are intended to boost up the morale of the sons in their fight against the wicked king. A reference to the transfer of leadership makes entry only near the end of the speech by assigning two of the sons with different duties. Simeon is to be listened as he is assigned with a paternal role (v. 65); while Judas will be the commander of the army (v. 66). The speech concludes with a call to avenge the wrong done to the people and to obey the commands of the law. While the speech exhorts them to be

[131] Phinehas and David represent the two major institutions in Israel: priesthood and monarchy.

[132] Consult also Num 25:1–13.

[133] Caleb means "dog" and the singular quality of a dog is faithfulness.

[134] See Num 14:24, 30; 32:12; Josh 14:14; Sir 46:7–10.

[135] Robert Doran, "The First Book of Maccabees: Introduction, Commentary, and Reflections," *NIB* 4:51.

faithful and zealous for the law, "there is no attempt to see the opponents as fellow human beings. War and the defeat of the enemy are glorified."[136] In the speech, the right to defend oneself and one's country is strikingly affirmed.[137] To preserve one's own heritage and culture when threatened, one had to defend oneself.

1.4. Drawing a Comparison between Miletus Speech and Ancient Speeches

The study of the above specimens helps us to draw a parallel between them and the Miletus speech. I will delineate the obvious parallels of few speeches with the Miletus speech in order to disclose how Luke was probably influenced by these literatures and conventions of the time. First, we begin with the speech of Cyrus followed by the speech of Hector. Although all the Greco-Roman farewell speeches presented above do not have notable parallels to the Miletus speech, the point of contact between them and the Miletus speech lies in the ethical exhortations. In short, various ethical considerations form the bulk of the speeches.

The first specimen, Cyrus' speech, is the most important, since it parallels the Miletus speech both thematically and structurally.

1.4.1. Xenophon 8.7.6–28 (Cyrus' Farewell Speech) and Miletus Speech

Xenophon, *Cyrus* 8.7.6–28	**Miletus Speech**
Reference to the last days (*Cyrus* 8.7.6)	Paul's declares that it is his last meet (20:25)
Antecedent history (*Cyrus* 8.6.6–8)	A short history of Paul's ministry (20:18b–21)
Reference to the efforts by which his friends were made happy (*Cyrus* 8.7.7–8)	Paul's work by which his friends were made happy (20:34–35a)
Transition to the present and future concern (*Cyrus* 8.7.9)	Transition to the present (20:22–27) and future concern (20:28–30)
Ethical advices (*Cyrus* 8.7.10–26)	Ethical exhortations (20:32–35)

[136] Doran, "First Book of Maccabees," 17. This line of thought of the book is similar to other Jewish scriptures. According to Susan Niditch, in killing human beings, Israelites function as agents of God's justice, requiting the sins and misdeeds of their opponents. For a detailed presentation see, *War in the Hebrew Bible: A Study of the Ethics of Violence* (New York: Oxford University Press, 1993), 15–21.

[137] The non-violence used by Mahatma Gandhi or Martin Luther King Jr. would not have served under the Seleucid regime. See Doran, "First Book of Maccabees," 18.

Instruction of Cyrus gets support from the history of the past (*Cyrus* 8.7.24)	Paul's instruction gets support from Jesus (20:35b)

1.4.2. Homer, Illiad 6 (Hector's Farewell Speech to Andromache) and Miletus Speech

The second sample is Hector's speech. According to Dennis MacDonald, Miletus speech strategically imitates Hector's farewell speech.[138] The speech and its context are quite elaborate making it difficult to decipher and pick out from the material the corresponding elements parallel to the Miletus speech.

Homer, *Iliad 6*	**Miletus Speech**
Hector decides to leave the battlefield and return to Troy (*Il.* 6.113–115)	Paul decides to go to Jerusalem (20:16)
Gathering together of the older women at the temple of Athena (*Il.* 6.269–276).	Gathering together the elders at Miletus (20:17)
Hector's lack of knowledge about the future (*Il.* 6.365–368)	Paul doesn't know what will happen to him in Jerusalem (20:22)
Future concern (*Il.* 6.430–434)	Transition to the present (20:22–27) and future concern (20:28–30)
Ethical advices (*Il.* 6.490–493).	Ethical exhortations (20:32–35)

Now we shall take two LXX samples in order to detect possible parallels between them and the Miletus speech.

1.4.3. Samuel's Farewell Speech and Miletus Speech

1 Sam 12:1–25	**Miletus Speech**
Addressing all Israel (1 Sam 12:1)	Addressing the elders of Ephesus (20:17–18a)
An indication about the last days (1 Sam 12:2)	Paul's declares that it is his last meet (20:25)
1 Sam 12:1–25	Miletus Speech

[138] Dennis R. MacDonald, "Paul's Farewell to the Ephesian Elders and Hector's Farewell to Andromache: A Strategic Imitation of Homer's *Iliad*," in *Contextualizing Acts: Lucan Narrative and Greco-Roman Discourse*, Todd Penner and Caroline V. Stichele, ed., SBLSymS 20 (Atlanta: Society of Biblical Literature, 2003), 189–203.

Reference to the honesty of Samuel (1 Sam 12:3)	Reference to the honesty and labor of Paul (20:26, 33–34)
Transition to the present (1 Sam 12:13) and prophetic view of the future (1 Sam 12:14–17, 25)	Transition to the present (20:22–27) and future concern (20:28–30)
Ethical exhortations to good behavior of the speaker (1 Sam 12:20–25)	Ethical exhortations (20:32–35)
The credibility of the instructions of Samuel gets support from Israel's past (1 Sam 12:24)	Paul's instruction gets support from Jesus (20:35b)

1.4.4. Tobit's Farewell Speech and Miletus Speech

Tob 14:3-11	**Miletus Speech**
Calling together the sons (Tob 14:3)	Calling for the elders of Ephesus (20:17–18a)
An indication about Tobit's death (Tob 14:3)	An indication about Paul's last meet (20:25)
Mention of antecedent prophecy (Tob 14:4)	A short history of Paul's ministry (20:18b–21)
Transition to the present "so now" (καὶ νῦν) (Tob 14:8)	Transition to the present "and now" (καὶ νῦν) (20:22)
Prophetic view of the future (Tob 14:4–7)	Prophetic view of the future and future concern (20:22b–23, 28–30)
Ethical exhortations to good behavior of the speaker using "and now" (καὶ νῦν) (Tob 14:8–11)	Ethical exhortations using "and now" (καὶ τα νῦν) (20:32–35)
Tobit uses the story of Ahikar to support his exhortation	Paul's instruction gets support from the words of Jesus (20:35b)

In addition, the Pauline instruction to support the weak in the Miletus speech is parallel to the charity instructions of Tobit. Though Paul does not explicitly ask the Ephesian elders to give alms (ἐλεημοσύνη) his command to support the weak in 20:35, together with the maxim of Jesus ("it is more blessed to give than to receive"), is a clear indication of the book's influence on Luke. Frequent occurrences of the term charity / alms (ἐλεημοσύνη) in the Book of Tobit (1:16; 4:7, 10–11; 7:7; 12:8–9; 14:2) and Luke-Acts (cf. Lk 11:41; 12:33; Acts 9:36; 10:2; 24:17) further confirms the above judgment.

Even though we have not drawn a comparison of all the above LXX-Intertestamental specimens with the Miletus speech, it can generally be said that they have many factors in common. Those four motifs identified in Jewish farewell speeches by Munck (see p. 30 above) are more or less present in all the speeches of the Jewish writings examined above. The same motifs are also present in the Miletus speech. Above all, what is clearly noticeable in these speeches is the ethical emphases they furnish.

1.5. Concluding Remarks

This chapter was an attempt to situate the Miletus speech within the broader context of ancient speech traditions. Coming to the farewell speeches examined we notice that the Greco-Roman death scenes and farewell words and speeches differ significantly in tone, situation, vocabulary, and rhetoric from the LXX and the Testament of Twelve Patriarchs. In Greco-Roman literature, the farewell speeches are delivered generally by statesmen or philosophers. They show much concern with suicide, the meaning of death, questions about noble deaths, and life after death. Most of this is alien to deaths and farewells in the Biblical traditions. Conversely, Greco-Roman death scenes lack the strong Biblical emphases on God's plan, people and covenant, or on theodicy and theological interpretation of history.[139]

One of the elements quite visible in all the farewell speeches, whether it is Greco-Roman, Jewish or New Testament,[140] is the ethical emphases they render. One of the major functions of such kind of speeches was to exhort the children or followers to lead a certain course of life or follow certain values. From the specimens examined we can reasonably conclude that ethics and morality play a significant role. The above analysis of ancient farewell speeches reveals that they function as some kind of aid material for the composition of the Miletus speech. Was Luke, in composing Miletus speech, more indebted to the Greco-Roman or Jewish materials? The observations in this chapter indicate that Luke was indebted to ancient documents in general but at least in the case of Miletus speech, his primary mold was Jewish materials[141] rather than Greco-Roman materials

[139] Kurz, "Luke 22:14–38," 261.

[140] For the influence of Greco-Roman literature on the farewell speeches see, John C. Stube, *A Graeco-Roman Rhetorical Reading of the Farewell Discourse*, LNTS 309 (London: T&T Clark, 2006); George L. Parsenios, *Departure and Consolation: The Johannine Farewell Discourses in Light of Greco-Roman Literature*, NTSup 117 (Leiden: Brill, 2005); Kurz, *Farewell Address in the New Testament*; and "Luke 22:14–38."

[141] For the influence of OT on the speeches in Acts see Kurichianil, "Speeches in Acts," 181–86.

Chapter 2

An Overview of the Pauline Speeches in Acts

This chapter's focus will be mainly on a general study of the Pauline speeches in Acts in comparison with the Miletus speech. Some general observations about the non-Pauline speeches in Acts may also be perused as part of our attempt to present a comprehensive picture of the Pauline speeches. Moreover, it will also investigate the narrative context, nature, and importance of the Miletus speech and how the speech differs from other Pauline speeches found in Acts.

2.1. Preliminary Observations

"What is the most striking feature of Acts?" The instant answer to the question will be this: "It is the speeches found in it." In fact, the speeches in Acts make up a third of its total material and this indicates their importance. All the speeches in Acts have a simple style and rhetoric. It was the mastery of Luke to attribute each speech to an appropriate character who is involved in the narrative.[1] The speeches of Acts focus continuously on the gospel message with a religious purpose, a trait that distinguishes Acts from other historiography. The speakers like Peter, Stephen, and Paul emphasize the divine plan and its fulfillment in the person of Jesus whose death and resurrection gave way to the action of the Holy Spirit at present.

It is not easy to say how many speeches are there in Acts, nevertheless the reader cannot miss the major speeches delivered by Peter, Paul, and Stephen. Acts, being an ancient work of history originated in the Greco-Roman milieu, demonstrates two Greco-Roman tendencies: (1) Insertion of

[1] See Keener, *Acts*, 1:316.

speeches into the narratives, and (2) the creation of speeches for the occasion and / or embellishment of them.

Since the speeches in Acts seem to be summaries they "are simply too concise for us to expect them to display the sort of eloquence typical of the elite historians' speeches,"[2] still they give sufficient information to reveal the authors' intent.[3] Lucan speeches in Acts differ considerably from those given by the Greco-Roman counterparts. The following chart illustrates the similarities and differences.

Greco-Roman Speeches	**Speeches in Acts**
These are placed in the mouth of important persons	These are placed in the mouth of important persons
These sketch the character of important persons	These sketch the nature of the history of salvation and the promise and fulfillment of the divine plan
These are generally long	They are short
These display divergent perspectives often with counter-speeches	These normally defend a single point of view
These may praise, persuade, exhort, entertain, defend, and accuse	These are more apologetic and deliberative
These reveal rhetorical composition in the written form	These manifest more evangelical concern and less rhetorical composition
These focus on important features in the narrative	These focus on the story of Jesus / church in the narrative
These have abundant indirect discourse	These have mostly direct discourse
These occur at crucial points in the action or in unusual and interesting situations to expose the events and facts	These occur at crucial points in the action or in unusual and interesting situations to interpret an event theologically
These show off historians' prowess	These convey theological motives

2.2. Some Important Features of Pauline Speeches in Acts

Two main protagonists of Acts are Peter and Paul. The first part of the Book of Acts (1–12) occupies a considerable space to report the speeches of Peter. The second part of the book (13–28) mainly reports the speeches of Paul. The person in whose mouth the speech was put is also important. In Greco-Roman

[2] Keener, *Acts,* 1:261.

[3] Keener, 1:260.

and Biblical tradition, speeches were usually put in the mouth of important figures to enhance the narrative's significance. With regard to the speeches of Acts in general it is noticed that in some of the speeches in Acts Luke is plainly not concerned with elegance of style or rhetorical effect, and Bruce comments, "It is curious how often the Greek becomes obscure when the apostles are speaking."[4]

Paul delivers 12 speeches in Acts of which two are evangelistic speeches to pagan audience, four are forensic speeches, four are addressed to the Jews, one is a paraenetic speech to the Ephesian elders and one is an exhortatory speech addressed to the fellow travelers during the sea voyage to Rome. It can be easily noticed that compared to Peter, there is a greater variety of speeches made by Paul. At Antioch of Pisidia we have a specimen of his missionary manner of reasoning with the Jews; in the speech at Athens of his unique way of appealing to the Greeks; in the Miletus speech of his earnestness in exhorting, strengthening, and comforting his devoted disciples; in the speech at Jerusalem of his manner of defense when attacked by his own people; in the speech before Felix of his strident apology before a Roman tribunal; in his speech before Agrippa of his way of personal appeal before a distinguished Jew;[5] and in the sea voyage speech of his manner of giving encouragement to a discouraged group.

Many features of the Pauline speeches are similar to the other speeches in Acts. The following features for example can be noticed as common to many speeches.

(1) The speeches in Acts have been composed first and foremost with a theological intent. Luke has inserted a number of speeches in the mouth of Peter, Paul and others to fit his theological purpose. It is in these speeches that Luke mainly explicates his theology and theological concerns. More than just placing speeches into the mouth of the protagonists of the story, Luke aims at something deeper. He conveys a theology, proclaims a message; he also defends and sometimes exhorts.

(2) Luke sees history as salvation history, not just chronological history. Therefore, he highlights the promise of God, fulfillment of the promise which climaxes in Jesus (cf. ch. 13) and in the Holy Spirit (2:17–21). Luke used the speeches in order to preach this message. Keener opines that Acts must include a significant proportion of material including speeches because proclamation is the focus of his work.[6]

---

[4] Bruce, *The Acts of the Apostles*, 126.

[5] The above ideas and phrases are from Gardner, "The Speeches," 395.

[6] Keener, *Acts*, 1:261.

(3) The speeches in Acts are neither long nor highly eloquent. Even though speeches could function to show off the writers polished rhetoric[7] no such attempt is visible in the speeches. They, more or less, state what is necessary for the speech and what is suitable to the occasion.

(4) Speeches are used to interpret events that are sometimes incomprehensible either to different groups of people, or due to conflicting strategies or procedures. So, the speeches bring out the issues in the narrative and many of the major themes, such as Christology, pneumatology, and soteriology, promise and fulfillment, repentance and forgiveness of sins, divine providence, and ethics, appear in the speeches.[8] "Whenever given an occasion to speak, the apostles try to convert the situation into an opportunity to proclaim the message of Jesus and convert others."[9]

(5) In the proclamations of Acts at least three main functions may be noted as belonging to speeches. They are apologetics, doctrinal teaching, and moral exhortation. No speech has been inserted into its place without a purpose. As we have noted above, the speeches are, in general, a vehicle for Lucan theology and concerns. So much so, that all speeches in Acts are proclamations. Therefore in the speeches of Acts one notices apology, doctrines, and paraenesis. Sometimes just one element may be present or an element may be completely shadowed by another.

(6) Insertion of quotations from the scriptures or other sources can be noticed, for example, at Acts 2:17–21, 25–28, 31; 4:11; 7:42–43, 49-50; 13:33b, 34b, 35b, 41; 15:16–18; 17:28; 20:35b.

The above six features apply to all the speeches of Acts including that of Paul. However, the following features are more specific to Pauline Speeches.

(1) Majority of Pauline speeches are forensic.[10] Paul is defending the Christian movement as a legitimate entity within Judaism and therefore he has done no crime to get any punishment from the political or religious authorities. Paul is defending Christianity, and Luke is defending Paul. One of the purposes of Acts is to defend Paul and his mission. Luke felt the need to do so, and therefore it was necessary and important for Luke to insert these defense speeches of Paul in Luke's history of the church.

---

[7] Cadbury, *The Making of Luke-Acts*, 184.

[8] Kennedy, *New Testament Interpretation*, 115.

[9] Kennedy, 140.

[10] Paul's defense speeches amount to half of his speeches put together, 73 verses in total.

(2) Paul delivers speeches mainly to the Gentile audiences, his speeches at Lystra and Areopagus, and speeches before Roman officials in chapters 22–26 are examples. Peter too does it once in Acts 10:34–43. It is natural that Paul should speak more to the Gentiles as he is set apart as an apostle of the Gentiles.

(3) In the speeches delivered to the Gentiles, Paul does not speak of Israel's history, unlike in other speeches delivered to the Jewish audiences. Israel's history is irrelevant to a pagan audience and Luke omits it and employs other means to flesh out the speeches. For example, the first person ('I' style) reporting of the conversion experience of Paul in the defense speeches which is unique.

(4) Paul delivers a farewell speech at Miletus whose form and content are completely different from the other speeches of Paul. This speech of Paul is exhortatory. Some specific Lucan and Pauline ethical concerns are visible in the speech, a fact that distinguishes the speech from other speeches. Most themes found in this speech have no parallels in the other Petrine (or Stephen's) speeches of Acts. Those themes dear to most speeches in Acts such as promise-fulfillment, divine providence and salvation history, and the doctrinal point of resurrection of the dead never appear in the speech, rather new themes appear in it. A similar exhortatory function of the sea voyage speech (27:21b–26, 31–34) makes it more or less thematically parallel with the Miletus speech.

2.3. The Function of Pauline Speeches within the Narrative of Acts

Schubert divides the speeches in Acts into three cycles. The first is from chapters 1–5, the second from chapters 6–20, and the final cycle from 21–28. In the first cycle the main theology of Luke is set forth. In the second cycle, Lucan theology is fully developed in its various aspects.[11] The division of speeches into three cycles, as done by Schubert, may not benefit us much as we see that this division appears imposed. All the speeches, whether Petrine or Pauline, have their particular function and a corresponding theology, mostly depending upon the audience for whom they were given. For example, divine plan, promise and fulfillment, resurrection, repentance, forgiveness of sins etc. are the main themes of Petrine speeches. All these themes reappear in the speeches of Paul as well. Besides these, Pauline speeches also contain other themes such as witnessing to the resurrection, devotion to the God of Israel, social concern, etc.

Within the proclamatory structure of the speeches, which function as deliberative, exhortatory, didactic, and apologetic, the main themes of Acts

[11] Paul Schubert, "The Final Cycle of Speeches in the Book of Acts," *JBL* 87 (1968), 2.

are also included. Speeches in Acts could include various categories and even shift from one to another in their different parts. The Pauline speeches include all the above functions but Paul's speeches are more apologetic and his Miletus speech stands out to be unique among the speeches. In the Miletus speech epideictic, deliberative and even defense categories interplay. Mixed rhetorical genres were common in some other ancient speeches.[12] The following paragraphs will give a comprehensive view of the Pauline speeches and how they function within the narrative as a whole.

2.3.1. An Overview of the Major Pauline Speeches

The first speech given in the synagogue of Pisidian Antioch is a mission speech. The purpose of this speech was to make converts. The speech begins with a Jewish story of salvation, as in some of the LXX speeches examined in the previous chapter, culminating in Jesus the savior. And this word of salvation has now sent to us (13:26). Paul makes a "theologically saturated survey of history, which ended in a Christological claim."[13] God acted in history to bring forward a savior from the line of David and this savior was rejected by the Jews, but God raised him from the dead. This short historical narrative is the foundation for Paul's proclamation of the good news (13:32) introduced with "we" (καὶ ἡμεῖς). The gist of the primitive preaching of Jesus' death, resurrection, and appearances (which also is the primitive Christology taught by Peter earlier) render the speech of Paul quite primitive. Paul recognized that the Jews should be the first recipients of salvation, hence, the Antiochean speech clearly underlines the Jewish priority of the reception of the word (13:32–33, 38, 46). The speech contains a number of scriptural quotations to prove his claims about Jesus. In any case, the first speech of Paul in the synagogue of Antioch was not accepted by some Jews who opposed him, which opened doors to Gentile mission (13:46–47).

The Speech of Barnabas and Paul at Lystra (14:15–17) is addressed to a Gentile Audience. The speech contains words of direct address to the audience, an appeal to the commonality of human nature, a mention of the gospel and an implication to natural theology. They make clear that all have same human nature, common origin, common destiny and functions.[14] Therefore, what is needed now is to turn to the living God, shunning all foolish things (idolatry—worshiping men as God). The speech contains no direct scriptural quotations, instead Paul appeals to natural theology revealed in scripture (Ex 20:11).

---

[12] David E. Aune, *The Westminster Dictionary of New Testament and Early Christian Literature and Rhetoric* (Louisville, KY: John Knox, 2003), 419.

[13] Soards, *Speeches in Acts*, 83.

[14] See Porter, *The Paul of Acts*, 138–139.

The Athenian speech of Paul (17:22–31) is significant for many reasons. It is the second speech of Paul directed to a pagan audience. Like the previous speech, this one also appeals to a form of natural theology which makes God known, and the speech ends with a reference to the resurrection. It otherwise does not follow the structure of the primitive kerygma nor has it any account of a Jewish salvation story. The speech on the other hand is against polytheism and idolatry. It emphatically states the need to worship a man, the one God has raised from the dead. It is curious to note that the speech does not directly mention 'Jesus' rather he is a man whom he has appointed (ἀνδρὶ ᾧ ὥρισεν). The speech could not gain many followers except a few, as they scoffed at him and some expressed that they would hear him another time, for he was speaking about the resurrection of the dead.

A variety speech, which resembles like Paul's letters, is delivered to the Ephesian elders at Miletus. I make no further comment on it here since the speech will be studied at length in the coming chapters.

Now I turn to the final set of speeches (chs. 22–28) which are all identified, except the penultimate one, as defense speeches as they are found in a forensic set up. Bulk of Pauline speeches makes this category. The apologetics of Paul are mainly present in the defense speeches (forensic genre); doctrinal teachings coupled with apologetics are found in the missionary speeches; and ethical exhortations linked with apologetics are characteristics of the Miletus speech. Doctrinal teachings and ethics, as per the Greco-Roman division of speeches, belong to the deliberative genre. One scholar has argued that Miletus speech belongs to the epideictic genre, a discussion I will reserve for a later chapter.

The enormity of defense speeches in Acts indicates that Paul was defending his mission as legitimate. The defense speeches are in the first-person style ('I' style),[15] and, notable here is the narration of his conversion experience twice (22:6–16; 26:12–18). The narration of his Damascus experience in first person is the center of the speech. The Damascus experience has already been narrated by Luke in chapter 9, but now Paul himself narrates it to emphasize the importance of the commission he received from the risen Lord. Paul defends his stance and what he is doing because his mission is not of human origin, but divine. Paul has not done anything against the Mosaic laws or customs; he speaks himself as an ardent observer of the same. This is well stated by Hansen, "The defense speeches are related uniquely to Paul's identity as a Pharisee and a Roman citizen,

---

[15] Schubert, "The Final Cycle," 4.

it seems clear that Luke's primary purpose is a personal defense of Paul's Jewish orthodoxy and legal innocence under Roman Law."[16]

Now, concerning the speech to the Jews of Jerusalem (22:1–21), four features are notable. They are Paul's word of direct address, mention of making a defense (ἀπολογία), recounting of his personal past, and emphasis upon Jesus.[17] What is more striking in the speech is his personal past (3–21). His Jewish identity, education, zeal for his religion, persecution of Christians, and his encounter with Christ etc. are retold in first person style.

The speech before Felix (24:10b–21) begins by stating that he is making a defense (ἀπολογέομαι). The main points of Lucan theology once again appear here. Paul reaffirms his singular devotion to the God of Israel and his faith in the Law and the Prophets (v. 14). He then states the hope in the resurrection of both the just and the unjust (v. 15). The speech also includes a reference to the alms for Jerusalem which ties to the social ethics of Luke-Acts. Paul ends his speech categorically stating that it is in respect to the resurrection of the dead that he is on trial.

The speech before King Agrippa (26:2–29) is the climactic defense speech of Paul. "Its point is that Paul, far from being a criminal, preaches in obedience to divine revelation and that his message is grounded in the historic hope of Israel and the Scriptures."[18] We may hold that more than defending himself of the charges brought against him, Paul is witnessing in his own defense.[19] The speech has the following features. (1) The *exordium* contains a *captatio benevolentiae*[20] in which Paul praises Agrippa for his familiarity with Jewish people and their customs (vv. 2–3). (2) Paul's continuity with the Jewish roots and his earnestness for his religious belief is stated, but now his trial is on account of his belief in the resurrection (vv. 4–8). (3) Paul begins his *probatio* (proof) by speaking of his conviction[21] for doing destructive things against the name of Jesus of Nazareth and it contains a short account of his actual persecution of the saints (vv. 9–11). (4) Paul retells of his conversion (vv. 12–18) where new narrative elements are added compared to the previous accounts of his conversion. Most notable is the mission of Paul called to open the eyes of the people so that they may turn

---

[16] G. Walter Hansen, "The Preaching and Defense of Paul," in *Witness to the Gospel: The Theology of Acts*, I. Howard Marshall and David Peterson, ed. (Grand Rapids: Eerdmans, 1998), 320.

[17] Porter, *The Paul of Acts*, 152.

[18] Keener, *Acts: An Exegetical Commentary*, vol. 4, *24:1–28:31* (Grand Rapids: Baker Academics, 2015), 3491.

[19] Witherington, *The Acts of the Apostles*, 736.

[20] Literally means "winning of goodwill." It is a rhetorical technique practiced by the ancients to capture the goodwill of the audience at the beginning of a speech.

[21] Paul considered that it was his moral duty to oppose the new sect and their claims.

from darkness to light and from the power of Satan to God, so that they may receive forgiveness of sins and a place among those who are sanctified by faith in Jesus. A third time the story of Paul's conversion is being mentioned here for Paul's mission is grounded on the charge from the risen Lord. (5) An account of Paul's ministry of preaching repentance both among the Jews and Gentiles (vv. 19–23). (6) Paul's declaration of sobriety and the demand to believe in the Prophets by seeking the king's conversion (vv. 24–29).

Luke narrates the sea voyage in more detail for the reason that he himself was a co-traveller ("we" section). Paul makes a speech during his sea voyage to Rome (27:10, 21–26, 31–34) which echoes divine vindication through storm, and shipwreck. This speech is unique, for many ethical themes dear to Luke appear in it. Therefore it will be studied in more detail than the other speeches in this section. On seeing the rough sea, Paul told the officers that the journey would be dangerous with loss of cargo and lives. But the captain and the owner of the ship paid no heed to his words but they convinced the centurion otherwise and continued with their journey. The ship then faced violent winds. All hope of being saved was lost but Paul stood up among them and spoke words of hope and encouragement (vv. 21–26). Such words appear again towards the end of the speech (vv. 33–34). The basis of his hope and encouragement is his faith in God who reveals mysteries and His plans cannot be thwarted.

We don't discuss here the ancients' beliefs of the reason for the storm (as storm in the sea for the ancients was often linked with the sin of a person boarded on their boat or ship at sea; cf. Jon 1:7–10), or the veracity of the story, or who were all involved in the first person "we," or the historicity of the speech itself. The intention of Luke in narrating the episode is clear. Luke's interest is in attesting the role of Paul as a servant of God and God would bring him to Rome regardless of all obstacles.[22] In doing so Luke is also vindicating Paul as an apostle to the Gentiles. Thus, apologetics and ethics intersect in the section. Luke also finds it suitable to produce a short speech of Paul which largely contains elements of Lucan ethics.

The speech develops the *ethos* of Paul by alluding to his warning, assurance, and instruction to protect everyone. Paul's concern for others, first and foremost, reinforces his positive *ethos*. In the speech, the ethics of encouragement and caring can be clearly found. Paul encourages them to take food and survive. He is not angry at the officers even though they did not heed his voice; he sees hope even in the present crisis even though his fellow travelers have already lost hope. He uses a proverb from the LXX (cf. 1 Sam 14:45; 2 Sam 11:14; 1 Kg 1:52; see also Lk 21:18) to reiterate the fact that God's care is total and he knows it through a revelation.

[22] Keener, *Acts*, 4:3569.

The speech itself is deliberative,[23] than anything else. It informs the reader of the courage of Paul, a courage that a philosopher should demonstrate when facing dangers. He should not fear death either.[24] The base for this courage is his faith in God. "A strong faith in God is the foundation for a life of encouragement."[25] Sometimes outward circumstances may run contrary, but everything will end as God has planned. Fear is the absence of faith (Lk 8:25; Mt 8:26); a man of faith is a man of courage. The speech then moves to the concern for the lives of the sailors who tried to escape. It seems that Paul is deeply concerned with the life of his fellow travellers, not only their physical life, but beyond; it links with the motif of salvation here (27:31) as this motif plays a crucial role in Luke-Acts. For Luke, salvation is not only bound with the world to come, but also with the life here below. Salvation of the body is as important as the salvation of the soul. Sharing and caring make sense only when the other is considered to be a person made up of body, mind and soul; but above all the other is created in the image of God.

Paul's encouraging words to eat food display his care for all, both believers and pagans. The travellers did not eat for fourteen days most probably due to sea sickness or they had lost hope. They thought that they would die in the sea and dying in sea would be cruel as such bodies will not get a burial.[26] In such a desperate state, Paul was encouraging them to eat. Not just once, but many times as the imperfect παρεκάλει indicates. This encouraging image of Paul is quite fitting here in the book as this is an important theme in it (see 2:44–45; 4:36–37; 11:29–30; 14:22; 20:34–35). For Paul, all must work for the common good, and he initiates it himself by caring for others on the ship. For Luke, Paul is a model of virtue.

2.3.2. The Apologetic Function of Pauline Speeches

Many scholars concur that one of the primary functions of Luke-Acts is apologetic. F. C. Baur for example, sees the purpose of Acts as apologetic.[27] G. Sterling suggests that Acts should be viewed as an "apologetic historiography." He argued that many early Greek historians were ethnographers who were interested in documenting "the land, the history, the marvels, and the customs of a people," but originally from a purely Greek perspective.[28] In

---

[23] Witherington, *The Acts of the Apostles*, 767.

[24] Numerous citations on the courage of philosophers can be found in Keener, *Acts*, 4:3627–29.

[25] Larkin, *Acts*, 373.

[26] See Keener, 4:3620–22.

[27] Ferdinand C. Baur, *Paul the Apostle of Jesus Christ: His Life and Works, his Epistle and his Teaching* (Peabody: Hendrickson, 2003), 6. Baur is one of the first to suggest the apologetic purpose of Acts.

[28] See Sterling, *Historiography*, 20–53.

their writings they demonstrated their cultural superiority. The priests of the Near Eastern world, among others, strongly felt the need to respond to the cultural imperialism of the Hellenists. In order to execute this plan effectively they used Greek language and literary forms; in the process they created "apologetic historiography."[29] These Jewish writers argued that their culture was older and greater than that of the Greeks.[30] Josephus' works are a perfect example of apologetic historiography. Sterling also classifies Luke-Acts into the genre of apologetic historiography.[31]

There is nothing solid that disapproves the apologetic nature of Acts. Historical foundation of the book is undeniable, and the apologetic aim, in fact, grows out of the established historical foundation.[32] Acts certainly function as an apology, and the apologetic thrust can be mainly seen in its speeches. A careful look at the speeches of Acts reveals that they often are responses to some issues, accusations, or misunderstandings. In other words one of the main thrusts of many of these speeches is their apologetic interest. Many of the speeches of Acts function apologetically for various audiences, such as Israel (7:2–53), philosophers (17:22–31), and Roman authorities (Acts 22–26). Even the speeches of outsiders, for example, Gallio (18:14–15), town clerk of Ephesus (19:35–40), Festus and Agrippa (26:31–32), are used for apologetic purposes.[33] Those speeches in forensic setting particularly serve an apologetic purpose.[34] Paul comes in direct confrontation with the Roman authorities towards the end of the book and all the speeches in chapters 22 to 26 serve this purpose. However, these speeches are not solely for defense purposes rather they are also a vehicle for theology and mission.

The speeches that ground gentile mission function in an apologetic way by emphasizing that the Jesus movement is thoroughly Jewish and hence

---

[29] Sterling, 55–136.

[30] Sterling, 137–225.

[31] Sterling, 311–89. Following Sterling, many others for example, Mason, and Johnson, view Acts through the lens of Apologetic Historiography. See Steve Mason, *Josephus and New Testament* (Peabody: Hendrickson, 1992), 196–97; Johnson, *The Acts of the Apostles*, xii. Useful here also is Keener's observations under the title "apologetic historiography" in *Acts*, 1:161–64.

[32] Baur, *Paul the Apostle*, 9. Baur suggests that those omissions and silence of names in Acts (episode of Peter and Paul at Antioch, omission of the name Titus in Acts) are in view of the apologetic character of Acts. See Baur, *Paul the Apostle*, 7. The vision of Paul is any proof of his apostolic mission. In this connection, the vision of Peter in Acts 10 and its acknowledgment by the primitive church is of importance as an indirect legitimation of the Pauline visions. It may be also noticed that in the Miletus speech, Paul makes efforts to defend himself and his works, thus rendering it some elements of defense.

[33] Keener, *Acts*, 1:448.

[34] Bruce, *The Acts of the Apostles*, 24.

not a disrespectable new cult.[35] It could also be said that Paul's evangelistic preaching, too, partly functions apologetically. For example, in 14:15 and 17:29–31 Luke finds common ground in belief, nonetheless, in 14:17 and 17:22–28, he also presents how the Gentiles see the God of the Christians thereby, defending "ethical monotheism."

Apologetic involves an agenda or purpose rather than a specific literary form. For this reason, it can overlap with various other types of historiography that are classified by form or topic.[36] It also explains why none of the forensic speeches exhibit a complete traditional rhetoric structure.[37] Nonetheless, various rhetorical elements such as *exordium, narratio, argumentatio,* and *propositio* found in such speeches indicate that Luke was familiar with the structures of the forensic rhetoric.[38] Bruce W. Winter suggests that Luke was indebted to the handbooks on forensic speeches for the judicial speeches in Acts.[39] Similar rhetorical elements are found also in many other speeches of Acts. The genre and structure of the judicial speeches in Acts are similar to the official proceedings of the Roman court. The prime difference is that the judicial speeches in Acts belong in a literary setting, whereas the official proceedings do not.[40]

Apologetic, though makes good sense, and is more evident in the defense speeches, is only one objective of the Pauline speeches in Acts. The defense speeches have other objectives as well. In general, the Pauline speeches, like most other speeches, aim at conveying the motif of the inauguration of the promised messianic era in the person of Jesus and that of the church as the new Israel of the same era. In the speeches, Luke goes beyond other Hellenistic Jewish writers in his overarching promise-fulfillment schema.[41] Within the promise-fulfillment schema other themes such as resurrection, divine plan, repentance, forgiveness, ethics, etc. do appear. To give an example of ethical emphasis, Paul's conversation with Felix, though not presented here as a speech, dealt with "righteousness, self-control, and the judgment to come. The reasons for taking up these topics for discussion,

---

[35] Keener, 1:267.

[36] Keener, 1:161.

[37] Aune, *Literary Environment*, 126.

[38] Rhetorical analysis of some speeches in Acts can be found in Kennedy's book, *New Testament Interpretation*, 114–40.

[39] For a comprehensive comparative presentation between court proceedings and forensic speeches in Acts see Bruce W. Winter, "Official Proceedings and the Forensic Speeches in Acts 24–26," in *The Book of Acts in Its Ancient Literary Setting* (Bruce W. Winter and Andre D. Clark, ed., vol. 1 of the *BAFCS*, Bruce W. Winter, ed.; Grand Rapids: Eerdmans, 1993), pp. 315–36.

[40] Winter, "Official Proceedings," 331.

[41] Keener, *Acts*, 1:164.

most probably, were aimed at correcting Felix's own wrong notions on spousal relationship and money. Felix's adultery (which is not mentioned by Luke), was a known fact and his desire for money from Paul gets a mention from Luke (24:26).[42] Mention was already made of the collection of Paul for Jerusalem as a gesture of sharing and caring. However, such themes get more space in the deliberative speeches.

2.3.3. The Deliberative Function of the Pauline Speeches

A number of speeches in Acts functions to fulfill a deliberative function. The speeches in chapters 1–20 are largely deliberative, seeking converts. Deliberative speeches are aimed at persuading someone to adopt a course of action. The evangelical or missionary speeches of Peter and Paul do mainly serve this function. The book, in fact, begins with a speech of Peter and in the succeeding pages few other speeches of Peter are recorded, all of which have mainly a deliberative function, even sometimes, as noted above, apologetic or exhortatory functions may intersect and overlap.

According to Keener, most evangelistic speeches in Acts will be largely deliberative, calling for conversion.[43] Deliberative speeches often reveal a didactic character. For example, the first speech of Peter contains doctrine of "apostolic succession" and the Pentecost speech contains doctrines of the "Holy Spirit," "salvation," and "resurrection." This is closely related to the deliberative nature of the speeches. The Greek verb and noun διδάσκω and διδαχή in their various derivative forms appear 16 times in Acts. However, within the speeches, the word does not appear but the speeches themselves are to be seen as the proclamation and teaching of the apostles at least in those contexts where the word appears in 4:2, 18; 5:21, 42; 11:26; 15:35; 18:11; 20:20; 28:31. It is also true that although forensic elements dominate the speeches in courts, other subordinate purposes may be visible there. For example in 26:29 a deliberative purpose is included. If we consider the speeches of Peter and Stephen deliberative, they also contain elements of defense,[44] for they seek vindication by defending the speaker's point of view.

Deliberative speeches aim at persuading the audience to change attitude, and to take a different course than the one now. Seen this way, the deliberative speeches include exhortatory function. There are two speeches in Acts that are more exhortatory ethical and less apologetic or missionary—the Miletus and the sea voyage speeches. The former is addressed to a

[42] See Schubert, "The Final Cycle," 13.

[43] Keener, 1:263.

[44] Heinz-Werner Neudorfer takes the speech of Stephen as a missionary speech. See "The Speech of Stephen," in *Witness to the Gospel: The Theology of Acts*, I. Howard Marshall and David Peterson, ed. (Grand Rapids: Eerdmans, 1998), 275–94. In my opinion it is also a defense speech.

Christian audience. It seeks a moral result, while the latter is addressed to a mixed group of travelers. It expects a boost in morale. Both speeches do not aim for converts, rather deliberations are rendered on different lines. I have already carried out a short study of the sea voyage speech, and so now it is required that the Miletus speech be examined in detail.

2.4. The Miletus Speech of Paul within the Pauline Speeches

Having examined the Pauline speeches in general, we now turn to the Miletus speech proper. We will only delineate its narrative context and nature here; a detailed theological exposition of the speech will follow in the succeeding chapters.

2.4.1. The Narrative Context of the Miletus Speech

The Miletus speech of Paul is the last public speech of Paul before his imprisonment. The speech is placed towards the end of his third missionary journey. After having established the church in Ephesus during his second missionary journey (18:19), he departed for a third journey from Syrian Antioch which would take him to the churches he established earlier, as well as, to found new ones. This journey took Paul back to Ephesus but Luke concentrates only on that narrative that unfolded in Ephesus (19:1–41). After the turbulent days in Ephesus Paul sailed to places like Troas, Philippi, Corinth etc. At this time Paul expressed his wish to go to Rome (19:21) but before that to return to Jerusalem by Pentecost (20:16). As he was in a hurry to get to Jerusalem he sent word to the Ephesian elders to meet him at Miletus. When the Ephesian elders gathered at Miletus, Paul delivered his speech to them.

2.4.2. The Nature of the Miletus Speech

Towards the end of the third missionary journey of Paul, Luke inserts the Miletus speech of Paul. This is the only speech in Acts delivered to a Christian audience. The speech is a pastoral-ethical exhortation given to a group of leaders by their beloved apostle and leader, Paul. This speech, compared with other NT material, is more akin to the theological framework of the Pauline letters. Not every theological consideration of Paul appears, or, again, no profound theological points have been made in the speech, however, few verbal and thematic parallelisms can be clearly seen. It might be that Luke wanted to relate his theological accents to that of Paul by placing the speech in the mouth of Paul. But, the speech itself is either material Luke inherited or his creation to strike a parallel between Jesus, the ethical teacher, and Paul. Paul is not only paralleled with Jesus in his teachings, but also in other respects. Just as Jesus preached and taught on his way to Jerusalem,

Paul is made to speak on his way to Jerusalem.[45] The speeches of Peter are all evangelistic speeches, sometimes involving elements of defense. On the other hand, Paul makes evangelistic, defense, and ethical speeches. It was the creativity of Luke to place two exhortatory ethical speeches (Miletus and sea voyage speeches) in the book. The sea voyage speech mainly has two functions. They are to encourage the audience not to lose hope and to place Paul as the hero in the story. But what is the function of the Miletus speech? Is it (1) to underscore the apostolic succession or (2) to parallel Jesus with Paul or (3) to underscore the pastoral duties of elders or (4) to defend Paul and his behavior[46] or (5) to emphasize certain exhortatory concerns, which always produce ethical exhortations, of Luke or (6) to collectively emphasize all the above five functions?

We cannot pin point a single objective of the speech.[47] Nonetheless, it seems that many purposes are at play, and, as we have already indicated in the introduction, various scholars have suggested different purposes of the speech, but a majority favor the exhortatory value of the speech.

2.4.3. The Ethical Character of the Miletus Speech

The speech may contain elements of defense or epideictic, but the primary being paraenesis. Paraenesis, which includes both persuasion and dissuasion, is integral to a deliberative speech. Earlier we have seen how the Greco-Roman genres function within their various writings. It seems that the Miletus speech has been composed making use of all three Greco-Roman genres (epideictic, deliberative, and forensic), but the dominant genre being the deliberative. Ethical and moral instructions are best found in deliberative genre than in any other. Miletus speech's ethical exhortations at its best are found in verses 32–35. Grace ethics, labor ethics, ethics of riches and poverty, ethics of giving, and contentment ethics play a key role in the pericope. The second part of this thesis will engage in a detailed study of the ethical emphases of these verses.

According to Jan Lambrecht, when Paul addresses the elders he gives them rules of conduct, his own behavior as an example, by which he motivates them.[48] In the same vein he suggests that in Luke's conception, Paul's primary purpose is probably not self-defense or announcement concerning his future, but exhortation.[49] This view has been affirmed by Barrett as he states: "In the

---

[45] See Johnson, *Acts of the Apostles*, who makes Peter and John, the apostles, as Jesus' prophetic successors, who repeat everything that Jesus did.

[46] Defending Paul is a major purpose of Acts; not only his theology and words need to be defended, but also his behavior and conduct.

[47] In a later chapter the purpose of the speech will be examined in detail.

[48] Lambrecht, "Paul's Farewell Address," 316.

[49] Lambrecht, 318.

speech of chapter 20 Paul is the chief and exemplary evangelist and pastor, who by word and example instructs the new generation in their duties."[50] In the Miletus speech we can say that Luke discloses his ethical agenda through the mouth of Paul. In his ethical orientation, Luke was closer to the historical Paul.[51] In the preceding pages a short description of the speeches in Acts has already been given. I observe the following differences and similarities in my comparison of the speeches in Acts and the Miletus speech.

Speeches in Acts	**Miletus Speech**
Have very few verbal or thematic similarities with the Pauline letters	Has many verbal and thematic similarities with the Pauline letters
Have ethical orientation but less compared to the Miletus speech	Is ethically oriented more than any other speech in Acts.
Are missionary in nature	Is exhortatory and ethical in nature
The addressees are Jews or Gentiles	The addressees are Christians
In a few instances narrate the historical past	Contains a retrospection of Paul's ministry
May contain elements of eschatology	Does have a prospection of Paul's life
Contain doctrinal elements	Contains minimum doctrinal elements
Are either deliberative or forensic	Contains deliberative, forensic and epideictic elements
Usually emphasize the resurrection (of Jesus), repentance, and fulfillment of the scriptures	Emphasizes Paul as a model, the importance of giving and caring.
Usually have a salutation (1:16; 2:29; 7:2; 13:15, 26, 38; 15:7, 13; 22:1; 23:1, 6; 28:17 see also, Ἄνδρες Ἰσραηλῖται "Israelites men" 2:22; 3:12; 5:35; 13:16; 21:28) and an invitation to listen (2:22; 7:2; 13:16; 15:13; 22:1; 26:3)	Has no salutation, no invitation to listen

[50] Charles K. Barrett, "Paul's Address to the Ephesian Elders," in *God's Christ and His People: Studies in Honor of Nils Alstrup Dahl*, Jacob Jervell and Wayne A. Meeks, ed. (Oslo: Universitet-forlaget, 1978), 108.

[51] Richard I. Pervo, "The Paul of Acts *and* the Paul of the Letters: Aspects of Luke as an Interpreter of the *Corpus Paulinum*," in *Reception of Paulinism in Acts = Réception du Paulinisme dans les Actes des Apôtres*, Daniel L. Marguerat, ed., BEThL 229 (Leuven: Peeters, 2009), 155.

Declare the identity of Jesus (2:36; 3:13-15, 20, 22, 26; 4:10; 5:31; 7:52, 56; 10:36, 42; 13:23, 33; 22:8; 22:14; 26:23)	Does not declare the identity of Jesus
Refer explicitly to the Prophets (2:16, 30; 3:18, 21, 24, 25; 7:42, 48, 52; 10:43; 13:27, 40; 15:15; 24:14; 26:22, 27, 28:25) and mention David (1:16; 2:25, 29, 34; 4:25; 7:45; 13:22 (2x); 13:34, 36; 15:16)	Has no prophetic quotation or mention of David.
Have many references to the Holy Spirit (1:5, 8, 16; 2:17, 18, 33, 38; 4:25; 5:32; 6:3; 7:51; 10:38; 11:12, 15, 16: 15:8; 21:11; 23:9; 28:25)	Has three references to the Holy Spirit (20:22, 23, 28)
Speeches in Acts	Miletus Speech
Usually have a call to repentance (2:38; 3:19; 5:31; 14:15; 17:30; 20:21 [implicitly]; 26:20 [implicitly]) and offer of forgiveness of sins (2:38; 3:19; 5:31; 10:43; 13:38; 22:16; 26:18)	Does not have a call to repentance or an offer of forgiveness but demands a change of attitude towards the weak

The first three points in the list, according to me, are the most important of all, namely, that the Miletus speech, unlike other speeches in Acts, contains many verbal and thematic parallels with the letters of Paul. The Miletus speech employs language familiar from philosophers and moralists, just as Paul's letters do.[52] Thus, it appears that the speech's ethical orientation is either the result of Lucan redaction of Pauline ethics or a portrayal of Luke's own community ethics. One thing is certain that the social ethics of Paul has a conspicuous similarity and relation with Lucan social ethics. In the following chapters I will examine these in detail.

52 See Abraham J. Malherbe, *Paul and the Popular Philosophers* (Minneapolis: Fortress Press, 2006), 152–54.

Part 2

The Ethical Emphases of the Miletus Speech: An Investigation into Acts 20:32–35

Chapter 3

Grace
A Gift Fundamental to Ethical Life

With this chapter we begin the evaluation of the ethical emphases of the Miletus speech. They are more powerful from verse 32 to 35. The theological accents, ethical themes, and emphases of these verses are recognizable also in the preceding verses of the speech (18–31); however these verses will not be studied at length here, but rather those verses relevant and related to this study will be examined as required in each case.

3.1. Preliminary Analysis of 20:32

This verse begins with καὶ τὰ νῦν which signals a dramatic shift in Paul's speaking and hence the phrase hints at a new theme or a change in the tone of Paul's speech. The statement in this verse, according to Keener, can go with the previous or the following unit, since there is no definite break in thought.[1] But it is clear enough to suggest that verse 32 is better linked to the following verses, for, καὶ τὰ νῦν functions aptly as a temporal clause with a change of tone from exhortation to a prayer. However, we should not forget that these verses are part of the same speech. For this reason it would be wrong to say that with verse 32 begins an entirely new unit or theme, for verses 32–35 are thematically connected to the previous verses, and, of course, they make a fitting and emphatic conclusion to the speech. These verses forcefully pronounce the new role the Ephesian elders are to assume imitating the example of Paul and ultimately of Jesus who is their supreme model.

---

[1] Keener, *Acts*, 3:3053.

We notice that within the speech the temporal clause καὶ νῦν is used two times (20:22, 25), a convention used several other times in the speeches (cf. 3:17; 7:34; 22:16; 26:6) and statements (10:5; 13:11; 23:21) of Acts. The use of the phrase in the Miletus speech functions as an invitation to change normal course of thinking or action for a new way of thinking and acting. The phrase found elsewhere in the speeches of Acts mostly functions in a similar manner.

A related form καὶ τὰ νῦν occurs in the verse under consideration (20:32) and also in 4:29; 5:38; 27:22. These instances are identical to the previous καὶ νῦν, and basically no new significance is attached to them. However, καὶ τὰ νῦν in 20:32 introduces a "shift in the tone and focus."[2] I concur with Soards and others who see a definite theological plan in verses 32–35 for καὶ τὰ νῦν introduces this plan. If we had a structure for the speech, it may help us recognize the significance of καὶ τὰ νῦν here.

Coming to the structure proper of the speech, there have been numerous attempts to construct it but no two commentators agree on a similar structure. And, that leaves most readers confused about its division, though this does not affect much the speech's theology and interpretation.[3] It can be clearly noticed that Luke employs in chapters 20 and 21, like in many other places in Luke-Acts, his favorite journey motif. By placing the Miletus speech at the center of Journey to Jerusalem (20:1–21:16). Luke wants to emphasize the importance of Paul's teaching precisely at this point.[4] Notice the structure suggested by Keener.

20:1–6: Travel
    20:7–12: Event
        20:13–16: Travel
            20:17–38: Event
        21:1–7: Travel
    21:8–14: Event
21:15–17: Travel

---

[2] Soards, *The Speeches in Acts*, 108.

[3] The structure of the speech has been drawn up by various scholars for example Dibelius who divides the speech into four parts: (1) vv. 18–21; (2) vv. 22–27; (3) vv. 28–31; and (4) vv. 32–35. See this division in "The Speeches in Acts and Ancient Historiography," 157. C. Exum and Charles Talbert have drawn up a chiastic structure for the speech. See "The Structure of Paul's Speech to the Ephesian Elders (Acts 20:18–35)," *CBQ* 29 (1967), 233–36; See also H. J. Michel who presents two parallel parts of the speech, verse 18–24 as parallel to 28–35. The first part is a personal section and the second is a paraenetic section, see *Die Abschiedsrede des Paulus an die Kirche: Apg 20:17–38*, pp. 26–27).

[4] In Luke, the important teachings of Jesus concerning discipleship, prayer, repentance, and the right use of wealth are given on his way to Jerusalem.

After a narrative about travel, an event takes place followed by subsequent travels and events. Paul's goal was to reach Jerusalem and then to Rome. Luke in a way provides compressed historical information about Paul's mission to remind the readers that Paul now leaves his successful Diaspora mission to return to Jerusalem.[5] In this rhythmic pattern, the Miletus speech steals the center place. As Paul is on his way to Jerusalem, he creates an occasion to meet the Ephesian elders at Miletus to instruct them about their most important obligation as leaders of the church.[6]

It seems that the speech is the most important event in the life of Paul in Ephesus. The following division I suggest for the speech will help to interpret the verse and the pericope fittingly which begins with καὶ τὰ νῦν. While the whole speech is one block of a single discourse, the speech itself may be broadly divided into three parts. (1) An account about Paul's past ministry (18b–21); (2) his present state and knowledge about his immediate future (22–27); and (3) his instructions to the elders for the future (28–35). The instructions given in the last part contain faith and / or pastoral matters (28–31) and ethics and morality (32–35). The second and third parts begin with καὶ (τὰ) νῦν. Moreover, καὶ τὰ νῦν in v. 32 makes a transition from the instructions concerning faith and pastorals to the instructions concerning ethics and morality.

This verse's main focus is on the λόγος τῆς χάριτος αὐτοῦ. Paul is commending the Ephesian elders here to the "word of His grace." This is a unique construction, for, similar constructions are found nowhere in the NT books except twice in Luke-Acts (Acts 14:3 and Luke 4:22). The usual constructions such as "word of God," "word of the Lord" etc. are frequent in the NT material; on the contrary, the "word of His grace" is unique here and therefore it seems to be more Lucan than Pauline. Tablets with curses excavated may indicate belief in demons and handing over their opponents to the gods of the lower world as it is reflected in 1 Tim 1:20. The counterpart to this is Acts 20:32 where Lucan Paul commends the elders to God and the word of his grace.[7] Although grace is a frequent Pauline term, the construction "word of His grace" most probably is a Lucan construction.

---

[5] Keener, *Acts*, 3:2947.

[6] Some scholars doubt the authenticity of the speech and its context. They opine that it was Luke who created an occasion for Paul to deliver the speech and the content of the speech. However, most scholars see this speech and its context as very original since there was no need for Luke to create a forged occasion for the speech or the speech itself at this point of the narrative. Moreover, the speech is very Pauline, though some Lucan features are distinct in it, and this is purely because of the theological and ethical affinity of Luke and Paul. These affinities will become clearer from this chapter on.

[7] See these points in Adolf Deissmann, *St. Paul: A Study in Social and Religious History* (London: Hodder and Stoughton, 1911), 73.

Who has "the power to build you up and to give your inheritance" (NJB): God or the "word of his grace?" The syntax rather seems to point to 'the word' as the referent of the relative ὃς. Syntactically the relative ὃς can be linked either to θεός or to λόγος.[8] Paul hands over his followers to the power of the word of His grace.[9] The structure of the speech above is clear enough apropos of a unit that is thoroughly ethical to suggest that "His grace" is emphasized in this verse more than God, because Paul sees grace as fundamental to ethics and morality.

The verb οἰκοδομέω[10] appears with a spiritual sense in Acts 9:31. In 20:32 the word is used not only in a spiritual sense but also in relational sense; the effect of the word of His grace should transform and build the Ephesian elders themselves and thus they build up the community of believers by rendering humble service to them by supporting the weak. What will enable them for this ministry is the word of His grace.

The word of His grace assures the inheritance to them among the sanctified. The sanctified are "set-apart ones," they are set apart for God, and they are the righteous or the remnant of Israel.[11] "Inheritance among those who are set apart" plays on the language of Israel's inheritance translated into eschatological terms in early Judaism.[12] Although this is an OT language for Israel, the same expression applies to Gentile believers in Acts 26:17–18. In Luke-Acts the inheritance includes especially "eternal life," the life of the kingdom (Lk 10:25; 18:18).

3.2. The χάρις Motif

Theologically the most important word in this verse is χάρις and therefore I begin this section with a short analysis of the term itself followed by its theological significance in Luke and Paul. χάρις is not a new word neither for Luke nor for Paul; it has been in use among the ancients even before the LXX period. J. Moffatt made a commendable study on the subject of "grace" and in his book, *Grace in the New Testament*, he expounds how the use of χάρις differs in its meaning in Greek and Jewish vocabulary. The term was in use

---

[8] See the comment of Fitzmyer in his commentary on Acts who links it with θεός, see p. 681.

[9] See for the material of this paragraph Marguerat, *Paul in Acts*, 43.

[10] The LXX word for Jeremiah's בָּנָה (to build) is οἰκοδομέω. Jeremiah has in mind the rebuilding of the people of Israel (e.g. Jer 1:10; 31:4, 28; 33 7; 42:10). Luke and Paul use the Greek word in its various forms many times. Luke never uses the word in the Gospel to indicate a spiritual building up of the community; in Acts it has been used in this sense only twice (9:31 and 20:32). Paul uses the word often in the sense of building up of the community (see Rom 14:19; 1 Cor 8:1,10; 14:4; Gal 2:18; 1 Thess 5:11).

[11] Keener, *Acts*, 3:3053.

[12] Keener, 3:3053.

in the Hellenistic circles. The profane use of the word in the ordinary sense would refer grace to showing favor, the lordly favor bestowed on a nation by Egyptian or Greco-Roman emperors. It also would mean the benefaction of one in power who grants some relief or practical benefit to his subordinates.[13]

Χάρις has been associated with supernatural power or aid closely connected with mystical or magical influence. It was also believed that there was a supernatural grace issuing from the other world; similarly the dead conveys some χάρις to the living.[14] The profane and the Hellenistic use of the word differed much in the later periods,[15] a topic into which I will not enter.

Coming to the OT use of the term, Hebrew חֵן is mostly translated in the LXX as χάρις.[16] חֵן is originally God's own power to impress, which he is able to bestow as a charisma which enables his people to create a favorable impression on those about them.[17] Another Hebrew word חֶסֶד also renders the meaning of χάρις, though the word is not translated as χάρις[18] but as ἔλεος except in Esth 2:9.[19] According to Conzelmann, χάρις is never a theological word in the LXX.[20]

Though the term grace has a special significance for the NT authors, two of them who have made abundant use of χάρις motif are Luke and Paul.[21] The concept of grace has already been present in the OT material. God's creation and election may be viewed as acts of grace. The three covenants, Abrahamic, Sinaitic, and Davidic, are based on grace.[22] Grace

---

[13] James Moffatt, *Grace in the New Testament* (New York: Richard R. Smith, 1931), 26.

[14] Moffatt, *Grace*, 28–29.

[15] For the development of the word in later antiquity see Moffatt, *Grace*, pp. 52–67; Hans Conzelmann and W. Zimmerli, "χάρις," *TDNT* 9:375–76.

[16] See Conzelmann and Zimmerli, "χάρις," 376–81. One of the arguments in favor of Luke's use and influence of the LXX is the usage of the LXX word χάρις throughout his two-volume work.

[17] John Nolland, "Grace as Power," *NT* 28 (1986), 29.

[18] Conzelmann and Zimmerli, "χάρις," 381–87.

[19] See also Sir 7:33; 40:17. The Book of Sirach, originally composed in Hebrew, was translated into Greek by the grandson of Sirach.

[20] Conzelmann and Zimmerli, "χάρις," 389.

[21] For the frequency of the word and its use in the NT see Klaus Berger, "χάρις," *EDNT* 3:457–460.

[22] These covenant formulae are similar to the royal treaties usually made between the king and the vassal. Accordingly, the vassals were to obey the conditions laid out in a contract for the full benefit of the contract. See Moshe Weinfeld, "The Covenant of Grant in the Old Testament and in the Ancient Near East," *JAOS* 90 (1970), 189–196.

was already there before any covenant was made.[23] In fact grace was the atmosphere and context into which the Decalogue is cast (Ex 20:1).[24] The Sinaitic covenant particularly calls for a total commitment and loyalty to the covenant stipulations through which grace becomes effective. According to Gordon Wenham, God's choice precedes man's obedience, but man's obedience is a prerequisite for knowing the full benefits of election.[25] Let us take Ex 19:4–5 as a specimen for evaluation. Three points are worth noting: firstly, the people see God's deeds in the past, secondly, they are called to obey him now, and thirdly, "if they obey" they will be his favorite people. Fuller benefits are added for obedience, but in the context of a grace already received and begun.[26]

One may naturally ask, "How then a person experiences grace if one is always obedient and law observing?"[27] Observing God-given laws does not nullify grace or grace did not mean observing no laws, or having grace did not mean all crimes are bypassed. It meant obeying the Lord and observing his ordinances. In fact, more grace will be given if people obey. "Obedience was not the source of blessing, but it augments a blessing already given."[28]

Both Paul and Luke draw much from the LXX notion of χάρις though the word is little used in the LXX sense. Grace is a central term in Acts and Pauline letters (often for his soteriology). Another important theological contributor is John who uses the phrase χάριν ἀντὶ χάριτος by which he describes how grace is contrary to the law, and the word χάρις becomes a synonym for Jesus (Jn 1:14–18). A striking factor here is the fact that Jesus never speaks about grace or a life of grace in any of the gospels. After the death of Jesus, His disciples applied the word to him, but that too in a minimal way.[29] I will briefly examine below how the word is used in Luke and Paul, since this is important for our analysis of the word in relation with the rest of the pericope.

---

[23] Grace of God was working from the beginning of creation and it continued to work. Grace was visible in God's election of people, Prophets and Kings; it was visible in His redemptive works, and it was visible in His guiding the history. In short, the whole history of Israel was the history of grace.

[24] Walter C. Kaiser, *Toward Old Testament Ethics* (Grand Rapids: Academie Books, 1983), 77.

[25] G. Wenham, "Grace and Law in the Old Testament," *The Highway,* accessed 20 May 2019, https://www.the-highway.com/law1_Wenham.html.

[26] Kaiser, *Old Testament Ethics*, 77.

[27] A similar rhetorical question in the negative is also asked by Paul, "Should we continue in sin in order that grace may abound?" expecting a negative answer.

[28] Wenham, "Grace and Law in the Old Testament."

[29] For the evangelist John, Jesus is Grace. See Jn 1:14–17.

3.2.1. χάρις in Luke-Acts

In Luke-Acts χάρις is used in two ways. (1) The "profane" sense of "favor," or "pleasure," occurs in Acts 24:27; 25:3, 9. The same profane use is also found in Acts 2:47; 4:33 but in the sense of "acceptance" and "blessing" respectively. (2) The "religious" use of the term can be found in Lk 1:30; 2:40; 2:52; 6:32, 33, 34; Acts 7:46; 7:10. Χάρις may be seen as instrumental in the spread of the church (Acts 11:23). Χάρις is generally used for the state of grace in 13:43 etc. One can notice people commended to the grace of God in 14:26 or to the grace of the Lord as in 15:40.

According to Luke's gospel, Jesus was God's manifestation of grace, a notion implicit in the other synoptics as well. Jesus becomes the personification of grace especially for the poor and needy through his words and action. In Luke 4:22 the "gracious words" is a synonym for the gospel.[30] People marvel at the words of Jesus. They marvel because the words are words of grace: the presence of χάρις makes a perceptible impact on the words.[31] Again, numerous vivid examples of the economy of grace, mostly healing miracles[32] and parables[33] are a feature of the Gospel of Luke. Healing miracles scattered throughout the gospel point to the overflowing grace of God tangibly manifested in history through the person of Jesus. The parables in the gospel are so attractive that the listeners are profoundly moved by them. Most of these parables are ethical; some proclaim the nature of the grace of God. For example, the parable of the Prodigal Son depicts the abundance of grace flowing through forgiveness.[34]

In Acts the Holy Spirit is the agent of grace and this Spirit is present with those who repent of their sins and accept Jesus as their Messiah and Lord (2:21, 38).[35] Where there is grace, there is the Holy Spirit and vice versa, no matter where the grace is found – in a community or person. It is intentional that Luke is making a parallel between the boy Jesus with χάρις (Lk 2:40, 52) and the young church with χάρις (Acts 4:33). They had 'great grace' is a reference most probably to the abundant spiritual blessings they experienced from the Lord or the respect they received from the society. The

---

[30] Moffatt suggests that Luke is using χάρις in 4:22 in its aesthetic sense, but there is more on his mind.

[31] For the idea, see Nolland, "Luke's Use of χάρις," 618.

[32] Healing miracles are found in Lk 4:31–39; 5:12–26; 6:6-11; 7:1–17; 8:26–56; 9:37–43; 13:10–17; 14:1–6; 17:11–19; 18:35–43.

[33] In particular are the parables of the Lost Sheep (15:3–7), Lost Coin (15:8–10), Lost Son (15:11–32), and the Great Dinner (Lk 14:16–24).

[34] See the presentation of S. Eastman, "The Foolish Father and the Economics of Grace," *ET* 117.10 (2006), 402–405.

[35] Kurz, *Farewell Address in the New Testament*, 42.

same idea has already been articulated in 2:47. The primitive Christians were "in favor" with all people. It is the result of "evangelistic success." Stephen is full of χάρις. Paul and Barnabas urge people to remain in χάρις. The use of the word 'grace' in Acts (e.g. 15:11; 18:27; 14:26; 15:40) is similar to the Pauline usage in many instances.

We are not entering here into an exhaustive discussion of grace according to Acts, but we focus only on those verses in the speech where the word appears. The "gospel of grace" and "word of His grace" used in the Miletus speech refer to the gospel of Jesus. It is unique to Luke to combine 'gospel' and 'grace' in 20:24. We find that Paul connects the word "gospel" with a genitive, such as we have in 'gospel of peace' or 'gospel of the glory of Christ' or 'gospel of your salvation' as in Eph 6:15; 2 Cor 4:4; Eph 1:13, but with an exception. He never uses the phrase, 'the gospel of God's grace,' although this would have been an apt formula for him. In all these instances their content may be gleaned from the context.[36] Here we need to ask: "What is the reason for Paul to speak of the "gospel of grace" (20:24) and the "word of His grace" (20:32) in the speech?" In the Miletus speech, the use of χάρις coupled with gospel is intentional because Paul repeatedly says that it is through the grace of God that he is an apostle of the gospel. A close association with Paul, perhaps, enabled Luke to hear often from him about the gospel and the grace Paul had received. Therefore, Luke might have found it fitting to use the favorite Pauline words by coining a phrase "gospel of grace" in the speech. The gospel also is the word / message. There isn't any conspicuous difference between gospel of grace and word of grace in 20:24 and 32. The usage 'to the word of His grace,' however, in v. 32 has a distinct purpose, which we will discuss little below.

3.2.2. *χάρις in Paul*

The word χάρις is a favorite term for Paul as he uses it abundantly in his letters. In fact, Paul opens his letters with a greeting of χάρις and εἰρήνη. It was also characteristic of Paul to close his letters with some reference to grace. The abundant use of the term and especially at the opening and closing of letters indicates the dominant place of 'grace' in his religious vocabulary, and as characteristic of his own message.[37]

In some of his letters he views grace as a favor pouring into human life. In this sense he speaks of abounding of grace (Rom 5:20; 6:1), the riches of his grace (Eph 1:7), the indescribable gift (2 Cor 9:14–15) and far surpassing in power any contrary force of evil (2 Cor 9:14) and filling life with hope and

---

[36] Conzelmann and Zimmerli, "χάρις," 392.

[37] Moffatt, *Grace in the New Testament*, 141.

strength. It is such a powerful grace that Paul wants the Ephesian elders to be filled with and he prays this for them in the Miletus speech.

Paul's use of the term χάρις suggests that it is a grace from the Lord, a free gift, just like faith. Grace is closely related to faith. In Romans and Galatians, grace is opposed to the Law. Paul speaks of salvation by faith, and those who do not believe in it are those who desert grace (Gal 5:4). By grace they were saved either from paganism, or sins, or immorality or false thinking and beliefs.

A brief survey of the use of χάρις in Pauline letters would reveal first of all that χάρις, the usual equivalent of OT חן for Paul, is not the same as Hebrew חן or ἔλεος of the LXX.[38] Paul never use the OT phrase "to find favor with" in his Letters. He has in mind a broader sense of ἔλεος quite often but does not quote any phrase about grace from the Old Testament.[39]

Secondly, the special office of Paul is an office of grace (Rom 1:5). It was given to him (Rom 12:3; 15:15). Actually his ministry is a ministry of grace (2 Cor 1:12, 15). Paul considers his own call, apostleship, and ministry as favors bestowed on him by the grace of the Lord. For Paul, "a right standing with God was wholly of grace."[40] Moving the focus from his understanding of grace as a personal gift and his own experience of the Lord's grace to that of the churches' reality, he can boldly claim that they have been saved by grace (Rom 3:24; 5:20; Eph 1:7); and now he wishes that the same grace may be with the churches. Whenever Paul greets the churches with the "grace of our Lord Jesus" it is a wish that the favor and blessings of the Lord Jesus be with them in the form of love, joy, and peace.

Thirdly, Paul demands that the members of the church demonstrate charisms and fruits of the grace of the Lord Jesus. By accepting Christ, they have received a special gift to live in His grace. When Christians are under grace, it means that they are under the power of God to live holy lives apart from man-made legal structures.[41] This would mean that they live without sin, loving one another, and helping one another. Grace is given to them to do good and to avoid evil. See for example, how Paul employs the word in various contexts. In Romans grace is a powerful gift to overcome sin (Rom 5:20). In Romans and Galatians χάρις is a gift, this idea is closely related to Acts 15:11, 18:27, and 20:24 where it is a favor granted through Jesus which one receives without observing the law or precepts. At the same time it is a

---

[38] ἔλεος is usually an equivalent for חֶסֶד in the LXX.

[39] See the explanation of this point in J. Moffatt, *Grace in the New Testament*, 37–42.

[40] Gary S. Shogren, "Grace–New Testament," *ABD* 2:1087.

[41] Shogren, "Grace–New Testament," 1087. It can also be noticed that for Paul grace is contrary to the laws of Moses or the works of the law.

creative force of sustainment which helps one to realize the working of the Spirit of Christ in him.[42]

Paul speaks of 'the grace of God' given to the churches of Macedonia (2 Cor 8:1). Though they are poor in possessions, they are rich in spirit (generosity) which causes abundant joy. Χάρις used in 2 Corinthians chapters 8–9 is related to giving. In 8:1, 9 and 9:8 χάρις refers to divine giving (God or Christ). In 8:4, 6, 7, 19 and 9:14 it refers to the Jerusalem collection, human work, and giving.[43] They contributed generously to Paul's collection for the Jerusalem church. The above observations point to the fact that for Paul, χάρις is not passive, but very active and dynamic, being actualized in the church (Phil 1:7). As grace is closely related to faith grace is morally vital by itself, it assumes that Christians demonstrate a life of love, since God has willed that man live in relationship.

3.3. Grace as Power

Grace is a gift from God. Grace should not be thought of as passive, as merely a favor of God or something that is associated with piety or docility, though these are manifestations of grace. It is better seen as a power from God. Seen this way it is "from above," from God.[44] Grace can be said to be the sum of the gifts and fruits of the Spirit, a power which enables a person to be a loving, active, and creative Christian. It is a "divine help whereby God moves a person to will and to act."[45] No person truly moved by grace can act amiss. So, grace is fundamental to ethical life.

Conzelmann in his article on "χάρις" takes the word χάρις to be a substantial power streaming down from the divine world. The use of χάρις as a substantial power is old, most probably of a late Hellenistic development, as Nolland proves it through few classical quotes.[46] Nolland analyzing Conzelmann's article observes that he grants a certain supernatural power as present in χάρις from the outset: the power of love or of the oath.[47]

In the Hebrew Bible, the equivalent for χάρις is חֵן as we have already noted. In Baruch 2:14, according to Nolland, χάρις is not simply a favor, but an endowment from God.[48] Daniel 1:9; Gen 39:21 and Prov 10:32 point to

---

[42] See Conzelmann and Zimmerli, "χάρις," 395.

[43] Orrey McFarland, *God and Grace in Philo and Paul*, NTSup 164 (Leiden: Brill, 2016), 207.

[44] The letter of James speaks of "wisdom" as the perfect gift from God, and this wisdom may be seen as a gift of the Spirit.

[45] Aquinas, *ST*, Ia-IIae 111.2.

[46] See John Nolland, "Grace as Power," *NT* 28 (1986), 26–29.

[47] Nolland, "Grace as Power," 26.

[48] Nolland, 31.

the fact that χάρις could be spoken of as a tangible reality, as a power given by God.[49] It is a power flowing down from God to man. In some of the extra Biblical Jewish writings traces of grace being spoken of as power may be found, for example as in the *Test. Jud.* 2:1. Here χάρις comes to Judah as super-human ability bestowed on him by God. In all these instances Grace is power, the divine power which redeems life and also uses it, rendering a man efficient for service.[50]

3.3.1. Grace as Power in Luke-Acts

In what manner does Luke use χάρις in his two-volume work? Is it only in the sense of God's graciousness or his good will? Or is it in the sense of something that is very dynamic? Some scholars see the use of χάρις in the NT as passive[51] on the other hand many other scholars consider the active or dynamic role of grace.[52] In many places in Luke-Acts the use of χάρις simply means favor (Lk 1:30; 2:52; Acts 2:47; 7:46; 24:27; 25:3 etc.); while in many other places an absolute use of χάρις can be noticed (Lk 4:22; Acts 4:33; 6:8; 7:10; 18:27).

There are other instances where χάρις is qualified by τοῦ θεοῦ or τοῦ κυρίου for example, Lk 2:40; Acts 14:3, 26; 15:11; 20:24, 32 etc.; and in Acts 14:26 and 15:40 where Paul and Barnabas initially and then Paul alone are handed over to the safe keeping of χάρις. God's grace is a power which is able to protect the travelling missionaries.[53] In Acts 18:27 χάρις is, most probably, a reference to an endowment of power which Apollos had received from God.

In Lk 1:28 Mary is full of grace and she has that divine power to face life's challenges. It was this power that helped her to set out for the hill country of Judea to serve Elizabeth. It was the same power that helped her to accept various life's trials and challenges.[54] Another example would be Acts 6:8 where a close relationship between grace and power is established. Again in 7:10, Stephen tells of the χάρις of Joseph that is perceptible to

---

[49] Nolland, 31.

[50] See Moffatt, *Grace in the New Testament*, 227.

[51] E.g., Jens W. Täger, *Der Mensch und Sein Heil: Studiem zum Bild des Menschen un der Sicht der Bekehrung bei Lukas*, SNT 14 (Gutersloh: Mohn, 1982), 221.

[52] E.g., John Nolland, "Luke's Use of *χάρις*," *NTS* 32.4 (1986), 614–20; Dupont, *Le discourse de Milet*, see especially pp. 235–84.

[53] Nolland, "Luke's Use of χάρις," 618.

[54] The culminating point of Mary's trial took place at the time of her son's crucifixion. The synoptic Gospels are silent about Mary witnessing the crucifixion of Jesus, but according to the Johannine account, Mary stood at the foot of the cross for which powerful grace would have been necessary (Jn 19:25–27).

Pharaoh. It is a grace given by God as a possession which creates an impact on those around.[55]

Grace is operative as power in the life of Jesus and the church. Paul personally experiences this grace, but now in his absence, the Ephesian elders must experience it and they should be guided by this grace, and Paul entrusts them to the care and protection of the Lord and to the word of his grace. The power is carried by the word as in Lk 4:22. Similarly the power of χάρις operating through the word is able to build up the Ephesian elders (20:32). According to Nolland, Luke's major theological use of χάρις is in reference to a tangible divine power dramatically present with Jesus and the church of Acts.[56]

3.3.2. Grace as Power in the Pauline Letters

Paul himself sees his apostleship as grace in Rom 1:5 and 1 Cor 3:10. χάρις plays an important role in the call and ministry of Paul. He is a witness to God's grace. Paul speaks of his commission received from the Lord as a means to serve and testify to all as a witness to the Lord (26:16). For Paul, other than his apostleship, the Gospel for the Gentiles (Gal 2:7) pertains to the realm of grace. For the churches, according to Paul, the reason for their faith in Christ and His mercy shown towards the churches is grace (Rom 4:16; 5:15, 17; 11:5; 1 Cor 1:4; 2 Cor 8:1).

Grace is an active favor for Paul, so he prefers χάρις to ἔλεος. Paul in using the term has in mind that grace is a power, a power to love. It is the will of God that the 'saints' live a clean and authentic life which is morally right which will be possible by the gracious call and choice of God's love in power. When Paul asks the Ephesian elders to care for the weak, it was a call to demonstrate the power of grace in all its magnitudes. "God is able to make all grace abound towards you that you may abound to every good work" (Col 1:10).

Grace opens up one into an ethical and moral person. This cannot be without χάρις being a power. A *locus* where grace is seen as divine power and its moral obligation emerges in 2 Cor 5:20 ff. Paul stresses the duty of using the blessing as God meant it to be used. Corinthians must be diligent in living up to the grace they have received, especially in giving a portion of what they have. Likewise, without being guided by the word of his grace the Ephesian elders will not have the mind of Christ who taught to give generously; they will not have the spirit of Paul who labored for his own and his companions' need.

---

[55] See Nolland, "Luke's Use of χάρις," 616.

[56] Nolland, 619.

3.4. The "Operative Grace"

The power of grace must produce fruits in the lives of the believers. So rightly the final lines of Miletus speech combine blessing (v. 32) and exhortation (vv. 33–35). The main thread of the blessing focuses on the word of God's grace.[57] William J. Larkin points out that grace is first of all a divine enabling for a person to believe and receive salvation (Acts 15:11; 18:27). Secondly it is a divine power and quality of life that becomes manifest in the lives of believers, so that it can be said that great grace rests on them or that they are full of grace (Acts 4:33; 6:8; 11:23).[58]

The use of χάρις in 20:32 is related to the power and strength the Ephesian elders need to possess for the edification of the community through sharing and caring. All Christians share the spirit of Christ. His grace propels them to unselfish love in the community. Anyone who thinks differently or acts in selfishness, or reluctant to share what one has for the common good, will perish like Ananias and Sapphira (5:1ff).

Grace is operative, in the sense that it is dynamic, productive, and relational. Grace received can only be the grace at work.[59] Paul reminds the Ephesian elders that the same grace is working in them for the service of the weak. Paul was already greatly aware of this reality and Luke picks up the same dynamic and relational aspect of grace in framing the Miletus speech. For Luke the good news is primarily for the poor. Jesus not only preaches the good news but also acts in favor of the poor being involved in their lives. Luke is convinced of the need for every Christian to be involved in the lives of the poor and needy, which would all the more be demanded of the elders.

Paul commends the elders to the word of God's grace so that grace may operate in them through personal goodness and by which they may form communities of sharing and caring. The prayer and wish for grace (v. 32) immediately follow ethical exhortations (vv. 33–35). The moral end of grace is that the Ephesian elders should be true pastors, should humble themselves to work, to share and care. Grace is received to be given, and in the giving and receiving of gifts, relationships are created and sustained.

In the Miletus speech, Paul himself becomes an example of operative grace. Grace should enable one to serve the society without being proud. The proud are tempted to neglect their humbler functions and duties because they think that humbler works are only for slaves and those in the low social strata. Such an attitude is detrimental to the formation of social fellowship.

---

[57] See Robert W. Wall, "The Acts of the Apostles: Introduction, Commentary, and Reflections," *NIB* 10:284.

[58] Larkin, *Acts*, 28.

[59] McFarland, *God and Grace*, 161.

Every society is comprised of members of different creeds and cultures; agnostics and atheists. We acknowledge that the Holy Spirit works even through these non-Christians and non-religious folk to act ethically and morally even so their moral concepts are different from that of the Christians. The Spirit is not a monopoly of the Christians, but bestowed on all (Acts 2:17) to produce repentance and ethical behavior. The sign of repentance and good actions in individuals indicates that some kind of grace is operative in and through all irrespective of their faith, race, or nationality.

3.5. Grace: Affinity of Luke and Paul

The χάρις-motif throughout Luke-Acts and Paul is a "special Christian development."[60] New Testament authors particularly Luke and Paul see χάρις as very dynamic and powerful. In the NT it is often seen in relation to its beneficial effects. It is not very difficult to determine whether Luke or Paul used the word first. Generally, it is considered that the Letters of Paul predate other books of the NT. This may indicate that the oft-used Pauline term has been borrowed by Luke without change in its meaning. In any case, it is essential to Luke's theology, and at the same time Luke is aware that it fits well with "Paul's gospel with its radical theology of grace" to which Luke himself testifies many times in Acts 13:43; 14:3; 15:11; 20:24, 32.

The Gospels, particularly Luke's, emphasize the moral and ethical demands of God's gracious purpose. Jesus himself speaks about and operates in accordance with the purpose of God. Although grace is a gratuitous favor given to us, it means for the Christian a certain ministry to others, and to this end "grace-gifts" (charisma) are bestowed. Both Luke and Paul will not compromise on that. Their proclamation constantly focuses on God's grace. Preaching and doing works of love and justice etc. flow from this basic message of grace.

The term χάρις can be translated as gracious work in 2 Cor 8:6, 7, 19, describing unusual generosity.[61] Grace is love demonstrated by giving.[62] So, one of the most important components of Grace is "giving." This "giving" grace of God in turn brings enablement to the helpless, especially the poor and persecuted. Luke also is aware that grace could work both ways, in the sense that it helps to realize love in the community, and communion and sharing can make individual and community to grow in grace. Grace is to be used for the edification of the church, and one should act as channels of

---

[60] We are not neglecting the presence of this motif in other NT writings and its vague form in the OT.

[61] Shogren, "Grace–New Testament," 1087.

[62] Shogren, 1086.

God's goodness and care. It is in this sense that Paul entrusts the Ephesian elders to the grace of God.

As we have seen above, grace is given or received for the edification of the church through charity and good works. It is to this grace that Paul commends the Ephesian elders. The use of the "word of His grace" is intentional here informing them that His grace alone can build them up as a community and this grace alone assures them the inheritance promised. The use of the "word of His grace" here has another connotation as well. Only by the word of His grace, a disciple is able to endure suffering and want for the sake of others and for the Gospel. It is very evident in the life of Paul and it must be so also in the life of the elders. This theology of grace of Paul runs parallel to Lucan theology of grace. When Luke says that Mary is full of grace, or God's grace was with Jesus, or there was great grace upon them all there is nothing to doubt that Luke is thinking in the thought line of Paul.

We judge it necessary at this point to dwell on Lk 4:22 where the gracious words of Jesus become the good news to the poor. This good news, known as the "Nazareth Manifesto" is a programmatic passage in the Gospel. With the Nazareth Manifesto, Jesus publicly initiates his ministry of love, service, and healing. The OT prophecies concerning the Messiah are now being actualized in the person of Jesus. Moreover, the manifesto indicates the ecclesial, social, and community dimension of Jesus' ministry.

We now compare the Nazareth Manifesto and the important speech Paul delivered at Miletus which is substantially similar to the former, and the latter becomes, as it were, the programmatic speech of Paul making it the 'Miletus Manifesto' of Paul. Thematically both manifestos include good news to the poor / weak.[63] Both are ecclesial and community oriented. The mission of Jesus was to bring good news to the poor; the mission of Paul was to preach the good news about Jesus, but now, the Ephesian elders are to continue with the same mission especially remembering the weak. The ecclesial, communal, and social dimensions of the good news are evident in both the speeches of Luke. There is nothing substantially different Paul is suggesting in the speech, but the speech has hardly any verbal affinity. This also may indicate that the speech is authentically Pauline; but put in words later by Luke recollecting the speech of Paul.

Again, the unique construction λόγῳ τῆς χάριτος αὐτοῦ is Lucan than Pauline. Similar construction found in Acts 14:3 and Luke 4:22 (λόγοις τῆς χάριτος) affirm the above argument. In the Pauline letters such a construction is not found although Paul frequently speaks of χάρις and λόγος. Other than the above unique construction, the speech reflects, at least in vv. 32–35, Pauline interests which are similar to Luke's. So it can be confidently said

[63] The poor are the weak, the blind, the lame, the captives, the oppressed etc.

that the speech was truly delivered by Paul which nevertheless came to be later noted by Luke in the Acts.

Observations so far point to the fact that both Luke and Paul see grace quite the same way, as a gracious favor and power for ministry and work of God. The use of grace in 20:32 is both in passive (in the sense of God's favor) and active (in the sense of power that is operative) sense, but the latter sense being dominant. The use of χάρις in the verse in this sense links it with the successive verses of the speech, indicating that χάρις is required for moral and ethical actions.

3.6. Grace: The Requisite for Ethics and Morality

The believers, according to Luke and Paul, are responsible for how they live. Therefore, in all their writings they insist on right behavior. For example, we notice passages such as Acts 2:43–46; 4:32–5:11; 11:27–30; 15:29; 20:28–35 and numerous such examples from the letters of Paul. A sample for insistence on ethical behavior may be found in 1 Cor 7:17–19. The whole letter in fact deals with many issues in the community in Corinth such as divisiveness (1:11–13; 11:13), tolerance of immorality (5:1–2), lawsuits between believers (6:1–8); licentiousness (6:12–20), wrong belief and pride (1 Cor 1:31; 4:7), and abuse of spiritual gifts (12–14).[64] Similarly in other Pauline letters there are abundant instances of exhortations to Christians to live in faith and to remain worthy of their calling, by acting and behaving morally and ethically right. They should not abandon their faith, but most importantly they should live a life worthy of their calling. Few examples are: Rom 12:9–21; 13:13; 2 Cor 13:5; Eph 5:3–20; Col 3:5–17.

It is grace that makes the ethical life of the believers possible. According to Paul, grace in a person ought to arouse some kind of moral consciousness. Paul seems to be more deliberately emphasizing this, which is also the reason for Paul to commend the Ephesian elders to His grace. Without the existence in Christ and the gift of the Spirit, there would be no ethical life.[65] They should not accept the grace of God in vain (2 Cor 6:1) rather perfect it. Paul makes attempts to demonstrate the way grace may be perfected in a person or group. In his book, *Paul and the Gift,* John M. Barclay classifies six perfections of grace indicated by Paul in his letters,[66] of which two are of some concern to us. They are "superabundance" and "efficacy." One is able to act in a truly "other oriented" way when he is

---

[64] See these points in Brad Eastman, *The Significance of Grace in the Letters of Paul*, SBL 11 (New York: Peter Lang, 1999), 49.

[65] Eastman, *Significance of Grace*, 213.

[66] The six perfections of grace are superabundance, singularity, priority, incongruity, efficacy, and non-circularity.

perfected by superabundance of grace. Similarly grace becomes efficacious in such moments, or better, efficacious grace is necessary for a man to live other oriented.

For Paul, human responsibility, reward, and dependence on God's grace go hand in hand.[67] Paul holds believers responsible for doing what is right but guided by the Spirit. To this end, he sees God's grace as an active force. For example, in Galatians, Paul speaks of faith working through love (Gal 5:6) and in 2 Corinthians, Paul values the voluntary nature of giving. Yet, the ability to love and give is a gift of God. "Although God makes certain behaviors possible, they still require human cooperation."[68] Ethical and moral actions are the result of the operation of grace (or spirit[69]) in the individual. Grace should not be taken for granted through laxity in one's social and ethical life. Without grace it is impossible to meet the ethical demands. Ethical imperative must be accompanied by grace and the empowerment of the spirit. In the words of Orrey McFarland, "Divine gift exists and works within insufficiency and inability."[70]

From what we have said so far on this point, one thing is obvious: the meaning of grace is crucial in understanding the ethics of the Miletus speech.[71] We have already examined enough how Luke and Paul understood grace. Both Luke and Paul have similar understanding about χάρις, and for them there is a constant divine power which enables Christians to moral duties. Thus, for Luke and Paul there is a moral dimension to grace (or faith). It is the ability to live up to the ethical demands of faith. To believe is to act Christian. Christians must allow Christ to live in them. Their behavior should correspond with their faith. Paul is entrusting the Ephesian elders precisely to this message of grace which alone can build them up by hard labor, generous giving, and caring (20:33–35) and which will give them the inheritance in return. In short in v. 32, we do not encounter a 'Paul of passive grace,' but a 'Paul of active grace.'

---

[67] Eastman, 90.

[68] Eastman, 90.

[69] In many places in the NT the spirit and grace seem quite the same (e.g. Acts 4:33; 6:8; 2 Cor 12:9; 2 Thess 2:16).

[70] McFarland, *God and Grace*, 175.

[71] Michael P. Cullinan, *Victor Paul Furnish's Theology of Ethics in St. Paul: An Ethic of Transforming Grace* (Rome: Editiones Academiae Alfonsianae, 2007), 127.

Chapter 4

Acts 20:33: Ethics of "Pure Intention"

After having entrusted the Ephesian elders to the word of His grace, which can build them up and give them the inheritance, Paul now boldly declares his status in relation to material things. "I have not coveted anyone's silver or gold or clothes." This small verse is directly linked to the last two commandments of the Decalogue[1] and at the same time evokes an indirect connection to a couple of other commandments, especially to the first, thereby making it a declaration pointing to an important element of the Pauline ethos. Therefore, our main focus here is to discuss the ethics found in this verse without neglecting the role and function of the verse within the speech.

4.1. Preliminary Observations of 20:33

Within the overall framework of the speech, verses 32–35 may be seen as the "closing *peroratio* with hortatory use of *exempla*." But D. F. Watson does not see verse 32 belonging to the closing *peroratio*.[2] I have already stated above, by drawing the structure of the speech, why vv. 32–35 is so closely related and is a single unit. Whatever may be the case, Paul's speech reaches

[1] According to the Catholic method of numbering, Ex 20:17 is treated as two commandments as in the case with Deut 5:21. In Exodus the injunction not to covet neighbor's house, wife, animals etc. is formulated as a single commandment, but in Deuteronomy it is divided into two. The development of the prohibitions against coveting (5:21a–b) by using two different verbs here demonstrate some kind of theological development. Coveting neighbor's "wife" is brought to the fore and placed as a separate commandment.

[2] Watson, "Paul's Speech," 207.

its stirring conclusion in these verses.[3] At the beginning of the speech Paul had already stated about his service rendered to the Lord in humility, tears, and trials and his faithful apostolic work in public and private (vv. 18b–20). He never shrank from declaring what was profitable, i.e., the whole counsel of God. Moreover his conduct was pure, pure from the blood of all men (v. 26).[4] This metaphor magnifies the crime Paul is disclaiming so that his contrary conduct appears even more exemplary.[5] He could honestly say that he was genuine to the core in his spiritual ministries, because he did not accept any wages from any of the churches; rather he found his own means of sustenance (Acts 18:3; 28:30 [most probably]; 1 Cor 4:12; 9:6). Now towards the end of the speech Paul again strikes a previous note and sets himself as an example to imitate as he himself coveted anyone's silver or gold or clothes.

One who finds inheritance with God requires no silver, gold, or clothing. By stating his uncovetous attitude towards material things, Paul becomes deliberative about the choice for the word of His grace. Paul's commendation of the elders to the word of His grace is applied to himself, that is, he wanted to be supported and guided by God's grace and not by the false promises of wealth. Thus this verse is directly connected to the previous verse. Paul's claim plays an important role in the Lucan narrative, which displays a devastating impact of greed (for example Acts 5:1–11; 8:18–24; 16:19–24). The speech thus moves more to its penchant ethical nature. In the verse Paul's claim is that he is different from the rest of the teachers/philosophers and preachers, who often sought monetary gains through their teaching and preaching. Many references within the NT indicate about the church leaders who preach for money (1 Cor 9; 2 Cor 2:17; 7:2; 11:7–13; 1 Thess 2:5; 1 Tim 6:6–10; 1 Pet 5:2). Keener observes that the ancient philosophers so often attacked each other that the abuse they heaped on each other became stereotyped—Epicureans were accused of hatred of humanity, Stoics and Peripatetics of greed. David Peterson suggests that Paul's humble disinterest in "silver"-based wealth sets him apart from the Ephesian magicians and shrinemakers[6] (19:19–27).

The key word in this verse is the verb "covet / desire" (ἐπιθυμέω). While translating the Hebrew books of the Bible, Greek translators used the word ἐπιθυμέω for the Hebrew דמח / אוה as is the case with the Decalogue. The appearance of the verb ἐπιθυμέω and the nouns silver, gold, and clothes

---

[3] Keener, *Acts*, 3:3054.

[4] Blood-guilt was a common image in the OT but v. 26 recalls Ezek 3:18–21 where a sentinel is held guilty of the blood of the wicked people if he fails to warn them.

[5] Watson, "Paul's Speech," 202.

[6] David G. Peterson, *The Acts of the Apostles*, PNTC (Grand Rapids: Eerdmans, 2009), 573.

as the object of desire make the verse highly reflective of the OT, particularly the last two commandments which have more to do with intention rather than action. In a section below we will discuss this topic at length.

4.1.1. The Objects of Greed in 20:33

As per the sequence of objects listed in the verse, they reflect the sequence in the OT (cf. Gen 24:53; Ex 3:22; Josh 22:8; 2 Kgs 5:5; Jer 10:9 etc.). We are not sure whether they are listed in ascending order of worth. It is possible that the sequence reflects listing of objects in an ascending order of value, for the wealth of many Orientals was mainly in clothing.[7]

Moreover, the sequence here—"silver," "gold," and "clothing"—is an example of "theoretical amplification by accumulation"[8] as in 20:19.[9] These objects stand for wealth, honor, and leadership. The list amplifies that Paul is in no way greedy.[10] Silver was the standard of exchange as the Hebrew word itself reveals, for the word כֶּסֶף was used for silver or money.[11] These objects were considered valuable and often appeared as objects of desire in the OT (Deut 7:25; Josh 7:21; 2 Kgs 5:22). Wars were waged not only to have power over other kingdoms but also to occupy their land and valuable goods such as silver and gold. For example the Aramean king Ben-Hadad as he captured Ahab says: "Your silver and gold are mine" (1 Kgs 20:3). Ben-Hadad takes everything Ahab priced (v. 6).

The command not to covet silver and gold of the images of pagan gods was given by Moses (Deut 7:25–26). Sometimes even the images themselves were made of silver or gold or jewels (Ex 32:2–4, 24, 31; Judg 8:24–27; 17:1-5; Isa 2:20; 31:7; Jer 10:4, 8-9; Ezek 16:17) and desiring them and appropriating them for oneself is the violation of the first commandment. The story of Achan (Josh 7:1–26), who covets a mantle, silver, and gold of Jericho and takes them (Josh 7:21), must be seen as a violation of the first commandment rather than an act of stealing. Other than the moral of this story[12] we are never told how silver, gold, and clothes ensnare one who covets it.

The mention of "clothing" among the coveted objects could rouse curiosity in the modern readers of the passage for modern men do not covet

---

[7] Watson, "Paul's Speech," 205; Hänchen, *Acts*, 594.

[8] See this in Watson, 205.

[9] The amplification is realized here through the use of depraved mental or physical state images.

[10] See Watson, 205.

[11] See E. E. Platt, "Jewelry, Ancient Israelite," *ABD* 3:824.

[12] Achan was put to death at the valley of Achor (Josh 7:25), warning them that everyone who violates the ban (*herem*) of God will be punished in such a way that they no more participate in the community.

clothing as such. The frequent reference to dress in the Bible indicates the social or symbolic importance of clothing in Israelite society.[13] We are not going to analyze all the significance of clothing in the Bible rather only point out that it was a symbol of wealth and social status. Some clothes could be more expensive than gold. Expensive clothing occupied a significant place at that time, and possession of many and expensive clothing was a standard to measure the wealth of a person. Expensive garments were part of wealth (Josh 7:21, 24; 22:8; 2 Kgs 5:5; Jam 5:2–3). Clothing appears in wills, divorce settlements, and dowries, sometimes alongside gold and jewels. Thieves also stole clothes left unattended, or from the backs of night travelers.[14]

Cloaks and other outer garments were more precious than inner garments. They were given as gifts (1 Kgs 10:25) and payment (2 Kgs 5:23; Prov 20:16). Garments also convey some kind of power (1 Sam 15:27; 1 Kgs 19:19).[15] Roman citizens were allowed to wear a semicircular dress draped around the body called 'toga'[16] but it seems that Paul did not wear one (cf. Acts 16:35–39). Two reasons for it may be drawn as Douglas R. Edwards notes: (1) Paul seems to be sacrificing his Roman citizenship symbol 'toga' for the sake of Christ or (2) the 'toga' he had might have been donated to a needy person. Paul is genuine especially in his attitude towards wealth. He did not covet anything, much less did he even want to be supported by the church and this is the important ethical point Paul was making. Paul's example is dominant here, for the church leaders should not be greedy (1 Tim 3:3; 1 Pet 5:2).[17]

4.2. Meaning and Attestation of "Greed" in the Scripture

4.2.1. ἐπιθυμία/, ἐπιθυμέω—Meaning

As already noted, the important motif at play in 20:33 is greed. Greed or covetousness is the strong wish to continuously get more of something.[18] It is an excessive desire to possess more than what one needs or deserves. The Greek words for greed are ἐπιθυμία and πλεονεξία.[19] While the former is

[13] Douglas R. Edwards, "Dress and Ornamentation," *ABD* 2:232.

[14] For these information see Keener, *Acts*, 3:3059.

[15] Elijah throws a mantle over Elisha indicating some kind of transfer of power.

[16] Edwards, "Dress and Ornamentation," 235.

[17] Didache exhorts the church leaders not to be greedy in *Did.* 11:6–9.

[18] "Greed," *Cambridge Dictionary*, accessed 2 March 2019, https://dictionary.cambridge.org/ dictionary/english/greed.

[19] πλεονεξία is attested both in the LXX and in the NT to mean greed. The Latin word for ἐπιθυμία or πλεονεξία is *avaritia*. Avarice, covetousness, lust, and craving are words synonymously used in English for greed.

mostly *vox media*[20] the latter is not.[21] The verb used in 20:33 is ἐπιθυμέω and therefore our focus falls mostly on this verb. Friedrich Büchsel claims that θυμός, a derivative of ἐπιθυμία is from an Indo-Germanic root.[22] In ancient Greek literature, the noun θυμός is taken to mean the vital force of animals or men. It then took the sense of desire, impulse, inclination, spirit, anger, sensibility, disposition, or mind. Θύω, a kin of θυμός, originally means a strong flow or movement of air, water, animals or men, in the sense of "to well up" or "to smoke" and the verb ἐπιθυμέω would mean "to covet / desire." In the pre-Socratic period the verb meant direct impulse towards food, sexual satisfaction etc. and also desire in general. In the Stoic period it is considered as a chief passion along with pleasure (ἡδονή), fear (φόβος), and pain / sorrow (λύπη).[23]

4.2.2. Usage of ἐπιθυμία/, ἐπιθυμέω in the LXX and Its Equivalent in the Hebrew Bible

The LXX uses ἐπιθυμία and ἐπιθυμέω predominantly for the constructs of the Hebrew stem חָמַד, אָוָהwhich mean "to desire." Desire can be considered ethically neutral when someone possesses certain material which is pleasant such as garment, food, treasures (see Gen 27:15; Dan 10:3; Ps 39:12; Ezek 26: 12; etc.).[24] Another word כָּסַף also, in few cases, function as a synonym for the above Hebrew words (see Gen 31:30; Ps 17:12; Job 14:15). All these Hebrew terms are translated as "to desire." However, the word frequently used for "to desire" is חָמַד. The meaning of חָמַד, to put in modern English, is "to have one's eyes on something."[25] אָוָה is synonymously used for חָמַד and this is supported by the parallel usages in Gen 3:6; more convincing examples are Prov 6:25; Ps 68:17; 45:12 and 132:13f.[26] The divine prohibition not to "covet" uses חָמַד in Exodus whereas Deuteronomy uses both the verbs simultaneously in the same verse (5:21).

The LXX use πλεονεξία for greed and the word always has a negative connotation.[27] Since πλεονεξία and ἐπιθυμία are synonymously used in the scriptures, especially in its negative sense, nothing compels me to make

---

[20] A word in itself having no positive or negative meaning.

[21] For consistency and simplicity sake I will be using the English word "greed" for the Greek ἐπιθυμία and πλεονεξία as far as the former does not carry the meaning "desire," in a positive sense.

[22] F. Buchsel, "ἐπιθυμέω, ἐπιθυμητής, ἐπιθυμία," *TDNT* 3:167.

[23] Materials for this paragraph are from Buchsel, "ἐπιθυμέω," 167–68.

[24] G. Wallis, "חָמַד," *TDOT* 4:456.

[25] Wallis, "חָמַד," 455.

[26] Günter Mayer, "אָוָה," *TDOT* 1:135.

[27] The NT also uses the word a few times.

any distinction between them in their meaning. Today the English words covetousness, avarice, and greed usually have a negative connotation while desire and longing are used as *vox media*.

4.2.3. The Use of ἐπιθυμία / ἐπιθυμέω in the NT

The words ἐπιθυμία and ἐπιθυμέω are common in the Epistles but rare in the Gospels.[28] Their usage, as in the LXX, is *vox media* also in the NT. Lucan attestation of the word is minimal in the Gospel and the only instance in Acts is the verse under our consideration. The word occurs in the NT several times to mean anger or wrath either, Divine or human. As *vox media* they may mean natural desire for food, longing (Lk 15:16; 16:21; 22:15; 1 Thess 2:17; Jam 4:2). It may also include desire for divine mysteries or something good (Lk 17:22; Phil 1:23; 1 Tim 3:1; Heb 6:11). In the negative sense they indicate evil desire (Mt 5:28; Mk 4:19; Rom 7:7; 13:9; 1 Cor 10:6; Gal 5:16; Rom 6:12; 1 Pet 4:2; Jud 16 etc.).[29]

Moving specifically to the usage in 20:33, Luke is using the word ἐπιθυμέω in the Jewish negative sense of covet or desire. This way the verse has an intrinsic link to the 9th and 10th commandment that prohibit desiring anything that belongs to others. All commandments have to do with the fidelity to one true God. Covetousness goes to the root of all. Both Paul and Luke see greed as something detrimental to the community and therefore both the speaker and the writer are engaged on this subject here, as various other examples from them will substantiate the point.

4.3. The Dangers of ἐπιθυμία / πλεονεξία in Luke-Acts

Not only Paul is speaking in the Miletus speech but also Luke. As indicated in the previous chapter, the Pauline theology of grace runs more or less parallel to Luke's; in the same way Paul develops the topic of greed quite parallel to that of Luke, differing only in its presentation. More than any other evangelist Luke graphically portrays the dangers of greed through parables and anecdotes.[30] At various occasions Paul speaks about greed and its dangers in the form of exhortations. Here we need to look into Lucan condemnation of greed in order to get to know his contribution to the subject; else, we will not be doing justice to this study. We will not be able to examine every specimen about greed in Luke or in Paul, nor does that come under the scope of this study. However, we will be examining the most important ones.

---

[28] See Hans Hübner, "ἐπιθυμία," *EDNT* 2:27.

[29] Information for this paragraph is from Buchsel, "ἐπιθυμέω," 167, 170–71.

[30] In these parables and anecdotes Luke never uses ἐπιθυμία or πλεονεξία to indicate greed, but the instances and their context make clear that they are told mainly against greed and selfishness. This is very evident from the context of the parable of the Rich Fool.

4.3.1. Greed Illustrated: Parables on Greed

The parable of the Rich Fool (Lk 12:16–21) is unique to Luke, and it seems that Luke has borrowed ideas from Sir 11:18–19[31] for the development of the parable.[32] Arland J. Hultgren classifies the parable as one of the four parables of exemplary behavior.[33] The parable is set in the larger framework of dispute over property (12:13–14) and anxiety over food and drink (12:22–31). What is also noticeable—this is important for us—that it is framed with warnings against greed (12:15 and 21).[34]

The parable is said in the context of greed, and the theme becomes more colorful as the parable echoes the greed of a man throughout the story in possessing and even accumulating wealth so that he might eat, drink, and make merry. There is no possibility of the man's desires getting quenched as God would intervene and demand his soul that very night. Selfishness manifested through greedy behavior is the object of condemnation here. The repeated use of "I" and "my,"[35] in the English translation of the parable conveys the meaning that the man is a personification of selfishness.

It is important for us here to note the application of the parable which is found in v. 21. According to Hultgren, verse 21 generalizes the parable but provides an application that differs from the meaning of the parable.[36] If we consider this verse an addition to the parable,[37] this kind of an interpretation has some weight. On the other hand, keeping it as belonging to the original parable—for there is nothing serious that suggests against this view —then the application is correct. One can only become rich towards God by generously giving to the poor. Not only does generosity function as an antidote for greed, but also as a necessity for every Christian.[38] Luke is convinced about this fact and it has been confirmed by various statements and examples within Luke-Acts to which we will turn in a later chapter. The parable forcefully invites

---

[31] One becomes rich by diligence and self-denial, and the reward allotted to him is this: when he says, "I have found rest, and now I shall feast on my goods!" he does not know how long it will be until he leaves them to others and dies.

[32] Somewhat similar passage appears in 1 Enoch 97:8–10.

[33] The others are parables of the Good Samaritan, the Rich Man and Lazarus, the Pharisee and the Tax Collector. See Arland J. Hultgren, *The Parables of Jesus: A Commentary* (Grand Rapids: Eerdmans, 2002), 92–128.

[34] Ideas of this paragraph are borrowed from Hultgren, *The Parables of Jesus*, 106.

[35] In Greek construction of sentences personal pronouns are not required with verbs since they are implied in the conjugation itself. But possessive pronoun μου, which means my/mine, is separately used many times.

[36] Hultgren, *The Parables of Jesus*, 107.

[37] Joseph A. Fitzmyer, *The Gospel According to Luke 10–24*, AB 28a (Garden City, NY: Doubleday, 1985), 971.

[38] In the catechetical books the virtue against greed is generosity.

the listener to be generous, and for Luke, generosity is the right way for the right use of wealth. Selfish and greedy persons should be remolded in the fire of generosity.

Moving to the next item, we focus on the parables in chapter 16. The whole of chapter 16 deal with possessions, a favorite topic of Luke. The parable of the Rich Man and Lazarus (Lk 16:19–31) was told in the contexts of swindling of money and greed, for Luke had already narrated the parable of the Unjust Steward (16:1–13) who was swindling money and the negative response of the Pharisees in hearing the parable and its application. For our purpose, therefore, it is better to consider here both the parables in chapter 16 together since both these parables are told to exhort the listeners about the right use of wealth and the dangers of greed.

The parable of the Unjust Steward is often considered by the scholars as the most difficult parable in the Gospels to interpret. It is not within our scope to examine the precise meaning or the difficulties attached to the interpretation of it, nonetheless, the application of the parable in the Lucan context warrants a "wise use of wealth" interpretation of the parable.[39] The unjust steward has been praised not because of his unjust actions, but because of his prudence that earned commendation by his master. There can be no doubt that the steward acted greedily by swindling the master's money but at the same time he acted prudently to secure his future for which he was praised. Verses 9–13, the application of the parable, is important here. Within the context of Luke's Gospel the parable is also interpreted in light of the responsible use of wealth as is clear from the applicatory verses; other interpretations are possible and can withstand but the most suitable being "the responsible use of wealth" interpretation.[40]

With the narration of the parable of the Rich Man and Lazarus, the picture becomes clearer. Those things already related deal with money (see especially vv. 9, 11, 13–15) and the parable is told immediately after (and within) a veritable catena of passages that speak of the dangers that

---

[39] Among the important scholars who favor this position are Alfred Plummer, *The Gospel According to St. Luke*, ICC (Edinburgh: T&T Clark, 1913), 380; Dennis J. Ireland, "A History of Recent Interpretation of the Parable of the Unjust Steward (Luke 16,1–13)," *WTJ* 51 (1989), 315–16; John Nolland, *Luke 9,21–18,34*, WBC 35b (Dallas: Word Books, 1993), 805; Dennis J. Ireland, *Stewardship and the Kingdom of God: An Historical, Exegetical, and Contextual Study of the Parable of the Unjust Steward*, NTSup 70 (Leiden: Brill, 1992), 97, 101; Darrell L. Bock, *Luke 2. 9:51–24:53*, BECNT 3b (Grand Rapids: Baker Book House, 1996), 1333–37.

[40] Since the parable is open to different interpretations, instead of arguing in favor of one or the other, it is better to approach the parable in a synthetic way. I have already suggested a "synthetic interpretation of the parable of the Unjust Steward" in my licentiate dissertation "Decoding Luke: A Synthetic Interpretation of the Parable of the Unjust Steward (Lk 16:1–13)" submitted in 2010 at the Pontifical Biblical Institute, Rome.

arise from greed.[41] By narrating the parable precisely at this location, Luke warns the rich about the danger of neglecting the needs of the poor. Greed or selfishness makes one slave of wealth and he does not even "see" the basic needs of his neighbor. Jesus communicates through the parable the great reversal of fortune; the one enjoyed good things in life is now tormented, and the tormented one is comforted in the bosom of Abraham. The parable is a motive for giving, that only by being generous and charitable with one's neighbor one is able to enter heaven.

4.3.2. Greed Condemned: Anecdotes on Greed

There are number of instances where greed is condemned and warned through various anecdotes in Luke-Acts. First of all, in his preaching John the Baptist demanded repentance from his listeners a repentance to sharing possessions and honesty. He addressed the greed of the tax collectors and asked them to avoid it (Lk 3:10–14).

Second, Jesus denounces the Pharisees and Scribes for their greed and wickedness and asks them to give alms (Lk 11:39–41). Pharisees ridiculed Jesus because he spoke about making friends with wealth (Lk 16:14), being faithful with wealth (Lk 16:10–11), and devoting oneself to God rather than wealth (Lk 16:13). By ridiculing Jesus the detestable greed of the Pharisees, more than anything, is visible. They again appear as persons who "devour widow's houses" (Lk 20:47). This behavior of the Pharisees goes directly against the Mosaic and prophetic call to protect the widows (Ex 22:22; Deut 24:19-21; 27:19; Isa 1:17; Jer 7:6 etc.).

Third, in 18:18–25 Luke presents a rich ruler who wished to inherit eternal life. But his attachment to wealth deterred him from following Jesus and thereby reaching his goal. The ruler went away sad for he was very rich. We are not told in the story what happened to the rich ruler after that; it is to be assumed that he could not be a disciple of Jesus on account of his inability to part with his wealth, as the text says he "went away sad" (see the parallels in Mk 10:22 and Mt 19:22). The rich man's attachment to wealth, we may say, is the outcome of his greed. In other words, a greedy person will be attached to his wealth and will lose eternal life.

Fourth, in his Exhortation to watch (Lk 21:34), Jesus warns the listeners to be on guard against dissipation, drunkenness, and the worries of this life. The Greek words used here κραιπάλῃ and μέθῃ for dissipation and drunkenness respectively point to the deleterious effect of greed especially if the greed is for food and drink. Luke may be also attacking Hedonism and Epicureanism here.

---

[41] Hultgren, *The Parables of Jesus*, 111.

Fifth, Judas is a greedy person and functions as a negative character in Luke-Acts. In Luke 22:3–6, Judas is a villain. He loved money more than his master and therefore he betrayed his master for a few pennies. The greediness of Judas resulted in his suicide about which information is reserved until Luke's second volume (Acts 1:18).[42] In any case, the point of Luke is clear: greed is an obstacle to discipleship.

Sixth, the famous story of Ananias and Sapphira (Acts 5:1–11) is told to exhort the disciples to watch against their greed. Anyone who is greedy will have all the chances to betray the community and God. Such people behave against the common good of the church and eventually will be cast out from the community. Ananias and Sapphira fell dead, may not be literally, but by their conscientious choice to be dead, indicating their non-belongingness to the community, for they are not worthy to have any participation in it. We notice that the story parallels in many ways that of Judas. Comparing the story of Ananias and Sapphira with information gathered about Judas from the Gospels and Acts, few points are similar. (1) Both stories depict greed for wealth. (2) Both involve some kind of deceit and betrayal. (3) The final result of the characters' greed for money is death.

Seventh, the episode about Simon Magus (Acts 8:18–24) communicates the greed of this magician at a different level. Here Simon, slightly differs from Judas or Ananias and Sapphira, for he is greedy not directly for money but for the "power" which the apostles had. The wickedness of Simon is that he offered money to get "this power" thinking that he could earn more money than before by the use of this power. He is indirectly greedy for money and moreover does not distinguish between the magical power and the power of the Holy Spirit. So his action gets a sharp condemnation from Peter: "May your silver perish with you" (8:20).

Last, the owner of the slave girl (Acts 16:16–19), the Ephesian shrine builders (Acts 19:23–28), and Felix the governor who expected a bribe from Paul (Acts 24:26) are examples of greed. In all these episodes they come across as plying their trade for money. In the first story they accuse Paul of causing disturbance in the city because the slave girl was freed from her spirit of divination and the owner of the girl lost income generated by her divinizing activity. In the second story, Demetrius instigates fellow workers to throw out Paul and his companions from the city which results in a tumult. These people are restless, for their business is affected by the presence and

[42] The text is not very clear as to how Judas died, perhaps by hanging himself or by falling down on something while hanging that caused his bowels to burst out. From the information we gather from the NT, we may conclude that Judas committed suicide by hanging (Mt 27:5) and while hanging he might have fallen off to the ground with such force that his bowels gushed out. Or it may be that in narrating the event Matthew and Luke transmit the tradition they have independently received.

miracles performed by Paul. Felix the Governor is more contemptable than the rest because though being a ruler with power and wealth, he was still greedy for money.

4.4. Condemnation of ἐπιθυμία / πλεονεξία in Paul

Paul constantly condemns or exhorts the churches against greed (Rom 6:12; 13:14; 16:17–18; 2 Cor 9:5; Gal 5:16; Eph 4:19, 22; 5:3–5; Col 3:5; 1 Thess 4:5; 1 Tim 6:9; 2 Tim 2:22; 2 Tim 3:6). He does the same with teachers (2 Cor 2:17; 7:2; 11:7–13; 1 Thess 2:5). Paul may see greed as a reality that taints human nature because of sin (Rom 7:8), which, however, at the same time is well within the control of man to overcome by the help of the Spirit (Rom 8:3–4; Gal 5:16). Paul, unlike Luke, treats the subject at a different level mostly on account of the epistolary character of his writings. Paul's method is characterized by the use of short exhortatory sentences as each occasion demands. The above references are enough to indicate the importance Paul gave to the subject of condemnation of greed. It is needless to examine these passages here. However, they indicate the congruence between Luke and Paul on the subject.

A passage that can help us delve into the meaning of 'coveting' is Romans, chapter 7:7–12. It refers to a commandment in the Decalogue, that is, "you shall not covet. . . ." While speaking about righteousness without the Law of Moses in Romans, Paul is also affirming the importance of the laws. In this effort to explain why the laws are actually made, he refers to the last commandments of the Decalogue. These commandments of the Lord are used to demonstrate how the laws function for the Israelites.

4.4.1. Rom 7:7: οὐκ ἐπιθυμήσεις

In Exodus 20:17 and its parallel passage, Deuteronomy 5:21, the last two commandments of the Decalogue can be found. Traditionally it is held that there were ten words spoken to Moses which, for Jews and Christians, are, as they term it, the Decalogue. The last words of the Decalogue prohibit desire for anything that is not yours. The coveted things, according to the 9th and 10 commandments, are wife and persons, property, and animals.[43] Everything that belongs to the other is the object of coveting.

Property includes land, house, fields, other material things such as money, gold, clothes, ornaments etc. Persons include male and female slaves and wife. Slaves are important for they contribute to the productivity and economic value of the master. One is also prohibited from coveting the wife of another. Another category of things is animals that were highly valued and

---

[43] This threefold categorization is confirmed also in Lev 27:1–25 although nothing about wife mentioned there.

occupied a high place in the culture's economy because they helped greatly to provide livelihood and sustenance of the households.[44]

4.4.1.1. Old Testament Background for οὐκ ἐπιθυμήσεις in Paul

We must assume that when Paul spoke about his not coveting silver, gold, or clothes, most probably he had in mind those wicked stories or proverbs concerning coveting found scattered in the Jewish writings. Coveting is a universal problem now and in the past. In the Bible, stories on coveting are told of the rich and the powerful such as David (2 Sam 11:2–27), Ahab (1 Kgs 21:1–16), and others; as well as of ordinary people such as Achan (Josh 7), Gehazi (2 Kgs 5:19b–27) etc. A suitable place to begin our study is with the story of Adam and Eve. This story is not to be discarded as scrap because of its mythical nature for even myths are a vehicle of powerful messages.[45] The origin of dangerous desire is in Eden; humanity is still grappling with it. The desirability of the fruit (Gen 3:6) leads to disobedience and selfishness. Adam and Eve, though technically did not covet another's property, coveted the glory and power belonging to God, which was even worse.

Achan coveted the silver, gold, and clothes of Jericho (Josh 7:21) which was then a pagan city, and naturally with his greed he became an idolater.[46] By his desire he did not violate another's right to own these objects, but still his action was against God's commandment because God had forbidden him to take anything from that pagan place. The incident involved a *herem*, or ban, which required that the goods of a conquered Canaanite city be devoted to the Lord and not coveted and taken as spoils by the Israelites (Josh 6:18). Achan's fate was a reminder of the consequences of greed.

A classic story about coveting another's land is the story of Naboth's vineyard (1 Kgs 21:1–16). King Ahab desired to buy a piece of land of his subject Naboth which was adjacent to the palace property. While it seems that Ahab's desire was reasonable, Naboth's reluctance to sell it was even more reasonable, as it was inherited as an ancestral property. As all efforts to acquire the land from Naboth failed, King Ahab, lured by his wife Jezebel, produced false witness against Naboth and put him to death. Being a king, coveting his own subject's small piece of inherited land was despicable; more heinous and horrible was the effort to appropriate the land of his subject by deceit! Though no reference is made to "coveting" in the story, it is still

---

[44] Ideas for this paragraph are from Patrick D. Miller, *The Ten Commandments*, Interp. (Louisville, KY: John Knox, 2009), 394.

[45] No myth has been simply told in the mythological world; they either teach us what to do and what not to do; what and how to be/not to be. They are vehicle of a considerable amount of ethos.

[46] We will later see how greed is idolatry for Paul.

a classic story that tells the heinousness and viciousness of the result of coveting.

The story of Gehazi[47] (2 Kgs 5:1–27) is another example of greed. We are told that Gehazi went after Naaman—when Elisha sent him off without accepting any gift in return for the healing performed on him—and solicited for a talent of silver and two changes of clothing. Elisha knew about it and when Gehazi presented himself before Elisha he said: "Is this a time to accept money and clothing, olive orchards and vineyards, sheep and oxen, and male and female slaves? Therefore, the leprosy of Naaman shall cling to you" (2 Kgs 5:27). Gehazi had accepted a talent of silver and two changes of clothing from Naaman, but then it was revealed to Elisha that Gehazi accepted olive orchards, vineyards, sheep and oxen, and slaves, besides money and clothing (2 Kgs 5:26). We are not sure why Elisha furnishes with a longer list of items Gehazi procured by deceit. The most probable answer to this is that it is a "theoretical amplification by accumulation." It might be that Gehazi, to satisfy his desires, bought with the gift of Naaman additional property including land, cattle, and slaves, but nothing is informed to the reader about it except that the reader is given the opportunity to assume it to have happened that way as the temporal setting is fast moving in many of the Biblical stories and the details often are omitted. Or it could also be that Gehazi had already accumulated these things using the privilege of being a disciple of Elisha, the miracle worker, but now that he has been caught red handed more information about his greediness were revealed / reported to Elisha. In any case, the moral of the story is clear: greed leads to deceit and destruction.

There are number of poignant stories that relate sexual greed in the Bible[48] and we will passingly mention here only two of them, namely the story of Joseph and Potiphar's wife and David and Bathsheba. Potiphar's wife tries to seduce Joseph, but Joseph proves himself a man in whom the spirit of God rests (Gen 41:38). King David blatantly violates the commandment of God. The greed of David was not so much for wealth, but for a person. He desired another man's wife and his desire led him to commit two grave sins: adultery and murder. The second last commandment "you shall not covet your neighbor's wife" has also been broken by David. In the Miletus speech however, Paul does not make even the slightest hint of sexual greed. Our text

[47] He was a disciple of Elisha.

[48] Many instances of rape (e.g. Gen 34:1–2) or desire for sex both natural (2 Sam 11:2–27) and unnatural (Gen 19:1–11) are due to the unbridled desire for sex. Another story is that of Susanna and the Israelite Elders, a story found only in the LXX and so we will not make any further mention about it.

refers to greed for silver, gold, and clothing. So we will limit our theological discussion exclusively to the meaning of v. 33.

Besides those stories that document greed, there are many wisdom sayings that condemn greed. Psalm 24:1–5 states the qualification of a person to be in the presence of the Lord. It is none other than one with "clean hands" and "pure heart." In other words, they are not greedy for money, but are righteous and truthful (cf. also Ps 73:13). See also other similar examples in Job 31:24–28; Ps 10:3; 15:5; 57:4; Prov 13:11; 15:27; 17:23; 21:26a. Eccl 5:10; Sir 31:1; 40:13.

More than any other data, Paul's statement "I have not coveted anyone's silver or gold or clothing" has more bearing to the two LXX passages: 1 Sam 12:3 and Ex 20:17 / Deut 5:21. We have already made some observations about the former passage in the first chapter and so now we are left with the latter, Ex 20:17 / Deut 5:21. The exposition of this commandment here will enable us to see the ethical dimensions of 20:33 in its right perspective, because for the Israelites and Paul the commandments function as fundamental norm and frame from which further discernment takes place.[49]

The Decalogue comes to us in two versions (Ex 20:2–17 and Deut 5:6–21) with certain theological development, the main one being the bifurcation of the last commandment of the Exodus version (v. 17) into two in Deuteronomy using two separate verbs (v. 21). The verb חָמַד, which means "to desire," is used in Exodus 20:17 and in the first prohibition in Deut 5:17. The first ban in Ex 20:17 prohibits desire for the house of one's neighbor, while the first commandment in Deut 5:21 prohibits desire for the wife of another. The Deuteronomic version makes use of another verb אָוָהfor the second prohibition. What effect does this achieve? How are we to understand these Deuteronomic developments?

First of all the Hebrew root words חָמַד and אָוָה synonymously used in Deut 5:21 underline the power of desire.[50] These verbs used in the Decalogue and elsewhere in the Bible have a legitimate object for desire, either some positive objects such as the law (e.g. Ps 19:9–10; 119:40) or negative objects such as property, persons etc. In many cases these verbs signal a negative sense, an "inordinate or ungoverned desire that leads to an act of taking what is desired."[51] Desire follows an act to take or possess what is desired as in the case of Achan, David, Ahab, Gehazi, and others.

---

[49] Patrick D. Miller, "Divine Command and Beyond: The Ethics of the Commandments," in *The Ten Commandments: The Reciprocity of Faithfulness*, William P. Brown, ed., LTE (Louisville, KY: John Knox, 2004), 14.

[50] See Miller, *The Ten Commandments*, 400.

[51] Miller, 390.

If one strictly applies the injunction applicable only to the "objects of neighbor" then the cases of Adam and Eve and Achan fail to be included in this slot. How should we proceed then? The commandment "do not covet your neighbor's property, or wife, or cattle" also includes that one should not covet the things belonging to God. In the instance of Adam and Eve there is no literal "neighbor" involved to whom belongs the object of desire. In their case God can be seen as a neighbor, in the sense that He is their creator and friend, who walks with them. The tree at the center of the garden belonged to Him and it was He who had ordered them not to eat of that tree. It belonged to God as He put a ban on them. But Adam and Eve in their greed disobeyed the mandate of God and sinned. In a similar fashion, Achan coveted the spoils of Jericho. Although there is no literal "neighbor" involved here, coveting the goods that belonged to God[52] was a crime. Coveting anything that belongs to God is dangerous, it was detrimental to Adam and Eve, and Achan as we know from their fate.

In this connection idolatry is the acknowledgment of other gods and giving glory to them instead of the one true God. The first commandment precisely prohibits the Israelites this and calls them to a total submission and rendering of glory to God alone. This is why the breaking of the first commandments begets the greatest condemnation in the Bible. According to Brian S. Rosner the first commandment issues the fundamental call to demonstrate absolute loyalty and devotion to God in all areas of life. It is the foundational commandment to the rest of the Decalogue.[53]

The issue of greed is a "high point" in the NT ethic. Both Luke and Paul, as seen above, are never tired of addressing this issue at various occasions. Greed is idolatry for Paul (Col 3:5 and Eph 5:5), in the sense that it can lead to idolatry.[54] This view consequently results in suggesting greed to be as contemptible as idolatry (Lk 16:13; Mt 6:24; Rom 16:18; Phil 3:19). The phrases in Ephesians and Colossians are formulated in order to magnify the sinfulness of greed.[55] No doubt that the expression in Colossians and Ephesians is to be viewed as a metaphor. When Paul compares greed to idolatry we must keep in mind that both greed and idolatry focused attention

---

[52] Under the ban (*herem*) Achan was not to appropriate any goods from Jericho. By the very ban, those goods were considered unholy. Moreover those goods without an owner naturally belonged to God.

[53] See Brian S. Rosner, *Greed as Idolatry: The Origin and Meaning of Pauline Metaphor* (Grand Rapids: Eerdmans, 2007), 71.

[54] It may be possible to hold that greed is as bad as idolatry. The internal evidences from his letters show that Paul was not having this in mind. For a different interpretation of the phrase "Greed is idolatry," see Rosner, *Greed as Idolatry*, 11–47.

[55] Rosner, 8.

on items made of gold and silver. These metals are associated in Jewish tradition with wealth and power; at the same time with idolaters and greedy.[56]

Greed contains an act of idolatry by focusing trust on material things or on one's own desire rather than on God (Eph 4:19; 5:5). It is also a sign of loss of faith (1 Tim 6:10).[57] Moreover the references in Phil 3:19 and Rom 16:18 may point to some kind of "figurative idolatry." They may refer to greed for wealth which is a hindrance to the true worship of God. Why should Paul consider this sin graver than other sins? Most probably, as Rosner puts it, greed for Paul stands in opposition to God.

Other than having an observable link between the first and the last commandments, there is an intrinsic connection between the last commandments and the 6th and 7th commandments. Unrestrained desire leads to stealing and adultery. A bird's eye view of the examples of greed in the Bible that we have dealt with allows us to arrive at such a conclusion. The commandments against coveting things or wife strike a relation with the commandments against stealing and adultery, since greed is the cause for theft, fornication, murder, lying etc. Thus, the commandment "You shall not covet" is retrospective of the rest of the commandments, and intrinsically related to all the other commandments of the Decalogue, especially to the first. Evil act is condemnable at the same time evil will (or desire) is equally so. It is from the evil desire every evil act originates. Thus coveting is considered as a chief sin. The Ten Commandments end with the injunction not to covet anything.

Another side of the danger of greed is that it is related to power. The dynamic of greed goes beyond material possessions, it can be an expression of power, to take advantage of others. In the above two examples of David and Ahab, one point that rings loud and clear is that "desire coupled with authority cannot stop doing whatever is necessary to get what is coveted."[58]

More than anything, the basis for Paul's condemnation on greed emerges from the life and example of Jesus received from the apostolic traditions. In all his letters Jesus is the perfect example of love, humility, obedience, service, generosity etc. He became poor so that we might be rich (2 Cor 8:9). Jesus' call to love, communion, generosity etc. are major themes for the evangelists, so also for Paul. Communion and community will be

---

[56] See this in the examples of the Golden Calf (Ex 32), Achan, and Gehazi. Though the same is not explicitly mentioned in the farewell speech of Samuel, the question "from whose hand have I taken a bribe to blind my eyes with it?" may point to some kind of allurement by gold or other costly objects.

[57] Konrad Raiser, "Theological and Ethical Considerations Regarding Wealth and the Call for Establishing a Greed Line," *ER* 63.3 (2011), 279.

[58] Miller, *The Ten Commandments*, 397.

destroyed when individualism creeps in. On the other hand love, generosity, and genuine care for one another will build up the community.

4.5. Desire: Action or Intention?

Desire in itself is neutral, as we have seen above, and is always a "movement of the will," which may or may not end up in a positive or negative action. By the use of separate verbs in the Deuteronomic versions of the Decalogue, some scholars have argued that Deuteronomic version shows evidence of a considerable refinement of moral standards extending the prohibition beyond the external act of actual appropriation, which is all that is forbidden in Exodus. But this argument has been criticized by William L. Moran.[59]

Moran argues that the use of חָמַד in Exodus does not refer to any act of appropriation although, as in the case with אָוָה, it may lead to an act of appropriation. I concur with the thesis of Moran and G. Wallis who favor that the commandment in both versions refers to the movement of the will, a thing to do with intention. For Wallis, חָמַד can be suitably interpreted in the framework of an ethic of pure intention.[60] Moran provides various use of חָמַד in the Bible as examples from which it can be concluded that the commandment does not refer to any act of appropriation. Wallis also observes that if it were to be so, then the necessity of the sixth and seventh commandment come under scrutiny. Therefore חָמַדdoes not refer to stealing or adultery *per se*, since other commandments deal with it.[61] Deuteronomy 7:25 is a good *locus* where the above point can been clearly noticed. Although Deut 5:21 includes some theological development, in essence, both versions point to the intentionality rather than resultative actions.

Paul never uses the word ἐπιθυμία / πλεονεξία to denote resultative actions of greed. The meaning of 20:33 therefore, refers to the intentionality rather than a performed action. Paul has not even "intended" to appropriate another's property, and so it is unthinkable of him to take illegal possession of anyone's property. Jesus had already taught that all evil comes from the heart (Mk 7:21–22). Desire must be controlled since the desired objects are of considerable value, otherwise people who desire these things will be in danger of committing other sins.

---

[59] For Scholars' argument and Moran's objections, see William L. Moran, "The Conclusion of the Decalogue (Ex 20:17 = Deut 5:21)," *CBQ* 29 (1967), 543–54.

[60] Wallis, "חָמַד," 457.

[61] The *Mitzvot* on coveting (265–66) is another clear example which claims that the commandment refers not to action, but to having the desire for what belongs to another and occupying one's mind with schemes to acquire it. The sin of coveting is the source of the urge to commit robbery. See Ronald L. Eisenberg, *The 613 Mitzvot: A Contemporary Guide to the Commandments of Judaism* (Rockville, MD: Schreiber Publishing, 2005), 288.

To conclude this chapter, we passingly mention 20:34–35 in which Paul is an example to imitate, for he conducts himself as a model for work, caring, and generosity. Such behavior of Paul itself is demonstrative of his attitude and pure intention. Verse 33, *prima facie*, appears to be Paul's claim that he is not covetous in his ministry even as Samuel wasn't (1 Sam 12:3–5). However, the observation of Christopher Hays concerning an import of this verse merits our attention. The triple objects of desire in v. 33 need not refer to covetousness *in se* as usually understood, but to Paul's lack of interest in silver, gold, and cloaks, which does not imply "an adjuration of desire for *great* wealth and thus derivatively, an eschewal of covetousness."[62] Lucan Paul condemns covetousness in any form and at the same time displays no desire for wealth in order to be supported. Lucan Paul might have tried to convey this understanding of the text, but in doing so he had LXX stories and terminologies in mind. Paul's letters assert, as we shall see later, that he, as a minister, did not ask for financial support. On the contrary he worked for a living and even gave part of it for the sustenance of others. The Ephesian elders must follow this example; that they should be generous in giving and not greedy. In a following chapter we will take up the "ethics of giving" as this topic is more suitable to inspect then than now.

[62] Christopher M. Hays, *Luke's Wealth Ethics: A Study in their Coherence and Character*, WUNT (Tübingen: Mohr Siebeck, 2010), 255.

Chapter 5

Acts 20:34: Ethics of Manual Labor

After his bold declaration about the pure intention of his past conduct now Paul emphatically states the custom of his manual work which the Ephesian elders were already familiar with. Such declaration itself is a proof of his pure intention and functions as evidence of his honesty to counter any charge made against him as greedy; for if he were greedy, then it was not at all necessary for him to work to support himself and others, on the contrary, he would have enjoyed the hospitality of others and could even press on others to provide for him. Quite the contrary, Paul worked with his own hands for the sustenance of himself and other ministers with him. This information from Paul is key to interpret the Lucan Paul's ethics of labor[1] at least in two of its aspects: (1) the importance and goal of work and (2) the dignity of manual work and workers. In this chapter we will examine specimens from Pauline and deutero-Pauline traditions[2] which would substantially contribute to this study.

---

[1] Labor ethics either as a subject of moral theology or as a theme in the Bible is a vast topic which includes different elements and aspects such as the purpose of labor, dignity of labor and laborers, just wages, slavery, exploitation of laborers, harassment and maltreatment at workplace, duties of workers, etc. By limiting the study only to Paul and Lucan Paul, the topic still remains vast; but, that which pertains to this study, namely, the purpose of work and the dignity of labor / laborers, however, needs to be considered as these two points are the focus of 20:34.

[2] "Deutero-Pauline traditions" of the NT are those letters attributed to Paul or writings in which Pauline tradition is transmitted.

5.1. Initial Comments on 20:34

Verse 34 calls the elders to witness to the truth of Paul's claim[3] as stated in the previous verse. The ethos of Paul and his example which appeared in the beginning of the speech (18b–21) reappears here but what is highlighted here is not his agonizing missionary activity as in 18b–21, but "working hands" and "working to support." Both vv. 18b–21 and v. 34 recount some amount of pain of labor and thereby underlines a similarity between the passages' ethos. The ethos of Paul found in vv. 18b–21 refers to a number of things which may also include a reference to his toil, most probably an indication to his manual work; but in the present verse Paul's ethos is narrowed down to the realm of manual work and its purpose.

The phrase, "You know yourselves" (αὐτοὶ γινώσκετε), here looks back to v. 18b although the verb used here is different (ἐπίσταμαι). Paul calls the attention of the elders to his practice of working with his own hands, a thing he did to sustain himself and his companions and by which he wanted to avoid burdening the churches wherever he might have stayed. Elsewhere Paul himself or Luke attests his habit of (manual) work (1 Cor 4:12; 9; 2 Cor 11:7–11; 12:13; 1 Thess 2:9; 2 Thess 3:7–10; Acts 18:3). For Paul manual work was a reason for his boasting on different occasions (1 Cor 9:15; 2 Cor 11:10).[4]

The striking word χρεία ("need") echoes the language of the apostles' speech to the Jerusalem community in 6:3.[5] This word is acrostic with χείρ ("hand") found in the same verse. "Hand" is a common term in the NT referring either to a part of the body (e.g. Mt 8:15; Mk 3:1; Lk 4:40; 6:1; Acts 3:7; 26:1; 28:3; 1 Cor 16:21; Gal 6:11; 2 Thess 3:17 etc. or also figuratively to the power of God or man (Lk 1:66; 23:46; Mt 17:22; Jn 10:39; Acts 5:12; 13:11; 2 Cor 11:33; etc.). Reference to "working with hands" is rare in the NT and such references are found in the proto-Pauline sources,[6] such as 1 Cor 4:12; 1 Thess 4:11 and in the deutero-Pauline traditions such as Eph 4:28, and here in Acts 20:34. These references are reflective of the use of χείρ in the Miletus speech.

---

[3] Watson, "Paul's Speech," 205.

[4] See Watson, 205.

[5] Soards, *The Speeches in Acts*, 108.

[6] We mean by "proto-Pauline sources" those authentic letters of Paul whose authorship is never disputed.

The verse ends by stating the purpose with which Paul worked: it sustained him and his companions. The aim of this statement of Paul in the verse is to provide a genuine work ethics for the Ephesian elders and the audience at large.[7] Since the verse's emphasis falls on "work" or "labor," in the following pages we shall orient our discussion in that direction.

5.2. Work in General: Scriptural Evidences

The Ethical concern of verse 34 may be detected by the Pauline example of work. Paul is advocating a specific work ethic here. Therefore, in this section we shall first present some important scriptural evidences of work ethic, without being exhaustive, and then examine proto / deutero-Pauline traditions which epitomize manual work ethics.

In scripture, the term "work"[8] is broadly used to describe diverse nuances, such as creation, effort, labor (both physical and spiritual), toil, service, even worship.[9] In the OT, work is a general term for various activities, such as physical work, mental work, obeying or disobeying the Lord, etc. More importantly it may be seen as a divine ordering for the life of man. It is part of the orderly structure of the world and man.[10]

In the OT, God is presented as one who creates everything out of nothing. The whole universe is the result of the work of God. Every now and then the leaders and Prophets of Israel proclaimed the mighty works of God, his creation, liberation, and protection (see Josh 24:31; Judg 2:7, 10 etc.). They even sang the perfection of his work (Ps 19:2; 8:3–8). Work is important and necessary for man because it is the will of God. He willed that man might collaborate with God, in some way, in the creative work of God. Negative actions of men such as idolatry (Deut 31:29; Jer 51:18 etc.) are metaphorically "evil works." Although work is important for man's sustenance, he is not to work on Sabbath (Ex 20:8–11). Why did God forbid work on a Sabbath? Because one should not be a slave to work or money rather one should respect God and his commands. "It is a recognition that work is a gift of God and not a tyrannical demon that rules us. It is also the recognition that all time belongs to God and therefore he is Lord over both his creation and time."[11]

---

[7] Other than providing a work ethic it also aims to present Paul as a model, a discussion we reserve for the next chapter.

[8] In English language, "labor" is a synonym for "work." In this thesis, I will be using both the terms interchangeably.

[9] Alan Richardson, *The Biblical Doctrine of Work*, EBS 1 (London: SCM Press, 1954), 13.

[10] See this in Richardson, *Biblical Doctrine of Work*, 23.

[11] Kaiser, *Old Testament Ethics*, 89.

In the NT God is the divine worker (Jn 5:17) and a farmer (Jn 15:1) images which are of course metaphorical. In John "sign" is synonymous with "work" (Jn 6:30; 7:21 etc.). The whole ministry of Jesus is referred to as "work" (Jn 17:4). Missionary activity for the sake of the Gospel is also a work but in a metaphorical sense (Acts 13:2; Phil 2:30 etc.). The Gospels contain no sayings expressly concerned with manual work.[12] However the apostles are presented as working; for they were fishermen. Jesus called Peter and Andrew while they were fishing; in the same way James and John were called while fishing (Mk 1:16–20). Matthew received his vocation as he was working at the tax booth (Mt 9:9). Moreover, there are parables and other examples that speak of men working, such as the parables of the Sower (Mk 4:3–9), Laborers in the Vineyard (Mt 20:1–16), the Two Sons (Mt 21:28–32), and the Talents (Mt 25:14–30). The Gospel of Luke narrates a unique episode in which a woman, Martha, is spoken of as engaged in serving Jesus and the apostles (Lk 10:38–42). Mary her sister is placed as a model against the activism of Martha, in doing so Mary becomes a model of "listening" the Word of God. Work may be abandoned in favor of a better cause, that is, for spiritual matters. But one should never neglect one's duties towards neighbor on account of "spiritual matters," lest one fails to be a "neighbor" to those in need as this concern is previously raised by Jesus in the parable of the Good Samaritan (Lk 10:30–37) where it is clear that the priest and Levite failed to be a "neighbor" to the man who fell among robbers.

In Acts and Epistles, the reader is informed about various people, particularly Paul working and to this we shall soon revert. In the vocabulary of Paul the word "work" has a number of connotations; first of all it is synonymous to Christian living (1 Cor 15:58; Phil 2:12-13); it can refer to good deeds (1 Cor 3:9; 12:6; 16:10; Gal 5:6; Gal 6:10) as well as evil deeds (1 Cor 5:2f; 2 Cor 11:13, 15; Gal 5:19; Phil 3:2; Rom 2:9; 7:5-20; 13:12). Moreover, Paul recalls his own (manual) work in a number of passages (1 Cor 4:11; 9:6, 15, 18; 2 Cor 6:5;[13] 11:23, 27).

Having drawn up a general picture of the idea of work in the scriptures, we assess that it would be impossible to proceed with this chapter without narrowing down the meaning of "work" to that sense in which it is used in Acts 20:34. In our discussion of the ethics of manual work we are neither referring to the work of creation which is attributed to God nor to the metaphorical reference to idolatry nor to the missionary activity for the

---

[12] See this idea in Göran Agrell, *Work, Toil, and Sustenance: An Examination of the View of Work in the New Testament, Taking in Consideration Views Found in Old Testament, Intertestamental, and Early Rabbinic Writings*, Stephen Westerholm, trans. (Verbum: Håkan Ohlssons, 1976), 85.

[13] Although 2 Cor 6:5 points to the work (κόπος) of Paul, it is merely placed as an item in the catalogue.

sake of the Gospel as projected in some places of the NT nor to any other connotations the word may have, but to the economic activity of 'manual work of men for sustenance and support' since Paul's reference in v. 34 is exclusively to this. In our examination that follows, we will therefore limit our area of research only to the instances and instructions of manual work found in Acts and Pauline letters and if needed other instances from elsewhere may be brought to attention.

5.3. Scriptural Foundation for the Labor Ethics of Paul

Paul speaks occasionally about his habit of manual work by which he was supporting himself and his companions. Although laborers deserve their wages (Lk 10:7; 1 Cor 9:4 etc.), Paul renounced this privilege as his economic life differed from other missioners. He found it rather important to work to earn a living. Paul's manual work of tentmaking recorded in Acts 18:3 is a clear evidence of his manual labor for his own sustenance. Paul himself attests his labor and toil on diverse occasions in his letters which indicate his habit of manual work. Why would Paul take his manual work so seriously?

The factors that influenced Paul in developing a manual work ethic or the reasons for Paul to see work as important was first and foremost the various Biblical concepts and precepts concerning work. The Mediterranean milieu mostly influenced by the Greco-Roman culture and philosophy would be another factor that influenced Paul in this regard. And finally, his own Jewish family upbringing must also be given due importance.

5.3.1. Biblical Notion and Precepts

Under this title we shall first examine the OT notion and precepts on work which most probably had a great impact on Pauline concept of work (ethics) and this will follow the notion and precepts of Jesus.

5.3.1.1. Torah, Historical, and Prophetical Books

We cannot underplay the Biblical influence Paul, as a Jew and Pharisee zealous for Judaism and its practice, had on the notion of work in general and the idea of manual work in particular.[14] God has placed man in the Garden of Eden to till it and care for it (Gen 2:15) which was a general task as a farmer or gardener. But with his sin and subsequent curse, man has to toil to earn his bread (Gen 3:17). Though the Genesis account is a mythical presentation[15] which relates the origin of man and his sin, it also tells the tale

---

[14] A fine description of Jewish attitude towards labor can be found in Arthur T. Geoghegan, *The Attitude towards Labor in Early Christianity and Ancient Culture*, SCA 6 (Washington DC: The CUA Press, 1945), 59–89.

[15] Modern scholars are of this opinion, but one may not hold that Paul kept a similar perspective of the text.

of the condition of man as one working always to sustain himself. In order to sustain themselves men were principally engaged in the manual work such as farm / field works, handicrafts, and textiles. In short, most manual works of Biblical time fell into one of these three categories.[16]

(1) First of all there are numerous references about farm work and its greatness. It is acceptable that bulk of the people was farmers (2 Macc 12:1). Farm work was important for grains, fruits, oil etc. and the yields of the farm were the outcome of manual work. Raising cattle also was part of farm work or even a hunter was "a man of the field" (Gen 25:27). Hard labor and farm work are created by God (Sir 7:15) and moreover the farmers are directly taught by God the art of cultivation (Isa 28:23–29). Farmers are called "tiller of the land" (Gen 4:2) and "planter of the field" (Gen 9:20) who dig the field (Is 41:5; Ger 51:23).

(2) Another important category of manual work includes handicrafts which comprise all types of work with metals, wood, stones, etc. (see Ex 39:8; Num 8:4; Isa 44:12 etc.). As in the case with farmers, even here it is God who gives spirit, skill, knowledge, and wisdom to craftsmen (Ex 35:31–35, 36:1). In the Bible work / workers with iron, bronze, jewels, and gold are considered important (Ex 37:1; Prov 17:3; Jer 6:29 etc.). Ceramic workers also occupied an important place in the Israelite society (1 Chr 4:23; Jer 18:3; 19:1; cf. Mt 27:7, 10). While handicraft works were generally positive especially those related to the objects of the cult and rituals (Num 10:2; 15:38 etc.), works involved with the production of idols were forbidden (Ex 20:4; 32:4ff; 34:17; Lev 26:1; Deut 4:16; 27:15; 31:29; 1 Kgs 12:28; Ps 106:19, 23, 39f.; 115:4; Isa 2:8ff; 44:9; Jer 10:3f; Hos 8:4 etc.). They will be cursed if they make idols and worship them (Isa 44:9; Jer 16:18; Ezek 36:18 etc.)

(3) Textile workers are another category who occupied an important place in the economy of Israel (see Ex 25:4–5; Prov 31:13). Some of them were specialized workers who were called *Kobes* (from the verb כָּבַס see Jer 2:22; Mal 3:2; cf. Mk 9:2). Abundant references to wool, linen, and other luxurious garments (Josh 2:6; 2 Kgs 23:7; Ezek 16:16; 27:7, 16; Hos 2:7 etc.) indicate the importance of textiles in the society.

In the Torah, historical, and prophetical books of the Bible there are many instances of individuals or community engaged in manual work, for example

[16] The ideas for the following 3 divisions of labor are taken from P. Imanuele Testa, *Il Lavoro nella Bibbia* (Assisi: Porziuncola, 1959).

Cain was a tiller of the ground and Abel was a shepherd; the work of both was manual. People at Babel were making a tower, which would naturally involve digging, carrying objects, work at kiln, masonry, carpentry, etc. all of which include manual work. The Israelites under the Pharaoh were engaged in building activity and field labor (Ex 1:11–14). The Exodus account is unique for it not only refers to manual work but also depicts the labor conditions in general which certainly manifest various ethical issues of labor. Ruth's story unveils in an agricultural setting where both the master and the laborers exchange greetings and blessings (Ruth 2:4). There are detailed building activities of King Solomon (1 Kgs 5:13–7:50), Ezra-Nehemiah etc. reported in the Bible. Elisha was ploughing when he was called by Elijah (1 Kgs 19:19). Jeremiah narrates how he was told to go to the potter's house and upon reaching there, he finds the potter working at his wheel (Jer 18:2–3).

In general, the abundant mention of manual work / workers in the Bible tells us that these are not undervalued in these documents rather manual work is seen as positive. Even those later redactors of Sacred Books did not find it embarrassing to narrate the doing of manual labor, let us say, of Gideon who was threshing wheat (Judg 6:11) or Saul who was ploughing with his oxen (1 Sam 11:5) or David who was a shepherd (1 Sam 16:11). There are many more examples of manual work but we need not cite more; the instances already quoted suffice to have an overarching picture of manual work and its place in the Bible. These books indicate or describe the type and nature of certain manual works usually done in the Israelite society. But specific ethical instructions regarding work are found in the Wisdom Books.

5.3.1.2. Wisdom Books

In the Wisdom Books we do not find a definition of work nor can we unravel an organic vision of work but the Biblical sages transmitted direct observations of realities.[17] For them work is a human reality, similar to the rest of the realities present in the Biblical realm. Wisdom Books mostly keep a positive attitude to manual work. More than any human work, God's work, His blessings are all that count. Only the blessings of the Lord make rich, and to this, hard toil has nothing to add (Prov 10:22 NJB). Similarly obedience brings blessings in one's work (see Ps 81:14ff.; 107:33ff.; Job 1:10; Prov 3:9ff.; 10:16; Eccl 2:24ff.), whereas disobedience produces curse in one's work (Ps 78:46ff.; 107:33ff.; Job 5:5; 27:13ff.; Prov 5:10; 10:16).[18]

---

[17] Nuria Calduch-Benages, "Il Lavoro in Proverbi e Siracide," in *Il Lavoro Opera delle Nostre Mani*, PSV 52 (Bologna: Centro Editoriale Dehoniano, 2005), 21.

[18] The evident blessing of God upon the laborers confirms the laborers' favorable position among the Hebrews. See, Geoghegan, *Attitude towards Labor*, 68.

5.3.1.2.1. Book of Proverbs

The Book of Proverbs mostly acclaims the zeal and diligence of a wise person. Most references to labor in the book pertain to manual work. The wise is active, laborious, and diligent as illustrated through the example of ants (Prov 6:6–11). The author rebukes the lazy with three warnings. Go to the ant, see their habit, and be wise. In Prov 30:24–28 ants along with badgers, locusts, and lizard are described as exceedingly wise. Among these animals, the ant, being wise, is active and diligent as against the fool. The lazy becomes a "prototype" of the fool (24:30). The book places diligence and laziness one against the other (10:4; 11;16; 12:11, 24, 27; 13:4; 28:19); at the same time it demands acquisition of wealth by labor (13:11). The book also praises skilled laborers (22:29). At the end of the book a wise and untiring worker is described (31:10–31). She is the opposite image of the lazy. It is highly interesting that the woman praised in the chapter is lauded mostly for her manual work and management of the household.

5.3.1.2.2. Book of Qohelet

The Book of Qohelet (Ecclesiastes) sees work and all enjoyment from it as a gift of God and the lot of man (Eccl 2:24–26; 3:22; 5:18–20; 8:15). While one is upon this earth, one must work, and by one's labor a person should also enjoy the fruits of his / her labor. Any work to secure a future and "workaholism" are futile (Eccl 2:22; 4:4–6) as Qohelet considers most of man's activities under the sun as "vanity" (הֶ֫בֶל cf. 1:14) including work and money (Eccl 5:9–11) without the blessings of God (Eccl 2:25). No direct reference to manual work may be found in the book, but as in the case with the Proverbs, here too, references to work are naturally and mostly linked to manual work.

5.3.1.2.3. Book of Sirach

The Book of Sirach (Ecclesiasticus) views the concept of work more or less in the same line with Qohelet, although some negative evaluation of certain work has been evident in it. But one must take into account that Sir 7:15 provides the most positive appraisal of manual work, for it says "Do not hate hard labor or farm work... ." The element common to both the books is God's blessing required for success of life rather than any willingness or personal effort, though these may benefit in the long run. In conclusion it could be said that generally the Biblical authors viewed manual work as positive as it was the most important thing required for sustenance in an agrarian society.

5.3.2. The Example and Teachings of Jesus

Another reason for Lukan Paul's positive view of work was the example of Jesus who labored as a carpenter for many years. The reaction of the people at the preaching of Jesus in the Capernaum synagogue points to the fact that carpentry was his profession (Mk 6:2–3). Therefore, it is to be assumed that Jesus worked to support his family, especially after the death of Joseph, his legal father. There are other telling examples of Jesus' manual labor about which Luke and Paul certainly knew. Jesus "condescended" to work like a slave (Mk 10:44; Jn 13:5, 12–14; Phil 2:7) and invites his followers to imitate Him in his manual work (Jn 13:15).

Some early authors have portrayed Jesus as scornful of work[19] but taking Gospels as sources for our reconstruction of Jesus' life and teaching, one can notice without doubt the emphasis He had given to manual work although His work was more of a spiritual nature during his public life. Christ's attitude to manual work is reflected in His life, selection of disciples, association with the working classes, and teaching. Paul, without doubt, learned and inherited this Jesus tradition through the apostles and other witnesses.

Moving to the teachings of Jesus concerning work, other than the aforementioned parables (see point no. 6.2) which refer to work and are told for an agrarian group, there is the example of slaves and steward whose duty is to work and manage a household, which definitely include a great deal of manual work (Lk 12:35–48; 17:7–10) but it need not involve hard farm work (Lk 16:3). The term steward (οἰκονόμος) is used both by Luke and Paul (Lk 12:43;[20] 16:1, 3, 8; 1 Cor 4:1–2; Gal 4:2), a term common to them. Jesus instructs his listeners to be like a faithful steward who is always vigilant and working (Lk 12:43).[21]

5.3.3. Greco-Roman Influence

The influence of Greco-Roman culture and philosophy in the life of Lucan Paul on the subject of manual labor may not be so decisive, since many of them considered manual work humiliating and especially trade in a workshop was kept apart for slaves and other people of the lower strata.[22] "The system of slavery was the greatest cause for the disesteem into which manual labor

---

[19] See the names of authors who picture a negative attitude of Jesus of labor in Geoghegan, *Attitude towards Labor*, 93.

[20] In the parallel passage, neither Mark nor Matthew introduces a new term as Luke does. Matthew contrasts faithful slave with wicked slave (Mt 24:45–51), whereas Mark gives a general instruction to be on guard (Mk 13:34). In Matthew the faithful slave is in charge of others' slaves but in Luke (12:41–48) the head slave gets a separate name, οἰκονόμος.

[21] Heinrich Schumacher even suggests that the allusions to labor in Jesus' teaching are intended to directly inculcate the duty [or dignity] of labor. See *Social Message of the New Testament*, RCS (Milwaukee, WI: The Bruce Publishing Company, 1937), 111.

[22] For a short presentation of stigma attached to manual work, see Ronald F. Hock, *The Social Context of Paul's Ministry: Tent Making and Apostleship* (Philadelphia, PA: Fortress, 1980), 35–37; Keener, *Acts*, 3:2722–25.

fell."[23] Manual labor, especially the menial ones were exclusively assigned for slaves.[24] Cicero *De off.* 1.150, Seneca *Ep.* 88.21, and Plutarch *Per.* 2.1 held a negative image of trade and manual work. This may be due to the philosopher's notion that concern for the common good of the state was considered higher than the individual good. In order to strive for this common good one must contribute to the state by philosophy and other intellectual contributions, which then was considered superior to various manual labors.[25] Nevertheless, this negative attitude to manual labor and trade need not be seen as the common opinion of all. R. F. Hock, in his analysis of the social context of Paul's ministry, slips up on the positive attitude many of the Greco-Roman philosophers and moralists had on manual work; as a result Hock sees no influence of Greco-Roman ideas on the custom of Paul's manual work.

On the other hand many moralists and philosophers of the time, like the Cynics and Stoics, demonstrated through their example and teaching that it is not slavish to take up manual work.[26] In fact engaging in or love of manual work is a virtue.[27] Musonius Rufus advised that toil is not something negative and that good achieved through toil lasts far longer than the toil itself.[28] Agricultural work was esteemed by all classes of Greek society.[29] Other examples of Greek authors who praise the value of hard work are Isocrates and Xenophon.[30] Even the privileged were, under certain conditions, encouraged to work.[31] So it was normal that the moralists encouraged the urban poor to work for their living. Dio Chrysostom recommended that the poor work with their hands (*Eub.* 7.124). Working with one's hand would meet one's needs, Dio concluded that there were many opportunities for making a living that

---

23 Geoghegan, *Attitude towards Labor*, 18.

24 Slave labor especially in Rome was shocking as one author notes that the number of slaves who labored there in 5 BCE were estimated more than 650,000.

25 See Geoghegan, *Attitude towards Labor*, 12. A stigma attached to the trades was that it left no desire for helping one's city or friends or for developing one's own soul (see Xen. *Oec.* 4.3; Luc. *Somn.* 10), accordingly artisans were regarded as incapable of achieving virtue (Xen. *Oec.* 4.3; Arist. *Pol.* 1319b. 28) or they were viewed as uneducated. See these references appearing also in Hock, *Social Context*, 36.

26 The Cynic Demetrius of Sunium worked as a porter in order to care for his friend in prison and thereby showed his friendship (Luc. *Tox.* 31).

27 Dio Chry. *Or.* 1.21.

28 Mus. Ruf. *Frg.* 51, as found in "Fragment LI," Google.com, accessed 3 March 2018, https://sites.google.com/site/thestoiclife/the_teachers/musonius-rufus/fragments/51.

29 Geoghegan, *Attitude towards Labor*, 27.

30 See Isoc. *Demon.* 9.21 and Xen. *Cyr.* 1.2.1; Plut. *Demosth.* 1.3; Plut. *Alex.* 40.2 who consider the love of toil as a virtue.

31 Plut. *De Vit. aer. al.* 830 A–B.

are neither improper, nor injurious to men who are willing to work with their hands (Dio Chry. *Eub*. 7.125).[32]

We do not know how much of Greco-Roman culture and practice has gone into the making of Lucan or Pauline manual work ethics. The general negative mentality towards slaves, manual labor / laborers weighs more than the positive mentality towards labor and laborers. It is also possible that Paul might have been voluntarily going against the negative mentality of the majority Greco-Roman populace. The general Greco-Roman negative mentality towards manual labor, triggered by the institutionalization of slavery, drove Paul to act reversely against it and to elevate it to the same status of any other job after the manner of Jesus, the carpenter and slave, his ultimate model.[33] Paul's willingness to do manual work in his own period thus becomes an example for the second generation Christians to imitate. We will be returning to this topic in the following chapter.

5.3.4. Jewish Practice and Family Upbringing

We have already stated that Paul's attitude towards manual work was positive, that he advocates his own churches to work and earn. Besides the Biblical examples and instructions about work and the example of Jesus, Paul could have been also influenced by his Jewish (Rabbinic) family upbringing custom which usually combined the study of Torah with practice of trade.[34] Many scholars suggest that Paul scrupulously maintained this tradition as a Christian preacher.[35] But it is still contentious why Paul worked with leather, something the Jews held abominable.[36]

Although Hock presents three objections[37] to the Jewish practice of learning and working simultaneously, he recognizes the possibility of learning a trade in a family setting, if not as part of formal rabbinic training.[38]

---

[32] For more on the attitude of ancients (Greeks, Romans, and Jews) towards work, see Geoghegan, *Attitude towards Labor*, 1–89.

[33] In his letter to the Philippians, Paul is explicit on the humility of Jesus who humbled himself to the point of taking the form of a slave.

[34] See Günther Bornkamm, *Paul*, D. M. G. Stalker, trans. (San Francisco: Harper & Row, 1971), 12; Hock, *Social Context*, 11; Mish. *Ḳidd.* 4. 79a.

[35] For example F. F. Bruce, *Paul: Apostle of the Heart Set Free* (Grand Rapids: Eerdmans, 1977), 107–108.

[36] Mish. *Kidd.* 4. 79a; See also Lev 11:39.

[37] First of all, Hock doubts that Paul was trained under Gamaliel (22:3); second, all who were trained under Gamaliel became scribes, and third, working alongside study of Torah began in mid-second century after Christ. These objections, according to Keener, do not stand (see Keener, *Acts*, 3:2725–26); there may be a grain of truth in them but other evidences are stronger

[38] Hock, *Social Context*, 23–24.

It must also be noted that the Jewish traditions did not always hold the same opinion on sages working "though it was more apt to present manual labor as honorable than do extant elite Greek sources."[39] Moreover, the extant Jewish sources reveal a high work ethic.[40] To conclude, Paul may not have been influenced by or slaved to a particular kind of thinking in his attitude to manual work; on the contrary it is highly possible that Paul, a learned Jew, influenced by various philosophies and opinions of moralists, including Jesus, shaped a work ethics for self and for the churches that was compatible to the work ethics of Jesus, a work-ethic that then became a norm for the churches. Luke is transmitting this work ethics through the Miletus speech.

5.4. "I Worked with My Own Hands": The Work Ethics of Paul

Paul plainly states his practice of manual work about which the Ephesian elders already knew. Not only in Ephesus but also in other places Paul worked for a living, a fact the Ephesian church as a whole most probably had known either through Paul himself or through the correspondence and communication of other co-ministers of Paul (for example Luke, Timothy, and others). Our task here is to glean instances from Paul's own letters and Acts to build a picture of Paul's custom of manual work to establish the dignity of labor and laborers, and the positive mentality Paul kept on manual work.

5.4.1. New Testament Attestation Regarding Paul's Manual Work

5.4.1.1. First Corinthians 4:12

This is the first instance (according to the order of books in the NT) where Paul himself testifies about his manual work. The context for this reference to manual work is the humble ministry of Paul and Apollos in Corinth who confront the wisdom of this world with the wisdom of Christ. In many ways the Corinthian wisdom was contrary to the wisdom of Christ. On this account, their ministry had become humiliating and distressful and an object of spectacle for the Corinthians. Paul mentions his own manual work as folly in the eyes of the world, that "he a learned teacher should assume

---

[39] Keener, 3:2726.

[40] Many quotes from the Wisdom Books, for example, generate a high work ethic. Similar instructions were given in *Test. Iss.* 5:3 (Bow down your back unto husbandry, and toil in labors in all manner of husbandry, offering gifts to the Lord with thanksgiving). Later Jewish sources are also helpful here since they reflect their earlier practices. Josephus observes that the Essenes labored during day in their community (Jos. *War* 2.131). Mish. *Aboth* 1.10 quotes the maxim of Shemaiah, the teacher of Hillel which reads: "Love labor." Positive attitude to labor was not common among the rabbis for some of them scorned worldly occupations. See this argument in Geoghegan, *Attitude towards Labor*, 77–78.

the contemptable condition of a mechanic."[41] In the catalogue of suffering (4:11–12), Paul's statement about working with his own hand appears as a disgraceful thing as most Greeks maintained. Nevertheless, Paul performed this for the benefit of the whole mission. Thus, the text clearly emphasizes that for Paul manual work became an inseparable part of his apostolic ministry.

Not only Paul is working with his hands, but also Apollos. The use of "we" serves to underline the fact that it is not Paul alone who is working but also "others," other apostles, thus making "work" an underlining character of all the apostles. The point is clear that having chosen to work with leather as their primary means of sustenance and having refused to accept any remuneration from the church, they have found themselves in the same situation of many artisans of the time who were making ends meet from a hard work which was excessively lengthy and carried out in difficult conditions.[42] Later in the letter Paul asserts "I worked harder than all" (15:10). It need not be an exclusive reference to the manual work of Paul but his missionary work in general. His working habit was also a reason for him to boast.

5.4.1.2. First Corinthians 9

This chapter in some way follows the thought line of chapter 4, which provides some insights into the nature of apostolic ministry at Corinth. In chapters 5–8 Paul first exhorts them through a letter concerning certain matters that have been reported to him and then answers their questions raised on various issues. After having addressed these Paul reverts to the question of apostleship in chapter 9. If Paul had explained the nature of his apostolic ministry in chapter 4, now he is defending some aspects of that nature as belonging to the rights of an apostle. One of the rights of an apostle is to get remuneration for the ministry performed. Yet, Paul renounced this right in view of the mission as a whole. By renouncing this right, Paul had to rely on manual work in order to maintain himself but this habit of Paul was criticized by the Corinthians. Some of the Corinthians considered it as menial (2 Cor 11:7) and a reason for humiliation.

Paul does not explicitly mention about his manual labor anywhere in chapter 9, but the main issue there was a disputation over Paul's manual work. The Christians there accused Paul and Barnabas for engaging in manual work (9:6), a thing considered shameful for the people there whose

---

[41] Thomas C. Edwards, *A Commentary on the First Epistle to the Corinthians* (London: Hodder and Stoughton, 1885), 112.

[42] Ideas for this paragraph are from Andrzej Gieniusz, "Paolo: Lavorare con le Proprie Mani e Compiere Fatiche Apostoliche," in *Il Lavoro Opera delle Nostre Mani*, PSV 52 (Bologna: Centro Editoriale Dehoniano, 2005), 185. Paul's workshop could have been in a small room of the ground floor which often was dirty, dangerous, and noisy. Paul might have worked even in the night as he sometimes indicates (1 Thess 2:9; 2 Cor 11:27).

attitude was conditioned by the predominant Hellenistic mentality. Being an apostle Paul had all the right, like the other apostles, to be supported by the church (9:4), to be accompanied by a wife (9:5) and to be free without doing any work (9:6). But quite differently Paul did work, did sacrifice the company of a wife and the remuneration from the church—all for the Gospel of Christ.

5.4.1.3. Second Corinthians 11:23, 27

Paul certainly refers to his manual work in these verses, though no explicit mention has been made about it. The Corinthian issues never got resolved or even subsided and therefore Paul had to write to them again. The issue of manual labor and Paul's self-sustenance again occupy a central place in the discussions here in chapter 11. Paul is highlighting the support he rendered to the Corinthian church and his habit of non-burdening of the community. He narrates his sufferings endured as an apostle and boasts about it. Paul also accuses those leaders[43] who boast according to human standards as false apostles (2 Cor 11:13, 18). Paul is different from other apostles precisely for the suffering endured for the Gospel which is not the case with the false apostles. Hence, he proves in this chapter that the mark of a true apostle is suffering. In the list of suffering[44] Paul mentions two times of his labor,[45] most probably indicating to his manual labor in Corinth and elsewhere. His suffering on account of manual work gets precedence over other items as κόπος (labor) is mentioned first in v. 23 and towards the end of the list at v. 27 along with another noun μόχθος (toil or hard labor) and thereby forming a thematic chiasm.[46] This may also indicate the importance and laboriousness of his manual work.

5.4.1.4. First Thessalonians 2:9

The reference to labor and toil (v. 9a) in this verse cannot be but a reference to the manual work of Paul and his companions. Paul calls the audience's attention to the custom of their (Paul and his companions) manual work. It also states the purpose of their work. This will be clearer in v. 9b in which their own habit of working night and day is in order not to burden the churches.

---

[43] The letters of Paul to Corinthians reveal that other than Paul and Apollos, there were other ministers of Christ who were not authentic, who were preaching differently than Paul and who were not working as Paul was, but were supported by the church there.

[44] A catalogue of suffering is listed at 2 Cor 11:23b–28.

[45] Reference to his labor and toil in vv. 23 and 27 uses the words κόπος twice and μόχθος once.

[46] Later, but chronologically prior to, in his instructions about manual work, Paul would use the same words at 1 Thess 2:9 and 2 Thess 3:8.

5.4.1.5. Acts 18:3

Obviously the most clear and direct evidence and attestation of Paul's manual work is found in Acts 18:3. While all the references to labor or toil in the above instances may give only a general indication to the manual work of Paul, Luke is specific about the nature of his work: "By trade they [Paul and Aquila] were tentmakers."[47] The most important point here is that the work they were associated with was manual.

Information gathered from Acts reveal that Luke's picture of Paul is more positive compared to Paul's own depiction of self in his letters. Paul was a Roman citizen, an elite figure in Acts but Paul presents himself as weak, foolish, and humble at many places in his letters (e.g. 1 Cor 4:11–13). Surprisingly the elite figure of Acts at the same time humbles to the level of a manual worker, a tent-maker. For Paul working at a trade had meant demeaning himself, taking on lowly status of a common laborer.[48] Paul's attitude towards manual work was positive that he even advocated it as a duty.[49]

How are we then to understand Paul's tent-making? Previously many scholars have attempted to explain it by suggesting that it was merely a following of a rabbinic custom of combining study and trade[50] or scrupulously maintaining this tradition.[51] Hock sees the reason for Paul's tent-making as something that he learned in a familial set up and continued later without diminishing the role of social and intellectual milieu.[52] Hock also suggests that Paul was making his workshop as a platform for evangelization.[53]

---

[47] This verse, as Keener and others observe, affronts a minor textual difficulty as of how to understand the word σκηνοποιός in 18:3. Is it tentmaker or maker of bed cushions (*lectarius* as in a Latin manuscript (h) or does it mean *sutor* (shoemaker) as Origen and Rufinus understood. The general understanding is that Paul's work involved something to do with leather; most probably he was a maker of tents with leather.

[48] See the discussion here in Ronald F. Hock, "Paul's Tent-making and the Problem of his Social Class," *JBL* 97 (1978), 562. Hock also suggests here that Paul's choice of language, namely (ταπεινόω) in 2 Cor 11:7 "to refer to his work reflects the snobbish and scornful attitude typical of upper-class Greeks and Romans."

[49] According to Hock, Paul's attitudes towards work are to be explained as "deriving from his Jewish upbringing and as differing sharply from attitudes in the Greco-Roman milieu." See Hock, *Social Context*, 11. But this thesis of Hock is one sided as he completely ignores the positive contributions made by the teachings of Greco-Roman moralists who advocated even humble work (albeit there was a tendency to disregard certain manual work).

[50] Bornkamm, *Paul*, 12.

[51] Bruce, *Paul*, 107–108.

[52] See Ronald F. Hock, "The Workshop as a Social Setting for Paul's Missionary Preaching," *CBQ* 41 (1979), 444–50.

[53] For Paul's missionary use of the workshop see Hock, *Social Context*, 7–42 and Hock, "The Workshop," 438–50.

Workshops were a *locus* for intellectual discourse, a convention that existed at the time of Paul.

We cannot exactly pin point any one of the above reasons as the specific reason for Paul's tent-making activity, but one thing is sure that some amount of Biblical-Greco-Roman-Jewish influence may have gone into the make-up of Pauline work ethics, particularly, the practice of a trade. The obvious reason for Paul's working at a trade was to support himself and others, and the first hand attestation of the fact by Paul himself at various places gives more weight to this argument. I would also view it as a conscious decision on the part of Paul to swim against the current, that is, to go against the negative mentality of the majority on manual work and to present himself as a model for others to take up manual work. Paul being a moralist himself, is instructing the audience to follow the ways of Jesus rather than pagan ways.

One may naturally ask, why tent-making and not something else? The simple answer may be that Paul learned the art of tent-making while still young and he could not have imagined putting his hand to work on another trade as his skill at another trade would be insufficient. Moreover being an itinerant preacher, Paul could not have then also established himself as a reputed skilled worker. Above all, it was the specific way for Paul to demonstrate himself as a model of humility and service.

5.4.2. Pauline Teaching Regarding Manual Work

In addition to the above New Testament attestation regarding manual work there are few instances of Pauline teaching concerning manual work about which a short analysis will follow below. We will examine both the authentic Pauline letters as well as the deutero-Pauline traditions. Naturally Acts 20:34 is the best example of Pauline teaching on manual work. Besides this few other instances found elsewhere are the following.

5.4.2.1. Ephesians 4:28

Paul engages in giving to the Ephesian Christians[54] various instructions among which is found an instruction to the thieves there who ought to work with their own hands not only for themselves but also to share its fruits with the needy. This verse is important for us for three reasons: (1) It speaks explicitly about manual work; (2) it is clear in stating the purpose of work: it is in order to have something to share with the needy; and (3) the verse reflects the schema and message of Acts 20:34. In Acts 20:34 Paul deliberates his habit of working with his own hands; using similar vocabulary Paul instructs the thieves in the Ephesian community to work

[54] Pauline authorship of the letter to the Ephesians is doubtful, but still there are few internal evidences that suggest the Pauline authorship. Traditionally it is held that this letter was written by Paul.

with their own hands. According to Acts 30:34 the purpose of Paul's work was for sustenance of self and other companions; similarly the purpose of work of the Ephesian thieves was to have something to share with the needy which would also include their self-maintenance.

5.4.2.2. First Thessalonians 4:11–12

In a general instruction to love (vv. 9–12), Paul gives a specific admonition to work with one's own hands (v. 11).[55] Paul's urging that the Thessalonians should work with their hands may suggest that the church was composed principally of manual workers.[56] The only use of χείρ in the letter (1 Thess 4:11) is reflective also of the use of χείρ in the Miletus speech (20:34). The phrase "we exhort you…to work with your own hands" is not an instruction to take up manual work[57] *per se*, that is, to take up work with physical hands, but to "work alone," "work personally." The finality of most work is to earn and therefore the instruction to work with your own hands is an instruction "to earn" by work, which naturally includes manual works. Thus, the meaning of Paul's teaching here is to earn a living for oneself[58] by engaging in any possible work.

Moreover, the purpose involved in manual work according to 1 Thess 4:11–12 is somewhat parallel to the purpose found in Acts 20:34–35. Steve Walton detects here three purposes involved in manual work: (1) to command the respect of outsiders and provide testimony to them (1 Thess 4:12a); (2) to secure financial independence by working (4:12b); and finally (3) to support the weaker members of the church (4:11) by means of one's work.[59]

Another important element for consideration often pointed out by scholars[60] is that the instruction to work was triggered by an eschatological concern. They have suggested that Paul was forced to give such instruction on work due to the unwillingness of many to work believing that the Lord would return soon. Hock downplays any eschatological concern in the instruction.

---

[55] Agrell, *Work, Toil, and Sustenance*, 96.

[56] Ernest Best, *A Commentary on the First and Second Epistles to the Thessalonians* (London: Adam & Charles Black, 1972), 176.

[57] This idea is already present in Gieniusz, "Proprie Mani," 177. The word used for manual work in the Greek sources is "άυτουργία" and the corresponding verb is "άυτουργεῶ."

[58] See Gieniusz, 178.

[59] Walton, *Leadership and Lifestyle*, 170. In 20:34 Paul himself provides the testimony to the church, whereas in 1 Thessalonians the members of the church there are the subjects of testimony.

[60] See for example names of a couple of German authors who argue in favor of an eschatological interpretation in Hock, *Social Context*, 43.

Since the instruction is placed along with concerns of holiness, and love,[61] Paul's precept on work may have been occasioned by a "stock concern,"[62] that in line with the moralists[63] and religious authors before him he may be addressing certain common concerns and is exhorting them as any teacher would. Eschatological concern most probably has less bearing on the idleness of people; the idleness might have been caused by the negative mentality of people towards manual work.[64] But for Paul and the Thessalonians it was to be an instruction that also values and even favors manual work. Paul or any moralists of the time would not settle with idleness and Paul would see that the most suitable and possible way an ordinary person could engage in life was by taking up manual labor, since the majority of people was farmers and craftsmen. In the church at Thessalonica there was widespread idleness which later becomes a topic for the Second Thessalonians.

5.4.2.3. Second Thessalonians 3:6–13

The instruction here longer than elsewhere in the NT material, suggests that idleness was a common phenomenon among the Thessalonians and that the command to work was a pressing need of the time for the Thessalonian church, and therefore the deutero-Pauline tradition repeats what Paul had already exhorted them. The Thessalonian Christian converts, most probably influenced by the Greco-Roman mentality towards work, were not willing to change by the previous instructions given, so it was needed that they be instructed again and the issue be taken up towards the end of the letter. In fact the author, transmitting the Pauline tradition,[65] was instructing them not to be slaves of pagan ideas of manual labor and trades. The point and content

---

[61] W. Bornemann discovers that the exhortation to holiness and love are spoken of as "God-willed, God-given, and God-taught" see Bornemann, *Die Thessalonicherbriefe*, KEK 10 (Göttingen: Vandenhoeck & Ruprecht, 1894), 158ff. Bornemann was the first to point out that the exhortation to work is not explicitly given a religious character, whereas the exhortation to holiness and love bears a God-imprint. As per this view, brotherly love cannot be said as the most natural motive for work. At the same time we must also view that even if brotherly love may not be the primary motive for work, work should also be performed keeping in mind our brothers especially the needy.

[62] Cf. Hock, *Social Context*, 46.

[63] Paul's instruction here should be regarded as reflecting his familiarity with the moral traditions of the Jewish and Greco-Roman philosophers.

[64] The members of the Greek society in general consisted of agricultural workers, craftsmen, textile workers, and slaves (who always undertook manual labor); a fair percentage of the citizens had to make their livelihood by working with their hands engaging in manual labor. There were some, who did not work, save only in the face of necessity.

[65] We hold that the Second Letter to Thessalonians originates from a deutero-Pauline tradition; nevertheless, its authorship is traditionally attributed to Paul.

of Paul's instruction in Acts 20:34 are reminiscent of Pauline Instructions in these passages.

5.4.3. "To Support Myself and My Companions": Primary Goal of Paul's Work

Paul as a travelling missionary stayed at Christian houses as a guest. This was usual at that time, but not more than three days (Acts 9:9; 28:7, 12) but under certain circumstances he would stay for seven days (Acts 20:6; 21:4). As an apostle of Christ, he could have imposed himself on a host for extended periods of time (1 Thess 2:7; 1 Cor 9:5–15). But Paul did not use this privilege so that the churches might not be burdened. Therefore, to support himself he had recourse to other means and Paul found tent-making as a means for that. Combining missionary preaching and manual work[66] meant "rising before dawn, toiling until sunset with leather, knives, and awls, and accepting the various social stigmas and humiliations that were part of the artisans' lot, not to mention poverty–being cold, hungry, and poorly clothed."[67] The expressions in 18:3 and 1 Thess 2:9 would mean that Paul worked hard for the Gospel night and day (1 Cor 4:12; 2 Cor 11:27). As per this account Paul preached every day there, but then he would have found time to work early in the morning or after his discourse in the σκολή (lecture hall).

For self-sufficiency Paul found tent-making as a means. It was Paul's policy to support himself (and others) by the work of his hands (1 Cor 4:12; 1 Thess 2:9). Luke does not refrain from reporting the ordinary work he did while living in a particular place. Why would Luke want to be accurate on this act of Paul? First of all it points to the genuineness of Luke in reporting certain facts since tent-making of Paul was a well-known fact among the churches of which Luke was a firsthand witness and of which Paul hints many times as we have examined above. Secondly for Luke and the second generation Christians Paul is a model, a model for manual work and charity.

An impressive study on the cultural and social world of Paul was made by Adolf Deissmann in his book *St. Paul: A Study in Social and Religious History*. His observation about Paul, according to me, is very appealing and accurate. Deissmann writes: "He [Paul] was much rather a plain and simple man whose trade was the economic foundation of his existence."[68]

---

[66] The work would involve both missionary preaching and manual labor (Acts 19:9).

[67] Hock, *Social Context*, 37. Artisans and unskilled workers of the city had to live in substandard conditions. The Cynics had to live in a public building and often had to resort to begging. See Hock, *The Social Context*, 30. Manual works were considered slavish. Instances of afflictions due to poverty can be found in the following examples: hunger and thirst (1 Cor 4:11; 2 Cor 6:5; 11:27), cold (2 Cor 11:27), and nakedness (1 Cor 4:11; 2 Cor 11:27).

[68] Deissmann, *St. Paul*, 51.

Deissmann places Paul "among the simple people of his own social class."[69] Simplicity, hard work, charity, humility, zeal, and suffering for the Gospel are the characteristics of the person of Paul. Although he appears to be learned, he is at the same time down to earth and practical. Paul's own tent-making and supporting himself and his companions thus have a deliberative function both in the proto and deutero-Pauline traditions.

Two texts, besides our verse, that report the purpose of work are relevant for our discussion here. They are Eph 4:28 and 2 Thess 3:6–13. Already in the 1 Thess 4:11–12 Paul had given them instruction to work quietly with their own hands. The same instruction is given to the Thessalonians again but slightly modified as is the case with 2 Thess 3:12. Here one of the purposes of work is explicitly mentioned: "to earn a living," whereas in 1 Thessalonians this fact is not overtly mentioned, though implied. Moving to the Ephesian text, the purpose of work is to share something with the needy but the text does not specify the purpose of work as self-maintenance, rather it is to be assumed that self-sustenance was the primary goal of work here. In any case, this text has more affinity with the Lucan account but the addressees are different: the instruction is given to the thieves in Ephesians, whereas it was given to the elders in the Miletus speech.[70] Luke is clearer on the matter here as the text itself gives no ambiguity with regard to the purpose of work: it is to support oneself and companions and to support the weak.

To conclude, Acts views (manual) work as positive, so do the writings of Paul. The positive view of work in Acts has been compared with the Pauline instances to see how they function in the overall work ethics of Lukan Paul. It was the conviction of Paul that manual work to a great extent complements his ministry, in the same way it should be in the lives of every member in the church who has the physical fitness to work. As already noted above, in the Greco-Roman world, to a great extent, manual labor was socially disesteemed. Paul's own example and teaching contributed greatly to the elevation of labor and laborers to a dignified state. Christianity thus from the beginning provided social recognition to the common working people and to the products of their labor.[71] The foregoing study of this chapter spells out the importance of labor and dignity of labor and laborers from the point of view of Biblical authors and especially of Luke and Paul.

---

[69] Deissmann, 6.

[70] Similar instruction given to thieves and elders in different context but to the same church is the primary reason to argue that the duty of every member of the church is to support the weak and needy; this duty is not exclusively given to the elders or leaders of the church.

[71] Raiser, "Theological and Ethical Considerations," 282.

Work must be performed not only for self-sustenance but also for the sustenance of others especially the needy. One must work for the common good, and collaboration for the common good is called "labor."[72] Paul's directive on this subject in the next verse opens up another ethical concern, the question of charity, which will be studied in a later chapter. But immediately after the reference to Paul's habit of manual work and its purpose, he presents himself as a model, and this will be the subject of our next chapter.

[72] G. B. Guzzetti, "Il Lavoro nei suoi Aspetti Morali," in *Il Lavoro: Encyclopedia*, Luigi Civardi e Pietro Pavan, ed. (Roma: Coletti Editore, 1963), 221.

Chapter 6

Acts 20:35 A: Paul as an Ethical Model

Acts 20:35 begins thus: "In all this I have given you an example." This affirmation of Paul naturally requires a scrutiny of the ethical significance of the use of 'example' in a speech or a narrative whose ultimate purpose is oriented towards 'imitation' of a model. To be a model for others involves imitation of the subject as a model. In the realm of ethics imitation of a person should be carried out only if that person is worthy of being imitated. In the proto-Pauline and deutero-Pauline traditions, Paul functions as a model for the churches, especially for the post apostolic churches. Paul in his letters establishes himself as a model for others. Imitation works as an ethical concept throughout these traditions.

Paul's words "in all this I have given you an example" at the conclusion of the speech can logically refer to every element related to Paul's apostolic life revealed through the speech, such as constant preaching, toil, suffering and tears for the Gospel, witnessing, perseverance, and giving warning. But here, in v. 35, it most probably refers only to the example of his manual work to support himself and others. The word πᾶς means all, every, or everything. The accusative form of πᾶς is πάντα which in our context means "in all this." Thus πάντα here is retrospective of Paul's manual work and support his companions (v. 34). It echoes the instruction of Paul concerning supporting the weak found in the same verse. When Paul speaks of being a model "in all this," there are basically two theses involved, namely, that he is a model of manual work, and that he is a model of charity especially by way of his conduct in supporting the weak.

In this chapter we shall examine the paradigmatic function of the figure of Paul in Acts revealed to us in the first part of this verse. In the previous chapter we have already learned that Paul's assessment of manual work itself is paradigmatic and thereby suggestive of an ethic of manual work. Here, therefore, we shall limit our study or focus more on the image of Paul as a paradigm of charity in supporting the weak.

6.1. "In All this I Have Given You an Example" (v. 35a): Preliminary Notes

Paul begins and ends his farewell speech by pointing to himself as a model for the church leaders at Ephesus. As pointed out earlier, Paul functions as a model not only for the leaders and believers of his own generation, but also for the leaders and believers of all ages. Lucan Paul here points to his examples, namely, of his manual work and support of the weak. The concluding verses of the speech (vv. 33–35) vocalize a self-defense of Paul against all criticisms lashed at him not only by his opponents or criticizers at Ephesus but also by such people in other churches. We learn from the letters of Paul that his defenses were related to areas of theology / doctrine, church structure / conduct, and various accusations brought against him regarding his ministry. The Miletus speech, in the thought line of Pauline letters, reveals that Paul is not willing to give room for any misunderstanding concerning the nature of his ministry and therefore defends his ministry in all its dimensions. For Paul Christian authority is for service and never for personal gain. He exemplified the true meaning of authority through his manual work and charity. He was a paradigm[1] then and is one now also. But why should Paul speak of himself being an example to be imitated? Certain ancient speech conventions seem to be at play here. We shall only make a quick attempt to indicate few textual evidences from the Greco-Roman world.

6.2. The Use of Examples and its Importance in the Greco-Roman World

Use of examples is an essential component of any speech, be it ancient or modern. The ancients have left many evidences of the use of examples in their writings. Examples were amply used as an integral component of argumentation in speeches. Most speeches, as we have already noted in the first chapter, were born in the court and assembly. Thus, the use of examples was important in forensic, epideictic, and deliberative speeches.

Aristotle proposed that in arguing a point one ought to resort to frequent use of example (παράδειγμα) to make the argument more convincing and compelling upon his hearers.[2] In a part of speech, proof is a major part

[1] Paul is the "model of labor" for the second generation Christians. He is the apostle of manual labor, who by his own example exalted labor, dignified every labor, proclaimed the duty of labor. See also Schumacher, *Social Message*, 177–80.

[2] Arist. *Rh.* 1394a; 1356b.

which consists of proposition, reason, proof of the reason, embellishment, and resume.[3] Embellishment is achieved through comparisons, examples, amplifications, previous judgments, and other means which serve to expand and enrich the argument.[4] Benjamine Fiore[5] notes that according to *Rhetorica ad Alexandrum* Anaximenes first explains negative examples, that is, ways of acting counter to the one proposed and errors committed by people in the past, both of which are to be avoided now.[6] Second, he supplements historical examples with recent examples.[7]

In addition to the use in the court and the assembly, the Greco-Roman rhetoricians identified the power of examples in the area of ethical exhortation. The objective of example is for imitation. Personal exemplification of the speaker functions at the level of ethos and is a motive for imitation.[8]

6.2.1. The Power of Examples in Ethical Exhortation

One of the characteristics of ancient exhortation was the provision of models for imitation.[9] *Encomia* were written precisely for this purpose. Ethical models were amply provided in almost all type of ancients' writings, inviting the audience / reader to imitation. Sometimes even the authors portrayed themselves as models as did Paul in his writings. For the Greco-Romans philosophers, personal virtue weighed more than their teaching. An example of a hero could motivate others to imitate him.[10] An incident narrated in Appollonius Rhodius will help us to better grasp this idea. As a group of people was travelling to Hellas they wanted to choose the most courageous man Heracles as their leader, but he did not consent to it because Jason had been their leader before. So Jason continued to lead the group and he was the first one to turn to work which motivated the followers.[11] One's conduct adds persuasiveness to one's speech. Aristotle says: "But an orator ought to be careful not only about his words but also about his personal behavior; regulating it according to the principles already laid down; for the manner of a

---

[3] Cic. *Rh. ad Her*. 2.29.46.

[4] Cic. *Rh. ad Her*. 2.29.46.

[5] See Benjamin Fiore, "Paul, Exemplification, and Imitation," in *Paul in the Greco-Roman World: A Handbook*, J. Paul Sampley, ed. (Harrisburg, PA: Trinity Press International, 2003), 228–29.

[6] *Rh. Alex*. 1429a.29–31; 1431a.26–27.

[7] *Rh. Alex*. 1430a7–9.

[8] See the importance of examples in Cic. *De Inv.* 1.30.49; Quint. *Inst.* 1.11.1–2. Also, in Plut. *Mor*. 7.539–547 an example is presented as an encouragement for success.

[9] Andrew T. Lincoln, *Ephesians*, WBC 42 (Dallas: Word Books, 1990), 310.

[10] See this in Pliny, *Ep*. 8.13; Sen. *Ep*. 6.5–6; Sen. *Ep*. 11.9–10; Ps. Isoc. *Demo*. 11.36.

[11] Ap. Rhod. 1.363–64.

man's life contributes to the persuasive influence which he exercise and to the establishment of a good reputation."[12]

Margaret Mitchell points out that deliberative proof by example functions with an implied or even explicit appeal to imitate the illustrious example (or avoid negative example). This appeal to imitate is in proof by example.[13] Deliberative texts and letters, characterized by deliberative proof by example, often combined with a call to imitation are found in deliberative texts. Such authors mostly in deliberative letters even add themselves as examples in addition to ancestors, deities, or historical persons. Such argumentations entreat the audience to imitate the behavior of the esteemed example (or not imitate a negative example). In fact, this is a distinctive element in deliberative rhetoric.[14] An example is like an analogy and applies to a particular without expressing a universal. This characteristic of enabling the audience to draw direct analogies from the exemplary situations to their own situations was well-suited for hortatory speeches and letters and consequently appeal to example became a distinctive feature of deliberative oratory and letters.[15]

6.3. Goal of the Use of Examples in the Scriptures

In general, all the characters in the LXX and in the NT are either positive or negative models, and a serious study on the subject will be a mammoth task, which is not really required in this study. Therefore only a few general remarks will be made here.

6.3.1. In the LXX

The most significant text in the LXX which conveys the imitation concept is Leviticus 19:2. Just as the Lord God is holy every Israelite ought to be holy. This holiness motif, as a means for ritual perfection has been introduced right from the beginning of the book, but the moral force of imitation of God only gets accrued from 11:44 and 45 running through the rest of the book and moreover, at intervals affirming the covenant obligation to be holy (Lev 19:2; 20:7, 26). The injunction to "be holy" is the direct call of God to imitate Him or to be like Him in the realm of His holiness. It involves imitating the qualities proper to God.

---

[12] *Rh. Alex.* 1445b.30–33. *Rhetorica ad Alexandrum* is attributed to Aristotle, but the general opinion of scholars today is that it was written by Anaximenes of Lampsacus.

[13] Margaret M. Mitchell, *Paul and the Rhetoric of Reconciliation: An Exegetical Investigation of the Language and Composition of 1 Corinthians* HUTh 28 (Tübingen: Mohr Siebeck, 1991), 42.

[14] See Mitchell, *Rhetoric of Reconciliation*, 45–46.

[15] Fiore, "Exemplification," 230.

Many characters in the LXX get a positive description of their conduct and relationship with God and / or fellow persons and they function as ethical figures or concrete models. Abraham, Joseph, Moses, Joshua, Caleb, Ruth, Samuel, David, Hezekiah, Josiah, Tobit, and similar figures are concrete positive examples. While this being the case, it is also true that the negative characters in it are examples of bad conduct who the Bible does not advocate as ethical models (e.g. Cain, the Sodomites, Achan, Gehazi, Jezebel etc.). Such characters do not function as models worthy of imitation. The Wisdom Books in particular draw examples from men, animals, and nature to provide concrete examples for imitation.

In connection with our topic, we have already examined the parallelism between Samuel's farewell speech and the Miletus speech. Samuel is defending his past temperate behavior of right intention. Samuel does not say that he has "shown an example" for the audience to imitate, nonetheless, in the speech he claims to hold genuine behavior which in turn aimed at emulating moral behavior from the listeners. In other words, the listeners are to imitate the behavior of the speaker. Similarly no explicit reference is made of Tobit as a model but the narrator's description about the character of the hero (Tob 1:3–20 [This is in first person]; 2:2–6; 4:3–11 and part of the protagonist's farewell speech (14:8–11) in particular attests the exemplary behavior of the speaker. Both Samuel and Tobit, as in the case of Paul, function as ethical models.

6.3.2. In the New Testament

Every imperative "follow me" from the mouth of Jesus is a summons to be a true follower of Jesus by imitating Him. Coming to the teachings of Jesus many of the parables contain ethical and moral exhortations and the characters in them that provide positive or negative images, the audience is asked to imitate or disown. For example, the audience is summoned to imitate the behavior of the Good Samaritan when Jesus says: "Go and do likewise" (Lk 10:37). In the parable of the Ten Minas (Lk 19:12–27), the master praises the good slaves for multiplying the mina which itself is an invitation to imitate the character of the good slaves. Reversely, the wicked slave is a negative example here and his terrible fate (vv. 24–27) further issues a warning to the audience. Leaders, such as the Pharisees and Scribes, are supposed to be models of imitation, but regrettably Jesus tells the people not to imitate them since what they do is contrary to what they teach (Mt 23:3).

In the farewell speech of Jesus (Jn 13–17), an episode of foot-washing is narrated at the beginning of the speech (Jn 13:1–15) and our Lord himself demands from the apostles that they imitate His example of foot-washing and everything that it entails; but here the idea of imitation has been communicated using a different language, "So if I. . .you also ought to wash one another's feet. For I have set you an example that you also should do as I have done to you" (Jn 13:14–15). The word used here for 'example' is ὑπόδειγμα which is synonymous to τύπος. The former word appears also in few other passages of the NT. In Hebrews 4:11 the author uses it for a negative example of disobedience. The Epistle of James holds the Prophets as ὑπόδειγμα of suffering and patience (Jam 5:10). For Peter, the destruction of Sodom and Gomorrah is an ὑπόδειγμα of warning to the ungodly (2 Pet 2:6). A remarkable passage that stalks many good examples of faith is Hebrews chapter 11.[16] But in all these no explicit mention is made about them as τύπος.

6.4. Paul and the Ethics of Imitation

Speaker's example was a source of authority for Christian exhortation, the other being recollection of Jesus' saying.[17] The example of the speaker worked as an ethical concept within Christian paraenesis which was in use within Greco-Roman and Jewish exhortations as we have already noted. Our study of the Greco-Roman and Jewish farewell speeches at the outset of this research has shown that the parting characters are models who operate within a certain ethical gamut and thus they function as paradigms. This they achieve mainly through their example and exhortations.

6.4.1. Ancients' Concept of Imitation

The ancients have stressed the importance of the use of examples in their writings as a means to urge imitation. Examples may be used for ethical purposes. They are important component in a persuasive speech or writing. Isocrates, a 5-4th century Attic orator is an important figure who has written conspicuously about the use of example for imitation. His contribution on the subject is mainly found in two of his works, *Evagoras* (see especially *Evag*. 74–77) and *Nicocles* (see especially *Nico*. 31–38). Isocrates' views on the use of example to urge imitation are salient. The important ones are: (1) where example serves explicitly hortatory ends, for the example itself provides for imitation (Isoc. *Evag*. 75). It is another way of saying, "an example is better than precept." "While no one can make the bodily nature resemble molded statues and portraits in painting, yet for those who do not choose to be slothful, but desire to be good men, it is easy to imitate the character of their fellow-men and their thoughts and purposes—those, I mean, that are embodied in the

[16] Michaelis also notes that in 3 Jn 11, Gaius should follow Demetrius who is praised in v. 12 and not Diotrephes who is denounced. It is a specific call to imitate the example of a good person. See "Μιμέομαι, μιμητής, συμμιμητής," *TDNT* 4:666.

[17] Kurz, *Farewell Address in the New Testament*, 49. In v. 35 Lucan Paul recollects one of Jesus sayings to emphatically present the theme of giving and caring. In the following chapter we will elaborate this.

spoken word" (Isoc. *Evag.* 75). (2) Exemplars who are close to the family are preferable (Isoc. *Evag.* 77); (3) that which shows exemplar's spirit is valuable and enlightened by people (Isoc. *Evag.* 74); and (4) the addressee (Nicocles) can himself expect to become a model of virtue as a result of striving (Isoc. *Evag.* 78).

In his work *Nicocles* one finds that the aim of Nicocles' virtuous conduct is to prevent criticism and to set an example (Isoc. *Nico.* 37–38). "If there are men whose reputations you envy, imitate their deeds. Whatever advice you would give to your children, consent to follow it yourself" (Isoc. *Nico.* 38). *Nicocles* 31–32 speaks about the importance of good name over wealth. Nicocles is to exercise self-control which will be an example for the rest.

In reality many of the Biblical stories and examples are aimed at urging imitation of the model figures which include, other than persons, even animals sometimes. So the concept of imitation was not alien to the Jewish world.[18] Two words that carry the sense of imitation are the Greek verb μιμέομαι (which means "to imitate") and the noun μιμητής (which means "an imitator").[19] Sometimes another noun τύπος (type, image, model) appears which in some cases implies an imitation from the reader since the model is worthy of imitation. But nowhere in the MT are Hebrew words that carry the meaning of Greek τύπος, used as a referent to any ethical model. The words μιμέομαι and τύπος hardly appear in the LXX.[20] Paul almost exclusively uses these words in his letters to endow a moral sense to imitation. Although Lucan Paul does not use these words in the Miletus speech, imitation of the speaker or the Lord is a goal of v. 35 and this he achieves through other vocabularies. In order to better understand the motif of imitation – imitation of Paul and the Lord – it is necessary that we consume few pages for a study of the concept of Imitation in Paul, including the deutero-Pauline instances.

6.4.2. The Concept of Imitation According to Paul

A short study on this motif will be useful here since Luke has placed the Miletus speech in the mouth of historical Paul and the content of the speech is very similar to that in Pauline letters.

---

[18] See details in Willis P. De Boer, *The Imitation of Paul: An Exegetical Study* (Kampen: J. H. Kok, 1962), 8–13.

[19] Paul uses different forms of μιμέομαι and always the plural form of μιμητής many times; the verb has the meaning "to imitate," "to mimic" and the noun has the sense "an imitator." Obviously an imitator enacts what is seen to be done by someone else as in Michaelis, "Μιμέομαι," 659.

[20] But appears in Wis 4:2; 15:9; 4 Macc 9:23; 13:9. The language "following YHWH" (Num 14:24; 32:11; Josh 14:8, 9, 14; 1 Sam 12:14; 1 Kgs 11:6; 14:8) may be seen as equivalent to "imitating Him." See Lincoln, *Ephesians,* 310–11.

6.4.2.1. Paul as a τύπος

In Paul's letters the term τύπος appears three times in connection with the idea of imitation (Phil 3:17; 1 Thess 1:6-7; 2 Thess 3:9). Τύπος as personal example in Hellenistic and Jewish literature carries strong moralistic accent.[21] In Phil 3:17 instead of the regular words such as 'imitator' or the verb 'imitate,' another word τύπος (example, type, or model) is used. Paul is the first τύπος for the Philippians. Τύπος is synonymous to μιμέομαι. When we talk about Paul as a paradigm, it is more about Paul's "showing" than Paul's "telling." Any manifestation of distinction between showing and telling is not our concern here, but rather his self-portrayal in the Miletus speech.

More than mere copying or imitation, Paul is a paradigm or *vorbild* (ethical example). In the mind of Paul, imitation entails that the object of imitation should be an authentic model: in most cases Paul is mediating the example of Christ, and so he claims to be an object of imitation. Whenever Paul says "be imitators of me" it is a call to imitate him of his behavior and way of thinking. In the ancient classical world teachers and philosophers were to provide good examples to the public and the society looked up to them as ethical figures for imitation.[22] Moreover, close association with and imitation of the teacher was encouraged at this period.[23] Paul functions as a *vorbild* especially in the sufferings of Christ his master. In Acts 20:34 Paul is a model not only of work, but also of the sufferings undergone on account of that work. Immediately after this Luke presents Paul as a *vorbild* of charity. For Luke Paul, more than anyone, is the model for the church(es).

This being said, we may conclude that every positive example, be it in the Greco-Roman, LXX or NT, is set before the reader as an example to imitate. Imitation of the model is the goal of setting that person as a paradigm. Among the NT authors Paul speaks often of the importance of imitating Jesus, himself, or a church. We shall engage into a study of Pauline instances of imitation since imitation works as an ethical concept both in the Pauline letters and the Miletus speech.

6.4.2.2. μιμέομαι and μιμητής in Paul and Pauline Traditions

Paul uses the verb μιμέομαι or the noun μιμητής to actualize the notion of imitation. Μιμέομαι has the sense "to imitate" "to mimic" to do what is seen

[21] See De Boer, *The Imitation of Paul,* 23.

[22] The philosopher's word alone, unaccompanied by the act, was regarded as invalid (Sen. *Ep.* 52.8–9; Dio Chry. *De Phil.* 70.6). The Cynic Demetrius of Sunium worked as a porter in order to care for his friend in prison and thereby showed his friendship (Luc. *Tox.* 31). This act was a concrete example of what he taught. Quintilian indicates that the character of the teacher is important, his purity, self-control, father figure, virtue. See Quint. *Inst.* 2.1–8.

[23] De Boer, *The Imitation of Paul*, 26.

to be done by someone else.[24] De Boer notes that the notion itself, however antedates the origin of human civilization. In fact, by imitating animals, men learned to build, to weave and the like. Men imitate other men, their practice, political, and cultural values, and they imitate even others' faith, values, and examples. Thus the word also found its way into the realm of ethics. Paul's was relying on the well-established Greek usage of "imitation."[25] Prior to the Pauline usage these words were still in use among the ancients.[26] The words, especially the verb, is adopted into ethical sphere and used there seriously.[27] Without any further discussion on the topic we now move directly into the Pauline and deutero-Pauline descriptions of imitation, especially those that derive from the use of the above words of imitation.

The verb μιμέομαι is not used by historical Paul rather he prefers the noun μιμητής to bid imitation. The verb is found in 2 Thessalonians and in the letter of John (3 Jn 1:11).[28] The word μιμητής is always used in plural and it is mainly used by the historical Paul. In the letters of Paul (including the deutero-Pauline letters) the words μιμητής, μιμέομαι, and its related forms appear 8 times. Five times it refers to the imitation of Paul himself or with co-missionaries (1 Cor 4:16; 11:1; Phil 3:17 [using the compound word συμμιμητής and the noun τύπος]; 2 Thess 3:7, 9); once to the imitation of churches / believers (1 Thess 2:14); once to the imitation of God (Eph 5:1); and once it points to the imitation of "us and the Lord" (1 Thess 1:6).[29] There are other passages that invoke imitation such as Gal 4:12; Phil 4:9 and Acts 20:35[30] which are thematically parallel to μιμέομαι but no verbal relation is seen. Thus, there are 7 instances of imitation texts in the authentic Pauline

---

[24] See Discourses of *mimesis* in antiquity in Castelli, *Imitating Paul*, 59–87.

[25] Democritus' famous saying is worth repeating here. "It is necessary either to be good or to imitate goodness" (Demo. Frg. 39). For more on this topic of imitation, see Benjamin Fiore, *The Function of Personal Example in the Socratic and Pastoral Epistles* (Rome: Biblical Institute Press, 1986), 184–90. For the moral significance of imitation, see De Boer, *The Imitation of Paul*, 7.

[26] De Boer asserts that the word μιμέομαι is as old as 6th century BC and has been in use throughout then on. See *The Imitation of Paul*, 1–16.

[27] Michaelis, "Μιμέομαι," 660.

[28] We are referring also to other occurrences of these terms in the NT to provide a general picture of the use of these terms in the NT.

[29] The passages in the undisputed Pauline letters, in which Paul explicitly calls on his audience to be like him, are the following (1 Cor 4:16; 11:1; Phil 3:17; 1 Thess 1:6). In the deutero-Pauline letters, the word μιμητής appears once in Eph 5:1 (cf. Heb 6:12), while 2 Thess 3:7–9 invokes the imitation using the verbal form μιμέομαι and the noun τύπος.

[30] Acts 20:35, though part of Lucan composition, can be grouped within "deutero-Pauline tradition" since the speech seems to be genuinely Pauline.

letters, whereas the deutero-Pauline tradition attests 4 samples of imitation texts bringing the total number of imitation texts to 11.

W. Michaelis identified three different uses of imitation terms in Pauline letters.[31] But if we take the deutero-Pauline letters and the Miletus speech in Acts also into account, the imitation texts may be grouped into four.[32] This is done without limiting the terminological affinity but broadening the horizon thematically to all the 11 imitation texts given above. Thus, the first group contains all the texts that render only a simple comparison and no conscious imitation is enjoined. These texts are 1 Thess 1:6 and 2:14 (cf. Heb 6:12).[33] The second group consists of texts that require following of an example (2 Thess 3:7, 9; Phil 3:17). The third category views obedience as predominant[34] (1 Cor 4:16; 11:1; Gal 4:12; Eph 5:1 and Phil 4:9) and the final one from a tradition on Paul consists of an Acts' text that views both imitation and obedience placed on equal footing (Acts 20:35).

6.4.2.2.1. "For You Became Imitators of the Churches of God": 1 Thessalonians 2:14

First Thessalonians 2:14 along with 1:6 (cf. Heb 6:12[35]) represent the first category that provides and constitutes only a simple comparison. There is no

---

[31] 1. Simple comparison, no conscious imitation (1 Thess 1:6; 2:14). 2. Following of an example (2 Thess 3:7, 9; Phil 3:17). 3. Obedience is predominant (1 Cor 4:16; 11:1; Eph 5:1; 1 Thess 1:6).

[32] It is difficult to categorize certain texts into one group or the other since extant imitation ideas in these texts are overlapping.

[33] The μιμητής idea appears also in Heb 6:12, where a simple comparison has been made. A comparison of Heb 6:12 with other similar imitation texts in the Pauline and deutero-Pauline specimens reveals that it enjoins a simple imitation.

[34] De Boer demonstrates that imitation and example refer to personal example than to obedience against the argument of Michaelis, for whom imitation implies primarily obedience to authority. Brian Dodd notes how Pedro Gutierrez understands imitation in Paul. It is in the context of the teacher-pupil relationship implied by spiritual parenthood. See Dodd, *Paul's Paradigmatic "I": Personal Example as Literary Strategy* (Sheffield: Academic Press, 1999), 22–23. See also a contrary opinion of Isocrates, "we ought not [behave] like children who learn from their parents" (Isoc. Frg. 74). While obedience is important 'the accent is put principally upon the paternal instruction which teaches the true way, to which the son must pay attention and obey.' What Dodd emphasizes in this regard seems the best. "Indeed, the model and the precept work hand in hand in Paul's moral instructions." See Dodd, *Paul's Paradigmatic "I,"* pp. 23, 26.

[35] In Heb 6:12 a simple comparison is made, but the author desires that the audience become imitators of those who inherited the promise through faith and patience. Obviously, the author has in mind those Jewish models of faith particularly Abraham since Abraham's faith and patience is immediately remembered (vv. 13–15).

demand in these texts to imitate or no obedience enjoined.[36] In 1 Thessalonians imitation involves a comparison of Thessalonians' experience of suffering for the Gospel with that of Paul, his companions (cf. also 2:2; 3:3–5), and the Judean churches (2:14). They have also become imitators of the Lord as is clear from the text. "The Lord's example precedes Paul's historically," but the Thessalonians are now imitating Paul their visible leader and guide whose example is the same as the Lord's.

In the category not only do Paul and the Lord become models of imitation but also other ministers with him and Judean churches. In this verse Paul expands the example and increases its force by including in it the other senders of the letter (Silvanus and Timothy 1:2; "us" in 2:15–16). This "establishes a bond between Paul and the audience by way of an appeal to emulate those who have the desired characteristics."[37] Paul is not singling out himself as a model, but he uses the first person plural "us" to indicate that he along with his co-ministers are models. The co-ministers have accepted Paul's version of the Gospel and they too have become examples by proving in their own lives its force by their faithfulness and determination.[38]

The Thessalonians became imitators also of the churches in Judea; the Judean churches suffered much from the Jews, while the Thessalonians suffered from their own compatriots (1 Thess 2:14). The reader is also given a glimpse of the manner of their suffering as is described in the following verses (15–16). In both cases Paul is using indicative mood and, according to Elizabeth Castelli, the import of Paul's use of the indicative in 1:6 and 2:14 is twofold. First, it is to describe a particular reality to characterize the behavior of the Thessalonian community. It is not an exhortation, but a clear statement of what is actually the case. Second, the syntactical distinction operates at the level of rhetoric, to place the Thessalonian community in a special position vis-à-vis other communities, and to heighten the praise which Paul is offering to the community.[39] They have performed their "mimetic role" and thus have become models for others.

Although Thess 1:6 comes across as a simple comparison, the next verse asserts the role of the Thessalonians as a model pointing to some kind of imitation in obedience. This may be the reason for Michaelis to classify it in the third category discussed above. Whatever be the case, the agent for

---

[36] Castelli has rightly noted that the usage μιμητής in both passages in 1 Thessalonians differs from the other passages like Phil 3:17; 1 Cor 4:16; and 11:1 because the Thessalonians texts describe a historical "fact" about *mimesis*, rather than exhorting the community to perform a mimetic act, see *Imitating Paul*, 92.

[37] Fiore, "Exemplification," 240.

[38] Ideas for this paragraph are from Fiore, "Exemplification," 239–40.

[39] Castelli, *Imitating Paul*, 92.

them to be an example is the Holy Spirit who bestows all graces. The grace they received empowers them not just to spread the Word as Paul does, but also to build up their own community in responsibility and loving care for each other.[40] Paul further calls for "ethical conformity" to his own pattern of behavior: he embodies what he expects of the Thessalonian community.

6.4.2.2.2. "Join in Imitating Me": Philippians 3:17

The texts of this category (Phil 3:17; 2 Thess 3:7, 9) represent imitation or the following of a model, which primarily centers on Paul and the co-ministers with him.

In Philippians, imitation is not simply copying a model but an expression of obedience, an example already given by Paul himself.[41] Paul uses "I / me" more than fifty times in the Letter to the Philippians and begins to propose himself as the paradigm of imitation (*mimesis*) as early as 1:12–26. He and the Philippians, by their baptism, are to conform their words and deeds to the life in Christ. They have to shape their lives to reflect their new identity. Paul can be an example because he is "in Christ" (1:1, 8, 13, 20–21; 3:7–10, 12).[42]

In the letter Paul provides examples of Timothy (Phil 2:19–24) and Epaphroditus (Phil 2:25–30) who were selfless in their conduct. But the greatest example of self-sacrifice is that of Christ himself and Paul wants the Philippians to imitate Christ. Paul himself is a model for the community because he is in Christ. Using συμμιμητής in Phil 3:17, Paul wants to communicate that those who do not join in imitating Paul are enemies of the cross of Christ.[43] The enemies of Paul are Christ's enemies also because they do not demonstrate a mature spirituality for their "minds are set more on earthly things" (Phil 3:19) than Christ. Paul is for such people an exclusive model since he has suffered loss and regarded all gain loss for the sake of Christ (Phil 3:7–8). Using different terminologies the call to imitate Paul appears a second time in 4:9. Philippians have already seen or known of his practice, teaching, trials, and imprisonment for the sake of the Gospel. So they know what and how to imitate.

Paul's suffering, teaching, and practice have been well reported in the deutero-Pauline tradition; a good example for this is second Thessalonians. Paul works for his own support (2 Thess 3:7, 9) and uses the language of recollection to direct the Thessalonians' attention to the various aspects of his example with which they are already familiar, a common hortatory

---

[40] Fiore, "Exemplification," 239.

[41] Michaelis, "Μιμέομαι," 668.

[42] Ideas for this paragraph are from Fiore, "Exemplification," 241.

[43] Castelli, *Imitating Paul*, 95–96.

technique.[44] Fiore also rightly states that his self-portrayal is both paradigmatic for those who conform to his model, and polemical against those who deviate from it.[45] In v. 7 the use of δεῖ is intentional and conveys an "oughtness" in their behavior. One notices the use of δεῖ in 2 Thess 3:7, which function as a kind of divine imperative.[46] Verse 9 aims to maximize the paradigmatic function of Paul and companions by holding them up as models whom the congregation should imitate.

6.4.2.2.3. "I Urge You, then, Be Imitators of Me": 1 Cor 4:16

The final category of imitation text draws in obedience as predominant. "First Corinthians offers the richest context for producing a reading of the discourse of *mimesis* in Paul's letters."[47] Corinthian passages (4:16 and 11:1) come before and after major topics of boasting, factionalism, disunity, false wisdom and knowledge, and self-interest.[48] To tackle these negativities in spiritual life, Paul counters them with lessons that highlight the imitation of Christ mainly that of His humility and self-abasement. Paradoxically, spiritual maturity is gauged with the device of humility.

All of first Corinthians is actually Paul's paraenesis concerning various matters and issues. In addition to its paraenetic purpose, it also has a deliberative purpose, and both are served by Paul's example.[49] Verse 4:16 may be seen as a conclusion to the discussion of the dispute which rose in the Corinthian church due to a false idea of Christian wisdom (1 Cor 1:18–3:4) and apostleship (1 Cor 3:5–4:17). The Corinthians must abandon all such false ideas and imitate Paul whose wisdom is coherent and compatible with that of Christ and whose apostleship is verified by the very nature of his apostolic ministry. They are to see a model in Paul who fathered them (1 Cor 4:15). Paul asks them to imitate him because he is imitating Christ.

The second instance (1 Cor 11:1) is a response to the false knowledge of the Corinthians. They are asked to do everything for the glory of God (1 Cor 10:31); they are to exercise true liberty which at the same time should not offend anybody (1 Cor 10:32). Paul is setting himself as an example for not offending anybody and doing all things at liberty and for the glory of God. Fiore observes that Paul inserts himself into each problem situation

[44] Fiore, *Personal Example*, 16–17.

[45] Fiore, *Personal Example*, 17; See also Beverly R. Gaventa, "Galatians 1 & 2: Autobiography as Paradigm," *NT* 28. 4 (1986), 321, 322; Abraham Smith, *Comfort One Another: Reconstructing the Rhetoric and Audience of 1 Thessalonians* (Louisville, KY: John Knox, 1995), 72.

[46] We shall explain the use of *δεῖ* as Divine imperative in the next chapter.

[47] Castelli, *Imitating Paul*, 97.

[48] See Castelli, 99; Fiore, "Exemplification," 241.

[49] Mitchell, *Rhetoric of Reconciliation*, 50–60; also Fiore, "Exemplification," 242.

(5:12; 6:12; 8:13; 9:12-15, 19–23; 10:28–11:1; 12:31–13:3; 13:11–12; 14:11, 14, 18) and thereby offers himself as an example of a non-divisive course of action that he hopes the community will follow.

6.4.2.2.4. "Become as I Am": Gal 4:12

The imperative "γίνεσθε ὡς ἐγώ" is similar to the exhortation "become imitators of me" examined earlier. The technical term μιμέομαι or μιμητής is lacking in the verse, still considering the whole context of the saying, the verse bears a clear notion of imitation. The Mosaic Law, its traditions, and practices now plays no role in the divine economy of salvation.[50] Galatians must understand this as preached by Paul through his words and life, whose version of the Gospel the Gentile Christians of Galatia should follow and not any other Gospel (Gal 1:6; see also 2 Cor 11:4). The Gentiles are called upon to free themselves from the law, and to do so by becoming like Paul.[51] Paul presents himself as an example of proper Christian freedom.

6.4.2.2.5. "Be Imitators of God": Eph 5:1

Among the texts that highlight obedience, the Ephesian text is unique since the "imitation" required is not of Paul or co-ministers with him, but of God—the "highest model possible."[52] Lincoln provides few Hellenistic Jewish writings as examples where the notion of imitating God was traditionally used.[53] God is depicted in the MT mostly as holy, just, showing steadfast love and mercy. Imitation of God therefore entails becoming like God as far as possible and the author of the epistle is most probably having this in mind in 5:1. The author demands that the Ephesians are to imitate God's forgiveness first, along with kindness, forbearance, tenderness, charity, and mutual love. Paul was not responsible for the conversion of the Ephesian church to Christ. Therefore this deutero-Pauline text would not and does not set Paul as a model; rather the model is God the Father. In this passage the usual Pauline style of proposing himself as an example is missing. A similar method may be also found in Col 3:13 where the Colossians are to imitate the Lord in forgiving each other. The Lord is a paradigm also in Rom 15:7 which refers to the acceptance of us (Paul and Romans) by Christ.

In these texts, thus, the primary model of imitation is God or Christ. The Ephesian text is important in our study because it complements Acts 20:35 where the ultimate model is Christ. Pauline concept of imitation

---

[50] For this idea see David M. Stanley, "'Become Imitators of Me': The Pauline Conception of Apostolic Tradition," *Bib* (1959), 875.

[51] See the idea appearing in De Boer, *The Imitation of Paul*, 193.

[52] The phrase "highest model possible" is from Lincoln, *Ephesians,* 310.

[53] Lincoln, 311.

establishes a hierarchical order and that order is: God or Jesus, Paul, and Christians. Acts 20:34–35 transmits, though not fully, this hierarchical order.

6.4.3. Christological Dimension of Imitation

It is hard to imagine why Paul does not call Christ directly a model for the Corinthians or he does not mention precisely in what connection Christ is a model for him.[54] In those specific imitation texts in the undisputed Pauline letters Paul is the model for the community, but Christ is the reason for Paul being a model. For example, in many places Paul urges the churches to follow the example of Christ (Rom 15:3, 5, 7; 2 Cor 10:1; Phil 2:1–11). The imitation is oriented towards the humble, welcoming, obedient, and crucified Christ. Paul's apostolic existence is fashioned by Jesus crucified and risen. In the imitation passages Paul's relationship with Christ as follower and apostle is expressed and legitimated.[55] The Christological dimension of imitation is consistent in all the instances above surveyed, with selflessness standing out as a way of being patterned after Jesus.

All the examples in the letters of Paul make it plain that one can be an imitator of Christ only by concrete obedience to the Word and will of the Lord. Paul refers to the obedient following as an expression of fellowship of life and will.[56] The element of obedience is clearer in 1 Cor 4:17. The imitation here is to follow His way (ὁδός) to accept His teaching (διδαχή) with its character and command; to follow what has been learned, received, heard, and seen in Him (cf. Phil 4:9). The reference in Eph 5:1 points to imitating God as an example, 5:2 then must be a reference to following the example of Christ. The reference to Christ is to be evaluated rather as an ethical motive which does not have to include the idea of imitation and example. Because in any imitation one cannot be equal to the model.[57]

6.5. Paul as a Model of Charity: The Collection for Jerusalem

An important element in the life of Paul, other than his habit of manual work, is his example of charity which is particularly revealed to us through his letters and Acts. In the Miletus speech, Paul exhorts the audience to take up even manual work and support the weak. Nowhere in his letters does Paul indicate what work he performed to support himself or his companions; for that one must have recourse to Acts as it explicitly mentions the nature of his

---

[54] Michaelis, "Μιμέομαι," 668.

[55] This is expressed in Fiore, "Exemplification," 242.

[56] In Paul both μαθητής and μιμητής look one and the same, though Paul does not use the former word. See Michaelis, "Μιμέομαι," 673.

[57] Michaelis, 671.

work (18:3). Nonetheless, exhortations to charity or sharing and caring are closer to Paul's own letters where similar instructions or echoes have been frequently found.[58] Pauline letters are actively involved about referring to the collection for Jerusalem, but Acts is rather passive about describing the collection,[59] nevertheless, the concrete examples of supporting the weak are described in the early chapters of Acts (6:1–5; 11:27–30). The Miletus speech puts plainly the exhortation to support the weak; but not how to do it; for that, one must have recourse to other texts of Acts and Paul's letters.

6.5.1. The Ethics of the Jerusalem Collection

The Jerusalem collection enters the discussion at least in five places in the NT (Rom 15:26–31; 1 Cor 16:1–4; 2 Cor 8:1–9:15; Acts 11:27–30; Acts 24:17).[60] What have the churches founded by Paul to do with Jerusalem Church that they should take a collection for the church in Jerusalem? Why should Paul demand a collection for the Jerusalem church and not for any other? We will be answering these questions as we proceed.

Acts gives us the impression that the Antiochean famine relief (Acts 11:27–30) was an altogether different collection unrelated to the one proposed by Paul to different churches.[61] As a matter of fact, Antiochean collection was the "first installment" sent to Jerusalem for the famine relief. Gathering information from Acts and relating it with the Epistles, one gets the impression that Acts 11:28–29 is the original reason for the collection. The reign of Emperor Claudius (41–54 CE) was marked with droughts and famines.[62] Judea was badly affected by the famine.[63] The time of the Apostolic Council (48 / 49 CE) coincided with the height of famine in Judea and probably Paul and Barnabas brought also the relief from the Antiochean church at this time.[64]

---

[58] Few examples, other than the ones mentioned already, are Rom 12:13, 20; 1 Cor 11:21–22; Gal 2:10; 5:6; 6:2. See also 2 Tim 6:18.

[59] According to Leander E. Keck, Luke is passive about the collection because he knew that it failed to do what Paul hoped it would. See "The Poor among the Saints in the New Testament," *ZNW* 56 (1965), 107.

[60] Another passage that most probably refers to the collection is Gal 2:10. This passage is the most important text that spurs the collection drive in the other letters.

[61] Proponent of this view is F. Randall. See "The Pauline Collection for the Saints," *Exp* 4th series vol. 8 (1893), 322.

[62] Gustav Stählin, *Die Apostelgeschichte: Übersetzt und Erklärt*, NTD 5 (Göttingen: Vandenhoeck & Ruprecht, 1962), 164.

[63] Jos. *Ant.* 20.101.

[64] Hieronymus Cruz, *Christological Motives and Motivated Actions in Pauline Paraenesis*, EHS.T 396 (Frankfurt: Peter Lang, 1990), 394. For the chronology of the famine and the

Antiochean relief for Jerusalem was sent through Barnabas and Paul and the question here is "Does this mission refer to their visit to Jerusalem before the Council?" Paul's own information about his visit to the Jerusalem authorities in Galatians does not speak of two visits. Lucan account gives us the impression that there were two distinct visits to Jerusalem, one before the Jerusalem Council and another to participate in the Jerusalem Council.[65]

Most probably Luke is only intending to tell the readers that the agents of the Antiochean famine collection were Barnabas and Paul and that they delivered it to the Jerusalem authorities; and in doing so Luke may be ignoring the time frame of the event. The reference in Acts 11:30 is a natural conclusion to the preceding material, but the reference in 12:25 appears to be placed more correct chronologically.[66] But even this observation of Keith Nickle is unreliable because Luke provides additional travel details of Paul before the actual commencement of the Jerusalem Council. In any case these issues are not important for us here but it needs only to be stated that after the Jerusalem Council there were subsequent efforts from Paul to collect money from all the Gentile churches for the assistance of Jerusalem.[67] So in the following pages we shall discuss about the efforts Paul made to collect money from the Gentile churches.

6.5.1.1. The Manner of the Collection

Although there were 'god fearers' among the Gentiles who bestowed benefactions upon the Jews,[68] the nature and manner of the collection was altogether different. As per the account in first Corinthians they are instructed to set aside a sum, whatever extra they earn, on the first day of every week (1 Cor 16:2). These directions had been already given to the churches of Galatia (1 Cor 16:1). We are not sure whether the information provided in

---

delivery of aid, see Keith F. Nickle, *The Collection: A Study in Paul's Strategy*, SBT 48 (London: SCM, 1966), 29–32.

[65] According to Cruz, it is more reasonable to conclude that Luke, confused with parallel traditions, speaks of two journeys, and Acts 11:30 and Acts 15 describe one and the same visit of Paul to Jerusalem, see his comment on this in *Christological Motives*, pp. 394–95. Absolute truth concerning the number of visits is difficult to establish. The fourteen year period of Gal 2:1 may point to a period between Paul's first visit and the second for the Council of Jerusalem. Acts is silent about the first visit of Paul if that occurred 14 years before the Jerusalem Council. The narrative differences between Acts and Galatians cast further doubts on the number of visits. If the Galatian information is to be viewed reliable, then Acts also should be viewed equally reliable.

[66] Nickle, *The Collection*, 31.

[67] Attempts for the collection are most explicitly presented in 2 Cor 8–9. For a good theological and spiritual commentary on 2 Cor 8–9 see Mark A. Seifrid, *The Second Letter to the Corinthians*, PNTC (Grand Rapids: Eerdmans, 2014), 314–67.

[68] They realized this through providing building, alms etc. See Lk 7:4; Acts 10:2.

the Corinthian text is a repetition of a directive or a request for a different method of collection contrary to the directives given to the churches in Galatia. It is most probable that Paul is utilizing the Galatian manner of collection since that is important and could be considered as the gist of all the directives. Apparently the Corinthians got the impression that the collection was in some sense obligatory, but Paul using "emphatic negatives" clarifies that it was not to be seen as mandatory.[69] The Corinthians have allowed Paul to assume that they were willing to participate in the collection.[70] Later the Corinthian church has expressed their perplexity over Paul's demand for a collection for the Jerusalem church, a reason for Paul to intervene and clarify the misunderstandings.

6.5.1.2. Interpretative Views on the Collection

The Gentile churches might have been to a varied degree perplexed over the collection; obviously the Corinthian perplexity over it is communicated to us by Paul himself. Not only the Corinthians but also the modern scholars are perplexed over the collection's theological motivations.[71] The amount of modern and contemporary writings on the topic illustrates how the scholars have been trying to understand the collection.[72] In this connection, I will passingly mention four main lines of interpretation.[73] (1) The collection as an eschatologically stirred event;[74] (2) the collection as an expression of the

---

[69] Negatives can be found in 2 Cor 8:8; 9:5, 7, revealing that the collection was not in any way being imposed upon.

[70] John C. Hurd, *The Origin of First Corinthians* (London: SPCK, 1965), 201.

[71] For the theological significance of the Collection, see Nickle, *The Collection*, pp. 100–43.

[72] See a short presentation on the subject in Julien M. Ogereau, "The Jerusalem Collection as Κοινωνία: Paul's Global Politics of Socio-Economic Equality and Solidarity," *NTS* 58 (2012), 362.

[73] See a similar mode of classification in Ogereau, "Jerusalem Collection" p. 361. Scholars' positions often overlap in this attempt, making it difficult for a neat classification.

[74] Johannes Munck, *Paulus und die Heilsgeschichte*, AJutT 26 (København: Universitets forlaget i Aarhus, 1954); K. F. Nickle, *The Collection*; *A Study in Paul's Strategy*; and Dieter Georgi, *Remembering the Poor: The History of Paul's Collection for Jerusalem* (Nashville: Abingdon Press, 1992) are the important monographs in which the eschatological aspects of the collection may be easily found. In Munck's book he also suggests that Paul used the Gentile's pilgrimage to Jerusalem as a model for the collection. The drawback of this opinion is that it is against Paul's intentions and theology. Moreover the recipients of the collection are the poor among the believers in Jerusalem and not the temple or Israel as a whole. See this in Samuel Auler, "More than a Gift: Revisiting Paul's Collection for Jerusalem and the Pilgrimage of Gentiles," *JSPL* 6.2 (2016), 146.

Gentile's moral and / or social obligation towards the Jerusalem church;[75] (3) the collection as an ecumenical offering;[76] and (4) the collection as a charitable act in the form of material relief.[77]

Most scholars have focused on the theological rationale of the collection, ignoring its more practical economic or even political implications.[78] In the following pages it will be clearer that the third and fourth interpretations most probably emerge from the actual Pauline intentions for the collection.[79] Various Pauline terms for the collection will orient our discussion concerning the purpose and implications of the collection.

6.5.1.3. Pauline Terms for the Collection

Various NT texts that mention the collection can help us to pinpoint the nature and purpose of the collection. Paul's report about it at various places is quite elaborative especially in Second Corinthians, but Luke has less interest in the matter. However, the Lucan word for the collection (Acts 24:17) is significant for our study as he proposes a new term for the collection which differs from the Pauline words found in his letters. As a matter of fact, all these terms are important as they indicate the purpose of the collection.

6.5.1.3.1. κοινωνία

A significant term for Paul is κοινωνία to describe the collection (2 Cor 8:4; 9:13; Rom 15:26[80]). Accordingly, it can refer to communion, fellowship, a

---

[75] Stephan Joubert, *Paul as Benefactor: Reciprocity, Strategy, and Theological Reflection in Paul's Collection*, WUNT 2.124 (Tübingen: Mohr Siebeck, 2000), sees this dimension of the collection as the prominent one. Related to this, but yet different, is the proposal of F. Randall, who suggests the collection as continuous and systematic almsgiving by deliberate act of policy. See "The Pauline Collection for the Saints," 322. It is also seen as an act of charity on the part of the Diaspora Gentile church and was seen as a substitute action for their sacrifices and circumcision. See Scot McKnight, "Collection for the Saints," in *DPL*, Gerald F. Hawthorne, and Ralph P. Martin, ed. (Downers Grove: InterVarsity Press, 1993), 145.

[76] Munck, *Paulus und die Heilsgeschichte*; David J. Downs, *The Offering of the Gentiles: Paul's Collection for Jerusalem in its Chronological, Cultural, and Cultic Contexts*, WUNT 2.248 (Tübingen: Mohr Siebeck, 2008). Closely related to the collection as an ecumenical offering, is the proposal of various scholars who suggest it as a sign of communion. See Ogereau, "Jerusalem Collection"; Hans D. Betz, *2 Corinthians 8 and 9: A Commentary on Two Administrative Letters of the Apostle Paul*, Herm. (Philadelphia, PA: Fortress Press, 1985), see especially p. 68; M. A. Seifrid, *The Second Letter to the Corinthians*; K. F. Nickle, *The Collection; A Study in Paul's Strategy*.

[77] This is found in Nickle, *The Collection*; Downs, *The Offering of the Gentiles*; McKnight, "Collection for the Saints," see p. 145.

[78] Few exceptions are Ogereau and Betz.

[79] The first two lines of interpretations manifest some flaws; explaining the reasons for these flaws is not the scope of this thesis and so we will not devote space for it.

[80] Romans 15:27 employs a verbal form (κοινώνω).

participation, or a contribution. Κοινωνία is a favorite term for Paul to speak about the life of Christian communities. In using this term for the collection, Paul was primarily emphasizing the direct expression of Christian fellowship through contributing relief funds.[81] Ogereau observes κοινωνία as a monetary contribution and distribution as for many translations of the NT (KJV [1611]; RSV, NAS, NIV, NJB). But κοινωνία is not monetary contribution anywhere in the Greek documents.[82] Analyzing various texts and examples, Ogereau concludes that κοινωνία "conveys the meaning of commonality, and by extension, of community on the basis of a common bond."[83] Therefore, the collection for Jerusalem was intended to be a sign of contributory participation in order to enhance communion. Behind all this is reflected the fellowship and incorporation of Christ of all of us.[84]

6.5.1.3.2. χάρις

One of Paul's favorite terms, χάρις, is used for the collection indicating that it is a gift or benefaction (1 Cor 16:3; 2 Cor 8:4, 6–7). Paul may have in mind the Greco-Roman concept of benefaction[85] but that is not the main reason for Paul to advocate the collection as we shall see soon. The term χάρις is used in some instances to the collection *per se*, or to God's favor enabling them to give (2 Cor 8:1, 9:8, 14). As noted in chapter 4, χάρις is a favor, God's enabling or power to fulfill a virtuous act. Second Corinthians chapters 8 and 9 draw the necessity of God's grace for an act of charity and the act of collection is an instance which manifests this distinction of grace.

As applied to the collection, 'grace' meant for Paul first and foremost the divine gift which enabled participation in the collection (2 Cor 8:6) in a Christian way which would involve an act of charity or a donation on the part of the members of the Gentile churches (1 Cor 16:3).[86] Secondly it was an expression of communion (2 Cor 8:4, 7). Thirdly the word is linked to the grace of the person of Christ (2 Cor 8:9), reiterating the fact that without the grace of Christ neither communion nor charitable acts are possible. And,

---

[81] Nickle, *The Collection*, 106.

[82] Ogereau, "Jerusalem Collection," 368.

[83] Ogereau, 372.

[84] Nickle, *The Collection*, 124.

[85] James R. Harrison, *Paul's Language of Grace in its Greco-Roman Context*, WUNT 2.172 (Tübingen: Mohr Siebeck, 2003), 294ff. More will be said about benefaction in the next chapter.

[86] Keck proposes a similar thesis. Paul sees the collection as an occasion for the grace of God to do its works in particular acts. See "The Poor among the Saints in the New Testament," 129.

finally, the term might have had a meaning in relation with the future effect of the collection, a result that 'relieves' and soothes (2 Cor 8:13).[87]

6.5.1.3.3. λογεία, *and* εὐλογία

The first word λογεία that denotes the collection is rare in the NT and it is used twice in consecutive verses in 1 Cor 16:1 and 2. The word is taken to mean as a "collection activity," or "reception of voluntarily contributed money." The word εὐλογία, a compound word, similar to λογεία in its meaning, is found in 2 Cor 9:5-6 and may be translated as a "bountiful / voluntary / real gift" (cf. NAS, NRS, NJB) or "blessing."

6.5.1.3.4. διακονία

The final Pauline term διακονία means a service or ministry (1 Cor 16:15; 2 Cor 8:4; 9:1, 12, 13) and this word seems to be more related to the overall mission of Paul in which the collection for the saints in Jerusalem becomes a particular ministry of Paul. As K. F. Nickle observes, the term διακονία initially meant 'waiting at table' and then extended to 'providing the necessities of life' and later it was generalized to mean simply 'service.'[88] Various accounts in Acts reveal that provision for the needs of the poor occupied a central place even within liturgical service (Acts 2:42; 6:1ff; cf. also 1 Cor 11:22). Similarly, needs of the poor in another community was meted out by other Christian communities, and so to denote this monetary collection, the term διακονία was used.

6.5.1.3.5. ἐλεημοσύνη

This word, a Lucan term, is commonly translated as mercy or pity shown in giving alms or charity. Quite contrary to the terms found in Paul's letters, Acts employs a different term ἐλεημοσύνη (24:17) for the collection; Luke places the term, a term more familiar to LXX and Luke, within a speech of Paul. The term used in Acts is important for us as it points to the purpose of the collection as seen through the eyes of Luke. This term ἐλεημοσύνη is found several times in Tobit which exclusively denotes alms and / or works of mercy and the same sense is generally reflected even in many Wisdom Books. Lucan import of the term in Luke-Acts conveys its theological importance for Luke and indicates how much ἐλεημοσύνη is important for a first century church's social setting.

---

[87] Ideas for this paragraph in Nickle, *The Collection*, 109–10.

[88] Texts such as Lk 12:37; 17:8 for waiting at table; Lk 8:3; 10:40 for providing for life; and Mt 25:42ff. for service.

6.5.1.4. Purpose of the Collection

The preceding terms identified for the collection may help us detect the purpose of the collection since these synonymous words function as a kind of substitute for the collection in the Pauline and deutero-Pauline traditions. Accordingly, it is highly possible that the purpose of the collection might not have been only one for there could have been more than one purpose for it. We will categorize the purpose of the collection into three: ethical and moral, reciprocal, and communitarian.

6.5.1.4.1. Ethical and Moral

At the ethical and moral level at least three considerations are important. Providing a good example, encouragement for equality, and exhortation to charity are the visible ethical and moral elements inherent in the collection. Accordingly, as one author points out, first of all within the Corinthian context, the Achaeans should provide a good example, which can be imitated by the Corinthians. Achaean's eagerness to contribute to the collection has stirred up most of the Macedonians (2 Cor 9:2), so that they too were willing to participate in the collection.

Providing a good example in this matter must be grounded in sound reason, for it is to bring about certain equality. Showing a good example as such is not the principal purpose of the collection, much more it is to bring about a fair balance (2 Cor 8:13). On the one hand, the saints in Jerusalem are poor due to socio-economic conditions; on the other hand most Corinthians are rich also for the same reason. Therefore, at the moral level, the latter have an obligation towards the former, and Paul sees the need for some sort of material equality and exhorts the Corinthians to take a collection for the church in Jerusalem. In the ethical and moral sphere it is to be seen as a duty in view of Christian charity.

6.5.1.4.1.1. An Act of Christian Charity

The poor is to be helped and this was part and parcel of the early Christians' ethical responsibilities.[89] Thus, assisting them in their material need or easing the burden of the Jerusalem Christians was one of the principal purposes of the collection. The whole enterprise may be called "a work of charity." "In fact this is the only purpose Paul himself explicitly speaks of"[90] (Rom 15:26; 2 Cor 8:13; cf. also Acts 24:17). In the realm of Christian ethics charity is the highest good. Therefore, the Gentile churches have a moral obligation towards their mother church in their time of economic need.

---

[89] Joubert, *Paul as Benefactor*, 113.

[90] Cruz, *Christological Motives*, 397.

Concern for the poor and needy was an important responsibility within Judaism. In order to address the issue of the poor and poverty within Judaism various measures had been taken by the recognized Jewish authorities.[91] As per the Gospel account, a concern for the poor was a dominant and well-remembered element in the ministry of Jesus. All the canonical Gospels record Jesus' deep concern for the poor and / or His exhortations to aid them (Mt 5:3; 5:42; 6:2; 11:5; 25:34ff.; Mk 10:21; 12:41; Lk 4:18ff. 11:41; 12:33; 18:22; 19:2ff.; Jn 13:29 etc.). Among the evangelists, Luke particularly emphasizes the need to "give to the poor" a motif dear also to Paul. Paul himself was eager to remember the poor (Gal 2:10) since concern for the needs of the poor was for him one of the expressions of fellowship in Christ. Christian charity for Paul was motivated by Christ and his example of love which accept all into a genuine fellowship (1 Cor 13:3; Rom 12:9–13). Moreover, true Christian charity is a matter of the heart; the attitude of a giver must be "ἐν ἁπλότητι" of heart, without having second thoughts about the donation,[92] manifesting itself by benefactions, liberality.[93]

It is important to note that Luke mentions no other purpose of the collection other than charity. In his defense speech before the governor (24:10–21) Paul spells out that the very purpose of his visit to Jerusalem was to bring alms and offer sacrifices. Luke is silent about other purposes mentioned by Paul in his letters. For Luke charity is important so also for Paul and he has already enjoined this as an obligation in the Miletus speech.

6.5.1.4.2. Reciprocal

Romans 15:27 sums up the reciprocal purpose of the collection. It was from the Jerusalem church that the Gospel reached the Gentiles, and for this reason the Christian community at Jerusalem is the mother church and the Gentile Christian communities must recognize the role of the mother church and be thankful to it. Since the gentile churches have received spiritual benefits from the church at Jerusalem, they owe to the mother church; the Gentile churches should now give material help to them (χάρις) in return. In Paul's conception reciprocity should be manifested through charitable acts. Paul sees a kind of "give and take" motive in the whole process. Hieronymus Cruz sees thanksgiving as the most important motive for the collection and the aid the Gentiles churches give to the mother church at a time of need becomes a

[91] For analogies to Paul's Collection in contemporary Judaism See Nickle, *The Collection*, 74–99.

[92] See "απλῶς," BDAG:104.

[93] This aspect is emphasized in Rom 12:8; 2 Cor 2:8; 9:11, 13, Eph 6:5; Col 3:22. See also 2 Cor 9:7.

concrete expression of their thanksgiving.[94] His observation is correct since genuine thanksgiving is not possible without being generous and charitable. Reciprocity is possible only when there exist care and concern for others and mutual love.

6.5.1.4.3. Communitarian

The collection was aimed also to promote communion. It was not a simple act of charity; it was aimed at communion as well. "It was the practical expression of κοινωνία across socio-cultural and ethnic boundaries. It was the manifestation of a persistent concern for socio-economic equality and solidarity within the Christ centered ecclesia."[95] Ogereau goes as far as to say that it was a practical embodiment of an ecclesiastical ideal, which itself seems to have been inspired by the 'community of goods' of the Jerusalem community.[96] This seems to be an overstatement since Paul does not in any way advocate a common possession of goods or selling everything to contribute to the common pool. On the contrary, Pauline instances will tell that he was more concerned about helping the poor and the needy which he was eager to do (Gal 2:10). Sharing and generous giving have more place in the thought pattern of Paul. Luke himself has advocated almsgiving and generosity throughout his two volume works. Common ownership of goods for a shorter period of the early church must be seen within the ethics of communitarianism and generosity and not the other way round.

The collection is a gift, a donation (εὐλογία). According to Mark Seifrid, "The gift, by its very nature and intent, constitutes Paul's attempt to bring the Corinthians (along with all other participants) into κοινωνία with all the other churches, and especially, of course, with the church in Jerusalem."[97] He hopes for unity among all the churches and communication between them. The Corinthians' gift is an expression of that unity.[98] Paul's announcement of the gift of the Macedonian churches serves this aim, even if he also thereby seeks to motivate the Corinthians to complete their promise (8:1–6).[99] Similarly Paul exhorts the Philippians to a life of communion (fellowship and sharing) and mutual support using the story of Christ. Their "doing" flows out of what Christ has given to them and has done for them,

---

[94] Cruz, *Christological Motives*, 397.

[95] Ogereau, "Jerusalem Collection," 363.

[96] See this in Ogereau, 363.

[97] Seifrid, *Corinthians*, 315.

[98] In advocating the collection, Paul may have wanted to offset the suspicions the Jerusalem Church seemed to have regarding his Gentile mission and consequently foster more trust in his leadership. See Cruz, *Christological Motivess*, 398.

[99] Seifrid, *Corinthians*, 315.

and indeed is a reception of the grace of Christ. Christ stands between Paul and other churches. Christ brings all of them into a relationship of giving and receiving. Human givers are finally receivers.[100]

Paul is also in some way engaging in economics, so that he may build up and care for the churches. His engagement in economics seems to be aimed at community building and charity as the NT documents him—a man of charity.[101] "Remembering the poor" (Gal 2:10) is what Paul was eager to do, and the Galatian text, if it refers to the collection, does not explicitly relate any purpose for it other than charity. However, at various places, Paul indicates his concern for community or communion of hearts which is the true mark of Christ's disciples. Paul's eagerness to help the poor (Gal 2:10) and the arrangement for the Jerusalem collection must be seen from this broader concern for building up of the community and thereby establishing the true communion of hearts. Is it possible to achieve communion without making efforts to solidarity and charity? Not at all. Paul's insistence on a collection for Jerusalem upon the many churches he founded, and Paul himself overseeing the manner of collection and taking it to Jerusalem, tell us how much he valued the collection as a symbol of communion and as a token of gratitude towards the mother church. Above all it stands as a concrete example of Paul's charity.

6.6. Paul as a Model for the Second-Generation Christians

We have already seen "how and why" Paul is a model of manual work and charity. At this juncture two important questions need to be answered: "Why is Paul a model in the Pauline and deutero-Pauline traditions especially in Acts?" and "How does Luke perceive himself and Paul in relation to the Twelve?"

Paul sees himself as a model[102] as he imitates Christ. He could not have held up another model, like Peter or any other apostle, since these first-generation apostles and disciples were not well-known to Paul's congregations. Paul sees himself as a tangible model for the Christians, but for him, the ultimate model is Christ / God. Deutero-Pauline traditions correspond with the Pauline self-conception of being a model / paradigm. The "memory of Paul" that lingered among the post-apostolic church was the primary reason for the origin of deutero-Pauline traditions. For Luke,

[100] Ideas for this paragraph are from Seifrid, *Corinthians*, 317.

[101] Testimonies from Paul's own writings and other deutero-Pauline traditions manifest that he spent money not on his upkeep alone but also on that of his co-ministers. In a particular instance he volunteered to redeem Philemon's slave, Onesimus (Philem 18–19), which also required a considerable sum.

[102] We cannot maintain that it was boastful or egoistic for Paul to point to himself as a model for the churches to imitate. This was an expected element in farewell discourses.

Paul represents all that the apostles were for the first-generation Christians. Thus, Paul becomes the primary role model for the post-apostolic readers, especially for the readers of Acts.

Coming to the second question, we answer that for Luke the apostles in Acts belong to a different temporal location. Luke never participates in the narrative with the apostles, but he does participate with Paul as a travelling companion. In the first chapters of Acts, Luke maintains a temporal distance from the events being narrated.[103] Thus until chapter 16 of Acts, the narrator is an "omniscient" third person and from ch. 16 on, the narrator identifies with the temporal location of Paul and of the reader.[104] Paul, though maintains some contacts with the apostles, is only a witness who belongs to the post-apostolic era. It is doubtful that Luke had any contact with the apostles, but he did maintain contact with Paul. For Luke,[105] Paul provides the primary role model for the post-apostolic second-generation Christians. According to Thomas Phillips, employing Paul as a role model makes a significant difference in at least one area – economic life. The pre-Pauline economic plan and community of goods were relevant only for the Christians of that period and not for the ordinary faithful of the second-generation Christians represented by Paul and Luke. A shift from the previous teaching can be detected in Lk 22:35–36, where a contradicting instruction of Jesus to the previous instructions (Lk 9:1–6 and 10:1–12) is given. The "ἀλλὰ νῦν" in 22:36, most probably, is a reference to the period of the church; the norm is different here from that of the period of Jesus. Therefore, the disciples are asked to take with them things for their sustenance and protection.

At the time of Peter, especially in the first few years of Christianity, communitarianism was the appropriate form and norm, but by the time of Paul and Luke, a different image of the community was formed, with Paul as the model for this new image.[106] Throughout Acts and Pauline letters, Paul conducts himself as a benefactor, dispenser of material gift to show that he was empathizing with the poor, especially with the church at Jerusalem. Empathy makes one to do what is necessary for the object of empathy. Paul does precisely this and thus becomes a model. Phillips notes that in the apostolic period, Peter functioned as the head by coordinating the economic status and life of the community (4:32–35; 5:1–11). But in the post-apostolic

---

[103] T. E. Phillips, "Paul as a Role Model in Acts," 51.

[104] See William S. Kurz, *Reading Luke-Acts: Dynamics of Biblical Narrative* (Louisville, KY: John Knox, 1993), 42–43. See also William S. Campbell's book *The "we" Passages in the Acts of the Apostles: The Narrator as a Narrative Character* (Atlanta: SBL, 2007).

[105] There were other writers other than Luke who found a role model in Paul, for example the authors of 2 Thessalonians, Ephesians, and Timothy.

[106] Phillips, "Paul as a Role Model in Acts" 55.

period, Paul functions as the norm[107] and ethical model as this echo in Paul's and Luke's writings. A shift in the economic dealings and structures is reflected in the Lucan writings and in the overall presentation of economic life of the early Christian community. It shifts from the early apostolic idea of Christians 'having everything in common' to the post apostolic idea of 'owning private property' and 'utilizing it for the needy.' Miletus speech reaches its climax by endorsing the ethic of giving which will be the topic for our next chapter.

---

[107] Jesus is the ultimate norm for Paul, Luke, and believers. However certain conduct of Paul may function as a norm for these Christians.

Chapter 7

Acts 20:35: Ethics of Giving

Paul ends his speech to the Ephesian elders thus: "In all this I have given you an example that by such work we must support the weak, remembering the words of the Lord Jesus, for he himself said: 'It is more blessed to give than to receive.'" Paul here arrives at the highpoint of his ethical discourse. He exhorts the audience to care for the weak. The climax of this climactic verse is a saying of our Lord which Paul utilizes from the oral tradition for an emphatic presentation of the thesis. It seems that the whole speech was delivered to arrive at this "stirring conclusion." Two points of this verse deserve elaboration. They are (1) the climactic maxim attributed to Jesus but used by Lucan Paul and its purpose and (2) the 'oughtness' of supporting the weak through giving / charity. In this chapter, therefore, we shall focus on these two points with a view to explain also the ethical (also moral) aspect of the verse.

7.1. Introductory Comments on Acts 20:35

So far, Paul has given a personal example of manual labor which he wishes his hearers will follow; but now he makes a close association between his example of work and supporting the weak, indicating the fact that his work was done with an aim to help the "weak." The weak, as in the perception of Luke-Acts, seem to be those of "low social status who tended to be marginalized in the Greco-Roman world, a condition found even in the Church."[1] The marginalized for Luke are the poor (e.g. Lk 4:18; Acts 11:27-30; 20:35 etc.) who would include the sick (Lk 4:31–41; 5:12–26; 6;6–11;

[1] Witherington, *Acts*, 625.

8:26–39; 9:37–43; 14:1–6; 16:19–31; 17:11–19; Acts 5:12–16; 9:32–35), the blind and lame (Lk 13:10–17; 18:35–43; Acts 3:1-10; 14:8–10), and women and widows (Lk 7:11–17; 36-50; 8:40–56; 13:10–17; 21:1–4; Acts 6:1–6). In our verse the "weak" most probably refers to those suffering from economic wants.

Lucan Paul sees "helping the weak" as an ethical duty and moral obligation. This aspect has been highlighted by the use of δεῖ, a word dear to Luke, to indicate a divine stipulation or personal / corporate obligation. In the previous chapter we have examined how Paul functions as a model and how the verb μιμέομαι and the nouns τύπος and μιμητής have been utilized to explain the μιμητής idea. In this connection v. 35 is important because here a call is made by Lucan Paul to imitate the speaker (Paul) but without using the above words of imitation but employing other vocabularies.[2] Further, Pauline instruction regarding helping the weak is authenticated by the words of our Lord since He Himself willed that such works should be performed when He said "It is more blessed to give than to receive."

7.1.1. The Use of δεῖ in Acts 20:35

At this point an important word that needs some discussion is δεῖ[3] used in the verse. Charles Cosgrove made a study of the word's significance in Luke-Acts to discover God's providence in these writings.[4] According to him δεῖ is used in Luke-Acts at least in 3 different ways: (1) as a divine necessity; (2) as "ordinary" usage which does not convey the idea of a divine necessity or compulsion; and (3) as a summons to obedience.[5]

Most uses of the term bespeak a divine necessity.[6] Cosgrove states: "Not all the uses of δεῖ in Luke-Acts express a divine must, but a majority

[2] The verb ὑποδείκνυμι used in 20:35 is not found in Paul but the noun ὑπόδειγμα in the sense of example in Heb 4:11; Jam 5:10; and 2 Pet 2:6. ὑποδείκνυμι is typically a Lucan word (cf. Lk 3:7; 6:47; 12:5; and Acts 9:16). This preference over verb to noun may point to Luke's later recording of the essence of the speech than to Paul's literal words at the time.

[3] δεῖ occurs 40 times in Luke-Acts. See the 6th edition of Moulton and Geden Concordance, I. Horward Marshal ed. (London: T&T Clark, 2002) pp. 188–89. The word appears 42 times according to the Moulton and Geden Concordance, 4th edition.

[4] Charles H. Cosgrove, "The Divine δεῖ in Luke-Acts," *NovT* 26 (1984), 168–190. He examined two authors who dealt with this theme namely Erich Fascher and Sigfried Schulz. According to the former, the Lucan idea of Divine providence is derived from the OT and Paul, whereas for the latter, it is from Hellenistic circles, see especially pp. 169–70.

[5] For our present purpose I have not followed the presentation order of Cosgrove, that is, point number two here is the last point in his article.

[6] Walter Grundmann, examining the word's meaning in its ancient literary context, states that the word expresses the "character of necessity or compulsion" in an event. In the language of philosophy, the term expresses logical and scientific necessities. See Grundmann, "δεῖ," *TDNT* 2:21.

do."[7] For example one can detect such use in Lk 2:49; 4:43; 9:22; 13:16; 13:13; 19:5; 21:9; 22:37; 24:7, 26, 44; Acts 1:16, 21; 3:21; 4:12; 5:29; 27:24. Acts 26:9; 27:21, 26 may be viewed as having this sense. In many instances fulfillment occurs by the divine will often expressed by the word δεῖ.[8] For example δεῖ has been frequently used in Acts 2:23; 4:28; 13:36; 20:27 etc. to prove prophetic fulfillment. Long-foretold prophecies are unfolded in these instances.

Jesus' passion is a divine necessity according to Lk 9:22; 13:33; 17:25; 22:37; 24:7, 26, 44; and Acts 17:3. Paul's Roman destiny is presented as God's plan and articulated three times in Acts (19:21; 23:11; 27:24) using δεῖ. Jesus and Paul "creatively participate" in the divine necessity. Instead of using the usual δεῖ, the same idea of divine necessity is expressed in Lk 9:31, 44 and Acts 26:23 using the verb μέλλω. Cosgrove concludes, "δεῖ is therefore a typical Lucan vehicle for describing the necessity that God's plan, expressed in Scripture, be fulfilled."[9]

Secondly, the "ordinary" use of δεῖ occurs thirteen times in Luke-Acts.[10] Examples are Lk 12:12; 13:14; 15:32; Acts 15:5; 16:30; 24:19; 26:9 etc. δεῖ indicates at times nothing more than practical necessity as is clear from Acts 19:36; 24:19; 25:24.[11] Ordinary use of the term corroborates no theological significance.

And finally, the divine δεῖ is a summons to obedience. Examples are Lk 4:43; 11:42; Acts 5:29; 9:16. "It confronts Jesus, Paul, or the Christian with marching orders."[12] The element of obedience can be also deciphered in Acts 20:35. Here obedience is made explicit by the use of δεῖ. In the realm of ethics obedience is a highly desired virtue. The use of δεῖ in v. 35, therefore, is an ethical one as Cosgrove rightly classifies the use of δεῖ here for ethical obligation.[13] The use of δεῖ is significant here since in the verse one finds an imperative to be obeyed or an ethical duty to be performed. Any negligence in performing this duty, then, is immoral and sinful.

---

[7] Cosgrove, "The Divine δεῖ in Luke-Acts," 172.

[8] According to Gregory Sterling, the fulfillment concept itself may be derived from a Christian attempt to relate the life of Jesus and the church to the OT (see Sterling, *Historiography*, 360). But it must also be noted that within the OT there already existed a promise-fulfillment pattern. Luke's deep knowledge of the LXX was instrumental in seeing the history in this way.

[9] Cosgrove, "The Divine δεῖ in Luke-Acts," 174.

[10] Cosgrove, 172.

[11] Soards, *The Speeches in Acts*, 28.

[12] Cosgrove, 189.

[13] Outside of Luke-Acts, the word's use has been briefly presented by Grundmann. See "δεῖ," *TDNT* 2:21–25. He notes that in the Greek circles the word may carry ethical and religious obligations.

By the use of δεῖ what is absolutely enjoined on the elders and believers is the charge to support the weak. Leaders (also believers) cannot shun away from this responsibility. They are to obey it and embrace it as an ethical and moral duty. In order to fulfill this task, they have a model, the working and giving Paul whom they can look at as a living model. Thus, the δεῖ connects between the model and action. In our case what does it mean? The ethical instructions of the speaker must be followed as the final instructions of a parting figure / leader, and the children / successors always obey the farewell words of a departing figure.[14] Thus, Acts 20:35 invites the audience to follow their leader who is also their model and to obey his words.

Another observation may be helpful here to better appreciate the significance of this verse and particularly that of δεῖ. Our thesis is that the use of δεῖ here is closely linked to our Lord's command and therefore δεῖ in this verse not only envisages a simple call to obedience but also a divine command to action. The word used in religious and ethical matters always requires fulfilling of religious or civil obligations which itself is seen as carrying out the will of God. The instruction found in this verse is, therefore, of primary importance. The command of the Lord at the end of the speech divinizes the δεῖ and the instruction as a whole by imparting a moral sense to the verse.

7.2. The Climactic Maxim (20:35b) as a Fitting Aphorism

The most important segment of the verse seems to be the climactic maxim "It is more blessed to give than to receive." In order to discover a full-blown ethics of 20:32–35 and especially that of v. 35, we first examine the use, purpose, and implications of the climactic maxim borrowed by the Lucan Paul from which we will be able to construct the ethical accents of the entire verse. Our study on this point is mostly based on the article of Robert O'Toole who examined the role of Jesus' saying in Acts 20:35.[15]

7.2.1. Ancients' Use of Maxims and Acts 20:35

Maxims give the speech an ethical quality and a clear moral purpose which increase the speaker's ethos.[16] Maxims should be brief and placed at the end of the sentence, or at the conclusion of an epideictic speech.[17] Maxim can also be called aphorism or gnome. Aphorism (χρεία) is a term referring to a popular wisdom saying. It refers to a concise, autonomous saying which gives pithy

---

[14] Instructions given by a parting figure is always considered to be important and even divinely revealed. This has been already indicated in the first chapter of this thesis.

[15] See Robert F. O'Toole, "What Role Does Jesus' Saying in Acts 20:35 Play in Paul's Address to the Ephesian Elders?" *Bib* 75 (1994), 329–49.

[16] See Arist. *Rh.* 1395b.

[17] *Rh. Alex.* 1441b, see especially 10ff.

expression to an insight about life.[18] In ancient societies, aphorisms typically functioned as vehicles for articulating and preserving traditional values and norms by expressing general and typical truths refracted through particular situations and occurrences.[19] Both attributed and unattributed maxims were memorized and passed on for centuries even in elementary educational settings.[20] While historians did not reproduce entire speeches verbatim, they could reproduce brief sayings in this manner.[21]

Maxims or proverbs[22] were amply used in Jewish circles. Wisdom Books contain innumerable pithy sayings which give a glimpse to the realities of life and thus they become important for the Jewish people. Some maxims in the Jewish circle were μακάριον related sayings (Job 5:17; Ps 1:1; 2:12b; 32:1; 40:4; 106:3; Prov 3:13; 28:14 etc.). Acts 20:35 uses a maxim which is a wisdom saying[23] in the form of a beatitude[24] (μακάριος). Lucan Paul uses it along with a comparative to express an ethical value judgment.[25] Beatitudes are normally personal, and absolute; but in our case it appears to bc impersonal and relative and is open to numerous applications.[26] At the same time it cannot be fully impersonal since more blessing is promised to "the giving." Some scholars have found more of Greek influence[27] in the sayings of Jesus while other scholars have detected both Greek and Jewish

[18] Arist. *Rh.* 1394b.

[19] James G. Williams, *Those who Ponder Proverbs: Aphoristic Thinking and Biblical Literature* (Sheffield: Almond Press, 1981), 36 & 40.

[20] Keener, *Acts*, 1:295. Keener also cites Hermog. *Progymn.* 4 & 8–10 and Sen. Y. *Ep. Lucil.* 33.7, texts that speak of passing on maxims from one generation to another.

[21] An elaborate description of the use and purpose of maxim can be found in Arist. *Rh.* 1394a–1395b.

[22] David E. Aune explains the distinction between a proverb and aphorism. Though an aphorism seems very close to a proverb, it is not quite the same. A proverb (γνώμη) is an unattributed saying which gives expression to collective wisdom and for that reason is accepted as true. The aphorism on the other hand is an expression of personal insight and vision, attributed to particular individuals, and often reflecting specific situations. See Aune, *Jesus, Gospel Tradition and Paul in the Context of Jewish and Greco-Roman Antiquity*: *Collected Essays 2*, WUNT 303 (Tübingen: Mohr Siebeck, 2013), 260.

[23] Most scholars agree on this. For example, see Hänchen, *The Acts of the Apostles*, 595; Witherington, *Acts*, 626; Keener, *Acts*, 3:3065. John J. Kilgallen, "Acts 20:35 and Thucydides 2.97.4," *JBL* 112 (1993), 314.

[24] Witherington, *Acts*, 626; O'Toole, "Jesus' Saying," 333.

[25] G. Strecker, "μακάριος," *EDNT* 2:376.

[26] See O'Toole, "Jesus' Saying," 333–34.

[27] For example, Hänchen argues that Luke has taken up a Greek proverb and placed it in the mouth of Jesus. It is Christianized by replacing the Hellenistic ἥδιον with the Biblical μακάριον. See *The Acts of the Apostles*, 595; and Joachim Jeremias, *Unknown Sayings of Jesus* (London: SPCK, 1958), 32–33. Kilgallen, opines that it is wiser to treat the wisdom saying of

influence.[28] The maxim anyway functions like a Greek aphorism, which at the same time is best understood in terms of a Jewish beatitude.[29]

Beatitudes[30] pronounce someone "happy" or "blessed." "In the Jewish context beatitudes were used above all in the wisdom paraenesis as an expression of the connection between a person's deeds and what happens to the person."[31] There exist several beatitudes in wisdom circles. These "wisdom beatitudcs are a didactic genre and serve to instruct"[32] (e.g. Prov 3:13; Sir 14:1; 25:8; 26:1 etc.).

In the NT μακάριος can have the general meaning "happy" or "good."[33] These meanings do not convey a futuristic dimension of μακάριος rather refer to happiness and goodness here in the present. Ulrich Luz notes that the goal of beatitudes is "not to give comfort by making promises about the next life" instead macarisms pronounce people happy in the present life.[34] This thesis appears to be credible, but the eschatological aspect and perspective of a macarism cannot be overlooked. In the Matthean and Lucan version of the beatitudes the use of future tense in the second clause of the beatitudes evidences this (see Lk 6:20; Mt 5:4, 5,6 etc.). The macarism used at Acts 20:35 relates primarily to the present, at the same time it relates also to the future, even if the future tense is absent in the sentence. Those who give are happy and blessed in the present life and they will be happy and blessed in the life to come, as they will get a just reward. Those who give less will be less happy and blessed.

Ernst Hänchen in his commentary on Acts has observed that the maxim's use here is influenced by Thucydides 2.97.4. It was the rule in the Persian Empire to give rather than to receive. John J. Kilgallen commenting on Hänchen's observation argues that Thucydides never wrote that it is better to give than to receive, but the opposite. If so, why did Hänchen give us this kind of an interpretation? It is not what he said becomes noteworthy, but

---

Jesus as borrowed from Greek and Latin citations which display or echo the idea of giving and receiving. See "Acts 20:35 and Thucydides 2.97.4," 314.

[28] E.g., Witherington, *Acts*, 626; O'Toole, "Jesus' Saying," 333–34.

[29] O'Toole, "Jesus' Saying," 333.

[30] The Hebrew equivalent is אַשְׁרֵי (construct form) with a predicate.

[31] Ulrich Luz, *Matthew 1–7*. James E. Crouch, trans., Helmut Koester, ed., Herm. (Minneapolis: Fortress Press, 2007, 187. Luz makes this observation following Kähler.

[32] Luz, *Matthew 1–7*, 187.

[33] Strecker, "μακάριος," 376. This observation following F. Hauck "μακάριος," *TDNT* 4:362–63.

[34] Luz, *Matthew 1–7*, 190.

what he surely would have said;[35] the parallel is not precise, it only reflects the sentiment.[36]

It is highly probable that Luke was summarizing the teaching of Jesus on the right use of wealth which he had already described through catchy sayings and parables (e.g. Lk 6:38; 11:41; 12:33; 8:1–3; 10:30–37; 16:1–12; 21:1–4 etc.) or it may be that Luke, influenced by Wisdom tradition, has utilized a maxim of beatitude. Lucan Paul's use of "It is more blessed to give than to receive" fits the two aforementioned suppositions.

7.2.2. Purpose and Implications of the Use of the Maxim in 20:35

O'Toole places Jesus' saying in Acts 20:35 in its general category. In doing so he depends on H. J. Degenhardt who identifies three typical aspects of Luke's redactional activity of passages which deal with possessions and their renunciation. They are (1) Jesus' words get transferred to the disciples and church leaders of Luke's time and these instructions impinge the community under certain conditions; (2) there is given the directives for mission, and advices and challenges for disciples; and (3) emphasis on almsgiving is now directed to the Gentile Christian communities. Evidently the maxim represents all the above three aspects. It transfers an instruction of Jesus to the Ephesian elders via Paul, and it challenges and advises the elders concerning their mission and above all calls them to charitable activity.[37]

In the speech Paul had previously exemplified himself as a true minister of the word; instructed the Ephesian elders of their duty; shown himself as a model; and in "all this" Paul was giving himself as a libation, yet he is glad and rejoicing.[38] All that Paul *was* and *is* reappears generalized in "It is more blessed to give than to receive."

The maxim refers back to the words of Jesus, which Paul "remembers" now.[39] This remembering "highlights" and "clarifies" Paul's motivation for assisting the weak. Gustav Stälin states: "*Das letzte wort, das Lukas von dem Missionar Paulus berichtet, ist ein wort Jesu; es soll als herrenwork entscheidende Richtschnur deinen* (cf. 1 Cor 7:10; 9:14; 11:23; 1 Thess 4:15) *darum ist die "Erinnerung" an diese worte so wichtig* (Acts 11:16; Jn 14:26; Lk 22:61; 24:6–8, 44; 2 Pet 3:1f.)."[40] Paul does remember the words of our

[35] Kilgallen, "Acts 20:35 and Thucydides 2.97.4," 313.

[36] Keener, *Acts*, 3:3065.

[37] O'Toole, "Jesus' Saying," 333.

[38] See the same idea in Phil 2:17.

[39] Although the saying of Jesus here comes from Lucan Paul, Paul's own writings draw a number of allusions to the sayings of Jesus. Redundancy of this topic leaves only a passing mention of it here. See a detailed presentation of the subject in David M. Stanley, *Pauline Allusions to the Sayings of Jesus* (Roma: PIB, 1961), especially pp. 26–39.

[40] Stählin, *Die Apostelgeschichte*, 271.

Lord as do Peter (Lk 22:61; Acts 11:16) and the women at the tomb (Lk 24:6–8). The word or message is grace (Acts 20:32), and it gives inheritance to all who are sanctified. We find a thematic link between the "giving" in Acts 20:32 and 20:35. In other words, "Acts 20:35 embraces the thought in Acts 20:32 that the power of God's word can build up the Ephesian elders and "give" them a share among the sanctified."[41]

The maxim at the end of the speech brings up the theme of the resurrection, which Luke had already brought in v. 32 using the term κληρονομία. In the speeches of Paul and Peter resurrection is a main theme. The blessedness intended in the maxim may be an immediate or future reality. However, it is better to see it more as a future reality, a participation in the kingdom of God. The word μακάριος[42] introduces a future aspect of life as this is evident in the entire Lucan writings (Lk 6:20–22; 12:32–33, 37–38, 43; 14:12–14; 23:29; Acts 20:35). For example, the beatitude "Blessed are you who are poor, for yours is the kingdom of God" (Lk 6:20) partly parallels Jesus' saying in 20:35; the difference, however, is that in Lk 6:20 the eschatological dimension is more perceivable.

Again, the maxim here recapitulates one of the main concerns of Luke and Paul, i.e., giving and supporting the weak. Beverly R. Gaventa observes that the single time a teaching of Jesus is quoted directly in Acts it pertains to the proper use of wealth.[43] We shall return to this theme soon but before that an overarching theme intrinsically connected to the whole speech requires some attention. The speech was primarily addressed to the Ephesian elders. They, as shepherds of the flock, have the duty to care for the flock. The use of μικρός ποίμνιον in Lk 12:32 and probable reference to church leadership strengthen the connection between these verses and Jesus' saying in the speech to the Ephesian elders. Thus the maxim is directed to the church leaders as similar concerns have been already addressed in Luke 12, especially in vv. 41–48. We can draw an immediate relationship with the maxim: blessedness is linked to leader's giving to those of the flock in need.[44]

The maxim in v. 35 unifies the entire speech. O'Toole has brilliantly showed, in his effort to establish the maxim in 20:35 as integral to the Miletus

---

[41] O'Toole, "Jesus' Saying," 335.

[42] The word means "blessed." A 'macarism' is a declaration of happiness or blessedness, it is a beatitude. Most NT macarisms are set in the context of eschatological hope and salvation, which is contrary to false happiness. The foundation for future blessing lies in the hope that God will "effect a reversal of all human values."

[43] Beverly R. Gaventa, *The Acts of the Apostles*, ANTC (Nashville: Abington, 2003), 290.

[44] Ideas for this paragraph are from O'Toole, "Jesus' Saying," 338.

speech, how Jesus saying in Acts 20:35 unifies the entire speech.[45] The main themes in the speech such as serving the Lord and believers, suffering for the Gospel, working night and day, caring for the flock, and reception of inheritance are reflected in this maxim. But, most importantly, the maxim connects to the ethical concerns of the preceding verses (32–35a). Grace is an integral component for giving; true giving blossoms through suffering, hard work, and in a spirit of generosity. Furthermore, faithful shepherds render service to their flock and, thereby, they generously "give" rather than selfishly "receive." Jesus's saying quoted here basically relates to his own life and ministry through which Jesus 'gave' his own life for us; and in a previous verse of the speech (20:28), Lucan Paul declares how God obtained the church of God with the blood of His own Son. Thus the Son becomes the "supreme model of giving." Not only our Lord, but also Paul is a model for Luke, especially his "self-giving, which is clearly advantageous to others and which shows affection and generosity."[46] The maxim is a fitting aphorism at the end of the speech, and on the whole the maxim posts an invitation to charity through the act of giving and this is the next point of this chapter.

7.3. Giving: An Important Lucan Theme

The final verse of the Miletus speech categorically states the 'oughtness' of supporting the weak. We have already analyzed the use of the ethical δεῖ in the verse as a vehicle for ethical and divine imperative. The ethical δεῖ demands from the audience concrete actions of charity, that is, the audience must support the weak by "giving;" this is the point emphasized in the verse and stressed by the maxim. As elsewhere in Luke-Acts, the Lucan Paul here too establishes his community and social ethics to which it is directed as a clarion call. Community and social ethics cannot be put into practice without concrete actions of charity, and Luke sees almsgiving as the specific way to support the weak in a predominant Gentile church for whom he writes. Giving as an expression of love is considered a supreme act in ethics and morality because love is the highest of all virtues. While the *summum bonum* is God himself the *summa virtus* is ἀγάπη which may be demonstrated in different ways, for Luke, however, it is primarily to be expressed in charity giving. At least here in the speech by the phrase "ἀντιλαμβάνεσθαι τῶν ἀσθενούντων" Lucan Paul intends charitable acts.

---

[45] O'Toole, 342–45.

[46] Watson, "Paul's Speech," 207.

7.3.1. Background for ἀντιλαμβάνομαι τῶν ἀσθενούντων and the Motif of Giving[47]

The topic itself is vast since it requires scrutiny of the subject found at least in the Greco-Roman and LXX writings, which mirror their customs, social and religious practices. Different forms of charity or philanthropic activity of a particular period can be understood only by examining the social ethos of the time.[48] Without being exhaustive, we attempt here to sketch few important elements and aspects related to the topic.

7.3.1.1. Greco-Roman Background

A. R. Hands notes that giving was largely one to one (to individual or corporate person) and hardly inspired by ethical or religious feelings. However, there was a general feeling of pity[49] for the poor and destitute. Information about the civil state overseeing charity work is scanty. This may be due to the misdirection of funds paid by wealthy individuals to the state or the tendency to neglect land given to the state.[50] Giving was performed for the welfare of the poor and destitute; it was done in the form of providing basic commodities, education, healthcare, and hygiene.[51] Most of the charity was done to individuals or community but almost always expecting a return.[52]

Ancient Greco-Roman people showed their concern for the other primarily through "gift-exchange" a practice, more than any other custom, that was very much part of that society. It operated at the level of various strata of society, "between groups and individuals."[53] Gifts were given to show gratitude which constituted the "bond" between individuals and groups.[54] Gift exchange was and is a common thing to do in any society although the mode and nature of it differed from place to place and culture

---

[47] Supporting the weak through various acts of charity and other forms of "giving" may be best understood as charity. Other words such as philanthropy, beneficence, magnanimity, liberality, and generosity are closely related to "giving" and sometimes synonymously used for the same.

[48] See this point in A. R. Hands, *Charities and Social Aid in Greece and Rome* (Ithaca, NY: Cornell University Press, 1968), 7.

[49] Pity should move people to give to the destitute. See the problem of "pity" in Bruce W. Longenecker, *Remember the Poor, Paul, Poverty, and the Greco-Roman World* (Grand Rapids: Eerdmans, 2010), 75–77.

[50] See Hands, *Charities*, 73 & 23.

[51] All these points are elaborated by Hands, *Charities*, pp. 62–146.

[52] Useful information on this is in Hands, *Charities*, 26–61.

[53] Joubert, *Paul as Benefactor*, 18.

[54] See Cic. *De Off.* 1.47; Sen. Y. *De Benef.* 1.4.2.

to culture.[55] Gift-exchange involves a dialectic of giving and receiving. The giver turns into receiver and vice versa. The most detailed work available on benefit exchange from the Greco-Roman world is Seneca's *De Beneficiis*. Seneca himself affirmed that the ethic of giving as an intrinsically rewarding experience.[56] Two practices that are closely related to and integral to gift giving are "patronage" and "benefaction" practices of the ancients.[57]

Patronage: This existed in general between rich and the poor. kings, officials, and the rich (for example, landlords) functioned as patrons of the lower-class including slaves.[58] The kings and officials gave benefits to those who had access to them and groups favored by them. Landlords bestowed benefits on tenants and other laborers. Clients were expected to give to their patron in return respect and greetings[59] which elevated the social status of the patron.[60]

There also existed relationship between Patron and Protégé (or superior and inferior friends). Since the use "patron and client" is demeaning, the idea of friendship relations between superior and inferior friends originated in the Latin circles. "The language of friendship was better suited to describe relations between socially disproportionate individuals involved in exchange relationships"[61] since the word *amicus* does not carry the distinction created by the use of the term "patron-client."[62] Patronage in its crude form consisted of giving at various levels of friendship relations and at the same time receiving honor and praise.

Benefaction: The topic of benefaction is elaborately treated in Aristotle's Nicomachean Ethics.[63] The virtue of "magnificence" implies generous giving usually by the nobles to individuals and community.[64] Public benefaction is

---

[55] See a short analysis of the topic based on two clan based societies' practice in this regard in Joubert, *Paul as Benefactor*, 19–21.

[56] Joubert, 41.

[57] Seneca's work "On Benefits" is an ethical treatise about how men ought to conduct themselves in the giving and receiving of favors and services. See Peter Garnsey and Richard Saller, *The Roman Empire: Economy, Society and Culture* (Berkeley: University of California Press, 1987), 148.

[58] Joubert, *Paul as Benefactor*, 24.

[59] Clients sometimes accompanied the patron in their business tour; they were expected to applaud the patron's speech in court. See Garnsey and Saller, *The Roman Empire*, 151.

[60] Garnsey and Saller, 151.

[61] Joubert, *Paul as Benefactor*, 29.

[62] The scope of our study does not include a detailed study on this topic; therefore we limit it to the bare minimum. For more information on this see Joubert, *Paul as Benefactor*, 29–37; Garnsey and Saller, 152–59.

[63] Book Four first treats liberality followed by magnificence.

[64] Arist. *NE*. IV.2.1ff.

the greatest and most honored[65] which include giving in service of the gods (public building, sacrifices, giving banquets, building ships of war etc.). The practice of benefaction of a magnificent man upon his community or city is rightly called euergetism. Every act of benefaction (euergesia) is to be explained by the generosity of the one who bestows benefaction.[66] In the art of rhetoric, Aristotle states that true wealth consists in doing good; in monetary donations, giving various gifts, and supporting others for their sustenance.[67]

A concrete and noble way to demonstrate euergetism was to provide bread for the hungry especially at the time of food shortage. However, assistance to the poor was not a moral obligation for the rich. Whenever the emperors or benefactors distributed money or materials it was given to the whole group without taking into account the financial status of recipients.[68] The euergetes were more concerned about their own social status and honor. For this reason more than alleviating others' needs, benefactors "frequently indulged in the more popular and glamorous benefits such as games, monetary handouts, and festivals."[69] We have already mentioned how Barnabas and Paul act as benefactors for the famine stricken church at Jerusalem by coordinating a collection. Quite contrary to the Greco-Roman notion of benefaction, Paul and Barnabas, and later Paul personally offered a Christian coloring to the idea of benefaction by asking and pleading with the Gentile Christians to support the needy in Jerusalem without expecting a human reward, but a Divine reward. Miletus speech is unique as it stipulates giving to the poor a moral obligation.[70]

7.3.1.2. LXX Background

The LXX contain various Jewish practices of supporting the weak by concrete acts of giving. These are the practices associated with the celebrations of the Sabbatical and Jubilee Year and the practice of Tithe. The LXX tradition addresses the situation of injustice and poverty in the above triple form. Moreover, the LXX displays various prophetic speeches and utterances that encourage helping or giving to the poor in addition to numerous wisdom sayings mostly found in the Wisdom Books.

---

[65] Arist. *NE*. IV.2.15.

[66] See this in Paul Veyne, *Bread and Circuses: Historical Sociology and Political Pluralism* (London: Penguin, 1990), 103–104. See the topic "euergetism" in Joubert, *Paul as Benefactor*, 51–58.

[67] Arist. *Rh*. 1361a especially 28–43.

[68] Joubert, *Paul as Benefactor*, 57.

[69] Joubert, 57.

[70] We will return to this point again at least a couple of times.

7.3.1.2.1. Torah Stipulations

Torah stipulations concerning giving derive from covenantal obligations articulated for the people of Israel because in a covenantal relationship fidelity to the covenant is paramount.[71] The people are to be loyal to their call, to the land, and to one another as a community which necessitated legislating various norms against injustice and oppression. At the same time, they were constantly stimulated to give generously to the poor and needy which itself ought to be an expression of their covenantal tie with God. "I am the Lord" (Lev 19:18) is the most important element in that covenant, and "you shall love your neighbor as yourself" is the second important. The following are some of the concrete occasions / ways of showing charity to the neighbor (one in need).

Sabbatical Year: The institution of the Sabbatical Year was in order that the land may rest and poor of the people may eat (Ex 23:10–11). In the Book of Leviticus (Lev 25:1–7) we may find an amplification of Ex 23:10–11. In the Sabbatical Year there were also the practices of release of debts (Deut 15:1–3) and the release of slaves (Ex 21:1–6). The purpose of the Sabbatical Year was to support the weak, i.e., the poor and slaves.[72]

Jubilee Year: The Jubilee Year came at the end of the cycle of 7 Sabbatical years. Leviticus specifies it as the 50th year (Lev 25:8–10). In the Jubilee Year those enslaved for debt were liberated, land of those families who were forced to sell it due to economic burden was restored to the owner.[73] Even though the primary theological basis for the Jubilee Year rests on the concept of land and the status of the Israelites (Lev 25), its central motive is redemption, both economic and social, whereby it involves supporting the weak. Redemption, after all, in Israelite context, was necessary for slaves and the poor. Thus, the Jubilee Year cannot be seen detached from carrying solid ethical accents. Viewing sociologically and religiously Sabbatical and Jubilee Years of the Israelites together, we can say that "not only in principle but also in reality their economic system was geared to the needs of the lowest in society, with the immediate goal of giving maximum assistance to the poor and the ultimate ideal that there should be no poor (Deut 15)."[74]

---

[71] See also Luke T. Johnson, *Sharing Possessions: Mandate and Symbol of Faith* (Philadelphia, PA: Fortress Press, 1981), 88.

[72] Ideas for this paragraph see Christopher J. H. Wright, "Sabbatical Year," *ABD* 5:857. Other than the Sabbatical Year, there was the annual right of gleaning in the fields, orchards etc. (Lev 19:9–10; Deut 24:19–22). It was intended to support the weak: aliens, widows, and orphans.

[73] Ideas for this paragraph are from Christopher J. H. Wright, "Jubilee, Year of," *ABD* 3:1025.

[74] Wright, "Sabbatical Year," 860.

One of the poignant passages that explicates the importance of supporting the weak is Deut 15:7–10. I will quote the text as it is, and it will help us to appreciate the Israelite system of aiding the weak.

> If there is among you anyone in need, a member of your community in any of your towns within the land that the Lord your God is giving you, do not be hard-hearted or tight-fisted toward your needy neighbor. You should rather open your hand, willingly lending enough to meet the need, whatever it may be. Be careful that you do not entertain a mean thought, thinking, "The seventh year, the year of remission, is near," and therefore view your needy neighbor with hostility and give nothing; your neighbor might cry to the Lord against you, and you would incur guilt. Give liberally and be ungrudging when you do so, for on this account the Lord your God will bless you in all your work and in all that you undertake. Since there will never cease to be some in need on the earth, I therefore command you, "Open your hand to the poor and needy neighbor in your land."

Tithe: Another institution that was established to help the poor was the Tithe.[75] Tithe is the religious act of giving a tenth for the support of a religious purpose.[76] A religious purpose then, naturally include the support of the priests and Levites who did not own land to cultivate. Deuteronomy 26 gives the impression that Tithe was enjoyed by the priests, Levites, and even worshipping family. Tithe has to be left in the local settlement, for the benefit of the Levites, who has no land of their own, for the strangers, the fatherless, and the widows (Deut 26:12).[77] Tithe for the most Biblical writers was giving one tenth to God. However, they also believed that by giving it one honors God, because giving to God equals giving to the poor and needy. We may conclude that in the practice of Tithe the Israelites pledged themselves for the care of the poor.

Other Torah Concerns: The Torah develops a sense of duty. An important Torah word, in this connection, is חֶסֶד since it implies beneficent action in the context of an enduring commitment between two parties,

[75] References to tithing in the Bible are relatively few, scattered, and diverse. It is mentioned in Gen 14 & 28; Lev 27; Num 18; Deut 12, 14, 26; Am 4; 2 Chr 31; Neh 10, 12, 13; and Mal 3.

[76] J. Christian Wilson, "Tithe," *ABD* 6:579.

[77] In other Biblical texts that deal with tithes, no mention is made about the proceeds of tithe going to the strangers, orphan, and widows. Obviously deuteronomic text indicates a development of the practice in Israel.

rendering assistance to one who is unable to help himself or herself.[78] The later prophetic saying "I desire steadfast love than sacrifice" (Hos 6:6) in fact represents what the Torah actually wanted to communicate through its various laws and charity institutions.

The destitute[79] occupied a significant role within Israel's ethos. This group became the focal point of Israel's almsgiving and care. "Giving" to the poor was a religious duty which often was seen as having reciprocity, a concept that particularly gained attention in the wisdom circles[80] and was carried forward in the Lucan and Pauline writings.

7.3.1.2.2. Prophetic Exhortations

Israelite Prophets had a unique role in raising their voice in favor of the weak. They took up the theme of supporting the poor from where the Torah had left off. Prophetic injunction concerning the need to support the poor is strong (Isa 1:17; Jer 7:6; 22:3, 16; Zach 7:10; Neh 8:10[81]) but their condemnation against all injustices done to and oppression of the poor is even stronger (1sa 3:15; 10:2; 32:7; 58:5–7; Jer 22:13; Ezek 16:49; 18:12; 22:29; Am 2:7; 4:1; 6:1, 4; 8:4–6; Mic 2:1–2). These Prophets also saw a breach of the covenant in oppression of the poor and needy (Isa 3:5; 5:7–10; 30:12; Jer 6:12–13; 8:10; Am 2:6–8; Hos 12:7–9; Mic 3:1–3 etc.). Under this title we could also include all the exhortation to charity made by Tobit and Esther. In a previous chapter we have already discussed about the almsgiving motif and its importance in the Book of Tobit. For Tobit true spirituality consists of charitable work and giving. The story of Tobit is a telling example of this. Since we have already dealt with the charity concerns of Tobit in chapter one, a word about Esther 9:22 would suffice here. The text "makes sending of gifts to the poor as a rule for the festival of Purim."[82] No celebration is truly possible without having to do something for the poor and needy.

7.3.1.2.3. Wisdom Books

Giving to the poor is a recurrent theme in the Wisdom Books. They speak of generosity and caring (Job 20:10; 31:16; Ps 9:18; 22:26; 41:1 [this verse expresses more or less the idea of Acts 20:35b using a μακάριος]; 72:4; 113:7). There are texts that contain explicit charity references such as Ps

[78] James K. Bruckner, "Ethics," in *DOTP*, David W. Baker, ed. (Downers Grove: InterVarsity Press, 2002), 228.

[79] Economically poor, widows, orphans, strangers were the so-called poor group (*anawim*) of Yahweh.

[80] Joubert, *Paul as Benefactor*, 96.

[81] *Rosh Hashana* was given a new meaning by Nehemiah here. It is not a day to weep and mourn, rather a day to rejoice and send food for those who do not have it.

[82] Raphael Posner, "Charity," *EJ* 4:569.

112:9; 132:15; 145:15, 16; Prov 14:21; 14:31; 19:17; 21:13; 21:26; 22:9; 28:27; 31:9, 20; Sir 3:30; 4:4; 7:10, 32 [this verse also contain the idea of the maxim found in Acts 20:35]; 12:4-5; 17:22; 29:8, 12; 29:9 [this text resembles Acts 20:35 because Paul's call to aid the weak finds its support in the words of our Lord; similarly Sirach exhorts the readers to support the needy for commandment sake]; 35:2–4; 40:17, 24. A person who has more is to share with the have-nots (Prov 3:27–28; 25:21–22; 28:27; 29:7). Supporting the poor and needy is important to these books. At the same time they condemn injustice and oppression of the poor and needy (Job 24:4, 9, Ps 10:9; 37:14; Prov 17:5; 22:22; Sir 4:1; 34:25). Job 22:5–9; 29:12–13 etc. speak of a reward for charity. Luke may have been more influenced and indebted to the Wisdom Tradition of Israel in matters of giving ethics.

7.3.2. ἀντιλαμβάνεσθαι τῶν ἀσθενούντων and the Giving Motif in the Lucan Writings

The phrase ἀντιλαμβάνεσθαι τῶν ἀσθενούντων does not appear anywhere else in the entire Luke or Paul or in the NT. However, the idea of supporting the weak is a recurrent theme in their writings for which they use other terms and vocabularies. In the LXX it is evident that any charity giving was aimed at the support of the weak. Similarly there are ample evidences indicating the recipients of charity giving as the poor and needy. Therefore, under this title, we shall only attempt to identify the sayings, anecdotes, parables, and exhortations that pertain to the theme of "giving" and make some observation about them. Such an approach to this topic is required since supporting the weak in 20:35 refers to charity giving. We begin with Luke who encountered the Gentile Christian world and who offered norms to address the weakness (poverty, sickness, and oppression) of the world he faced.

7.3.2.1. Giving Motif in the Lucan Writings

In the NT, in general, there is no mention of Tithe, observation of Sabbath or Jubilee Year, but there are powerful exhortations to give charity in order to help the poor and the needy. Here we shall first examine instances from the Gospel of Luke followed by the instances from Acts.

7.3.2.1.1. Giving Motif in the Gospel of Luke

7.3.2.1.1.1. In Chapters 1–9

The Gospel of Luke opens by striking the chord of service (Lk 1:8), which requests generous giving of time and energy. Mary's visit to her cousin Elizabeth (Lk 1:39–45) is another example of generous giving of time, money, and energy. Mary's song of praise (Lk 1:46–55) extols the God who generously gives by filling the hungry with good things (v. 53). In his preaching, John the Baptist asks the ordinary people to share their food and clothes with those who do not have (Lk 3:11). As the soldiers ask what they should do he replies them to be content with the wages they get (Lk 3:14); to the tax collectors he asks that they be content with what is due to them and not to extort money (Lk 3:13).

The "Nazareth Manifesto" (Lk 4:18–19) is a "programmatic text" that graphically portrays the mission of Jesus to the weak. The text read from Isaiah picks up the language of the Torah especially that of Jubilee release.[83] Vocabularies such as "poor," "captives," "blind," and "oppressed" evoke the aspect of weakness associated with such people. The text clearly points to the role of Jesus as one anointed by God for salvation of the weak. Jesus came to "give" integral salvation, if not wealth and fortune.

God supports the poor and weak; this has been sharply presented in the Lucan version of the beatitudes (Lk 6:20–23). Just as God gives and shows mercy, the believers are to give and show mercy. 'Showing mercy' and 'giving' are often synonymous terms in the Bible. Luke 6:29b–30 invites the believer to give to everyone and do good to others, making the beneficiaries of Christian giving as "everyone." The giving of a Christian ought to be liberal (Lk 6:38). This verse is one of the highpoints of the Lucan ethics of giving. Ethics of giving begin to accelerate from here on in the Lucan writings. This verse is placed within the discussion of judging others and that itself may call for a different interpretation of the verse other than material generosity. Luke connects the verse with the rest of the passage and makes an obvious point regarding forgiveness. Forgiveness entails generosity of the heart; without the generosity of the heart any talk on forgiveness remains only a lip-service and will not achieve the desired results. This point has been confirmed by the preceding section on love of enemies and the believers mentality towards their enemies (Lk 6:27–36).

Greed and its effects have been vividly presented in the Lucan writings (see ch. 5) but so are giving and its benefits. Luke 6:38 begins and ends with 'giving and getting' forming a thematic chiasm. One is to give and its benefit will be that the giver will get back in return. Openhanded generosity is the point of the verse here. Thus, this verse is closely linked to Acts 20:35. He who extends liberality does so with the expectation that he will be the recipient of God's unfathomable generosity (also in Lk 18:29–30). Moreover Lk 6:38 demarcates the theme of giving in a unique way as the nature of giving is established here. One is invited to give a good measure, pressed down, shaken together and running over. The instruction to generous giving here is followed by various concrete examples of liberal giving climaxing in the example of the Poor Widow (21:1–4).

---

[83] John Nolland, *Luke 1:1–9:20*, WBC 35a (Dallas: Word Books, 1993), 197.

Along with the Twelve there were also some women who were disciples of Jesus and they provided for the entire group out of their resources (Lk 8:1-3). What is impressive about the account is that the women were generously supporting Jesus and the apostles.

7.3.2.1.1.2. In the "Central Section"

Parable of the Good Samaritan: Generous giving is the antidote against greed. How can one give generously? And what are the concrete ways to exhibit generous giving? The parable of the Good Samaritan sheds light in answering these questions. Although the story was told to explain "who is my neighbor," the parable at the same time contains other motifs that are dear to Luke, for example, the theme of generous giving. To be a good neighbor involves caring and being generous. Not only did the Samaritan take care of the man who fell among the robbers by treating and taking him to an inn but also spent his resources on the injured man. Thus the parable, other than brilliantly answering the question "who is my neighbor," also brings out the motif of caring and the right use of wealth. "Showing mercy"[84] for Luke then involves caring and generous giving.

Martha and Mary: Martha and Mary share their home and resources on Jesus and his disciples (10:38–42). The incident may be a reflection of the first century situation, where showing hospitality to travelling missionaries was required. At the same time it also teaches the dual duties of the friends of Jesus—loving service and worship.

Luke 11:41: The topic of greed and its remedy continues in the next chapter. The Pharisees get a sharp condemnation from Jesus for being full of greed and wickedness (11:39) and the cure for their greed is to give alms so that everything will be clean for the greedy Pharisees who are evidently unclean within. A classic expression of Jewish piety is almsgiving and it is clearly important for Luke. While Luke is concerned about almsgiving, in reality, he is also warning them about the destructive potential of wealth.[85] Justice and the love of God (11:42), for Luke, are intimately linked to charity as voiced previously by the Torah and Prophets.

Parable of the Rich Fool: While the greed of the rich fool (12:16–21) is graphically narrated, this negative example also functions for the purpose of positive edification. One should not be greedy, but should think about God and others as well. The conclusion of the parable of the Rich Fool makes it clear that the parable was told to create a sense of otherness. Certainly the evil of greed is addressed in the parable, but it proposes a remedy as well: instead of storing up treasures for oneself, one should be rich toward God,

---

[84] The Hebrew word חֶסֶד is equivalent to the Greek ἔλεος used in Lk 10:37.

[85] Nolland, *Luke 9:21–18:34*, 664.

that is, one should store up treasures in heaven through generous giving to the needy. "The point could be generalized to all acts of compassion."[86] Taking the parable within the broad context of the "central section" and particularly of chapter 12, stewardship of wealth may be seen as paramount. For Luke stewardship of wealth mainly involves in almsgiving.

Luke 14:13–14: This passage is thematically parallel to Acts 20:35 because both speak of giving to the weak and the eschatological reception of reward. The inability of the weak to invite you in return is the reason for Jesus to exhort the audience to invite precisely such people for a banquet. Hospitality shown towards others with the view of receiving the same in return has no merit. When it is shown without expecting anything in return, it becomes generosity. The thought here invites comparison with various other themes, but especially with that of almsgiving.[87]

Luke 14:28–32: Jesus provides two examples of prudence in his exhortation on the cost of discipleship (14:28–30 and 31–32). These examples are provided so that the disciples of Jesus may weigh and judge well the pros and cons of leaving everything for the sake of Christ. Jesus' call to give up 'all' is an invitation to give to charity which is the qualification for discipleship (Lk 18:22). One must choose between God and wealth / mammon. A disciple must realize that it is better to "give" and become a disciple of the all-powerful God rather than "not give" and become a slave of money. Although the passage primarily speaks about discipleship, it also speaks about the "giving up" of possessions. Any giving up of possessions is not without some benefit to the other, and in Luke's conception, giving up of possessions will benefit the weak.

Parable of the Unjust Steward: The parable (Lk 16:1–13) was told to inculcate prudence, the prudence a disciple should have in dealing with money and the kingdom of God. At the outset of the parable, the steward is squandering his master's property, and comes across as dishonest. Even when his master finds out his dishonest behavior, he continues his dishonesty by falsifying accounts and winning clients for himself. But, this negative image suddenly becomes a positive one as the listeners are advised to learn from the astuteness of the dishonest steward. The parable might have been told to inculcate prudence, but with the material added to the parable (vv. 8b–13), it takes on a "wise use of wealth" application, since the main concern of vv. 8b–13 is instructions concerning the use of wealth. Verse 9, one of the parable's applications is clear: to make friends with money, i.e., do charity to the poor and they will become mediators for you to get to heaven. This verse is significant here because it explicitly states the invitation to "make friends

---

[86] Nolland, 688.

[87] Other thoughts are reciprocity ethic and generosity of God.

for yourselves by means of dishonest wealth" and in the Lucan context it is through almsgiving.[88]

Parable of the Rich Man and Lazarus: In the parable, the rich man could not enter heaven, not because he failed to sell all that he had, as was presented elsewhere (Lk 14:33; 18:22) but because he failed to care for the poor. He ignored to share his material blessings with the needy. Wealth *per se* is not evil or bad, but one's disposition to it makes it either good or evil. The rich man could have been a generous benefactor, but his focus was on enjoying life in extravagance. He had been blessed generously by God and in return he should have also generously helped the weak. He had been instructed through the Law and the Prophets (Lk 16:29) what his priorities were and how he ought to pay heed to them. Helping the poor and needy is never a secondary concern for the Law and Prophets. The Gospel affirms the Law and Prophets as still valid and makes mercy and genuine love radical qualities for the kingdom of God.[89] Lazarus' "longing to be fed"[90] is similar to the prodigal son's longing for food. Lazarus's longing for food was genuine as it might have been caused by social, religious, and economic factors; whereas the prodigal son's longing for food was caused by his own fault and yet he is later fed by his father. Jesus reminds the listeners of the importance of giving to the needy without analysing too much about the causes of poverty.

Rich Ruler: Another explicit mention concerning the topic of 'giving' is found in the story of the "Rich Ruler" (Lk 18:18–25) especially if we couple the sequential episode of the blind man with this story. Even though the story here deals with discipleship and its challenges yet at another level it also unfolds the theme of giving. Nathan Eubank notes "Almsgiving—albeit in its most extreme form—is presented in the story of the rich man as the culmination or perfection of the commandments."[91] The reluctance of the rich man to follow Jesus (v. 23) has been compensated by the blind man (Lk 18:35–43) who followed Jesus (v. 43). How did the blind man follow Jesus? In order to appreciate the fervor of his following, we need to look into the parallel story in Mark (Mk 10:46–52) where the blind man is depicted as having a mantle, the only valuable possession he might have had, and when Jesus called him he ran to Him throwing off the mantle, indicating that the blind beggar was willing to 'let go' of even his only treasure. When the

[88] See the discussion of the theme in F. E. Williams, "Is Almsgiving the Point of the 'Unjust Steward'?" *JBL* 83 (1964), 293–97; Johnson, *Sharing Possessions*, 18.

[89] See also Nolland, *Luke 9:21–18:34*, 832–33.

[90] Fitzmyer, *The Gospel according to Luke,* vol. 2, 1131.

[91] N. Eubank, "Almsgiving is 'the Commandment': A Note on 1 Timothy 6:6–19," *NTS* 58.1 (2012), 147.

evangelist says that the blind man followed Jesus, it also means that the blind man fulfilled the requirement for discipleship, by giving up all that he had.

Zacchaeus Episode: Giving ethics in the Gospel of Luke reaches its penultimate climax in the story of Zacchaeus (Lk 19:1–10). Apparently, a rich man, who has swindled money from others, is the hero of the story here. Many Lucan motifs, other than almsgiving, may be verified in the story such as repentance and conversion, Jesus' association with sinners and outcasts, discipleship, salvation of the lost. One theme that is very evident and striking in the story is the theme of giving. Zacchaeus makes a resolution to give half of his possessions to the poor, and to give four-fold to them from whom he has defrauded. Zacchaeus gives the fruits of his labor to others, a fact revealed to us through his words "half of my possessions, Lord, I will give to the poor." He gives, much more than he ought,[92] to those who were victims of his fraudulent tax-collection. In the story, there is no mention of Zacchaeus selling all his materials, but he does charity, and makes reparation for the injury done through his past actions. Zacchaeus is the positive counterpart of the rich young man who could not make it to eternal life, on the other hand Zacchaeus, another rich man, is assured of salvation because of his repentant and generous action. Giving is always accompanied by receiving and here in the story Zacchaeus receives salvation, the ultimate goal as indicated by Jesus in the Gospels. Concerning the reception of the final reward, we have already commented enough in the previous section of this chapter. These observations indicate that the story strikes many thematic parallels with Acts 20:32–35, such as themes of avoidance of greed, giving, and blessedness of giving.

Parable of the Ten Minas: Through the parable (Lk 19:11–27) the disciples are exhorted to use wealth properly. They have to faithfully trade with their minas so that they may receive more wealth to trade with and make further use of. Though the parable can be looked at from different angles, we focus only on the giving side of it. In trade, there is giving and receiving. But if one is not willing to trade, he cannot be part of the giving-receiving cycle. Jesus says: "To those who have, more will be given." Why does this happen? Because quite often those who have are those who have worked hard and exercised proper stewardship over their wealth. Such disciples will always flourish and prosper. Seen this way proper use of wealth, especially by charitable giving, fetches more wealth. There is no gain in hoarding

---

[92] According to the Torah, stolen goods were to be restored but how the restitution is to be done differs from object to object and period to period (see Ex 22:1, 4; Lev 6:25; 2 Sam 12:6). In some cases four-fold restitution was a Roman practice to which Luke may be referring. See Nolland, *Luke 18:35–24:53*, 906.

possessions one has; possessions, generously given by God, should be used for the service of the poor and needy which in turn makes one prosper.

7.3.2.1.1.3. Jesus Ministry in Jerusalem

Question about Tax Payment (Lk 20:20–26): Here the aspect of giving gets a civil dimension. Charity giving may be voluntary and liberal, but tax paying is not. Disciples of Jesus, as citizens of a country, should give tax to the civil authorities for the good functioning of the state. In any case, payment of tax here does not even slightly allude to any form of almsgiving or charitable contribution to the state, but at the same time, citizen's tax may sometimes function as a help for the poor and needy. While the disciples of Jesus are urged to generously give, they are obliged to give tax to the state.

Widow's Offering: Gospel of Luke may suggest three climaxes concerning giving ethics. The first is 6:38, a saying of Jesus, during His ministry in Galilee; the second is the story of Zacchaeus (19:1–10) which takes place on His way to Jerusalem; and the third is the incident of the widow's offering (Lk 21:1–4) that happened in Jerusalem. All these three climaxes may have been provided to intensify the giving ethics of Lucan Jesus.

All are invited to generous giving. It does not matter whether one is rich or poor, man or woman, faithful or pagan, giving is always needed and it benefits the weak. The story of the widow's offering is a powerful example of generous giving with love and devotion. Love doesn't calculate—it spends lavishly! Jesus drove this point home to his disciples while sitting in the temple and observing people offering their tithes. Jesus praised a poor widow who gave the smallest of coins in contrast with the rich who gave greater sums. How can someone in poverty give more than someone who has ample means? Jesus' answer is very simple—love is more precious than gold!

Through this story Luke wants to communicate that giving is not reserved only to the rich, but it can be performed by anyone who has the love of God and neighbor. Lucan ethics of giving sketched in the first volume literally gains momentum in 6:38, as we have already noted, and it reaches its climax in the story of the widow's offering. Everyone can and must give for the support of the weak. True love of God and neighbor is the driving force for generous giving. Both Lk 6:38 and 21:1–4 speak about lavish giving, and this was necessary for the Lucan church. Since the poor are always with us (cf. Mt 26:11; Mk 14:7; Jn 12:8) the invitation to generous giving is a demand and obligation that stands to this day.

7.3.2.1.2. Motif of Giving in Acts

The Early Christians: The Book of Acts continues the thematic rhythm of Luke and as expected the theme of "giving" is a main concern also for Acts. The primitive church is presented as a group of people that gives for the common good. As we see in Acts 2:44–45; 4:32–35, the disciples in the Jerusalem church sell property and they keep everything in common. These examples must be a response to the primitive church's responsibility to support everyone and give to everyone according to the need of each.[93]

Barnabas: He is introduced in the narrative as one who has sold his field to meet the needs of the church (4:36–37). There was a man called Joseph and the apostles named him Barnabas, which means "son of encouragement." Most probably they did so because of his behavior; for he was willing to give away his possessions for the common good. Barnabas' willingness to sell his property and give the proceeds to the apostles is especially mentioned in the narrative with a deliberative function, namely that by this action he 'encouraged' others also to give, for which he himself first becomes a model.

Tabitha: She is described as a woman of charity (9:36–39). We are not sure what good works she did or how she performed acts of charity. It may be assumed that she was honestly practicing the divine injunctions to care for the needy. Her death most probably created a great vacuum in the community.[94] Peter fills that vacuum by raising her up. The miracle performed on her may be also seen as a reward for her good works and charity, as the theme of retribution is very strong in Luke-Acts.

Cornelius: He also comes across as a man of charity (10:1–2). Though a Gentile, he was God-fearing and observed many of the Jewish practices like Sabbath, dietary laws, synagogue service etc. Above all he was known for his loving concern for the poor and for making available provisions for them.[95] Later in the narrative we are told that he is reckoned as righteous by his almsgiving (10:31).

Barnabas and Paul: They take the role of representatives in delivering relief to the famine hit people (11:27–30). Later Paul is presented in the Miletus speech as a perfect model of work and generosity.[96]

---

[93] Robert Tannehill notes that Jesus command to "sell" and "distribute" the proceeds to the poor (Lk 18:22) is being actualized in the early Jerusalem church by their selling of goods and distributing the proceeds to those in need.

[94] Simon J. Kistemaker, *Exposition of the Acts of the Apostles* (Grand Rapids: Baker Book House, 1990), 360.

[95] Kistemaker, *Acts of the Apostles*, 371.

[96] Since in the previous chapter this topic has already been adequately covered, we will not say anything more on it.

Lydia: She is generous as a hostess (16:14–15, 40). In the account itself there is nothing to suggest that she was doing good works or charity, but her "God-fearfulness" and hospitability indicate something unique in her character – generosity.

Acts 24:17: In his defense speech before Felix, Paul is explicit about his intention to come to Jerusalem: to bring alms to my nation and offer sacrifice (24:17). Something very interesting to note here is that even within a defense speech, Luke inserts a reference to the collection as alms. Much differently from Paul's own view on the collection, the purpose of it is plainly given here and for Luke Paul comes to Jerusalem with "alms."

Malta Event: Faced by a shipwreck, the travelers took refuge in an island called Malta and the people there showed great kindness towards the refugees (Acts 28:1–2). In ancient times survivors of shipwrecks who managed to reach unknown shores faced either death or they were made slaves,[97] but in Malta things were different. The people there showed φιλανθρωπία which would include providing accommodation facility and also catering to the needs of 276 people (Acts 27:37) for three months (Acts 28:11). Luke towards the end of his literary work picks up again and for the last time the theme of φιλανθρωπία, which naturally would involve generous giving and genuine care. Such an attempt from Luke seems to be deliberate. It is meant to show how important the theme was for him.

All these instances in Acts are examples of giving and generosity. These examples do not warrant the complete renunciation of wealth from the disciples, but they create a positive image of right attitude towards wealth.

7.4. Ethics of Giving in the Pauline Writings

This topic is vast; however, without a short presentation of it here our thesis would remain incomplete. Miletus speech, although found in Acts and composed by Luke, is a speech most probably delivered by the historical Paul and for which reason it can provide a glimpse into some aspects of his theology and ethics. The whole speech contains various theological and ethical elements; the prominent one being community ethics. For Paul the essence of community ethics lies in κοινωνία and διακονία. Lucan Paul does not use these terms in the Miletus speech (except the word διακονία which he has used once) but the whole speech is oriented toward and aimed at establishing the importance of κοινωνία and διακονία in Christian communities. "Giving" is intrinsic to κοινωνία and διακονία, a fact established by Lucan Paul especially in the latter part of the speech. What Lucan Paul highlights in the speech is compatible and coherent with Paul's own information about the same. It will not be possible here to examine each and every instance of

[97] Kistemaker, 947.

giving ethics in the Pauline writings, albeit the more important ones will be examined.

According to Paul there is a "social and theological" reason to give. These reasons have been mainly found in 2 Cor 8–9. In the social realm, Paul expects some kind of equality and communitarianism. Paul's intentions seem to have extended beyond the mere alleviation of poverty by means of charitable giving. He appears to have aimed at reforming the structural inequalities apparent in the early church (1 Cor 11:17–22) by fostering socio-economic ἰσότης between Jews and Gentiles by establishing a global, socially and ethnically inclusive κοινωνία among them.[98] Moreover Paul sees God as the source of all created and non-created things. He is bountiful and His giving is entirely due to his own generosity. Therefore, those who have been blessed by God are obliged to give to the less privileged and serve them in their need.

The clearest and thought through example of giving is none else than Paul's tireless and determined efforts for the Jerusalem collection. Paul's collection for the Jerusalem church is a concrete example of communion, service, and exertion in order to strike some kind of balance between the haves and the have-nots through the act of giving. In the previous chapter (see 7.5) the matter has been discussed in detail and therefore we skip all the references in Paul's letters related to collection as an act of giving and we will only examine other clear instances related to the ethics of giving.

Romans 12:7–8, 13: The first specimen we will examine is Rom 12:7–8. Paul exhorts the Romans to serve and give generously. Service in v. 7 can carry many meanings including that of giving in charity. Roman text most probably alludes to the participation of the Jerusalem collection since Paul himself has defined it as a service (see 2 Cor 9:12). "The ἐν τῇ διακονίᾳ in this verse is not simply tautologous, but underlines the basic character of a charism for Paul as grace (χάρις) coming to visible expression (χάρισμα),"[99] and so making a link between grace and giving as in the case with Acts 20:32–35. ὁ μεταδιδούς ἐν ἁπλότητι in v. 8 carries the sense that the one who gives / shares should be generous, that the giver should show liberality. In other words, let there be no double-mindedness in giving. Wholehearted giving is the point here.

Closely related to the above is Rom 12:13 where Paul asks the Romans to contribute a share in the needs of the saints and to be hospitable. Paul certainly has in mind the Jerusalem collection[100] as he exhorts them to provide a share for the needs of the saints. Besides, as already noted, genuine

[98] See these ideas in Ogereau, "Jerusalem Collection," 377.

[99] James D. G. Dunn, *Romans 9–16*, WBC 38b (Dallas: Word Books, 1988), 729.

[100] Same view of Dunn, *Romans 9–16*, 743.

hospitality involve generous giving and sharing. It should be extended to the strangers as well and not reserved just to the neighbors or friends.[101] It is a requirement for bishops (1 Tim 3:2; Tit 1:8), and the Miletus speech may also reflect the leader's need to show hospitality to the needy since the speech is primarily addressed to the πρεσβύτεροι.

2 Corinthians 9:6–11: Although the text falls within the ambit of the discussion of Jerusalem collection, 2 Cor 9:6–11 invites discussion because these verses offer varied theological outlook on giving. The text reflects an agrarian background. Givers should be generous. Verse 6 echoes positively Prov 11:25 and negatively Prov 22:8. One who sows sparingly is a metaphor for one who gives niggardly. Second, Cor 9:6 echoes Lk 6:38 because both have in common the aspects of giving and receiving. As long as one is unwilling to let go one's money that person will run into sadness and loss of joy (Deut 15:10). An aphorism used from Prov 22:8 was aimed at presenting the thesis convincingly. Moreover, such an idea clearly reflects the LXX thought (Sir 4:10, 14; 13:26; 26:4; 35:7). Besides, it is God who gives to each blessings and wealth so that one can in return be generous. Paul is not only speaking about material prosperity *per se* but also about the abundant grace they have received.[102] As receivers of both grace and material wealth, the Corinthians must come to the aid of the poor. They have to open their hearts[103] in giving. Their giving should be shaped and propelled by the grace of God. Those who give liberally will receive liberally; only a spiritual person can see this theological dimension of giving.

Galatians 2:10: Another important text that can educate and enlighten us on this theme is Gal 2:10 in which Paul indicates a decision of the Jerusalem Council (Acts 15) that they (Paul and companions) should "remember the poor," a decision unrecorded in Acts. It is quite puzzling how Luke could have missed out on this important decision of the council which could have provided the cutting edge for Lucan social ethics.[104] Although its mention is lacking in Acts 15, similar concern appears

---

[101] Robert Haldane, *Exposition of the Epistle to the Romans* (Escondido, CA: Electronic Edition by the Ephesians Four Group, 1999), 577.

[102] Also Ralph P. Martin, *2 Corinthians*, WBC 40 (Dallas: Word Books, 1986), 292.

[103] Earlier Paul might be alluding to this when he said: "Our heart is wide open to you" (2 Cor 6:11) and "Open wide (your hearts) to us also" (2 Cor 6:13; similarly 7:2) can be seen as closely related to the idea.

[104] Such omission is unusual for Luke. See how in the account of the healing of a centurion's servant (Lk 7:1–10) Luke omits certain elements found in Matthew (especially Mt 8:11–12) but adds a piece of discourse that is important for Luke (Lk 7:5). In Acts 15 the whole discussion concentrates on the mode of inclusion of Gentiles into the Christian community and the author is least interested in any other issues of the early church, a reason most probably for the exclusion of Galatian detail in Acts 15.

analogously and very powerfully in another context, in the Miletus speech, which allows us to think that Luke might have reserved the mention of it until here or compensated for the accidental omission of it in Acts 15. Anyhow, Paul's mention of it in Galatians allows us to establish the social / communitarian concern of Paul that is similar to Luke.

We assume that at the Jerusalem Council, the Christians at Jerusalem were acknowledged as "the poor" and a collection was agreed upon for the Jerusalem church. The Antiocheans were the first to acknowledge this fact and for that reason gave their approval to the agreement. Later most of the Gentile Christians also acknowledged the need to support the mother church which enhanced the interconnectedness and the feeling of solidarity between different groups.[105] Paul's usage "πτωχῶν ἵνα μνημονεύωμεν"[106] in the verse has an ethical coloring. The verb 'remember' then draws our attention to the apostolic preference for the poor in general and not a preference for the Jerusalem poor. It would also seem that the word does not carry the meaning of helping them materially. It is a call to remember the poor, but caring for them materially is not really substantiated by the verb μνημονεύω here. Nonetheless, it must be affirmed that the phrase "we remember the poor" is primarily an invitation to cater to the materially poor. The Galatian text may allude to the collection but it does not refer only to the collection, but to the apostolic preference for the poor in general.[107]

Having said this, it is also possible to establish that Paul's eagerness to remember the poor mostly consisted in supporting the poor in Jerusalem and other churches. It is not a one-time job or enterprise, but an ongoing activity as Richard Longenecker rightly observes in his commentary on Galatians.[108] According to him remembering is an inner attitude of recognition, gratefulness, and financial aid. To remember the poor in Galatians therefore refers primarily to economic or material assistance although it does not exclude "moral assistance." From the Miletus speech it is clear that the act of remembering also included supporting his companions who were not materially rich.

Galatians 5:6: Two passages that make allusion to giving are Gal 5:6, and 1 Thess 5:14. One thing particularly notable in Gal 5:6 is that Paul emphasizes the ethical dynamics inherent in a faith life.[109] Discussions on faith at least in Galatians and Romans suggest that it is a passive reality,

---

[105] For these ideas see Georgi, *Remembering the Poor*, 39.

[106] For a detailed study of this phrase in Gal 2:10 see Longenecker, *Remember the Poor*, especially pp. 108–219.

[107] See Georgi, *Remembering the Poor*, 40.

[108] See Richard N. Longenecker, *Galatians*, WBC 41 (Dallas: Word Books, 1990), 60.

[109] Longenecker, *Galatians*, 229.

something purely worked by God. All the same, Paul does not in any way deny the human efforts necessary for an authentic faith life, which may be termed as love. Love is not passive, it is active and manifested in various ways, especially in generous giving. Paul will not compromise on that, because love is the fulfillment of the Law and the Prophets. "Faith" and "love" cannot be viewed as "theory" and "practice" both are interrelated, having the features of receiving, enabling, and giving.[110]

Ephesians 4:28: A document that clearly points to some form of giving is Eph 4:28. Since the Ephesian text has been studied in a previous chapter, we refrain from making any further comments on it.

I Thessalonians 5:14: Like the previous text of Galatians even here nothing specific about giving is seen. But the appearance of ἀντέχομαι τῶν ἀσθενῶν in the verse is parallel to ἀντιλαμβάνομαι τῶν ἀσθενούντων of Acts 20:35. Paul uses a different verb, ἀντέχομαι, but having the same sense of Lucan Paul's ἀντιλαμβάνομαι. By employing these verbs, both Paul and Luke want that the community and the leaders should support the weak, those weak in faith, morals, and money. A comparison between Paul's letters and Lucan writings concerning various examples of support to the weak, sharing, caring etc. point to the fact that both Luke and Paul wanted Christian communities to be little welfare states practicing mutual aid among its members in all respects.[111] A special responsibility is placed on the shoulders of the leaders of the church, but all can contribute generously to this end. Assistance to the weak is the point here and this naturally involves generous giving of one's resources.

7.5. From Ethical Concern to Moral Obligation

To conclude this chapter and the second part of the thesis we shall note few important observations gathered from chapters 4–8. It is clear from the arguments of these chapters that ethics is primary there. But in the last verse (v. 35) it may be observed that from ethical concerns the speech turns into moral precepts. Thus, work at a trade (or some kind of work), supporting the weak, and charity are moral obligations of leaders and Christians.

Both ethics and morals deal with "good" or "bad" and "right" and "wrong" respectively in human conduct. Ethics refers to rules or principles of conduct usually provided by an external source. They are guiding principles which help the individual or group to decide what is good or

---

[110] For the ideas of the last part of this paragraph see Hans D. Betz, *Galatians: A Commentary on Paul's Letter to the Churches in Galatia*, Herm. (Philadelphia, PA: Fortress Press, 1979), 264.

[111] For this idea see Frederick F. Bruce, *1 and 2 Thessalonians*, WBC 45 (Dallas: Word Books, 1982), 126.

bad.[112] On the other hand, morals are concerned with principles of right and wrong.[113] The above distinction between ethics and morals allows us to establish the speech's transition from ethics to morality. Lucan Paul's use of the term δεῖ is key to establish this transition. We have already confirmed the role of δεῖ in v. 35 as ethical and even having a divine facet. Accordingly, supporting the weak constitutes a necessity in the moral realm and therefore any failure to do so will be considered as wrong. Thus, the Miletus speech towards its end decisively turns out to be deliberating moral obligations.

Lucan Paul here enjoins supporting the weak as an obligation. He encountered poverty and want in the Greco-Roman world as well as among Christians who were part of this larger world. Thus, he sees assisting the weak as a principal duty of Christians especially that of the leaders of the church. Lucan Paul will not compromise on any failure to help the poor and needy, because that is what precisely Jesus did and taught. For Lucan Paul assisting the poor and needy is characteristic of a good conduct; moreover, that is the right thing to do for such people. The best way to assist the weak is to "give" them a share of what one possesses. For Jesus himself said "It is more blessed to give than to receive."

Our research so far has proved that Luke and Paul agree on various points and themes such as grace, avoiding greed, importance of work, supporting the poor and needy, and charity. In fact, these are important theme characteristics of the Miletus speech and, therefore, the speech, it can be said, is composed by Luke after having recalled to mind historical Paul's speech. At the same time, it provides the author's own coloring to the speech with regard to its language, structure and themes. The manner of unfolding the speech indicates that Lucan Paul wanted the audience to consider it 'right' to work and support the weak. Reversely, it would be 'wrong' not to work and support the weak. Thus, Lucan Paul is moralizing the conclusion of the speech or culminates and ends it in a moral tone leaving the windows open for the future Christians to stretch out their heads to see the world with the eyes of moral vision which will favor the poor and needy.

---

[112] See "Morals vs Ethics," *Keydifferences.com*, accessed 8 February 2019, https://keydifferences.com/difference-between-morals-and-ethics.html.

[113] See also J. Anna, "Ethics and Morality," *Enc. of Ethics* 1:485–87.

Part 3

Theological Ethics, Ethical Concerns, and Prospects of Acts 20:32–35

Having closely analyzed the ethical emphases of the concluding part of the Miletus speech and having gathered up some important concerns of the whole speech, we now consider it appropriate to begin the next chapter outlining the purpose of the speech. Since we notice an interplay of theology and ethics in the whole speech, it is crucial to delineate these purposes at least for two reasons. (1) It will help us to discover and highlight to a greater extent certain theological and/or ethical accents (theological ethics) of the speech. This will be the topic of the following chapter. (2) It will also enable us to draw up some ethical concerns and prospects related to the pericope. This will be the subject of the final chapter of this thesis.

Chapter 8

Interplay of Theology and Ethics in the Miletus Speech

In this chapter each objective of the speech and its related theological underpinnings will be simultaneously assessed. We have not entered into a thorough study of the whole speech. However, the overall examination of the various motifs of the speech so far reveals that the speech could not have had a single purpose; rather Luke might have interwoven and communicated several motives in a single episode yet without losing focus on his prime concerns. Lucan Paul's social ethic and the ethic of imitation get upper hand in vv. 32–35. But the rest of the speech reveals that there have been other motives for its composition. In the following pages we shall look into five principal purposes of the speech that Luke might have had in mind at the time of the composition of the Miletus speech. They are randomly presented below without taking into consideration the order of importance, or appearance in the text, or information gathered comparing them with other Lucan or Pauline writings. Moreover, certain points presented under a particular heading may intersperse with other purpose(s) in the list and thus there may be some intentional overlapping in the presentation of these purposes.

8.1. The Purpose of the Miletus Speech

8.1.1. Transfer of Authority and Mission through Commissioning

First of all, within Luke's narrative, it is possible to demonstrate and justify transition of authority and mission in the church from Paul to the elders as a major purpose of the Miletus speech.[1] The speech reflects the character of a commissioning scene[2] in which Paul passes on his care for the Ephesian church to its elders. We will begin by analyzing the context, audience, and the style of the Miletus speech in order to explain this point adequately. The matrix Luke used to produce the Miletus speech seems to be the farewell speeches in the LXX and Jewish documents that depict commissioning scenes and / or transfer of power to successors in which instructions were given either to children[3] or to disciples. Jacob, Moses, Elijah, Samuel and Tobit bless and instruct children / disciples so that they follow the leader in his spirit and that they practice what has been instructed to them.[4]

Let us examine the immediate chronological context of the Miletus speech. Paul stayed in Ephesus for three years (Acts 20:31; cf. 19:10) and preached the word, first in the synagogue and when some stubbornly refused to believe him and spoke evil of him he left them and changed his platform of preaching to the lecture hall of Tyrannus (19:9). Let us assume that Paul was winning many souls at Ephesus and was laying hands on some alongside to be leaders of the church whom he later called to Miletus to address them (20:17). As Paul was travelling hastily to Jerusalem (20:16), winding up his other missionary activities in Greece, Macedonia, and Troas (20:1–12), he also foresaw the end of his life and therefore called the elders of Ephesus to Miletus and delivered a speech to them. The whole speech has the character of a "commissioning scene" where transfer of authority, giving of instructions, and the entrustment to God are usually made. Commissioning of successors or transfer of authority was usually done through a (farewell) speech and blessing of the audience towards the last days of the leader figure. We have already qualified the Miletus speech to fit this genre since it fulfills the requirements for being called a farewell speech.

No scholar of Luke-Acts would doubt the purpose of Miletus speech as involving some kind of transfer of power for missionary service. For example Robert W. Wall sees it as a 'succession speech.'[5] The purpose of this farewell speech, according to Thomas M. Budesheim, is to commission

---

[1] Kurz, "Luke 22:14–38," 265. Kurz notes here that transition of authority as the first application of Jewish historiography.

[2] In the LXX many commissioning scenes are recorded such as Moses' commissioning of Joshua (Deut 31:1–23); Samuel's commissioning of Saul (1 Sam 9:27–10:16); and Mattathias' commissioning of Judas and Simon (1 Macc 2:49–69).

[3] Children would include grand children or even great grandchildren.

[4] Here one may recall my comparison between Miletus speech and LXX speeches in the first chapter which disclosed Miletus speech's greater affinity to LXX farewell speeches than to Greco-Roman farewell speeches. However, the ethical and moral instructions given in the speech have clear affinity to the Greco-Roman counterparts.

[5] Wall, *The Acts of the Apostles,* 279–86.

Paul's successors for ministry.[6] It was customary, in ancient times, for a departing person to exhort his successors. Paul, as he bid farewell to the Ephesian elders, his successors in that city, confirmed their authority, as is clear from verse 32.[7] Verse 32 is mostly loaded with vocabularies[8] that suit a commissioning narrative and the preceding and succeeding verses are like defenses made and exhortations given that characterize a commissioning scene.

The audience that was summoned to listen to him was the πρεσβύτεροι / ἐπίσκοποι.[9] The speaker's entrusting the elders to God and the word of His grace is a wish and a prayer of blessing. Again the instruction to watch over the flock in vv. 28–31 is given to the elders, thus indicating that from now on it will be their duty to "watch over" them especially from false teaching or heresies.[10] The authority for "missionary service" is now completely given to the elders,[11] since Paul, as a leader and pastor, will no longer be physically present with them.[12] Miletus speech, towards the end of his third missionary journey, marks the end of a whole period in the life of the church, and for Luke the speech may serve as a vehicle for the transition of mission and authority from the second generation to the third.[13] Paul may function like a bridge between the second and third generations since he is presented as belonging to both. Luke presents Paul having contact with the first-generation apostles,

[6] See the article of T. L. Budesheim, "Paul's Abschiedsrede in the Acts of the Apostles," 9–30.

[7] Lambrecht, "Paul's Farewell Address," 309.

[8] One may not detect these vocabularies in the LXX commissioning scenes, but related vocabularies and overall presentation of the speech favor our thesis.

[9] In Acts 20:17 πρεσβύτεροι were summoned from Ephesus to Miletus but later Lucan Paul uses another word ἐπίσκοποι in v. 28 to identify the same group. The first use might be anachronistic (reflecting usage during the time when Luke wrote Acts) but the second term is what Paul uses precisely for the Ephesian elders. See this observation in Witherington, *Acts*, 611.

[10] Dibelius, "Speeches," 157; and Hänchen, *Acts of the Apostles*, 596–97 observe this heresy as Gnosticism. See also Watson, "Paul's Speech," 189.

[11] Even while Paul was with them there were elders and overseers who exercised some form of leadership in the church, but the *capo* was Paul himself.

[12] One is immediately redirected to the commissioning of the apostles just before the ascension of Jesus. Jesus gathers them, strengthens and blesses them, and gives them instructions (see Lk 24:36–53).

[13] Cf. Lambrecht, "Paul's Farewell Address," 333. For Lambrecht, the address is from Paul, of the first generation to the second, since it is possible to count Paul as one of the first generation apostles as he was a contemporary of Jesus and the Twelve and had close ties with the apostles after his conversion to Christ. It is best, however, to take Paul as belonging to the second generation and the transfer of authority to the third generation, represented by the Ephesian elders.

at the same time he is different from them. He is autonomous and his *modus operandi* is, at least in certain matters, different from that of the Twelve and the "acknowledged leaders." For Luke, although Paul has some link with the first-generation apostles, belongs to the second-generation Christians and Luke, the author of Acts, identifies himself with this group.

The authority transferred to πρεσβύτεροι / ἐπίσκοποι comes directly from the Holy Spirit and not from any human person. The speech categorically states the source of power for the ordained leaders of the church—it is from the Holy Spirit. Luke highly values the Spirit's guidance in church leadership (Acts 13:2, 4). Since the elders are ordained ministers, they possess authority and know the whole counsel of God (Acts 20:27). This leaves no room for false teachers and teaching in the church of God nor can the false teachers "claim secret Pauline teaching unknown to those in apostolic succession. There is a continuity of faith from Paul to his successors who possess the deposit of faith."[14] Moreover, the price for the church of God is the blood of His own Son (v. 28) and therefore it is supremely important that the precious church of God "believes, hopes, and lives" in Christ.

The transfer of authority is not the sole point here but also the transfer of important teachings of Jesus and the transmission of valuable traditions about Him along with it. Not only do the teachings of Jesus and traditions about Him are transferred, but teachings and traditions concerning Paul are also transmitted to the next generation. Important exhortations of Paul are now also transferred to the elders. The apostolic message without adulteration has to be passed on faithfully to successors. Acts 20:32–35 is unique that it deals with both the transmission of Jesus' teaching through Paul and Pauline teaching and tradition through Luke.

8.1.2. To Highlight the Importance of Paul

Luke highlights the importance of Paul by drawing parallel from sources important for him. One of the features of Lucan writings is the use of parallelism in describing events, places, and persons.[15] The practice of using parallelism in a speech or literature is called "syncresis." Not many scholars have identified the use of parallelism to highlight a purpose in the Miletus speech;[16] but they have only identified it as one of the prominent features of the speech. But we take it as a technique employed in the speech for obvious

---

[14] Watson, "Paul's Speech," 189.

[15] The purpose of Luke is to show parallels but the technique by which he does it is *syncresis*.

[16] According to Kurz it is reasonable to suggest that Luke's plan to have a farewell speech by Paul in Acts 20 may have inspired him to insert a parallel one by Jesus here, since there is so much evidence for parallelism between Jesus and Paul in Luke-Acts. See Kurz, "Luke 22:14–38," 257.

reasons. In a previous chapter we have already compared the farewell speech of Jesus in Luke with the Miletus speech of Paul. Here we are not concerned about 'how parallel' the Miletus speech is with other farewell speeches found in the LXX or NT, rather, the idea of syncresis here pertains to the attempt and skill of Luke to produce a farewell speech by Paul paralleling many aspects and elements found in the LXX, Gospel of Luke,[17] and particularly the farewell speech of Jesus.[18] In doing so Luke achieves certain goals.

A feature of Miletus speech is that it parallels with the farewell speech of Jesus in Luke (22:14–38). For example, just as Jesus prepares the apostles for the time without him being physically present (22:14–23; 31–32) so does Paul the Ephesian elders. Jesus looks back to the mission of the disciples (Lk 22:35) so does Paul look back to his mission. Just as Jesus exhorts the disciples (Lk 22:24–30; 36-38) Paul too exhorts the Ephesian elders; just as Jesus speaks of his suffering (Lk 22:15–16; 21) Paul too speaks of his impending suffering; just as Jesus teaches them about humility and service (Lk 22:24–27) Paul too teaches them about the same; just as Jesus is a model of service (Lk 22:27) Paul too is a model of service; just as Jesus predicts his own rejection and passion (Lk 22:15–16; 22) Paul predicts his own persecutions, imprisonments, and the imminent wolf attack on the church of God. Moreover, the affirmation of Acts 20:28 is being related to Lk 22:20.[19] These examples demonstrate the Lucan eagerness to show a parallel presentation of the Miletus speech with the farewell speech of Jesus (Lk 22:14–46).[20] Since we have already drawn parallelism between

---

[17] Various scholars have already pointed out the thematic parallelism between various narratives of the Gospel of Luke and Acts. For example, the prologue in Luke (1:1–4) is parallel to the prologue in Acts (1:1–5); the preparation for the birth of the messiah in Luke (1:5–80) is parallel to the preparation for the birth of the Church (Acts 1:4–26); the overshadowing of the Holy Spirit upon Mary (Lk 1:26–35) is parallel to the descent of the Holy Spirit on the disciples (Acts 2:1–4); the proclamation of John the Baptist and Jesus (Lk 3:1–17; 4:16–30; etc.) is parallel to the proclamation of the apostles (Acts 2:14–42; 4:8–22; etc.); the miracles of Jesus (Lk 4:31–37; 5:12–16; 5:17–26; 7:11–17 etc.) are parallel to the signs and wonders performed by the apostles (Acts 3:1–10; 5:12–16; 9:32–35; 36–41 etc.); the travel account of Jesus (Lk 9:51–19:27) is parallel to the travels of Paul (Acts 13:4–21:14); the ethical teaching of Jesus through various parables (Lk 10:30–37; 12:15–21; 16:19–31) is parallel to the ethical speech of Paul to the Ephesian Elders; the trials and last days of Jesus in Jerusalem (Lk 19:28–23:12) are parallel to the trials of Paul in Jerusalem and his days in Rome (Acts 21:15–28:22).

[18] Syncresis may be made with Greco-Roman specimens examined in the first chapter. But since most obvious parallelism can be drawn from LXX and Lk 22:14–38, we refrain from entering into the Greco-Roman samples for syncresis.

[19] This point is noted by Lambrecht.

[20] A comparison between Lk 22:35–38 and Acts 20:34–35 may be forced upon in this connection, for, just as the disciples are told in Luke to carry money and sword for their sustenance and protection, Paul in Acts also owns money for self-sustenance, but the difference is that he earns it mainly through manual work.

the Miletus speech and other LXX speeches[21] repetition of the same here is omitted.

The journey motif is a prominent feature of Luke-Acts and it is colorfully presented in it. Luke records the journey of Jesus to Jerusalem in Lk 9:51–19:27 and the material that comprises this part is called by some scholars the "central section" of the Gospel. Most important teachings of Jesus, as scholars point out, can be found in the central section of the Gospel. Jesus' main teachings are recorded in this section especially through vivid parables and strident exhortations. Four main recurring themes in this central section are discipleship (9:57–10:42; 11:27–28; 12:35–48; 13:22–30; 14:25–35; 18:18-30; 35–43), prayer (11:1–13; 18:1–14), repentance (11:29–32; 13:1–9; 15:1–32; 19:1–10), and right use of possessions (12:13–48; 16:1–31; 19:1–27). In fact, these are some of the main teachings of the apostles as reported in Acts and these themes are integral to the Miletus speech.

Luke creates a Journey to Jerusalem section (20:1–21:16) in Acts but due to the peculiar nature of this journey, the usual Lucan themes and teachings do not appear or Luke could not incorporate them here as he did in the Gospel. But the themes that remain scattered in the Gospel are presented more concisely in the Miletus speech, which Luke found as the best *locus* for proclaiming his important themes and concerns. Miletus speech is distinctive in that it contains all the above four important Lucan themes and, in addition, the speech is also a testimony to Paul's ministry performed so far and is "a summary of Paul's central message to a church he had founded."[22] Therefore "it is not unreasonable to claim that the speech is the most important paragraph in Acts"[23] and can be called the central part of the journey to Jerusalem section of Acts.[24]

Further support for this claim may be found in the way Luke presents Paul's travel to Jerusalem to suffer there which parallels Jesus' travel to Jerusalem and his trials there to suffer and die. Luke makes Paul travel to Jerusalem to be tried before religious and civil authorities[25] which has been

---

[21] Miletus speech's parallelism in words and thoughts with many of the farewell speeches of the LXX has been already detected in chapter one. Therefore we avoid drawing any comparison with them here.

[22] Keener, *Acts*, 3:2946.

[23] See Barrett, "Paul's Address to the Ephesian Elders," 107.

[24] A contra view may be seen in Francis Pereira's book (*Ephesus: Climax of Universalism in Luke-Acts: A Redaction Critical Study of Paul's Ephesian Ministry (Acts 18:23–20:1)*, Anand: Gujarat Sahitya Prakash, 1983), in which the writer notes several points to show the parallelism between Jesus' Galilean ministry and Paul's Ephesian ministry. See pp. 65–74.

[25] According to Christopher Hays, the essential agenda of the speech is to demonstrate first Paul's intentionality in going to Jerusalem to be arrested according to the plan of God. See Hays, *Luke's Wealth Ethics*, 254.

already a motif in the Gospel. However, there is no mention of the death of Paul in Acts.[26] By placing the Miletus speech at the center of Paul's Journey to Jerusalem (20:1-21-16), Luke might want to emphasize the importance of Paul's teaching on various points that have already appeared in Luke's central section and in the farewell speech of Jesus.[27]

Still we need to consider some points related to the Greco-Roman writings, LXX and the Testament of the Twelve Patriarchs. Many of the major elements of the farewell speeches of these ancient documents, such as various ethical exhortations, declaration of innocence, portrayal of genuineness, reception of revelatory details etc. reappear in the Miletus speech creating a syncresis with them and are probably to be understood in the Greco-Roman narrative-rhetorical setting as providing an example of how a leader in the post apostolic tradition should behave and give instructions to those under his ministry.[28]

Based on the above observations we can confidently say that one of the purposes for the composition of Miletus speech was to present a parallel primarily between Jesus and Paul and between some of the Lucan teaching in the third Gospel and Acts; secondarily between the conduct and character of ancient figures and Paul. A key question then would be "why does Luke want to show Paul in such a way that by employing syncresis he is made to parallel Jesus in words and deeds?" The answer is simple, because for Luke Paul is not a mean figure, rather for the generation he represents he is a model just as Jesus and other ancient figures were models for the people in their own time. In other words, using parallelism Luke wanted to highlight the importance of Paul.

---

[26] The abrupt ending of Acts may be because Luke did not want to report the death of Paul in Rome, which would break the syncresis with Jerusalem since Jesus died there (It is unimaginable to think that Luke did not know the last days of Paul in Rome). If he had died in Jerusalem, or somewhere in Palestine, he would have certainly reported it. Paul is parallel only to Jesus' trials in Jerusalem and before the Roman authorities but not to his death in Jerusalem. However, in the speech Paul himself foretells of his suffering and possible death (vv. 23–25).

[27] Syncresis is however broken if we take into account the place of the Miletus speech at the center of the Journey to Jerusalem. In the Gospel of Luke, the farewell speech of Jesus is placed at a moment when Jesus is in Jerusalem, in fact after having completed His journey to Jerusalem and after having performed some ministry there. Lucan focus in the farewell speech of Paul in Acts at that place thus falls on his ministry and teaching rather than on geographical or temporal location. In other words, Lucan parallelism is made of the teachings of the journey section of the Gospel and the teachings of the journey section of Acts. Thus, the parallelism does not concern itself with temporal locations or time of the speeches.

[28] P. Elbert, "Paul of the Miletus Speech and 1 Thessalonians: Critique and Considerations," *ZNW* 95 (2004), 259.

8.1.3. To Provide a Pastoral Testament and Testimony

Some scholars have noted and a couple of them have tried to establish that the speech's purpose was to provide a pastoral testament of Paul, the missionary and pastor.[29] Not only does it provide pastoral laws for the leaders, but it is also a testimony of Paul's pastoral work. The Miletus speech "is a fine summary of Paul's ministry as the apostle of the Gentiles; it is a sort of retrospection on his life and ministry as well as on the principles that guided him all along. Paul the man, his ministry, his convictions, all boil down to whatever is said in this speech."[30] "Perhaps Luke, who presents Paul as a spirit-empowered evangelist, includes this speech to round out his portrait of Paul as a charismatic missionary[31] to Jews and Gentiles."[32]

In Acts Luke presents Paul as the greatest missionary and preacher of the word. He is also the ideal preacher for Him. Luke has this in mind throughout the book.[33] As a preacher and missioner, he himself testifies his own apostolic activities and the sufferings undergone for that sake. One of the key words in the speech that expresses the mission of Paul is "witness" (20:21, 24, 26). His call was above all to witness to Jesus and His resurrection. In Paul's letters (including the deutero-Pauline) this witnessing aspect gets some importance (Rom 1:9; 1 Cor 1:6; Eph 4:17; 2 Thess 1:10; 2 Tim 1:8). Luke, being aware or even having firsthand experience of Paul's shepherding and witnessing activities, presents a very 'witnessing Paul' throughout Acts but above all in the Miletus speech and the whole speech becomes as it were a pastoral testimony of St. Paul.

Luke describes Paul as a pastor of the flock and witness to Jesus and how he unceasingly preaches the message amidst all oppositions and trials. His testimony was not limited to the Jews alone but it was open to the Gentiles also because he never shrank from proclaiming the word of His grace or suffering for the Gospel. He defended the true belief about Jesus Christ opposing every form of heresy in the churches and, in fact, a main concern of Paul in the speech was for the Ephesian church against λύκοι βαρεῖς (20:29), who would appear to destroy her with false teachings. The

---

[29] A staunch proponent of this idea is Dupont in *Le Discourse de Milet: Testament Pastoral de Saint Paul (Actes 20:18–36)*. See also Richard I. Pervo, *Acts: A Commentary*, Harold W. Attridge, ed. (Minneapolis: Fortress Press, 2009).

[30] John Kuruchianil, "Portrait of a Minister of the Word in (Acts 20:13–35)," *BiBh* 37 (2011), 247.

[31] In the LXX there are charismatic figures like Moses, Joshua, Elijah, Samuel, and others. Here we are made to recall the figure of Samuel who delivers a speech (1 Sam 12:1–25) which contains his ministry of apology, exhortations, and warnings for the Israelites.

[32] Elbert, "Critique and Considerations," 259.

[33] Kuruchianil, "Portrait of a Minister," 247.

future predictions in Paul's farewell speech have a specific function in Acts, which as Kurz points out God knew and so prepared the church for what was to come. This is an important function in Biblical historiography (e.g. Deut 31–34; Jos 23–24; Tob 14:3–11).[34] An ethic and theology of vigilance is precisely the point here. The importance of vigilance, sobriety, being awake and alert, appear a number of times in Luke and Pauline letters (Lk 12:15, 37; 17:3; 21:34; 22:36; 1 Cor 16:13; 1 Thess 5:6, 10; Col 4:2) and are often related with eschatology. Eutychus fell down and died (20:9) which was caused by his sleep, but metaphorically, as one author notes, it may be seen as an example of lack of vigilance and its consequence.

His portrait as a "true shepherd" is particularly appealing here. Luke creates a true shepherd image of Paul who gives his life for the sheep.[35] Lucan Paul describes the Ephesian elders as watchmen of the flock (v. 28). This presentation seems to be borrowed from Ezekiel 34:1–8. It is the rule of law that shepherds watch over the flock like Jesus who shed even His blood to redeem the Church.[36] False teachers, the wolves, destroy the Church and this false image of shepherds immediately takes us to Ezekiel 34 where a severe condemnation of selfish shepherds is made.[37] Quite contrary, Paul is a true shepherd who teaches them the right faith and who is even willing to die for the sake of his commitment to the mission. Ethics of right teaching is emphatically presented here; true pastors need to teach Christian values and they are not to seek money or personal interest. Such commitment to ministry is required of all leaders and thus the whole speech may be regarded as a pastoral law for the Ephesian church leaders and ministers of post Pauline period.[38]

A true witness of the Gospel not only preaches with his mouth but also feels with his heart and acts with his hands. This is being exemplified in Paul as he was even willing to stoop down to work with his own hands to support the weak. Oral proclamation should be substantiated and accompanied with concrete deeds of charity. In every instance Paul is a model and a perfect witness of the Gospel. Paul's examples and exhortations do set forth values that should guide the exercise of leadership in the church.[39] In short, Miletus

[34] Kurz, "Luke 22:14–38," 267.

[35] For more on this see Bernard Aubert, *The Shepherd-Flock Motif in the Miletus Discourse (Acts 20:17–38) Against Its Historical Background*, SBL 124 (New York: Peter Lang, 2009).

[36] Keener notes the plausibility of Paul's speech making fuller, Midrashic reference to the texts in Ezek 33–34.

[37] Lövestam even argues in his article ("Paul's Address at Miletus") that the Miletus speech's order of presentation is influenced by Lucan Paul's use of Ezekiel, 33–34.

[38] Luke may also want that these pastoral laws may provide some guidelines for the Christian leaders everywhere and at all time.

[39] Larkin, *Acts*, 297.

speech offers a pastoral testament and testimony of Paul who is not only their shepherd and leader but also their model and inspiration.

8.1.4. Apology for Paul

One can also argue that the Miletus speech, in the thoughtline of the Greco-Roman history and historiography, was an apology for Paul and his ministry.[40] This partially explains why there is "Paulinism" in the Miletus speech or why it is more Pauline than Lucan. The apologetic features of the speech can be deciphered from within the speech itself and they are not very slight. There are many indications especially in the first half of the speech (20:18–27) that it was made in defense of what Paul had been teaching and doing. Certain indications elsewhere in the Pauline and deutero-Pauline writings confirm that Pauline legacy did come under attack (2 Tim 1:15) and some criticism was raised during his ministry (Rom 3:8; 2 Cor 6:8; 11:4–6, 12-15; Gal 4:16–17). Luke therefore may have some apologetic reason for defending Paul's legacy.

In the speech first of all Paul defends himself against various accusations launched at him by some Christians. Marie-Eloise Rosenblatt sees the Miletus speech basically as a defense against accusations.[41] Paul faced much opposition as a missioner and often encountered opponents within the Christian communities. For example, the divisions in the Corinthian church and related issues (1 Cor 1:10–4:21), the teaching of a different gospel in Galatia by some (Gal 1:6–9), and the heretical teachers in Ephesus (Acts 20:28–31). In Ephesus, Paul finds many such opponents who even taught differently than Paul. The missionary efforts of Paul, his willingness to suffer for the Gospel, his manner of behavior with and within the churches, his attitude towards labor and the poor all have the characteristics of an apology for what he was doing. He may be also defending himself against a "charge of heresy[42] with a sure appeal that he is guided by the Holy Spirit and not by any other spirit."

---

[40] The hypothesis that the whole Book of Acts is an apology written to defend the early church and its mission as accomplished through the apostles and Paul has not been favored by the modern scholars. Gaventa argues that the purpose of Acts is apologetic to convince the Roman officials about the credibility of the Gospel. See *Acts of the Apostles*, 48. It is possible to view it as an apologetic for Christianity before a wider Roman audience. See Burridge, "Gospels and Acts," 210. For literary and social dimensions of Luke's apology for Paul see John T. Carroll, "Literary and Social Dimensions of Luke's Apology for Paul," in *Society of Biblical Literature 1988 Seminar Papers*, David J. Lull, ed. (Atlanta: Scholars Press, 1988), 106–18.

[41] Marie-Eloise Rosenblatt, *Paul the Accused: His Portrait in the Acts of the Apostles* (Collegeville: The Liturgical Press, 1995), 62–68.

[42] Many scholars opine that the false teaching appeared in the form of Gnosticism. Other than Dibelius, "Speeches," 157 and Hänchen, *Acts of the Apostles*, 596–97, scholars like H. Schürmann, "Das Testament des Paulus für die Kirche: APG 20:18–35," in *Unio Christianorum:*

Secondly Paul defends himself against "utilitarianism."[43] He has not taken advantage of anyone. Rather he worked hard night and day for the Gospel without expecting any financial gain. Luke seems to be particularly defending Paul's habit of manual work, and his method of charity.

And finally, for Luke's audience his "apologetic for Paul is also an apologetic for his Gentile mission and a model of commitment to that mission."[44] In the Pauline letters Paul himself claims that he is an apostle, but in Acts no such claim is ever made. In fact, Paul does not qualify to be called an apostle yet Luke may support Paul's claim to be an apostle, an apostle of the Gentiles. Nowhere in Acts Luke explicitly support this claim as Paul does (e.g. Rom 11:13). This he does in Acts, especially in the Miletus speech, by portraying in a convincing manner Paul's mission and his ethos. It may have been also in the mind of Luke to describe and defend the "apostolicity" of Paul through the Miletus speech.[45]

8.1.5. Deliberative Purpose

Deliberation in speech and literature involve presentation of facts to be deliberated and exhortations to be made. We have already seen that ancient literatures often emphasized the words of a dying person as having a paraenetic function. All that Paul says to the Ephesian elders may be seen as presentation of facts and exhortations for them from a parting figure. It seems that the most important purpose of the Miletus speech was deliberative as it exhorts on different topics and deliberates the importance of Paul as a model. Luke realizes this through the figure of Paul by transmitting that image across all periods and for all Christians.

Festschrift für Erzbischof Dr. Lorenz Jaeger [. . .]. (Padeborn: Bonifacius Druckerei, 1962), 108–46 and Lambrecht, "Paul's Farewell Address," 311 also identify the danger that Paul was concerned about as Gnosticism. Cf. Michel, *Die Abschiedsrede des Paulus and die Kirche*, 82–83. It cannot be absolutely verified that the Ephesian heretics were the Gnostics.

[43] See another defense of Paul in Lambrecht, "Paul's Farewell Address," 306–307.

[44] Keener, *Acts*, 3:2995.

[45] I refrain from developing this point here since it will take considerable space. For the benefit of the present thesis, we note the following. First, Paul's manner of missionary activity coupled with exhortations described in Acts 20:19–21 and vv. 27–35 is similar to the apostolic activity described in various places of Acts. Second, the spirit guidance is a mark of the apostles and Paul too is guided by the Spirit (Act 20:22–23). Third, the speech makes clear that Paul's ministry was from the Lord. It was a ministry of grace (Acts 20:24). Paul's letters document the ministry of grace and apostleship he received from the Lord (e.g. Rom 1:5; 15:15; Gal 1:15; 2:9). And finally, the exhortations which Paul give in the speech contain apostolic authority.

In chapter one, we have discussed some features of an epideictic speech that has the characteristics of panegyric speeches or encomia. Miletus speech discloses, indeed validates, some features of a panegyric as shown by D. F. Watson.[46] Since encomia are usually written in praise of a person or place, the Miletus speech comes across to the reader as a praise offered to Paul by a travelling companion. In fact the whole Book of Acts appears to be an encomium of Paul.[47] Praise of Paul[48] is important for Luke since the audience is invited to learn and imitate from the model figure. Given this character, it may be said that Luke praises Paul using a speech Paul might have had given some time before the actual composition of Acts.

While one may notice panegyric elements in the speech some of it were precisely used for transmitting and commending Pauline tradition. Luke seems to be hailing the 'Pauline way' rather than the 'apostolic way' in some regard.[49] Steve Walton examining the Miletus speech states three conclusions of the speech and one of which is that Luke "seeks to pass on and commend Paul's tradition."[50] Clear manifestations of this are apparent in the Miletus speech. Paul remains as a symbol of the Christian movement in providing legacy for the church.[51] In Luke's view, Paul is the perfect model in his own time as a witness, missionary, and pastor.

Almost all scholars who examined the speech[52] identify the deliberative purpose of it especially in the last part of it (vv. 28–35), since these verses are exhortatory all through. Even D. F. Watson who views the speech through the lens of epideictic rhetoric does not fail to affirm the deliberative function of it.[53] For Luke's own audience, the portrayal of Paul may well function epideictically, but within the narrative world, the use of oneself as ethical and

---

[46] The article of Watson proposes epideictic character of the speech. See "Paul's Speech," 184–208.

[47] Miletus speech may be considered as a part of the whole encomium which is Acts.

[48] Praise of Paul is closely related to apology for Paul, yet in the literary level they are different.

[49] The apostles were more radical; they are presented as not possessing private property or money. Paul's conduct is quite different from that of the apostles.

[50] Walton, *Leadership and Lifestyle*, 212.

[51] Brawley, "Paul in Acts: Aspects of Structure and Characterization," 103, mentions how Jacob Jervell characterizes Paul through the Miletus speech in "Paulus in der Apostelgeschichte und die Geschichte des Urchristentums," *NTS* 32 (1986), 382–83.

[52] See for example scholars who have already been cited like, Dibelius, Barrett, Budesheim, Lambrecht, Hemer, Gaventa, Talbert, Fitzmyer, Johnson, Witherington, Bock, Soards, Marshall, and Keener.

[53] Watson argues that Luke may weave in deliberative or judicial elements while remaining especially epideictic, emphasizing Paul as a model more than giving an apologetic for him (see "Paul's speech," 191).

moral example within a speech could have a deliberative function (e.g. as in 1 Cor 9).[54] Moreover "simple exhortations, without necessarily referring to a model, by themselves are deliberative by the very nature of their paraenetic function."

Luke was not only writing history but also preaching. In this effort, he did not strictly follow the Greco-Roman conventions of rhetoric which is evident in the Miletus speech. The speech has the characteristics of epideictic, deliberative, and even judicial. Luke's speeches serve multiple functions and therefore, the usual epideictic character of farewell speeches took other characters as well. In any case the very nature of the concluding verses makes it very deliberative. It provides exhortations to work, imitate a model, and support the weak by giving. Not only Jesus' teaching is deliberated here but also Paul's and Luke's.

As already elucidated the speech bears ethical and moral tenors. The ethical and moral exhortation here, as in most Greco-Roman, LXX, and Jewish testaments, serve a deliberative function within the narrative world.[55] The deliberative purpose of the speech can only be appreciated in comparison with the whole plot of Luke-Acts. Acts follows those themes and patterns of the Gospel; for example, the theme concerning universality, Holy Spirit, discipleship, prayer, repentance, right use of wealth and generous giving, retribution, etc. are the main themes in Luke-Acts. In every sense the Miletus speech is concerned with and engaged with these themes especially through exhortations which make it by and large deliberative.

As already noted, Paul was clearly a model of manual work and charity besides being a model of suffering and missionary work. He was a true pastor and leader who was always guided by the Holy Spirit and / or grace and who never acted selfishly or cunningly. His convictions are principally echoed in the final part of the speech making it more deliberative than the rest of the speech. These images of Paul were something that Luke wanted to communicate. Keener points out that "the deliberative function is captured in hortatory applications today often for leadership formation." The final chapter of our thesis will examine especially these hortatory applications for us today.

---

[54] Keener, *Acts*, 3:2995.

[55] Keener, 3:2995.

An observation related to this topic is the example of Paul himself in matters of money. Paul in Acts (also in Paul's Letters) is an extrovert who is engaged with economics to achieve certain objectives or fulfill certain tasks. According to the first chapters of Acts apostolic practices especially on economic matters were different from the Pauline practice[56] as is evident from the latter chapters of Acts. We are more interested about the period of Paul where Paul's own way of testimony and economic practices were different from the apostolic way of testimony and economic practices. Luke recalls the foundations of teachings and practices important to Luke's readers, such as the example of "Paul who does not seek money from those he serves." This character of Paul differs in matters related to the teachings of Jesus in Lk 9:3 and 10:4 and even contradicts it; but it is to be considered as Paul's intention to render the later instructions of Jesus (Lk 22:35–38) and apostolic practices more absolutely than the previous missionary instructions / practices and may also imply that missionary methods need not be uniform everywhere but depends on place, culture, and social situations. So, "changes in conditions can justify changes in methods."[57] Luke seems to be deliberating this change in missionary practice in the Miletus speech.

8.2. Normative Function of the Figure of Paul

It is not out of place to say that Luke, through this speech, finds a normative and moral function in the figure of Paul. Paul and his practices are normative for the Gentile churches and the second-generation Christians. Paul is also a paradigm for them especially for Christian ministry and in economic practices. In the early chapters of Acts Christianity is presented as maintaining communitarian features, most probably spearheaded and motivated by "initial religious enthusiasm" or "eschatological expectation," but for the latter chapters of Acts communitarianism was not the norm, instead Luke presents Paul as a norm and model for the believers' faith, mission, and economic life. Bernhard Weiss suggests that social and economic structures of the early Christianity provided normative lessons about Christian love, identity, and unity of the church.[58] T. E. Phillips observes that contrary to the pre-Pauline communitarian conception of economic life, Paul himself functions as a norm and ethical model for the second generation Christians in matters of faith and social life, especially in the area of economic life, which in the mind of Paul, was more capitalist, and was characterized by earning for sustenance by work

---

[56] This point is made by Phillips in his article "Paul as a Role Model in Acts: The We Passages in Acts 16 and Beyond."

[57] Ideas for this paragraph see Kurz, "Luke 22:14–38," 266.

[58] See Bernhard Weiss, *Die Apostelgeschichte* (Leipzig: J. C. Hinrichs, 1983), 100. This point of Weiss is also noted by T. E. Phillips in his article "Paul as a Role Model in Acts," 56–57.

and giving generously for the sustenance of others. Back in the time of the apostles, Peter as their primary spokesperson, communitarianism was the appropriate norm for the church. But 'now,' in the time of the narrator, that appropriate norm had been replaced by private keeping of goods. After the apostolic times, the readers, who stand with Paul and Luke, should imitate their role model, Paul the reliable witness.[59]

What did Paul do or how is he a role model for the second-generation Christians? How is he a bridge between second and third generations? The Miletus speech provides the basic information and insight on this. Paul functions as an ethical model in economic matters in particular. Paul's manual work and his earnestness to help others are prominent. According to Tannehill, Paul's work (1) ends the necessity of taking contributions from others and (2) enables Paul to help his co-workers and the sick or economically weak.[60] Moreover, his own work as a tentmaker indicates that he considered all work as honorable. It also points that there should not be any discrimination of persons on the basis of the work they do.

He is a model and norm for the Christians of the second and subsequent generation. We assume that he was a man of adequate wealth, or it was not necessary for him to work and earn to support himself. Yet he earns money and uses it on himself and others, he worked with his own hands to support himself and others. Paul's character is unique here since he crosses all the boundaries of economic life of the apostolic conception of community of goods. He is thus a model of manual work. Secondly, he used his resources and proceeds from his manual work to extend a helping hand to others[61] and thus he is a model of charity. For Luke's own audience the *vorbild* of Paul has had a deliberative function. Paul as a model serves as an example for the church.[62]

The Jerusalem collection is the concrete example of Paul's initiative on charity, care, and love for the Jerusalem community. According to Phillips Paul's post-apostolic life and his participation in the ordinary economic life of the world provide the role model image of Paul for the post-apostolic times. The image of Paul is offered as an example. This is a true image of Paul; it proclaims how much he values community and their well-being.

Paul had sufficient means for self-support and he also supported others (Acts 20:34). He instructs the Ephesian elders to work, share and care for the

---

[59] Phillips, "Paul as a Role Model in Acts," 56–58.

[60] Tannehill, *The Narrative Unity of Luke-Acts*, 2:260.

[61] Already mention has been made of the Pauline effort for the collection and Paul's willingness to set free a slave, Onesimus.

[62] We have already examined various Pauline and deutero-Pauline texts that support this view. To this we shall also add 1 Cor 15:10 and 2 Tim 1:13.

flock. These instructions of Acts echo also in his letters informing the reader that the image of Paul drawn by Luke is a genuine one, and it is an ideal image that can remain as a norm for all time.

8.3. Lucan Paul's Imperative as a Moral Duty

Pauline ethics can be treated as imperative and his theology as indicative.[63] According to W. Dennison, Pauline indicative always precedes the imperative.[64] But according to Victor Furnish Pauline theology and ethics are integrally related;[65] this is also supported by H. Cruz who sees Paul's theology and ethics as two sides of a coin.[66] The same can be said also of Lucan theology and ethics. They are integrally related and are inseparable. Miletus speech confirms the interrelationship between theology and ethics as conceived by Lucan Paul. Paul's mission provides the crucial link between his theology and ethics[67] and the speech in a nutshell gives how this mission so far was, how it should be in future, and describes various aspects of that mission combining theology and ethics.

Imperatives demand concrete actions. Pauline imperatives are many as we see them in his letters.[68] Pauline imperative is a human response to the grace and gift of God given to us. Baptism makes one belong to this imperative spectrum as it is an imperative placed on us.[69] Not all Pauline imperatives are morally relevant or applicable for the Church today (e.g. 1 Cor 13:34; Eph 6:5 // Col 3:22) but the majority are. Imperatives concerning love, humility, service, charity, and the importance of leading an authentic Christian life are never inapposite for the Church at any period. In the line of Pauline letters, the Miletus speech commands the audience to follow the

---

[63] In Rudolf Bultmann's opinion Paul's theology can be regarded as "indicative" and ethics as "imperative." See his article "The Problem of Ethics in Paul," Christoph W. Stenschke, trans., in *Understanding Paul's Ethics: Twentieth Century Approaches*, Brian S. Rosner, ed. (Grand Rapids: Eerdmans, 1995), 195–216.

[64] See his article "Indicative and Imperative: The Basic Structure of Pauline Ethics," *CTJ* 14 (1979), 55–78.

[65] The integral relationship between theology and ethics of Paul is explained by Victor P. Furnish. See especially pp. 224–26 in *Theology and Ethics in Paul* (Nashville: Abingdon, 1968). Furnish produces examples such as Rom 1:5; 6:1–14; and the first letter to the Corinthians for the integrality of theology and ethics.

[66] See *Christological Motives*, 24.

[67] Michael D. Barram, *Mission and Moral Reflection in Paul*, SBL 75 (New York: Peter Lang, 2006), 140.

[68] For a comprehensive discussion of Pauline indicative and imperative, see Willi Marxsen, *New Testament Foundations for Christian Ethics*, O. C. Dean, trans. (Edinburgh, T&T Clark, 1993), 180–224; Assisi Saldanha, "Rediscovering Paul: The Indicative and the Imperative," *ITS* 45 (2008), 381–419.

[69] Saldanha, "Rediscovering Paul," 389.

instructions given. As repeatedly noted, the use of δεῖ in the speech (v. 35) gives these words of Paul an imperative character. It is in this verse that Pauline imperative is categorically a moral duty. The call that is given is not a simple imperative, but an obligation, failure of which is a sin. Thus, supporting the weak is a moral duty for all Christians, especially for the leaders of the church.

In the last verses of the Miletus speech, Lucan Paul moves from providing ethical instructions to mandating moral obligation. Paul's own life, his style of ministry, his sufferings and pain for the Gospel, his hard work and teachings etc. provide ethical flavor to the speech. But it is obligatory for the elders to support the weak because Christ himself taught to give than to receive. Here, Luke may see Paul as a norm, but Paul himself sees Christ as the ultimate norm. Since Christ himself has shown and demanded from his followers to give to the poor and help the needy, any failure to help the poor and needy is a sin. To put it in plain words, it is our moral obligation to support the weak.

8.4. Ethics of Poverty and Riches

Poverty and riches is a major theme in Luke-Acts. It will not be a light task to study this topic[70] in detail nor is it required here. However, I will try to pin point a couple of aspects related to it taking into consideration Acts 20:32–35 which contributes significantly to this Lucan theme.

No other NT author has communicated the value of poverty and the evil of riches as did Luke, who from the beginning of the Gospel extols poverty and sees a "potential danger" in the accumulation of wealth. This same idea has been repeated in the Book of Acts in a number of narratives. Researchers on the theology and ethics of Luke-Acts will be literally handicapped if they do not understand the meaning of Luke's wealth ethic. R. J. Karris has gone to the extent of arguing that "poor and rich" constitutes the *sitz im leben* of

---

[70] A number of monographs and articles have appeared on this topic of poverty and riches in Luke-Acts. Important ones are Hans-Joachim Degenhardt, *Lukas Evangelist der Armen: Besitz und Besitzversicht in den Lukanischen Schriften: Eine Tradition-und Redaktionsgeschichtliche Untersuchung* (Stuttgart: Kath. Bibelwerk, 1965); Walter E. Pilgrim, *Good News to the Poor: Wealth and Poverty in Luke-Acts* (Minneapolis: Augsburg Publishing House, 1981); Luke T. Johnson, *The Literary Function of Possessions in Luke-Acts*, SBLDS 39 (Missoula, MT: Scholars Press, 1977); David P. Seccombe, *Possessions and the Poor in Luke-Acts*, SNTU Serie B 6 (Linz: Plöchl, 1982); Johnson, *Sharing Possessions: Mandate and Symbol of Faith*; Hays, *Luke's Wealth Ethics: A Study in their Coherence and Character*; Robert J. Karris, "Poor and Rich: The Lucan *Sitz im Leben*," in *Perspectives on Luke-Acts* (Danville, CA: Association of Baptist Professors of Religion, 1978), 112–25. The theme has been partially treated in many commentaries and monographs for example Jaques Dupont, *Le Beatitudini,* vol. 1 (Roma: Paoline, 1972), and J. Dupont, *Le Beatitudini*, vol. 2 *Gli Evangelisti* (Roma: Paoline, 1977).

Luke-Acts.[71] Luke's concern for the neglected widows, poor and sick, so evident in Luke-Acts, and those materials dealing with the rich / riches need no further explanation here.

The poor in Israel were given care and protection by the enforcement of religious norms, but these norms were often disregarded and as a result the poor suffered mostly at the hands of the rich who were least bothered about them and who showed no justice and mercy in their dealings with these unfortunate ones. Similarly, Luke saw a disparity between the haves and the have-nots in the Gentile world in which the rich often oppressed the poor, disparaged their work, and held them as sub-standard folks. There was little possibility for the poor to become rich or to go up the ladder of social status. Benefaction, patronage, and even friendship were shown on the principle of 'gain'[72] and this was a big disadvantage for the poor as they often did not gain the fruits of benefaction or patronage as they would have merited. Faced with a situation such as this, Luke wanted his readers to think differently and act concretely and proposed a new vision of benefaction and euergetism. In Luke's conception the best possible way to make use of one's wealth is through almsgiving to the poor which is an expression of visible support for them. Luke stresses this aspect frequently in Lk 11:41; 12:33; 18:22; Acts 9:36; 10:2; 4:31. Luke finds support for this not in a vacuum but from the LXX, Jewish tradition, teachings of Jesus, and examples of Paul on which he is dependent.

As already noted, for Luke and Paul, wealth *in se* is not evil and the possession of it can be a great means to help the poor and needy. Wealth is good only if it is used correctly and wisely. All the paraeneses of Luke-Acts regarding wealth have this overarching concern. Paul is a pointed weapon used by Luke to confront the enemy of misuse of wealth. Unlike Paul in his letters, Luke is not eager to report Paul's poverty, hunger, and want. It is also visible that the Gospel of Luke deals extensively with poverty and its theological dimensions. But these concerns are minimal in Acts and, more than the early church's poverty or the apostles' or Paul's poor style of life, Luke is rather concerned in Acts about their manner of earning wealth and its Christian use. An obvious point of contact for this is Acts 20:34-35.

Paul is a model for the correct Christian use of wealth. The stories of Zacchaeus (Lk 19:1–10), poor widow (Lk 21:1–4), Barnabas (Acts 4:36–37; 11:28–30), and Cornelius (Acts 10:2) in particular are concrete examples of the Christian use of wealth. We have already examined other paraeneses and instances of generous giving in Luke-Acts, which contribute substantially to this thesis, and in all these instances Lucan emphases are clear. "Giving"

---

[71] Karris, "Poor and Rich: The Lucan *Sitz im Leben*," 112–25.

[72] This has been already explained in ch. 8.

and "sharing" one's resources with others are a fundamental quality and requirement for being a true Christian. Paul's example of giving here is not an appendix to the rest of the items of the Lucan theme of correct use of wealth but it is integral to the theme as a whole. In short, a high point of the ethic of poverty and riches may be found in the Miletus speech.

Chapter 9

Ethical Vision and Implications of Acts 20:32–35

An "ethical rhetorical turn" taken in the field of Biblical studies demands a deeper commitment to ethical interpretation of Biblical passages which in turn directs Christians to a greater involvement in the lives of the people by promoting human values and redressing various wounds of the world. Biblical ethics is mostly exhortations. It is a call to conversion and a challenge to decide in favor of what is morally good. It envisions creating a better Church and world where the poor and needy are always taken care of, and where human dignity is always maintained. Based on the study of Acts 20:32–35, we will present in this chapter the ethical visions and implications that derive from it.

9.1. Let Grace be the Guiding Force

Luke and Paul share in common not only the notion of grace but also consider it as a power and force for performing ethical and moral duties and obligations. Right from the beginning of the Gospel Luke understands grace as a gift and quality operative in the lives of Mary and Jesus. In chapter 4 of this thesis we have already pointed out its relational dimension and power to carry out loving ministries. Luke 6:33–34 in this connection can provide us with more insights to explain the significance of grace and what it envisions for us Christians. "If you do good to those who do good to you, what benefit / credit is that to you?" The English equivalent used in our translations for the Greek χάρις is credit, benefit or profit. There is no χάρις that you can claim to hold if you do good only to those who do good to you.[1] Grace is given to do good to all. The emphasis falls both on "doing good" and "to all." Let grace be the guiding force in you to do good to all. St. Paul also concurs on this that a Christian should bear fruit of the Spirit and consequently must be able to do good to the household of faith and to all (Gal 6:10).

Similarly Jesus asks, "What χάρις do you have if you only lend to those who lend you? (Lk 6:34). There is no true grace in you if you are not willing to give to the one who need money or things. Give to everyone who begs from you (Lk 6:30). Paul instructs the Romans to demonstrate true Christian love according to the χάρις given to them. Certain charism may make one a specialist in certain type of ministry, like prophecy, teaching, ministering, leadership etc. (Rom 12:6–8). But grace is given to all that they may demonstrate genuine love of a Christian as specified in Rom 12:9–21. The guiding force for this love is χάρις which is bestowed upon all the baptized. We have already examined that Acts 20:32–35 fits this pattern. Both in Luke and Paul it is crystal clear that χάρις is intrinsically related to doing good to all and giving to all in need.

According to Acts, the apostles and disciples found favor with all people (2:47); moreover, in the church there was great grace (4:33). Stephen was full of grace (6:8). Barnabas saw the grace of God upon the Antiochean church (11:23). The missioners (14:26; 15:40) and believers are commended to the grace of God. Paul and Barnabas urge their listeners to remain in the grace of God (13:43). Paul commends the Ephesian elders to the grace of God (20:32). The elders, who now are the listeners, are soon to become the missioners stirred by grace. Whether it is the missioner, or the believer, χάρις is the guiding force of that person. By the Christian baptism everyone receives charisms, which is "a word or action which brings to concrete expression God's gracious outreach to humankind, which serves as "a means of grace.""[2] Grace is the "source and measure" of all charisms. Paul exemplifies a grace-filled Christian life and leadership; the Ephesian elders also must demonstrate the same. The Fathers of the Church and the theologians after them hold grace as a unique gift of God for authentic Christian life. For example, St. Augustine said that even in the midst of present evils all good men are helped by grace;[3] and according to Thomas Aquinas a person's relationship with God and with others can be perfect only by grace. An individual duly fulfills the commandments of God by the

---

[1] In a parallel passage of Matthew (Mt 5:46) the word χάρις is not used, but μισθός which would mean reward, wage.

[2] Dunn, *Romans 9–16*, 734.

[3] Augustine, *The City of God against the Pagans*, Book 22. 22.

same grace. Even a person's destiny to everlasting life depends on grace.[4] St. Alphonsus says that grace of God is the highest and best good one can possess;[5] God in his goodness grants to everyone the grace of prayer by which one is able to obtain all other graces which one needs in order to keep the commandments of God.[6] In short, a person cannot wish and do any good without grace.[7]

Today all leaders and believers are called to be guided by grace to fulfill their task. They require this grace above all for generous giving and humble work. Grace gives gifts, at the same time it demands from the leaders and believers to give gifts liberally to others without counting the cost. Often people lack spiritual resources to want to give generously. The rich need the grace of God to boast not in their wealth, but "in being brought low," to know that every act of generous giving is from above, by the grace of God (Jam 1:10, 17). We all need to know that "accumulation of wealth is folly but sharing is wisdom and a simple expression of hope." Acts 20:32 envisions and implies that the words and actions of leaders and Christians are charisms that originate from grace.

9.2. Leaders Must Have Pure Intentions

An action and its consequences are evaluated by its intention. One is responsible for the choices one makes. Paul's statement, "I have not coveted anyone's silver or gold or clothes" reiterates the fact that his conduct and behavior among the Ephesians (and among other churches) were with a pure intention. He ministered to them not desiring anything in return but in humility, simplicity, and even laboring night and day.

Church leaders must have pure intention in all matters, especially in matters of money. The Miletus speech envisions that church leaders conduct themselves devoid of all greed for money, position, and fame. They are first and foremost ministers of the Word and sacraments and therefore they ought to attend to it first and do it with pure intention. They are not to serve the Church to have a cushy life, or to find ways and means to amass personal wealth, or to burden the community, or to aim for fame and power. In simple terms, a minister's intention should be pure in all that he does. It is disheartening that some leaders do not conduct themselves with pure

---

[4] *ST* I-IIae Q109 a1–4.

[5] Alphonsus M. de Liguori, *The School of Christian Perfection*, Cornelius J. Warren, trans. (Boston: Mission Church Press, 1910), ch. 1, section "A living Faith," www.ecatholic2000.com, accessed 1 June 2019, https://www.ecatholic2000.com/liguori/school/perfect.shtml.

[6] Alphonsus M. de Liguori, *Prayer: The Great Means of Obtaining Salvation and All the Graces which we Desire of God*, Part 2, ch. 2, Catholic Treasury, Accessed 1 June 2019, http://www.catholictreasury. info/books/prayer/pr19.php.

[7] *ST* I-IIae Q109 a2.

intention, they misuse people's money or property by being extravagant, feeding the overfed, living luxurious life etc.; or some enter into money making business or trade. When intentions are not pure, church leaders are easily seen disobeying authority, encouraging factionalism, even overtly accusing another in public and before the media. The clear manifestation of all these can be noticed now among the leaders of the Catholic Church.

All faithful, the Church leaders especially, are called to hold pure intentions in everything that they do. Evil intentions brooding in the heart are the cause of every evil acts (we have already explained this in ch. 5). Paul testifies that all through his ministry his intentions were pure especially with regard to material things and money. Paul never burdened the church and never wished anything for personal gain instead, he supported them from his own resources. The Miletus speech envisions that ministers should not burden the church community in anyway, rather they should help it. They should not exploit the church, but generously provide for it.

9.3. A Call to Generous Giving

As the field of a rich man produced abundantly, he said to himself "What should I do?" (Lk 12:16–17). He wanted to store up all the produce for his future enjoyment. The parable gives not the slightest hint that the man wanted to use his wealth, the blessing of God, in the service of the poor and needy. This selfish attitude of the man earns a sharp condemnation from Jesus. The question posed by the rich fool was similarly asked by the audience of John the Baptist (Lk 3:10) and the early converts at Jerusalem (Acts 2:37) but their question was a genuine one with a desire to effect a change in their style of life. In Luke's view every person ought to ask oneself, "What must I do with my wealth / talents?" because everyone can be in some way an instrument of God's grace to another. The primary vision and prospect of Acts 20:34–35 is that it aims at personal conversion, first, by one's willingness to see that there are poor and needy everywhere and next, in wanting to address such a situation, making a personal introspection, "what should I do with my wealth?" Paul's behavior indicates the positive personal engagement with his wealth.

Care for the poor and support of the weak is a major concern of the OT as we have already seen. Luke makes it a major theme in his writings; it is Lucan Paul's swan song in the Miletus speech. Support of the weak was thought by both Luke and Paul to be a necessary hallmark of Christians.[8] In their conception, Jesus does not condemn wealth justly possessed and rightly used, but He condemns it if not shared and given generously.

---

[8] See this idea also in Longenecker, *Remember the Poor*, 1.

Support of the poor was firmly rooted within their understanding of the internal matrices of the Good News.[9]

We have already noted how the conception of the possession of wealth came to be altered in the Lucan writings. Luke in the first part of Acts presents a picture of the "homegrown church" and as per this account it was possible and ideal for a short period and for a small community to keep everything in common under the leadership of Peter and the other apostles. The early converts were encouraged to give generously to the common pool so that there would be no needy person. There also existed absolute freedom for all converts to decide either to sell their property for the common pool or not. But once one decided to donate towards the common pool no foul play was tolerated; any deceit performed invites self-destruction as Luke is eager to narrate in the story of Ananias and Sapphira at the beginning of Acts (5:1–11). All are to give voluntarily and generously for the well-functioning of the community in good intention and disposition.

But later the economic policy of the Jerusalem church was no longer relevant or even practical as the church began to grow both numerically and geographically. In the second part of Acts, Luke presents the picture of the "global church" and their *modus operandi* especially in economic matters. Sharing possession was the character and nature of the early Christianity in Jerusalem. But things were different among the Gentile Christians. We are no longer told anything about the common ownership of goods, but each family or individual owned property. Paul primarily represented the new economic practices at that time as this has been transmitted to us by Luke. It can be reasonably assumed that the economic practices of Jerusalem itself might have got changed after the first generation apostolic period.

Paul, as we have seen, is not averse to private ownership of goods. However, at the same time he also exemplifies how those goods ought to be used in the service of others. In a global church where some of its members were rich and others poor the best way to press for some kind of equality was generous giving (especially of the rich). Both Luke and Paul are consistent on this matter. With the rise of the urban Christians outside of Palestine, redistribution of wealth from a common pool ceased to be an issue for it could not be supported anymore for practical reasons. The issue rather centered on the conversion of the wealthy to the point of their sharing and liberally giving to the poor,[10] which appeal resonates in the writings of Luke and Paul.

---

[9] Longenecker, 12.

[10] Bruce J. Malina, "Wealth and Poverty in the New Testament and Its World," *Interp.* 41 (1987), 366.

The inspiration they got for this was from our Lord. For both Luke and Paul the motive for giving is first and foremost borne out of the teaching of Jesus himself who commanded to give generously. The ministry of Jesus for the poor and weak, his parables, and sayings exemplify Jesus' own attitude to charity and they form the core of Jesus' teaching on giving as well. However, the application of this teaching took two forms, one in the primitive Jerusalem church and another in the Gentile churches. Paul utilizes the teaching and example of Jesus and in the final verse of the Miletus speech, Paul ultimately resorts to the teaching of Jesus rather than the content of Paul's own exhortation to prove the necessity of being charitable.[11]

The teaching of Jesus alone is not the motive for giving, for according to Paul there is also another theological dimension to it. Because we are members of Christ's body, we must take care of the other in every possible way.[12] Since Christ was poor, in every poor person we see Christ. So whenever we do a small act of charity, it is done to Christ as well. The Church is the body of Christ and when any member suffers poverty or hunger or want, it's the body of Christ that suffers. Since the Church is the body of Christ, it is the duty of every member of the Church to support and help the other in such a way that every wound in the body of Christ may be redressed.

Furthermore, wealth is considered a blessing from God[13] and, therefore, it must be used for the benefit of the community and especially for those who are unable to find sustenance for themselves, viz. the poor, widows, and orphans. Sharing possession was a "symbol of faith" in the primitive church. However, greed lurked on the way of Christians' journey of generosity. The story of Ananias and Sapphira powerfully proclaimed the destructive potential of greed and unbelief and the ensuing deceit displayed in their unwillingness to fully part with their possessions.

The Lucan and Pauline exhortations in line with the teaching of Jesus on almsgiving and charity were practical efforts to address the challenge of poverty and wealth within the early Christian community. As the early church remembered Jesus and His words through the breaking of the Bread and Word, it also remembered Jesus' specific teaching on various matters, all these shaped character and community in the early church. Their call to generous giving, which obviously found its roots in Jesus' teaching and His

---

[11] Luke and Paul colorfully transmit Jesus' teaching on generous giving at various points of their writings as we have already investigated.

[12] B. B. Barton, D. Veerman, and N. S. Wilson, *Romans*, LABC (Wheaton, IL: Tyndale, 1992), 240.

[13] Both for Luke and Paul wealth is a blessing if it is used for the needy. It is a grace, a blessing, if liberally given to the poor and needy. One of the terms Paul used for the collection is "grace" as made clear in chapter seven. The collection is equated with grace, and it primarily involves liberal contribution of money.

memory, and the socio-political milieu of the time were instrumental for the church to instruct and encourage her children to generous giving. The memory of Jesus formed a tradition of generosity and justice[14] which was later emphasized by the first century writers and the Fathers of the Church. The *Didache*, a document that is born in the first century, contains various ethical teachings and partly addresses the issue of wealth and poverty. It encourages cheerful giving to the needy hoping that God would pay them back in return (see *Did.* 4:7, 9–11). Allen Verhey notes that the Emperor Julian the apostate himself praised the charitable efforts of the Christians. In his efforts to restore Hellenism in the empire he suggested to learn from the Christians their practices of hospitality to strangers, attending to the proper burial of the poor and feeding the hungry, whether Christian or not.[15]

After the apostolic period, the Fathers of the Church took up the challenge of instructing the faithful. The patristic injunction to generosity[16] was primarily born from the command of our Lord to "give." The Fathers of the Church encountered widespread greed as a social issue in the Roman Empire. The tightfistedness of the rich was a greater threat to the empire than that of the barbarians' incursions from outside. It was a greater problem than drought.[17] In such a milieu the command and practice of the Lord and their interpretations by the Fathers of the Church gave rise to "institutional responses" to the needs of the poor. "Supporting the weak" was seen as a communal responsibility. "The very presence of the poor testified to the moral failure of the community." Poverty and wealth are interdependent. Anyone, or any group who wants to alleviate poverty, hunger, and homelessness must first deal with the issue of wealth. In fact, Jesus, Paul, and the Fathers of the Church followed this thought line.

However, later Aquinas brings in the element of natural law to giving or charity. "Whatever certain people have in superabundance is due, by natural law, to the purpose of succoring the poor."[18] He does not limit the act of giving only to the superabundant, but since there are many who are in need, each one is entrusted with the stewardship of his own things, so that out of

---

[14] See these points in Allan Verhey, *Remembering Jesus: Christian Community, Scripture, and the Moral Life* (Grand Rapids: Eerdmans, 2005), 306.

[15] Verhey, *Remembering Jesus*, 308.

[16] A neat presentation on 'giving' and 'social aspect of the believer according to the Fathers of the Church' may be found in William J. Walsh and John P. Langan, "Patristic Social Consciousness," in *The Faith that Does Justice: Examining the Christian Sources for Social Change*, John C. Haughey, ed. (New York: Paulist Press, 1977), 113–51.

[17] See these and similar thoughts in Cyprian, *Treatise 5, An Address to Demetrianus* (*ANF* 5:457–65).

[18] *ST* II-IIae Q66 a7.

them one may come to the aid of those who are in need.[19] Such practices, in their various forms, must be followed even to the present day.[20] But a wrong understanding and use of private property is a real impediment to realize a society envisioned by Jesus and the Church.

The Church, acknowledging a communal responsibility, began to undertake concrete acts of charity such as providing food, shelter and clothes for the needy among other social and charitable ministry. Down through the centuries the Church as an institution tried to answer this question especially when there were economic crises, famine, wars, and natural calamities. The Church in the modern and contemporary times is particularly engaged in a great amount of social and charitable ministry. She has realized that "the presence of the poor is not a curse," it is a blessing so that her faith may be active and relevant. In those places where there are no poor and no social issues, faith is as it were dead and no concrete actions are required there to demonstrate one's faith, other than occasional gathering for prayer and worship.

Luke-Acts presents a series of stories and exhortations that deal with both greed and generosity, as already elucidated. These ethical and moral stories are being retold to us today. Some of these include the radical call to sell one's possession to follow Jesus, some others insist on giving up all possessions, but most examples urge on sharing one's possessions. The first two options are difficult, though possible, but the third option is the best for all Christians.[21] This having said, we are not very sure why Luke makes Jesus demand a complete renunciation of possession to follow Him, or why a contrary view is found towards the end of the Gospel and in Acts.[22] But it is clear that in Acts a total renunciation of possessions is never a demand from the apostles, though many of the early Christians did away with their possessions for the common good. But there was a freedom to keep for oneself and family the wealth they possessed. The picture is clearer in the latter part of Acts. We neither see any Gentile church keeping everything in common, nor Paul himself renouncing his wealth completely, on the contrary, private ownership of goods was the norm at that time. Hence, there are the constant reminders especially to the wealthy to give generously to the poor and needy. The world in which we live is not much different from the one Luke and Paul encountered. We are challenged in our day to give generously

---

[19] *ST* II-IIae Q66 a7.

[20] Raiser, "Theological and Ethical Considerations," 284.

[21] Personalist readings of Luke depict Luke as offering a myriad of ethical options. See Hays, *Luke's Wealth Ethics*, 264.

[22] We have already suggested in a previous chapter a couple of possibilities for this dichotomy.

to the poor and the needy, to take up the issues of poverty, hunger, famine, homelessness, and deprivation.

In a church where there are poor, every member ought to ask "What should I do?" Similar questions were asked by John the Baptist's audience (Lk 3:10, 12, 14), as a soliloquy by the rich fool (Lk 12:17) and the unjust steward (Lk 16:3), and by the audience of Peter at the Pentecost speech (Acts 2:37). The first and last group asked the question after having been touched by the Word. They were made to realize that faith and conversion must be accompanied by practical decision and ethical attitudes. The rich fool on the other hand asked himself the same question to gratify himself and to secure his future. The unjust steward also asked it to find a solution to the current problem in the hunt for securing his future. In the third Gospel, in addition to the Zacchaeus narrative, the parables of the Rich Fool (12:16–21), Unjust Steward (16:1–13), Rich Man and Lazarus (16:19–31) (these parables are also examples of ill use of wealth), provide powerful instructions on the prudent use of wealth. Those instances of giving in Acts further enhance this point. Above all Lucan Paul sets an example of the prudent use of wealth. Even today the best way to support the weak is to provide for them, especially through generous alms and charitable actions.

The magic that can unlock the hearts of the people is charity and this vision is being mirrored in the conclusion of the Miletus speech. What a difference it would make if the whole world believed in giving and so set to conquer the world by loving the poor. The Church has been throughout the past twenty centuries spending her energy in different ways to reduce poverty and hunger. Some twelve centuries after Jesus and Paul, Aquinas taught about the liberal use of money which belongs to the realm of justice. Accordingly use of money consists in parting with it.[23] Through the social teaching of the Church of the 19th and the 20th century,[24] the Church deliberated more clearly and eloquently her vision for the world and encouraged people to responsible social conduct by sharply condemning every form of greed. I am aware that a fundamental duty of every leader and Christian is to teach

---

[23] *ST* II-IIae Q117 a5 and a4.

[24] Pope Leo XIII's epoch making social encyclical *Rerum Novarum* (*RN*) inaugurated this process which was then succeeded by a number of social encyclicals and other church documents. Important ones are Pope Pius XI's *Quadragesimo Anno* (*QA*), an encyclical on the reconstruction of the social order published on 15 May 1931; Pope John XXIII's *Mater et Magistra* (*MM*), an encyclical on Christianity and social progress published on 15 May 1961; Second Vatican Council's *Gaudium et Spes* (*GS*), pastoral constitution on the Church in the modern world promulgated on 7 December 1965; Pope Paul VI's *Populorum Progressio* (*PP*), an encyclical on the development of peoples published on 26 March 1967; and Pope John Paul II's *Centesimus Annus* (*CA*), an encyclical on the hundredth anniversary of *Rerum Novarum* published on 1 May 1991.

generosity to others, especially to the rich so that there may be, among the people, some material equality as envisioned by Luke and Paul.[25] This duty of every Christian has a binding force as it is normative to every Christian. This is reiterated by Pope Pius X and for him it is an obligation of charity for the rich and for those who have means, to help the poor and needy, according to the precept of the Gospel. This precept is of such binding force that, at the Day of Judgment, as our Lord Himself tells us, a special account of its fulfilment will be required.[26]

No one lives for one's personal advantage in a community; one lives for the common good as well, so that an individual may creatively aid or contribute to those in need by serving their need. In line with the Gospel teachings and other NT exhortations[27] the social encyclicals promote the right use of wealth by both the wealthy and poor, and the dignity of labor and laborers.[28] One Gospel-oriented priority is the proper use of wealth through charity. From the time of Jesus and Paul to the present time Christianity has always upheld the system of private property,[29] at the same time it

---

[25] There is no distinction between rich or poor, Jew or Gentile, men or women. Many misunderstand the word "equality" assuming that it stands for equality in anything and everything. Equality depends on historical, cultural context, and the term cannot be viewed as absolute norm for all time and culture. For Luke and Paul equality is the status of all before God. Equality may be particularly desired in economic affairs. This was the ideal vision of the primitive church, but it worked, as we have seen, only within Jerusalem. Luke faced a disparity in the distribution of wealth among the Gentile communities and he addressed the issue through parables, anecdotes, and sayings. Luke and Paul are aware that it will not be possible to make a community equal in everything, but they challenge the rich to giving, aiming at some kind of equality.

[26] See Pope Pius X, *Motu Proprio*: *Fin dalla Prima*, ix.

[27] Acts 20:34–35 and Jam 1:9–11; 2:1–8; 5:1–6 are key texts in this regard.

[28] See this aspect is emphasized especially in *MM*, 14–27.

[29] The Popes never condemn capitalism on principle but denounce its abuses in practice. Still its practical abuses and organizing principle of economic activity, competitive profit seeking etc. have not been sufficiently attended to. See Denis Goulet, "Economic Systems, Middle Way Theories," in *Readings in Moral Theology no. 5: Official Catholic Teaching*, Charles E. Curran and Richard A. McCormick, ed. (New York: Paulist Press, 1986), 341. The fundamental accusations against capitalism are that it is individualistic, materialist, and anarchic. At times it is also suggested that capitalism fosters inequality (although comparisons are seldom undertaken with respect to inequality under other historical systems). See the above observations in Michael Novak, "The Bias against Democratic Capitalism," in *Readings in Moral Theology no. 5: Official Catholic Teaching*, 331. However it must be noted that private property is not a "primary right," it is only secondary as conceived by Aquinas. One does not necessarily have to own private property to have one's primary rights such as food, shelter, and clothing respected. See this idea in Marvin L. Mich, "Commentary on *Mater et Magistra*," in *Modern Catholic Social Teaching: Commentaries and Interpretations*, Kenneth R. Himes, ed. (Washington DC: Georgetown University Press, 2005), 200. The purpose of private property

has condemned the neglect of justice and stewardship on the part of the people especially the rich. Ownership of property has a social character that the owners must take into account not only their own advantage, but the common good.[30] Therefore, ownership of property and superfluous income oblige one to charity, and liberality.[31] A roadblock to charity and generosity is greed which is condemned as idolatry by Paul (see ch. 5) and seen as a root sin by the Fathers of the Church and the modern popes.[32] Today greed (in its various forms such as hoarding, adulteration, charging high interest, use of false measures and weights, charging high agent fees or brokerage) is taken in stride as something normal, and one appears ethically so indifferent concerning it, that hardly any religion and social activists speak of it as an ethical or moral issue. For people find nothing wrong in not sharing one's legally acquired wealth, or the tendency to make excessive profits, or living luxuriously with one's justly earned wealth. But the modern social encyclicals address these issues by challenging our presuppositions on the matter.

The rich can surely be an instrument of alleviating poverty if they attend to the needs of the poor around them first, and then by listening to the cries of the poor from the four corners of the world. Proper distribution of wealth is needed to attain the common good of all and when that happens, there is true social justice and human dignity. *Pacem in Terris* of John XXIII stresses on the need to give more attention to the less fortunate members of the society, and Drew Christiansen sees it as an anticipation of the insightful expression, "the preferential option for the poor,"[33] which would spearhead the encyclical *Populorum Progressio*. Since the appearance of this encyclical the churches all over the world deliberately opted for the poor and have drawn out programs for their advancement in various ways. They have understood that development is social as well as individual and that we are all part of a larger network and each and every individual is linked to all other persons, and therefore each individual has a duty towards all others.[34]

Many people think that it is the duty of the rich to give. Not only the rich but everyone has the obligation to give. Even the poor widow gave alms (Lk 21:1–4). In the same way with the little one has, one must reach

---

is for sustenance of oneself and the family along with providing for the human race. See Pope Pius XI, *QA*, 45–46.

[30] Pope Pius XI, *QA*, 48.

[31] Pope Pius XI, *QA*, 50-52.

[32] The Popes, like John XXIII, Paul VI, and John Paul II strongly condemn greed in their social encyclicals.

[33] Drew Christiansen, "Commentary on *Pacem in Terris*," in *Modern Catholic Social Teaching: Commentaries and Interpretations*, Kenneth R. Himes, ed. (Washington DC: Georgetown University Press, 2005), 228.

[34] Pope Paul VI, *PP*, 17.

out to others, because after being content with all that one has, one is less likely to enter into the act of giving. So, no matter how poor one is, still one can contribute to the welfare of others. One can point to thousands of examples of generous giving and hard work of ordinary poor people. If poor people can achieve great feats, how much more the rich? One can finger count examples of business tycoons, celebrities, or wealthy who help the poor and, in contrast, the needy who sometimes give more than half their income. But most of the rich are selfish and proud, who want to create a kingdom of power and glory for themselves and often neglect the poor and the needy. A roll call is given to all especially the rich to give generously for the building up of the communities and individuals. If all the rich were to seriously heed the voice "give generously" there would not have been many poor in this world.

Luke instructs that when people "give" they should give to the poor, the maimed, the lame, and the blind (Lk 14:13, 21). Those who wish to follow Jesus must be willing to sell all that they have and give to the poor. Zacchaeus gave half his wealth to the poor; and the poor widow put into the treasury all she had to live on. The fellowship early Christians at Jerusalem maintained indicates their willingness to share and hold everything in common, through which they were also proclaiming that they were responsible for one another. Barnabas sold his property and placed it at the feet of the apostles. Cornelius and Lydia were examples of charity. Most importantly Paul spent his wealth for the service of the needy. These and other narratives in Luke-Acts illustrate the correct Christian use of wealth, irrespective of them being rich or poor.

"Man is an answerer, engaged in dialogue and responding to actions upon him."[35] This is all the more true of a Christian as the Catechism of the Catholic Church (CCC) states that man responds to his vocation through the exchange with others, mutual service and dialogue with his brethren.[36] This communal and dialogical nature of Christian faith demands promotion of welfare and justice in society because "moral imagination" of Christians is shaped by the teaching of Christ and the Church. Accordingly love is the central point of Christian ethos because Jesus is the absolute norm of morale as he "brought to fulfillment the deepest aspirations of mankind." For this reason Paul, in many cases, relies ultimately on Jesus for his moral teaching as he does in Acts 20:35. Our real strength is in the willingness to care and support each other. It's a simple universal principle that in giving that we

---

[35] James F. Childress "Scripture and Christian Ethics," in *Readings in Moral Theology No. 4: The Use of Scripture in Moral Theology*, Charles E. Curran and Richard A. McCormick, ed. (New York: Paulist Press, 1984), 277.

[36] Catechism of the Catholic Church (Vatican City: Libreria Editrice Vaticana, 2005), 1879.

receive. "By getting things we make a living, by giving we make a life." It is hard to make people believe that in giving life one becomes happier or it is the means to get abundantly in return. Acts 20:34–35 envisions communities where generous giving is their hallmark.

Giving should be generous otherwise it does not merit a virtue. For example, if something is required of us, then doing that is not to be considered a meritorious conduct. If a person is hungry, the action of someone offering that person food cannot be called a generous act, because the recipient really needs that food. That act may be called an act of charity.[37] Though charity is important for both Luke and Paul, they also speak abundantly of generous giving. Generosity involves giving and doing more than required. It is not a simple act of charity, but it is an excellent act of giving, a charity without any boundaries. It is giving rightly to the right people, the right amount at the right time with pleasure.[38] It was a virtue so important for Jesus and Paul; it is important for us because we also live in a similar interdependent world. The problem is not so much wealth as such, but its excessive accumulation and imprudent use of it.

A person can have a lot of money and still live a very poor life and a person can have no money at all and live a really rich life. What makes a person rich is not how much that person has, but how much that person gives. An act of giving to the needy is a sign of one's empathy for that person in need. It is an act of kindness. When it comes to empathy or kindness, the size of a person's wallet doesn't matter. When it comes to giving, the size of one's heart is the only thing that matters. We must also know that one simple act of generosity can snowball into more and more act of kindness and giving. It doesn't matter how much we have to give, however big or small, true giving always returns positivity to our lives.[39] Giving is always rewarding as the conclusion of the Miletus speech is clear on this. Give with your whole self, like the poor widow (Lk 21:1–4), love with your whole heart, and your life will be full of happiness. One small step, one small act will create a ripple. You may not see its effects often, but the effect is big.

The message "give" is posted at the heart of all Christians especially the rich, that they may be generous and responsible for one another. Pope Francis in one of his general audiences said that people who are unable to give are slaves to possessions. The purpose of wealth is to serve others and promote human dignity. Life is for loving and giving and not for amassing

---

[37] See these expressions in Lester H. Hunt, "Generosity," *Enc. of Ethics* 1:602.

[38] Arist. *NE* 1120a 12-13. See more on liberality, prodigality, meanness in Arist. *NE* 1120a–1122b. Aristotle's definition of liberality restricts imprudent distribution of money to others.

[39] Thoughts here are from various messages I received on WhatsApp.

possessions.[40] Everyone comes into this world with nothing and leaves this world with nothing. "It is what one does between one's birth and death is all that counts." Many rich who earn huge sum as profit or salary or wages do not know what to do with their income, and often these people live a luxurious and unaccountable life. Acts 20:32–35 envision that Christians should know the purpose of wealth and that they learn to use it responsibly. This takes us to the next point.

9.4. A Call to Christian Responsibility

The poor are so not because they are always at fault but because of the circumstances and social situations in which they live. The rich are so not always because of their merit or hard work but because of certain advantages and opportunities they have. Therefore, everyone has the obligation to help the poor without examining too much the causes of their poverty. In simple terms an ethic of responsibility is also envisioned in Acts 20:32–35.

When we speak of responsibility it is always *for* something and *to* someone.[41] This is slightly different from the ethics of duty, which includes carrying out a specific duty. For example it is the duty of the teacher to teach at allotted periods. But it is her responsibility to care for the students in general or to cooperate to maintain discipline at the school. Responsibility is in question when one is answerable for a particular social, political, or religious situation, for carrying out a complex task, or when one is ultimately answerable before the law or God for the consequences of one's actions.[42] Paul's final words envisage the need for care of the poor and needy as a responsibility of the Ephesian elders and Christians. They are, to certain extent, responsible *for* the misery of the poor and they are responsible *to* God and one another in all that they do. Giving financial or moral support to a needy or weak person under certain circumstances may be a specific duty of the Christians, but giving generously for the support of the poor is a responsibility of every Christian.

Another aspect in this regard is the co-responsibility one ought to have for the other. God asks Cain a fundamental question "Where is your brother?" Cain replies, "Am I my brother's keeper?" (Gen 4:9). We could say that Luke-Acts try to answer the above question in a very touching and colorful way. It constantly tells us that every needy person is my neighbor and

---

[40] "Pope at Audience: Life is a Time for Giving not Possessing," *Vatican News*, accessed on 5 April 2019, https://www.vaticannews.va/en/pope/news/2018-11/pope-francis-general-audience-7-november-you-shall-not-steal.html.

[41] Robert Spaemann, "Christian Ethics of Responsibility," in *Moral Truth and Moral Tradition: Essays in Honor of Peter Geach and Elizabeth Anscombe*, Luke Gormally, ed. (Dublin: Four Courts Press, 1994), 134.

[42] Spaemann, "Christian Ethics of Responsibility," 134.

brother. The parable of the Good Samaritan, for example, vividly portrays the care the Samaritan rendered to the man who fell among the robbers. The Samaritan sees it as his responsibility because for him everyone, irrespective of caste or class, is his neighbor. Through the parable of the Rich Man and Lazarus a similar lesson is again taught, and the moral of the story is clear: that the rich man ought to have been responsible for the poor in general, and he had had a specific duty to care for Lazarus. This story is typical of Luke both in its perspective on rich and poor and in the reversal of the fortunes of the rich man and Lazarus.[43] These parables are told that the audience may be conscious of their responsibility for the other. We are our brothers' keeper. Spaemann states that 'my brother's keeper' is the key word for a Christian ethic of responsibility. If your brother is hungry or needy or homeless or without clothes you have an obligation to feed him and provide for him. The Miletus speech brilliantly answers the question "who is my neighbor?" and Paul exemplifies as a model who is very much concerned for the neighbor. Paul as a pastor and leader assumes great responsibility for the churches' faith and practices, their economic condition and behavior. So he instructs them about various aspects of their faith and practices and exhorts and encourages them to lead an authentic Christian life which will be characterized by love, humility, and service.

The rich man who did not assume any responsibility for Lazarus could have defended his stand for not helping Lazarus "with the argument that one should not interfere when God is punishing a person."[44] In our world there are many such people who refuse to help the poor and needy. They often blame the unfortunate ones for their misery. I have come across so many broken families due to the drinking habit of the husbands, or their irresponsibility towards their wives and children. When these desperate and heavy-laden women and children ask for some kind of monetary help to lead a dignified life, no true pastor could refuse to help them just because their husbands or a member in the family is irresponsible towards them.

In the OT the institutions like the Jubilee Year, Sabbath, and Tithe were established so that Israel as a people might fulfill their corporate responsibility towards the poor and needy. The NT does not speak about these institutions nor does it propose them as means to alleviate poverty and need. On the contrary the NT recommends generous giving. Various instances in Luke-Acts are an obvious place to find support for this claim. "Christian" responsible use of wealth is a central theological point in Luke-Acts. "Some materials in Luke-Acts primarily concentrate on this motif, while in some other materials the motif appears secondary to the main subject." Those

---

[43] Fred B. Craddock, *Luke*, Interpr. (Louisville, KY: John Knox, 1990), 195.

[44] Craddock, 196.

narratives and references about almsgiving and the parable of the Rich Man and Lazarus are to be acknowledged as belonging to the former, while some parables and narratives in Luke-Acts touch upon the latter. We have already examined these instances in chapter eight.

The Church has a corporate responsibility towards the poor and needy.[45] Generous giving is always a relevant and noble virtue that can contribute greatly to the welfare of the poor people. Church leaders ought to be responsible with the church resources such as funds, movable and immovable property, donations, and offering so that they may fulfil the corporate responsibility towards the unfortunate. All resources must be used for the benefit of others, especially for the poor and needy. There is a growing tendency among clerics and laity to misuse money or property received as donations and offering. Many parishes spend huge sums in order to construct new buildings or to beautify existing ones. Some pastors use up donations and offering neglecting the poor and needy and some others use them to lead a luxurious life. In some places priests constantly ask the faithful to donate money so that church buildings, institutions, and business may prosper. In some cases, the money collected from the people for the poor does not reach them. And this is certainly not the responsible use of wealth.

And finally Christian responsibility is a call to solidarity[46] which one needs to demonstrate in the society. The social doctrines of the Church emphasize this point enough and more. For example, CCC articles 1939–1942, speak about human solidarity. Socio-economic problems can be resolved only with the help of all forms of solidarity: solidarity of the poor among themselves, between rich and poor, of workers among themselves, among nations and peoples, between workers and employers.[47] Church leaders can efficiently function as facilitators of solidarity in the society.

9.5. Imitation of Jesus and the Saints

The Miletus speech envisions that Christians imitate Jesus and his faithful servant Paul; in imitating Paul they ultimately imitate Jesus because Paul's imitation is geared up and shaped up by the Lord. It can be reasonably argued that Christians' imitation of Paul can be extended to the imitation of saints since they too imitate or bear witness to Christ. Christ is the ultimate norm for all while all other laws and norms are secondary. Jesus is the norm for us Christians who are a big family united in love. The Church is the mystical

---

[45] *GS* 40–41 speak about the importance of being responsible. Moreover almost all the social documents of the Church directly or indirectly address this subject.

[46] Solidarity is the natural unity that unites the members of a society: family, clan, tribe and people. See Testa, *Il Lavoro nella Bibbia*, 76.

[47] CCC, 1941.

body of Christ and, thereby, we the members are called to love as Jesus loved. The manifestation of this love in the community makes the Church a community of love. Saints like Paul, Barnabas, Francis of Assisi, Vincent de Paul, Alphonsus Maria de Liguori, Mother Teresa and others are models who transmitted the values of Christ in their own way and time. Certain values such as solidarity, caring, and generosity are the results of genuine love.

The whole enterprise of imitation suggests that any imitative practice is oriented towards cultivating virtues and in the Pauline and Lucan context virtues such as humility, generosity, repentance and conversion, suffering with joy, and endurance are of foremost importance. The leaders of the church, especially priests of the church have an obligation to imitate Jesus and "to give an example of every virtue, of zeal, of humility, of charity, of modesty, etc."[48] Secondly, genuine imitation demands the good of the other. This may involve vicarious suffering for the other, or willingness to bear burden or let go of something on another's behalf. Giving of a financial gift is only an outward manifestation of such suffering and burden bearing. Thirdly, the goal of imitation is for the edification of the Church. Particular churches can be models of generosity, solidarity, endurance of trials, communion, etc.[49]

9.6. Uphold the Dignity of all Labor and Laborers

Paul deliberately chose manual labor as a means of sustenance although it was not required of him. Most people of the time treated manual work / workers with contempt but unlike them Paul saw in every worker / work a value and upheld its dignity. Jesus himself was a manual worker who was Paul's model. We have already noted these facts in a previous chapter. Acts 20:34–35 envisions that every Christian have the mind of Christ and of Paul towards manual work and workers and it implies that every Christian seriously endeavor to imbibe the same Christian spirit and bear fruits in his / her own life. The Church, following the teaching and example of Jesus, has been more deliberative on the dignity of labor and laborers and she has been comprehensive and outspoken in her teaching on it. An overview of some of the Church documents will reveal that how much the Church has contributed to spread the awareness of dignity of every work and worker. Pope John Paul's encyclical *Laborem Exercens* is unique here as it seems to have followed the teachings of Paul on labor. The encyclical proclaims the necessity of work for sustenance and contribution to the social development.[50] Work is something

---

[48] Alphonsus M. de Liguori, *Dignity and Duties of the Priest or Selva*, E. Grimm, ed. (New York; Cincinnati; Chicago: Benziger Brothers, 1889), 235.

[49] Ideas for this paragraph are from Michael Jensen, "Imitating Paul, Imitating Christ: How does Imitation Work as a Moral Concept?" *Churchman* 124.1 (2010)," 32–33.

[50] See this idea in the preface of *Laborem Exercens* (*LE*) of Pope John Paul II issued on 14 September 1981.

that corresponds to man's dignity, it expresses this dignity and increases it. This ethical dimension of work is an element so important[51] for the present day.

9.6.1. Importance and Dignity of Manual Labor

God dignified manual labor by "portraying himself as a manual worker whose fingers formed the universe." God works for six days: the first image that one gets of God is that he is a worker and he rests only on the seventh day. The Book of Genesis also describes how labor is man's lot from his beginning. Man is born to toil (Job 5:7) and there is no escape for him from it. The many references to various manual works in the Bible, be it farm work, crafts, textiles, or any particular work such as making the ark or the tabernacle or the temple, are indications of the great importance work, particularly manual work, has in the Jewish society. Thus in the Bible both manual and intellectual works are presented as having more or less the same dignity. Yet among the Israelites manual labor was mostly performed by the poor.

Jesus' birth into a carpenter's family and his labor as a carpenter for long years is basic to the correct view of the dignity of labor. He was most intimately connected with the labor world. For Jesus every work is important and deserves respect because no work is menial or inferior. Joseph Husslein observes "All honest labor, of head or hand, was held in honor by Him."[52] By becoming a slave and doing the work of a slave, Jesus raises the dignity of every slave on par with the Divine. Jesus' friendship with fishermen, tax collectors etc. testifies his own positive attitude to such labor and laborers. Moreover, many of the parables Jesus told are taken from the labor world.

With the life and example of Christ, the Greco-Roman predominant negative attitude towards manual work to some extent gets reversed among the Christians. Paul's own example was a key factor that contributed to this ideological reversal. However, in practice many Christians looked down upon manual labor, particularly works like domestic works (cooking, washing etc.), works in the fields (digging, planting, and harvesting, etc.), and works linked with trade (work at diary, carpentry, masonry, butchering etc.), which were mostly done by the poor or slaves. Paul's own example of manual labor and his attitude towards it is clear enough to suggest that every work is a good thing, unless otherwise, such as stealing, prostitution etc. which cannot be considered as good work (Eph 4:28); and every good work is for the benefit of the individual and community. Every work, whether it is intellectual, manual, official, or clerical, has its own dignity. Reference to Paul's manual labor at Acts 20:34–35 and elsewhere in his own letters

---

[51] *LE*, 9.

[52] Joseph Husslein, *Bible and Labor* (London: Sands & Co., 1924), 172.

absolutizes the dignity of every labor; and this is a great contribution of the Lucan Paul to Christian social ethics.

The official teachings of the Catholic Church do not include any elaborate discussion on the dignity of varied labors,[53] but they deal with it within the treatment of the "dignity of human person, which may be viewed as the cornerstone of *Gaudium et Spes*," the Pastoral Constitution on the Church in the Modern World. Long before the issuance of this document, Leo XIII in his encyclical *Rerum Novarum* had exhorted the faithful to give due respect to workers by giving them just wages and respectful treatment.[54] This itself was a reminder to hold every work as divinely ordered and planned.

Dignity of every labor is reiterated in *Laborem Exercens* as it particularly dignifies agricultural works. We may extend this dignity given to agricultural labor to other forms of work that are considered low-class or sub-standard. The general tendency is to look down upon agricultural and other forms of manual work. But these works are essential for the survival of the humanity. One must not see manual work as slight or undesired, after all Jesus was a manual worker for the major span of his life, and Paul upheld the dignity of manual work by resorting to it himself. "The teaching of Christ on work through the example of his life during his years in Nazareth finds a lively echo in the teaching of the apostle Paul." Labor, whatever kind may it be, "is not a disgrace for those who perform it; it is an honor, because it supplies an honest means of sustaining life."

9.6.2. Dignity of Laborers

Right from the first pages of the Bible there are indications about the dignified state of all labor and laborers. All laborers are created by God, redeemed by Jesus, and judged by the merits and demerits of each, this is the "Christian democracy."[55] The dignity of Christians derives from Christ as it is clear from the Miletus speech. Acts 20:28 indicates the special emphasis laid on the dignity of the person and on the preciousness of the ransom. The people of God are His by right of purchase (this is analogous to what in ancient times was customary when slavery prevailed).[56] The Church is called the Lord's by the qualification that it is "bought with a price" (1 Cor 6:20; cf. also Rom 14:8-9; Tit 2:14).

---

[53] *Laborem Exercens* includes a section on the dignity of Agricultural work. See *LE*, 21.

[54] *RN*, 20 and 39–46.

[55] Joseph Husslein, *Work, Wealth, and Wages* (Chicago: Matre & Company, 1921), 99.

[56] George Smeaton, *The Doctrine of the Atonement according to the Apostles* (Peabody: Hendrickson, 1988), 97.

Acts 20:34–35 is helpful to visualize a Christian treatment of workers and a Christian perception of dignity. The Christian perception of dignity bases itself on Acts 20:28, which provides respectful treatment to all laborers, since all labor is divinely willed. Thus dignity of labor and laborers is inseparable one from the other; if a laborer is treated badly or shown bias on account of the work he does, it is also an indication that the work he does is sub-standard or menial for the one who shows bias. Paul's own example here indicates that he neither held any work menial nor was disrespectful to workers for the kind of work they did. Human society is characterized by diversity, for example, different race, color, physical features, gender etc.[57] and to make these elements uniform would be the destruction of society itself. Though they may be pluriform and unequal by way of nature, the possession or dispossession of these elements cannot be used to deny them equal dignity as persons.[58]

A man's dignity does not depend on the work he does, but rather for whom it is done: all who are engaged in work merit honor and status irrespective of the work they do, because all are called by God for a specific type of work. Objectively there is no hierarchy of work, but some works are more necessary and some less; some directly related to man's lives, existence, common good, and his necessity but some are not.[59] This being true, subjectively one is free to attend to any work, intellectual or manual, white collar or blue collar.

An important issue here is that the Bible comes across to the reader as showing bias against certain groups of people, not so much their work. The crystal-clear example is the acceptance of slavery. The OT accepted slavery, and the NT never spoke against it and even Paul exhorts the slaves to be obedient to their masters and accept their authority (Eph 6:5; Col: 3:22; Tit 2:9).[60] The Catholic Church until the 20th century did not definitely speak against every form of slavery; rather she had supported the practice of "just slavery." There was a growing sentiment among some theologians of the early centuries that slavery was incompatible with the Christian conception of charity and justice. But many others including the influential Aquinas accepted "penal slavery" subject to certain restrictions. Throughout Europe

---

[57] CCC paragraphs 1934–38 provides more insights on the equality and differences among men.

[58] Husslein, *Work, Wealth, and Wages*, 99.

[59] Ideas for this paragraph are from Guzzetti, "Il Lavoro nei suoi Aspetti Morali," 225.

[60] For more on this see A. J. Harril, "Paul and Slavery," in *Paul in the Greco-Roman World: A Handbook*, J. Paul Sampley, ed. (Harrisburg, PA: Trinity Press International, 2003), 575–607. For slaves and slavery among the Greeks, see Nick Fisher, "Citizens, Foreigners, and Slaves in Greek Society," in *A Companion to the Classical Greek World*, Konrad H. Kinzl, ed. (Malden: Blackwell, 2006), 327–49.

by the end of the medieval period enslavement of Christians had been mostly abolished but enslavement of non-Christians was permissible. It was only gradually that any form of slavery was seen as against the mind of Christ.

A breakthrough in the social ethics of the Church was made by Leo XIII in his encyclical *Rerum Novarum* which calls for respectful treatment of all persons especially the laborers. To see a laborer as a commodity is the greatest possible evil done against a laborer. Dignity of laborers is at stake when there are child laborers, poor wages, and dangerous working conditions. Moreover, when a laborer's status and worth are measured on the basis of the work a person does, again dignity of laborer is highly at risk. Just wages,[61] better working conditions, and the right to associate were primary components of workers' dignity. Human dignity is more important than human rights since rights are rooted in human dignity. *Rerum Novarum* also points out that the equality of all men is contradicted by every fact and condition of human life. Although everyone does not do the same work or the profession of people is not the same for all, it certifies that it is God's order and not man's. But at the same time we must raise our voice against every injustice and abuse that exists in our society. Following *Rerum Novarum*, all the social teachings of the Catholic Church give due importance to the dignity of all individuals, particularly of laborers.[62]

A culture which recognizes the eminent dignity of the worker will emphasize the subjective dimension of work. The value of any human work does not depend on the kind of work done; it is based on the fact that the one who does it is a person. Here we have an ethical criterion whose implications cannot be overlooked. Thus every person has a right to work, and this right must be recognized in a practical way by an effective commitment to resolving the tragic problem of unemployment.[63] Unfortunately in many

---

[61] All social encyclicals give due attention to the promotion of just wages. See for example *RN*, 43. *LE*, 19 is very forceful on this as it says "wages, that is to say *remuneration for work,* are still a *practical means* whereby the vast majority of people can have access to those goods which are intended for common use: both the goods of nature and manufactured goods. Both kinds of goods become accessible to the worker through the wage which he receives as remuneration for his work. Hence, in every case, a just wage is the concrete means of *verifying the justice* of the whole socioeconomic system and, in any case, of checking that it is functioning justly."

[62] See this point emphasized in *GS*, 12, 19–22. *GS* 29 is prophetic as it says "Equal dignity of persons demands that a more just and humane condition of life be brought about. For excessive economic and social differences between the members of the human family or population groups cause scandal, and militate against social justice, equity, dignity of human person, as well as social and international peace." The same ideas are reflected in *LE*, 21–25; CCC, 129–33.

[63] See these points in Congregation for the Doctrine of the Faith, *Instruction on Christian Freedom and Liberation*, 22 March 1986, 85.

parts of the world certain works are still considered sub-standard and there aren't enough laborers to do such works, which causes the problem of unemployment among those who have pursued professional courses as the country or society is not equipped to offer desired works to all these professionals. Moreover, those who have pursued a professional course are unwilling to choose a work that is considered low-standard. The only solution for these issues is a subjective and collective attitude change stimulated by the attitude of Jesus and Paul.

This being said we also encounter a world where women are paid less and treated badly at work places. Equal pay for equal work is a distant dream for women in many societies of the world. Women have a unique role in the society which must be respected and allowed to flourish. The true advancement of women requires that labor should be structured in such a way that women do not have to pay for their advancement by abandoning what is specific to them and at the expense of the family, in which women as mothers have an irreplaceable role.[64] A similar mother role is played by Catholic nuns, all over the world, whose service is often taken for granted, and in many cases they are underpaid by the clerics or their service is not at all taken into account. The domestic services of nuns are often given little recognition. According to a recent report some of them work in bishops' or cardinals' residences, others in the kitchen linked with clerics or church institutions; some are employed for the service of men in the church, and they work from dawn to late night, having no fixed time table and yet their remuneration is slender. More saddening is the fact that these nuns are not invited to sit at the table at which they serve. Is it normal for a consecrated man to be served by another consecrated person? Consecrated people destined to domestic work are almost always consecrated women.[65] It is true that all consecrated persons are at the service of the Church but at the same time their dignity must be always upheld.[66] Clericalism may impede the growth of women and the Church and the idea that women are of less worth than men sabotages the dignity of women.

---

[64] *LE*, 19.

[65] See the above observations appeared in "The (almost) free Work of Sisters," *Matters India*, accessed on 8 April 2019, http://mattersindia.com/2018/10/the-almost-free-work-of-sisters/.

[66] Pope Francis addressing the International Union of Superiors General, the main umbrella group of nuns, on 9 May 2019 told them that their vocation is service, not servitude. He also urged religious sisters to just say no when clergy want to use them as maids. See "Pope vows to fight nun abuse, urges service, not servitude," *Cruxnow.com*, accessed on 29 May 2019, https://cruxnow.com/vatican/2019/05/10/pope-vows-to-fight-nun-abuse-urges-service-not-servitude/.

The above points presented in this chapter are the important visions and implications of Acts 20:32–35 for us today. Since I have examined the text through the ethical lens, its vision is formed and its implication for us today is detected primarily with the help of the narratives about Jesus and Paul, and the teachings of the Church. The challenge before every Christian and church leader is to translate these great examples and teachings into action. For that, ultimately, one needs to have recourse to the grace of God as did Paul for himself and for others.

General Conclusion

This study is unique in its emphasis on ethics and theology. It has highlighted the mutuality of Biblical theology and ethics which, in fact, are two sides of the same coin. In general, it has shown the overarching ethical concern of the Miletus speech, but it has examined specifically the ethical content of the final part of the speech, and this my attempt is original in the ethical and theological field. The following pages present a summation of the theological-ethical findings of this study.

By situating the Miletus speech in its Jewish and Greco-Roman context, some important observations have been made. First, the Miletus speech is a farewell discourse that was composed in the tradition of the LXX and Jewish farewell speeches. The forensic, epideictic, and deliberative elements found in the speech derive also, to some extent, from Greco-Roman (farewell) speeches. It is an undisputed fact that the NT authors borrowed many elements from their literary world, culture, and society. This explains why the form and certain elements of the Miletus speech are akin to Jewish, LXX, or Greco-Roman speeches. It was customary for ancient writers to include ethical and moral instructions in their Works. This was especially true for farewell speeches, and Luke is clearly following this convention.

An important point that has been repeatedly noted in this thesis is the evident LXX influence of and on Luke. Many of the themes found in Luke-Acts have an LXX stamp. The placement of the Miletus speech towards the end of Paul's missionary journeys, the speech's farewell character, its subject matter, and paraenesis correspond to LXX farewell speeches. We conclude that Luke was indebted to the LXX more than to any other ancient document for the Miletus speech. At the same time, it does not discount Lucan indebtedness to other literatures and conventions of the time.

Speeches were regularly given by the ancients at various places and events. These speeches constituted a major part of Greco-Roman and Jewish literature. Acts is unique for the many speeches of different individuals that are included in it. All the speeches in Acts, including the Miletus speech, were given shape by Luke. Nevertheless, it was easier for Luke to form the Miletus speech as its content was available to him while he was a travelling companion of Paul and was present, most probably, at the time the speech was delivered. This is a speech delivered for a public occasion but, inserted into the "we section" that suggests that Luke was present at the Miletus discourse. This firsthand information of Luke strengthens the credibility of the content of the discourse. Since the speech came from the mouth of Paul himself, it is not surprising that it is akin to the letters of Paul.

We have also discussed the similarity of the speech to the Pauline materials by examining the figure of Paul in Acts. One originality of this study is that it has identified and clarified most of the issues related to the figure of Paul therein. Accordingly, we have concluded that any information that differs in Acts need not be considered as something invented by Luke to prove his points or to convincingly present facts. Nor should it be construed as a sign of Luke's ignorance about Paul; rather it would show that by "writing independently" of Paul, Luke might have overlooked the exact time of certain historical events, or that he did not possess the exact details of many events that were transmitted to him through oral tradition or a third person account. Incompatibility in a couple of historical details should not be viewed as a sign of error or disagreement in facts or theology. The value of Acts in this regard lies in the additional information Luke furnishes about Paul which serious scholars regard as irrefutable. Thus, Acts is to be considered as reliable as the letters of Paul.

Granted that the speech appears to be akin to certain sections of Pauline (and deutero-Pauline) letters, Luke might not have used them for the composition of the speech, although he might have had some knowledge of them. We determined that the resemblance of the speech to letters is due to three reasons. First, the speech was delivered to a Christian audience and thus truly reflected Paul's discourse in a similar situation.[1] Second, Paul's letters were always addressed to Christians in Gentile territory. Thus, it was quite natural for Paul to have delivered to Christians a speech similar to the content of his letters, rather than a speech similar to one that aimed at making converts, as in his missionary speeches. Third, each letter of Paul was written with specific purposes to address diverse issues. It is evident that some concerns of these letters, with which Luke himself was familiar (though

[1] Unfortunately, we do not have any such speech recorded in the NT save the Miletus speech; various sections of Pauline letters may be considered as speeches in written form. This can explain well the Miletus speech's resemblance to Paul's letters.

without a direct dependence on them), are brought under one umbrella in the Miletus speech; thus, the speech is typically Pauline.[2]

In our study of the Miletus speech various ethical and theological concerns of it have been highlighted. In the second part of this thesis we have examined Acts 20:32–35 in detail and identified the ethical emphases found in it. Using various texts related to Acts 20:32–35 and the Pauline corpus, we have been able to demonstrate the coherence in the ethical teaching of Luke and Paul. The speech is parallel to the content of Paul's letters; one can notice, especially in Acts 20:32–35, a blending and coherence of Lucan-Pauline thoughts at four points and they spearhead the ethical evaluation of it.

First, this is seen in their use of the word χάρις which is used abundantly and somewhat identically[3] in their writings. Grace is a gift of God, at the same time it is active and a power. When the gift of God is channeled to the good of the community, it becomes active, powerful, and strengthens bond—it is grace. It is impossible to be a true Christian without creatively and actively demonstrating "grace working through love." Effective love must consider an individual's deepest needs and concerns.

Second, various references to work in the Pauline Corpus and the mention of the same in Acts 20:34–35 share the same theology and ethics of both Luke and Paul. This again evidences the Lucan and Pauline agreement in their teaching on labor.

Third, the important Lucan paraenesis on "giving," the most important ingredient of the 'right use of material possessions,' is similar to Pauline paraenesis, which views wealth mainly as gifts for διακονία and κοινωνία. Luke offers "different options" for Christians who wish to follow Jesus or help the poor;[4] it could be by the selling of (all) goods and giving the proceeds to the poor (Lk 18:22; Acts 2:44–45; 4:36–37), or by contributing for the benefit of the community (Acts 11:29–30), or through almsgiving (Acts 9:36; 10:2). We may conclude that the Lucan call to charity and generosity becomes analogous to the Pauline vision of διακονία and κοινωνία, although these may have other meanings for Paul. Various examples in Luke-Acts suggest that Luke is quite clear and emphatic on the use of wealth for sustenance and charity. The Lucan stereotypical call to almsgiving, several parables in the Gospel, the exemplary figures of

[2] But the speech is in Luke's wordings. It is also noticeable that certain major topics of Romans and Galatians, for example, justification by faith and baptism are absent in the Miletus speech.

[3] In different places the word may have a slightly different meaning depending on the context. I have not entered into a thorough discussion on the topic in this thesis.

[4] We have not made any attempt to explain the reason for Luke's suggestion of various options as this was not the scope of our study.

charity in Acts, and the paraenesis in the final part of the Miletus speech all point to this. Similarly, in Paul's conception, wealth is both for oneself and for other needy persons in the community. Paul does not offer various options as does Luke, but the Miletus speech presents Paul's option: one may work and earn for the sustenance of self and others.

Fourth, and closely related to the above, is the Lucan concept of social ethics[5] which is parallel to the Pauline position. This is dealt with in chapters 6–8 of this thesis. A comparison between Pauline letters and Acts 20:32–35 shows that Paul's practical example of charity, in the form of his collection for the Jerusalem Church stood at the center of his entire social ministry. Our study concluded that the collection for Jerusalem was the principal model act of charity by Paul and his communities, although it was undertaken to realize other purposes. It was a painstaking effort by Paul to carry out this project. The clarion call of Luke in favor of the poor, weak, and needy is the high point in Lucan social ethics, and this call is made throughout Acts, particularly in the Miletus speech.

In the Miletus speech Lucan Paul does not explicitly refer to the communitarian life, or collection, but speaks generally of supporting the weak. He continuously supported himself and his companions by laborious work as is recorded also in some of the Pauline Epistles. The climactic maxim in the Miletus speech, which is similar to Lk 6:38 and 2 Cor 9:7, may be considered as the core of the wealth ethics of Luke and Paul. In the latter reference ("God loves a cheerful giver") Paul utilizes an aphorism that reveals his outlook on giving. This thesis repeatedly demonstrates that the wealth ethics of Luke and Paul correspond and that the emphasis on the motif of giving is an important component. Christ is the "real motive" in Pauline and Lucan paraenesis. The work ethics, imitation ethics, and giving ethics are characterized by their Christological motives. Paul used the most profound motives at important points; Lucan Paul's use of Christ's words at the end of the speech reiterates the importance of giving. Moreover, it is imposed on the audience as an obligation. Christ's words and generous giving are the "real motivating force for Christian action." Generous giving was a thing so relevant for the Gentile Christians in their time; similarly, Lucan Paul tried to provide directions for their moral behavior by using Christ's own example.

In this study I have tried to elaborate the ethic of imitation according to Paul since it is a major theme in the Miletus speech. Though there are many theological and ethical affinities between Luke and Paul, when it comes to imitation terminology, Luke is not enthusiastic about it, and the

[5] A few instances characteristic of Acts' community ethics may be noted in chs. 6–8 of this thesis but there is no detailed discussion of them.

only place there is some verbal affinity is in Acts 20:35, and here it follows the Pauline pattern—the imitation of Paul first and then of Jesus. Thus, the Christological dimension of imitation in the speech is parallel to the idea of imitation in the Pauline letters. Imitation in Acts 20:34–35 is limited to the realm of manual work and supporting the weak; but the imitation in Paul's letters embraces other moral realms. Nevertheless, Paul's concise testimony about his own missionary life in the speech may be viewed as an example for the Ephesians and future leaders of the church to imitate; thus, the whole speech has savors of *mimesis*. For Luke, Paul is a model since he fulfils the requirements for being a model; but the ultimate model for Paul is Jesus. The final call is to imitate Jesus who is their moral imperative; thus, imitation works as a "moral concept" in the Miletus speech and Pauline letters.

Luke narrates Paul's virtues so that Christians may be edified by it. I am convinced that just as Paul provided a model of Christian giving, care, and work, present day Christians must imbibe these qualities so that they too can be ethical models for the society and church in which they live. First, Christians can be models by their charitable actions. The perfect way of charity is by Giving. Christians must be willing to give from the little they have, and they must be willing to work to support themselves and others especially the poor and the needy.

Again, the examination and elaboration of the purpose(s) of the speech has provided a solid evidence for the coherent and eloquent interplay of theology and ethics in the Miletus passage. The originality of this study also includes an elaborate study of the purpose of the speech. Among the purposes of the speech, the deliberative function is the most apparent, the most important point being the ethical paraenesis which brings the speech to a close. These paraeneses remind the Ephesian elders of their duty to be true pastors, models, and missionaries. They reiterate the right attitude that leaders should possess concerning grace, labor, wealth, and giving.

In Luke's conception, Paul plays a normative function for the second-generation Christians. By portraying Paul's lifestyle of manual labor and self-sufficiency Luke shows that Paul fulfilled the standard claims of virtuous character espoused by the ancients.[6] Nevertheless, he is an apostle who monitors and supervises the community in the absence of the first-generation apostles. Paul is a role-model for the second-generation leaders and Christians especially in the realm of economic life. Instead of being the "first recipient" of charity, he works with his own hands to provide for himself and others. In short, three normative conclusions may be drawn from Luke's view of Paul in Acts 20:34–35: (1) Paul, as an apostle and

---

[6] Abraham Smith, *Comfort One Another: Reconstructing the Rhetoric and Audience of 1 Thessalonians* (Louisville, KY: John Knox, 1995), 38.

pastor, is a norm for the post apostolic churches; (2) Paul's practice of private ownership of goods is acceptable and it became the norm in the gentile churches; (3) following the example of Paul, leaders and Christians are to work and help others.

Not only Paul is a normative figure, but the final exhortations given to the elders have a normative character; they are imperatives, they demand absolute obedience, and hence the following of them is morally obligatory. An important duty of a Christian, then, is to support the weak. For this, they must go to the extent of working and providing for others. Christians and leaders must humble themselves even to the point of taking up manual labor for this purpose. Christians should have the right attitude towards wealth so that they may use it responsibly; the wealthy must give generously to the poor; moreover, they ought to know how and when to use their wealth for the service of the needy.

Our examination of the selected text proves that it is a relevant one for present-day Christians. It challenges the Church and her members to a socially oriented ethical life, for which God's grace is necessary. Without the grace of Jesus neither communion nor charity is possible. We conclude that only truly grace-filled individuals can strip themselves of greed, demonstrate generosity, undertake manual labor, be examples to others, and above all have the mind of Christ, who said, "It is more blessed to give than to receive." The guidance of grace should be present among individuals and communities.

The Church, as a community of persons and an institution, has the duty to be involved in the social life and issues of her members and seek remedies for them. One of her prime ministries must be to extinguish the physical hunger and thirst of the people and her children. This implies a great responsibility whereby the Church today must primarily deal with the issue of wealth and private property. Only a right attitude to wealth can inspire and motivate people to create generous hearts. Responsible use of wealth is the main point here. Through an awareness of their responsibility for every individual in society, Christians should come to respect people and their struggles in life, to elevate the dignity of every labor and person to achieve the desired Christian standard.

Bibliography

1. Primary Sources

Alexander, T. D., and D. W. Baker, Ed. *DOTP*. Downers Grove: InterVarsity Press, 2003.

Aquinas. *ST*.

Arnold, B. T., and H. G. M. Williamson, ed. *DOTHB*. Downers Grove: InterVarsity Press, 2005.

Augustine. *Confessions*. In vol. 1 of the *NPNF*. Series 1. Edited by P. Schaff. 1886–89, 14 vols. repr. Peabody: Hendrickson, 1994.

Aune, D. E. *The Westminster Dictionary of New Testament and Early Christian Literature and Rhetoric*. Louisville, KY: John Knox, 2003.

Balz, H., and G. Schneider, ed. *EDNT*. 3 vols. Grand Rapids: Eerdmans, 1990–93.

Becker, L. C., and C. B. Becker, ed. *Encyclopedia of Ethics*. 3 vols. New York: Routledge, 2001.

Biblia Hebraica Stuttgartensia. Fifth edition. Stuttgart: Deutsche Bibelgesellschaft, 1997.

Biblia Sacra iuxta Vulgatam Versionem. Stuttgart: Württembergische Bibelanstalt, 1969.

CCC. Vatican City: Libreria Editrice Vaticana, 1993.

Chrysostom, J. *Homilies on the Acts of the Apostles*. In vol. 11 of the *NPNF*. Series 1. Edited by P. Schaff. 1886–89, 14 vols. repr. Peabody: Hendrickson, 1994.

Congregation for the Doctrine of the Faith. *Instruction on Christian Freedom and Liberation*. 22 March 1986.

Cyprian, *Treatise 5, An Address to Demetrianus*. In vol. 5 of the *ANF*. Edited by R. Alexander and J. Donaldson. 1885–87. 10 vols. repr. Grand Rapids: Eerdmans, 2001.

Danker, F. W. et.al., ed. *A Greek-English Lexicon of the New Testament and other Early Christian Literature.* 3rd edition. BDAG. Chicago: The University of Chicago Press, 2000.

de Liguori, A. M. *Dignity and Duties of the Priest or Selva.* Edited by E. Grimm. New York: Benziger Brothers, 1889.

DMT. Compiled under the Direction of Francesco Cardinal Robert. Edited under the direction of P. Palazzini. London: Burns and Oats, 1962.

Freedman, D. N., ed. *ABD.* 6 vols. New York: Doubleday, 1992.

Hawthorne, G. F., and R. P. Martin, ed. *DPL.* Downers Grove: InterVarsity Press, 1993.

John XXIII, Pope. *MM.* Encyclical on Christianity and Social Progress. 15 May 1961.

———. *PT.* Encyclical on Establishing Universal Peace in Truth, Justice, Charity, and Liberty. 11 April 1963.

John Paul II, Pope. *LE.* Encyclical on Human Work. 14 September 1981.

———. *Centesimus Annus.* Encyclical on the Hundredth Anniversary of *RN.* 1 May 1991.

Kittel, G., R. E. Pitkin, and G. Friedrich, ed. *TDNT.* 10 vols. Translated by Geoffrey and W. Bromiley. Grand Rapids: Eerdmans, 1981–82.

Leo XIII, Pope. *RN.* Encyclical on Capital and Labor. 15 May 1891.

Loeb Classical Library. For all citations and quotations of classical literature including Philo and Josephus. Cambridge: Harvard University Press, 1928–35.

Longmann III, T., and P. Enns, ed. *DOTWPW.* Downers Grove: InterVarsity Press, 2008.

Marshall, I. H., ed. *Moulton and Geden Concordance to the Greek New Testament.* 6th ed. London: T&T Clark, 2002.

Novum Testamentum Graece. Nestle-Aland 28th edition. Stuttgart: Deutsche Bibelgesell-schaft, 2012.

NJB. London: Darton, Longman & Todd, 1985.

NRSV Catholic Edition Bible. Bangalore: Theological Publications in India, 1993.

Paul VI, Pope. *PP.* Encyclical on the Development of Peoples. 26 March 1967.

Pius X, Pope. *Motu Proprio*: *Fin dalla Prima.* 18 December 1903.

Pius XI, Pope. *QA.* Encyclical on the Reconstruction of the Social Order. 15 May 1931.

Septuaginta. Edited by A. Rahlfs. Stuttgart: Deutsche Bibelgesellschaft, 1935.

Skolnik, F., and M. Berenbaum, ed. *EJ*. 22 vols. Second Edition. Detroit: Thomson and Gale, 2007.

Vatican II. *LG*. Dogmatic Constitution on the Church. 21 November 1964.

Vatican II. *GS*. Pastoral Constitution on the Church in the Modern World. 7 December 1965.

2. Secondary Sources

Agrell, G. *Work, Toil and Sustenance: An Examination of the View of Work in the New Testament, Taking in Consideration Views Found in Old Testament, Intertestamental, and early Rabbinic Writings*. Translated by Stephen Westerholm. Verbum: Håkan Ohlssons, 1976.

Allen, O. W. *The Death of Herod: The Narrative and Theological Function of Retribution in Luke-Acts*. SBLDS 158; Atlanta: Scholars Press, 1997.

Argyle, A. W. "The Influence of the Testaments of the Twelve Patriarchs upon the New Testament." *ET* 63 (1951–52): 256–58.

Aubert, B. *The Shepherd-Flock Motif in the Miletus Discourse (Acts 20:17–38) against Its Historical Background*. SBL 124. New York: Peter Lang, 2009.

Auler, S. "More than a Gift: Revisiting Paul's Collection for Jerusalem and the Pilgrimage of Gentiles." *JSPL* 6.2 (2016): 143–60.

Aune, D. E. *The New Testament in its Literary Environment*. Philadelphia, PA: The Westminster Press, 1989.

———. *Jesus, Gospel Tradition and Paul in the Context of Jewish and Greco-Roman Antiquity: Collected Essays II*. WUNT 303. Tübingen: Mohr Siebeck, 2013.

Baltzer, K. *The Covenant Formulary in Old Testament, Jewish, and Early Christian Writings*. Philadelphia, PA: Fortress Press, 1971.

Barbi, A. "Il Paolinismo degli Atti." *RivBib* 34 (1986): 471–518.

Barclay, J. M. *Paul and the Gift*. Grand Rapids: Eerdmans, 2015.

Barram, M. D. *Mission and Moral Reflection in Paul*. SBL 75. New York: Peter Lang, 2006.

Barrett, C. K. "Paul's Address to the Ephesian Elders." Pages 107–21 in *God's Christ and His People: Studies in Honour of Nils Alstrup Dahl*. Edited by J. Jervell and W. A. Meeks. Oslo: Universitetforlaget, 1978.

Barton, B. B., D. Veerman, and N. S. Wilson. *Romans*. LABC. Wheaton: Tyndale House Publishers, 1992.

Bauckham, R. *Jesus and the Eyewitnesses: The Gospels as Eyewitness Testimony*. Grand Rapids: Eerdmans, 2017.

Baur, F. C. *Paul the Apostle of Jesus Christ: His Life and Works, his Epistle and his Teaching*. Peabody, MA: Hendrickson, 2003.

Bayer, H. F. "The Preaching of Peter in Acts." Pages 257–74 in *Witness to the Gospel: The Theology of Acts*. Edited by I. H. Marshall and D. Peterson. Grand Rapids: Eerdmans, 1998.

Best, E. *A Commentary on the First and Second Epistles to the Thessalonians*. London: Adam & Charles Black, 1972.

Betz, H. D. *Galatians: A Commentary on Paul's Letter to the Churches in Galatia*. Hermeneia. Philadelphia, PA: Fortress Press, 1979.

———. *2 Corinthians 8 and 9: A Commentary on Two Administrative Letters of the Apostle Paul*. Hermeneia. Philadelphia, PA: Fortress Press, 1985.

Birch, B. C. "The First and Second Books of Samuel: Introduction, Commentary, and Reflections." Pages 947–1383 in *Numbers, Deuteronomy, Introduction to Narrative Literature, Joshua, Judges, Ruth, 1 & 2 Samuel*. Vol. 2 of *NIB*. Edited by L. E. Keck. Nashville: Abingdon Press, 1998.

Bock, D. L. *Luke 2. 9,51–24,53*. BECNT 3b. Grand Rapids: Baker Book House, 1996.

———. *Acts*. BECNT. Grand Rapids: Baker Academics, 2007.

Bodner, K. *1 Samuel: A Narrative Commentary*. Sheffield: Phoenix Press, 2008.

Boling, R. G. *Joshua: A New Translation with Notes and Commentary*. AB 6. Garden City, NY: Doubleday, 1982.

Bonz, M. P. *The Past as Legacy: Luke-Acts and Ancient Epic*. Minneapolis: Fortress Press, 2000.

Borgmann, P. *The Way according to Luke: Hearing the Whole Story of Luke-Acts*. Grand Rapids: Eerdmans, 2006.

Bornemann, W. *Die Thessalonicherbriefe*. Göttingen: Vandenhoeck & Ruprecht, 1894.

Bornkamm, G. *Paul*. Translated by D. M. G. Stalker. San Francisco: Harper & Row, 1971.

Brawley, R. L. "Paul in Acts: Aspects of Structure and Characterization." Pages 90–105 in *SBLSP* of 1988. Edited by D. J. Lull. Atlanta: Scholars Press, 1988.

Bruce, F. F. *The Acts of the Apostles: The Greek Text with Introduction and Commentary*. London: Tyndale Press, 1951.

———. *Paul: Apostle of the Heart Set Free*. Grand Rapids: Eerdmans, 1977.

———. *1 and 2 Thessalonians*. WBC 45. Dallas: Word Books, 1982.

Bruckner, J. K. "Ethics." Pages 224–40 in *DOTP*. Edited by D. W. Baker. Downers Grove: InterVarsity Press, 2002.

Budesheim, T. L. "Paul's Abschiedsrede in the Acts of the Apostles." *HTR* 69 (1976): 9–30.

Bultmann, R. "The Problem of Ethics in Paul." Translated by Christoph W. Stenschke. Pages 195–216 in *Understanding Paul's Ethics: Twentieth Century Approaches*. Edited by B. S. Rosner. Grand Rapids: Eerdmans, 1995.

Burridge, R. A. "Gospels and Acts." Pages 507–32 in *Handbook of Classical Rhetoric in the Hellenistic Period 330 BC–AD 400*. Edited by S. E. Porter. Leiden: Brill, 1997.

———. *What are the Gospels? A Comparison with Greco-Roman Biography*. Second Edition. Grand Rapids: Eerdmans, 2004.

Butler, T. C. *Joshua*: *13–24*. WBC 7b. Grand Rapids: Zondervan, 2014. [Second Edition].

Cadbury, H. J. *The Making of Luke-Acts*. London: Macmillan, 1927.

Calduch-Benages, N. "Il Lavoro in Proverbi e Siracide." Pages 21–37 in *Il Lavoro Opera delle Nostre Mani*. PSV 52. Bologna: Centro Editoriale Dehoniano, 2005.

Campbell, W. S. *The "We" Passages in the Acts of the Apostles: The Narrator as a Narrative Character.* Atlanta: SBL, 2007.

Carey, C. "Rhetorical Means of Persuasion." Pages 26–45 in *Persuasion: Greek Rhetoric in Action*. Edited by I. Worthington. London: Routledge, 1994.

Carroll, J. T. "Literary and Social Dimensions of Luke's Apology for Paul." Pages 106–118 in *SBLSP* of 1988. Edited by D. J. Lull. Atlanta: Scholars Press, 1988.

Castelli, E. A. *Imitating Paul: A Discourse of Power*. Louisville, KY: John Knox, 1991.

Charles, R. H. "The Testaments of the Twelve Patriarchs in Relation to the New Testament." *Exp* 7 (1909): 118–19.

Childress, J. F. "Scripture and Christian Ethics." Pages 276–88 in *Readings in Moral Theology No. 4: The Use of Scripture in Moral Theology*. Edited by C. E. Curran and R. A. McCormick. New York: Paulist Press, 1984.

Christensen, D. L. *Deuteronomy 21:10–34:12*. WBC 6b. Nashville: Thomas Nelson Publishers, 2002.

Christiansen, D. "Commentary on *Pacem in Terris*." Pages 217–43 in *Modern Catholic Social Teaching: Commentaries and Interpretations*. Edited by K. R. Himes. Washington DC: Georgetown University Press, 2005.

Civardi, L. and P. Pavan, ed. *Il Lavoro: Encyclopedia*. Roma: Coletti Editore, 1963.

Clements, R. E. "The Book of Deuteronomy: Introduction, Commentary, and Reflections." Pages 269–538 in *Numbers, Deuteronomy, Introduction to Narrative Literature, Joshua, Judges, Ruth, 1 & 2 Samuel*. Vol. 2 of *NIB*. Edited by L. E. Keck. Nashville: Abingdon Press, 1998.

Cone, O. *Paul: The Man, the Missionary, and the Teacher*. London: Adam & Charles Black, 1898.

Conzelmann, H. *The Theology of St. Luke*. Translated by Geoffrey Buswell. London: Faber and Faber, 1960.

———. *Die Apostelgeschichte*. Tübingen: Mohr Siebeck, 1972.

———. *Acts of the Apostles: A Commentary on the Acts of the Apostles*. Philadelphia, PA: Fortress Press, 1987.

Collins, J. J. "Testaments." Pages 325–55 in *Jewish Writings of the Second Temple Period: Apocrypha, Pseudepigrapha, Qumran Sectarian Writings, Philo, Josephus*. Edited by M. E. Stone. CRINT 2.2. Assen: Van Gorcum, 1984.

Cosgrove, C. H. "The Divine δεῖ in Luke-Acts." *NT* 26 (1984): 168–90.

Craddock, F. B. *Luke*. Interpr. Louisville, KY: John Knox, 1990.

Cruz, H. *Christological Motives and Motivated Actions in Pauline Paraenesis*. EHST 396. Frankfurt: Peter Lang, 1990.

Cullinan, M. P. *Victor Paul Furnish's Theology of Ethics in St. Paul: An Ethic of Transforming Grace*. Rome: Editiones Academiae Alfonsianae, 2007.

Curran, C. E. and Richard A. McCormick, ed. *The Use of Scripture in Moral Theology*. New York: Paulist Press, 1984.

De Boer, W. P. *The Imitation of Paul: An Exegetical Study*. Kampen: J. H. Kok, 1962.

Degenhardt, H. *Lukas Evangelist der Armen: Besitz und Besitzversicht in den Lukanischen Schriften: Eine Tradition und Redaktionsgeschichtliche Untersuchung*. Stuttgart: Kath. Bibelwerk, 1965.

Deissmann, A. *St. Paul: A Study in Social and Religious History*. London: Hodder and Stoughton, 1911.

Dennison, W. "Indicative and Imperative: The Basic Structure of Pauline Ethics." *CTJ* 14 (1979): 55–78.

Dibelius, M. *Studies in the Acts of the Apostles*. Edited by H. Greeven. London: SCM Press, 1973.

———. "The Speeches in Acts and Ancient Historiography." Pages 138–85 in *Studies in the Acts of the Apostles*. Edited by H. Greeven. London: SCM Press, 1973.

Di Lella, A. A. "The Deuteronomic Background of the Farewell Discourse in Tobit 14:3–11." *CBQ* 41 (1979): 380–81.

———. "A Study of Tobit 14:10 and its Intertextual Parallels." *CBQ* 71 (2009): 497–506.

Dodd, B. *Paul's Paradigmatic "I": Personal Example as Literary Strategy*. Sheffield: Academic Press, 1999.

Doran, R. "The First Book of Maccabees. Introduction, Commentary, and Reflections." Pages 1–178 in *1 & 2 Maccabees, Introduction to Hebrew Poetry, Job, Psalms*. Vol. 4 of *NIB*. Edited by L. E. Keck. Nashville: Abingdon Press, 1996.

Downs, D. J. *The Offering of the Gentiles: Paul's Collection for Jerusalem in its Chronological, Cultural, and Cultic Contexts.* WUNT 2.248. Tübingen: Mohr Siebeck, 2008.

Dunn, J. D. *Romans 9–16*. WBC 38b. Dallas: Word Books, 1988.

Dupont, J. *Le Discourse de Milet: Testament Pastoral de Saint Paul (Actes 20:18-36)*. LeDiv 32. Paris: Cerf, 1962.

———. *Le Beatitudini.* 2 vols. Vol. 1 *Le Beatitudini*. Parola di Dio 7. Roma: Paoline, 1972. Vol. 2 *Le Beatitudini: Gli Evangelisti*. Parola di Dio 14. Roma: Paoline, 1977.

Eastman, B. *The Significance of Grace in the Letters of Paul.* SBL 11. New York: Peter Lang, 1999.

Eastman, S. "The Foolish Father and the Economics of Grace." *ET* 117.10 (2006): 402–405.

Edwards, D. R. "Dress and Ornamentation." Pages 232–38 in vol. 2 of *ABD*. Edited by D. N. Freedman. 6 vols. New York: Doubleday, 1992.

Edwards, T. C. *A Commentary on the First Epistle to the Corinthians*. London: Hodder and Stoughton, 1885. [Second edition].

Eisenberg, R. L. *The 613 Mitzvot: A Contemporary Guide to the Commandments of Judaism*. Rockville, MD: Schreiber Publishing, 2005.

Elbert, P. "Paul of the Miletus Speech and 1 Thessalonians: Critique and Considerations." *ZNW* 95 (2004): 258–68.

Enslin, M. S. "Luke, The Literary Physician." Pages 135–43 in *Studies in New Testament and Early Christian Literature: Essays in Honor of Alen P. Wikgren*. NTSup 33. Edited by D. E. Aune, H. J. Cadbury, and A. P. Wikgren. Leiden: Brill, 1972.

Eubank, N. "Almsgiving is 'the Commandment': A Note on 1 Timothy 6:6–19." *NTS* 58.1 (2012): 144–50.

Exum, C. and C. Talbert. "The Structure of Paul's Speech to the Ephesian Elders (Acts 20:18–35)." *CBQ* 29 (1967): 233–36.

Fiore, B. *The Function of Personal Example in the Socratic and Pastoral Epistles*. Rome: Biblical Institute Press, 1986.

———. "Paul, Exemplification, and Imitation." Pages 228–57 in *Paul in the Greco-Roman World: A Handbook*. Edited by J. P. Sampley. Harrisburg, PA: Trinity Press International, 2003.

Fiorenza, E. S. *Rhetoric and Ethic: The Politics of Biblical Studies.* Minneapolis: Fortress Press, 1999.

Fisher, N. "Citizens, Foreigners and Slaves in Greek Society." Pages 327–49 in *A Companion to the Classical Greek World*. Edited by K. H. Kinzl. Malden: Blackwell, 2006.

Fornara, C. W. *The Nature of History in Ancient Greece and Rome*. Berkeley: University of California Press, 1983.

Furnish, V. P. *Theology and Ethics in Paul*. Nashville: Abingdon, 1968.

Fitzmyer, J. A. *The Gospel According to Luke X–XXIV*. AB 28a. Garden City, NY: Doubleday, 1985.

———. *The Acts of the Apostles: A New Translation with Introduction and Commentary*. New York: Doubleday, 1998.

Gärtner, B. *The Areopagus Speech and Natural Revelation*. Uppsala: Gleerup, 1955.

Gardner, P. "The Speeches of St. Paul in Acts." Pages 379–419 in *Cambridge Biblical Essays*. Edited by H. B. Swete. London: MacMillan, 1909.

Garnsey, P. and R. Saller. *The Roman Empire: Economy, Society and Culture*. Berkeley: University of California Press, 1987.

Gaventa, B. R. "Galatians 1 & 2: Autobiography as Paradigm," *NovT* 28.4 (1986): 309–26.

———. *The Acts of the Apostles*. Abington New Testament Commentaries. Nashville: Abington, 2003.

———. "Theology and Ecclesiology in the Miletus Speech: Reflections on Content and Context." *NTS* 50 (2004): 36–52.

Geoghegan, A. T. *The Attitude towards Labor in Early Christianity and Ancient Culture*. The Catholic University of America. SCA 6. Washington DC: The CUA Press, 1945.

Georgi, D. *The Opponents of Paul in Second Corinthians*. Philadelphia, PA: Fortress, 1986.

———. *Remembering the Poor. The History of Paul's Collection for Jerusalem*. Nashville: Abingdon Press, 1992.

Gieniusz, A. "Paolo: Lavorare con le Proprie Mani e Compiere Fatiche Apostoliche." Pages 175–96 in *Il Lavoro Opera delle Nostre Mani*. PSV 52. Bologna: Centro Editoriale Dehoniano, 2005.

Goodenough, E. R. "The Perspective of Acts." Pages 51–59 in *Studies in Luke-Acts: Essays in Honor of Paul Schubert*. Edited by L. E. Keck and J. L. Martyn. London: SPCK, 1968.

Goulet, D. "Economic Systems, Middle Way Theories, and Third World Realities." Pages 340–65 in *Readings in Moral Theology no. 5: Official Catholic Teaching*. Edited by C. E. Curran and R. A. McCormick. New York: Paulist Press, 1986.

Guzzetti, G. B. "Il Lavoro nei suoi Aspetti Morali." Pages 209–49 in *Il Lavoro: Enciclopedia*. Edited by L. Civardi, and P. Pavan. Roma: Colletti Editore, 1963.

Hänchen, E. *Die Apostelgeschichte*. 4 vols. Göttingen: Vandenhoeck & Ruprecht, 1956–1977.

———. *The Acts of the Apostles: A Commentary*. [Trans. of *Die Apostelgeschichte*]. Oxford: Basil Blackwell, 1971.

Haldane, R. *Exposition of the Epistle to the Romans*. Escondido: Electronic Edition by the Ephesians Four Group, 1999.

Hallo, W. W. "The Birth of Rhetoric." Pages 25–46 in *Rhetoric before and beyond the Greeks*. Edited by C. S. Lipson, and R. A. Binkley. Albany, NY: State University of New York Press, 2004.

Hands, A. R. *Charities and Social Aid in Greece and Rome*. Ithaca, NY: Cornell University Press, 1968.

Hansen, G. W. "The Preaching and Defense of Paul." Pages 295–324 in *Witness to the Gospel: The Theology of Acts*. Edited by I. H. Marshall and D. Peterson. Grand Rapids: Eerdmans, 1998.

Harrelson, W. "The Significance of "Last Words" for Intertestamental Ethics." Pages 203–13 in *Essays in Old Testament Ethics*. Edited by J. L. Crenshaw and John T. Willis. New York: KTAV, 1974.

von Harnack, A. *The Acts of the Apostles*. Translated by J. R. Wilkinson. London: Williams & Norgate, 1909.

Harril, A. J. "Paul and Slavery." Pages 575–607 in *Paul in the Greco-Roman World: A Handbook*. Edited by J. P. Sampley. Harrisburg, PA: Trinity Press International, 2003.

Harrison, J. R. *Paul's Language of Grace in its Greco-Roman Context*. WUNT 2.172. Tübingen: Mohr Siebeck, 2003.

Hays, R. B. *The Moral Vision of the New Testament: Community, Cross, New Creation. A Contemporary Introduction to New Testament Ethics*. San Francisco: Harper San Francisco, 1996.

Hays, C. M. *Luke's Wealth Ethics: A Study in their Coherence and Character*. WUNT 2.275 Tübingen: Mohr Siebeck, 2010.

Hemer, C. J. *The Book of Acts in the Setting of Hellenistic History*. WUNT 49. Tübingen: Mohr Siebeck, 1989.

———. "The Speeches of Acts: I. The Ephesian Elders at Miletus." *TynBull* 40.1 (1989): 77–85.

Hock, R. F. "Paul's Tent-Making and the Problem of his Social Class." *JBL* 97 (1978): 555–64.

———. "The Workshop as a Social Setting for Paul's Missionary Preaching." *CBQ* 41 (1979): 438–50.

———. *The Social Context of Paul's Ministry. Tent Making and Apostleship*. Philadelphia, PA: Fortress Press, 1980.

Hollander, H. W. *Joseph as an Ethical Model in the Testament of the Twelve Patriarchs*. SVTP 6. Leiden: Brill, 1981.

Horn, F. W. "Holy Spirit." Pages 260–80 in vol. 3 of *ABD*. Edited by D. N. Freedman. 6 vols. New York: Doubleday, 1992.

Horsley, G. H. R. "Speeches and Dialogues in Acts." *NTS* 32.4 (1986): 609–14.

Hultgren, A. J. *The Parables of Jesus: A Commentary*. Grand Rapids Eerdmans, 2002.

Hurd, J. C. *The Origin of First Corinthians*. London: SPCK, 1965.

Husslein, J. *Work, Wealth, and Wages*. Chicago: Matre & Company, 1921.

———. *Bible and Labor*. London; Edinburgh: Sands & Co., 1924.

Ireland, D. J. "A History of Recent Interpretation of the Parable of the Unjust Steward (Luke 16:1–13)." *WTJ* 51 (1989): 293–318.

———. *Stewardship and the Kingdom of God: An Historical, Exegetical, and Contextual Study of the Parable of the Unjust Steward*. NTSup 70. Leiden: Brill, 1992.

Jensen, M. "Imitating Paul, Imitating Christ: How does Imitation Work as a Moral Concept?" *Churchman* 124.1 (2010): 17–36.

Jeremias, J. *Unknown Sayings of Jesus*. London: SPCK, 1958.

Jervell, J. "Paulus-Der Lehrer Israels: Zu den Apologetischen Paulusreden in der Apostelgeschichte." *NT* 10 (1968): 164–90.

———. "Paul in the Acts of Apostles: Tradition, History, Theology." Pages 297–306 in *Les Actes des Apôtres: Traditions, redaction, théologie*. Edited by J. Kremer. BEThL 48. Leuven: Leuven University Press, 1979.

———. "Paulus in der Apostelgeschichte und die Geschichte des Urchristentums." *NTS* 32 (1986): 378–92.

Johnson, L. T. *The Literary Function of Possessions in Luke-Acts*. SBLDS 39. Missoula: Scholars Press, 1977.

———. *Sharing Possessions: Mandate and Symbol of Faith*. Philadelphia, PA: Fortress Press, 1981.

———. *The Acts of the Apostles*. Sacra Pagina 5. Collegeville: The Liturgical Press, 1992.

———. "Luke-Acts, Book of." Pages 403–20 in vol. 4 of *ABD*. Edited by D. N. Freedman. 6 vols. New York: Doubleday, 1992.

Joubert, S. *Paul as Benefactor: Reciprocity, Strategy, and Theological Reflection in Paul's Collection*. WUNT 2.124. Tübingen: Mohr Siebeck, 2000.

Karris, R. J. "Poor and Rich: The Lucan *Sitz im Leben*." Pages 112–25 in *Perspectives on Luke-Acts*. Danville, CA: Association of Baptist Professors of Religion, 1978.

Kaiser, W. C. *Toward Old Testament Ethics*. Grand Rapids: Academie Books, 1983.

Keck, L. E. "The Poor among the Saints in the New Testament." *ZNW* 56 (1965): 100–29.

———, and M. J. Louis, ed. *Studies in Luke-Acts: Essays Presented in Honor of Paul Schubert*. London: SPCK, 1968.

Keener, C. S. *Acts: An Exegetical Commentary*. 4 vols. Grand Rapids: Baker Academics, 2012–15.

Kennedy, G. A. *The Art of Persuasion in Greece*. New Jersey: Princeton University Press, 1963.

———. *The Art of Rhetoric in the Roman World 300 BC–AD 300*. New Jersey: Princeton University Press, 1972.

———. *New Testament Interpretation through Rhetorical Criticism*. Chapel Hill, NC: The University of North Carolina Press, 1984.

Kilgallen, J. J. "Acts 20:35 and Thucydides 2.97.4." *JBL* 112 (1993): 312–14.

Kistemaker, S. J. *Exposition of the Acts of the Apostles*. New Testament Commentary. Grand Rapids: Baker Book House, 1990.

Klein, W. W., C. L. Blomberg, and R. L. Hubbard. *Introduction to Biblical Interpretation*. Nashville: Thomas Nelson, 1993.

Knox, W. L. *Acts of the Apostles*. Cambridge: University Press, 1948.

Kolenkow, A. B. "The Literary Genre "Testament."" Pages 259–67 in *Early Judaism and Its Modern Interpreters*. Edited by R. A. Kraft and G. W. E. Nickelsburg. SBLBMI 2. Atlanta: Scholars Press, 1986.

———. "The Genre Testament and Forecasts of the Future in the Hellenistic Jewish Milieu." *JSJ* 6. (1975): 57–71.

Kugler, R. A. *The Testament of the Twelve Patriarchs*. Sheffield: Academic Press, 2001.

Kurichianil, J. "The Speeches in Acts and the Old Testament." *ITS* 17.2 (1980): 181–86.

———. "Paul in the Acts of the Apostles." *ITS* 45.3 (2008): 255–93.

———. "Portrait of a Minister of the Word in (Acts 20:13–35)." *BiBh* 37 (2011): 247–303.

Kurz, W. S. "Luke 22:14–28 and Greco-Roman and Biblical Farewell Addresses." *JBL* 104.2 (1985): 251–68.

———. *Farewell Addresses in the New Testament*. Collegeville: Luturgical Press, 1990.

———. *Reading Luke-Acts: Dynamics of Biblical Narrative*. Louisville, KY: John Knox, 1993.

Lambrecht, J. "Paul's Farewell Address at Miletus: Acts 20:17–38." Pages 307–37 in *Les Actes des Apôtres: Traditions, rédaction, théologie*. Extrait. Edited by Gembloux and J. Duculot, Leuven: Leuven University Press, Date not Available.

Larkin, W. J. *Acts*. IVPNTC. Downers Grove: InterVarsity Press, 1995.

Lentz, J. C. *Luke's Portrait of Paul*. SNTSMS 77. Cambridge: Cambridge University Press, 1993.

Liefeld, W. L. *Interpreting the Book of Acts*. Grand Rapids: Baker Books, 1995.

Lincoln, A. T. *Ephesians*. WBC 42. Dallas: Word Books, 1990.

Lövestam, E. "Paul's Address at Miletus." *ST* 41 (1987): 1–10.

Long, B. O. *1 Kings with and Introduction to Historical Literature*. Grand Rapids: Eerdmans, 1984.

Longenecker, B. W. *Galatians*. WBC 41. Dallas: Word Books, 1990.

———. *Remember the Poor: Paul, Poverty, and the Greco-Roman World*. Grand Rapids: Cambridge: Eerdmans, 2010.

Lüdemann, G. *Early Christianity according to the Traditions in Acts: A Commentary*. London: SCM, 1987.

———. Assisted by T. Hall. *The Acts of the Apostles: What Really Happened in the Earliest Days of the Church*. Amherst, NY: Prometheus, 2005.

Luz, U. *Matthew 1–7*. Translated by James E. Crouch and Edited by H. Koester. Herm. Minneapolis: Fortress Press, 2007.

Macatangay, F. M. *The Wisdom Instructions in the Book of Tobit*. Berlin; New York: De Gruyter, 2011.

MacDonald, D. R. *Does the New Testament Imitate Homer?: Four Cases from the Acts of the Apostles*. New Haven, CT: Yale University, 2003.

———. "Paul's farewell to the Ephesian Elders and Hector's Farewell to Andromache: A Strategic Imitation of Homer's *Illiad*." Pages 189–203 in *Contextualizing Acts: Lucan Narrative and Greco-Roman Discourse*. Edited by T. Penner and C. V. Stichele. SBLSymS 20. Altanta: SBL, 2003.

Maddox, R. *The Purpose of Luke-Acts*. Göttingen: Vandenhoeck & Ruprecht, 1982.

Malherbe, A. J. *Moral Exhortation: A Greco-Roman Sourcebook*. Philadelphia, PA: Westminster Press, 1986.

———. *Paul and the Popular Philosophers*. Minneapolis: Fortress Press, 1989, 2006.

Malina, B. "Wealth and Poverty in the New Testament and Its World." *Interp.* 41 (1987): 354–367.

Marguerat, D. L. ed. *Reception of Paulinism in Acts = Réception du Paulinisme dans les Actes des Apôtres*. BETL 229. Leuven: Peeters, 2009.

———. *Paul in Acts and Paul in his Letters*. WUNT 310. Tubingen: Mohr Siebeck, 2013.

Marshall, I. H. *Luke: Historian and Theologian*. Carlisle: Paternoster, 1970.

———. *The Acts of the Apostles: An Introduction and Commentary*. Leicester: InterVarsity Press, 1989.

Marxsen, W. *New Testament Foundations for Christian Ethics*. Translated by O. C. Dean. Edinburgh: T&T Clark, 1993.

Mason, S. *Josephus and the New Testament*. Peabody: Hendrickson, 2003.

Martin, R. P. *2 Corinthians*. WBC 40. Dallas: Word Books, 1986.

McCarter, P. K. *I Samuel: A New Translation with Introduction and Commentary*. AB 8. Garden City, NY: Doubleday, 1980.

McFarland, O. *God and Grace in Philo and Paul*. NTSup 164. Leiden: Brill, 2016.

McKnight, S. "Collection for the Saints." Pages 143–47 in *Dictionary of Paul and his Letters*. G. F. Hawthorne, and R. P. Martin, ed. Downers Grove: InterVarsity Press, 1993.

Mich, M. L. "Commentary on *Mater et Magistra*." Pages 191–216 in *Modern Catholic Social Teaching: Commentaries and Interpretations*. Edited by K. R. Himes. Washington DC: Georgetown University Press, 2005.

Michel, H. *Die Abschiedsrede des Paulus an die Kirche: Apg 20:17–38: Motivgeschichte und Theologische Bedeutung*. SANT 35. München: Kösel Verlag, 1973.

Miller, P. D. "Divine Command and Beyond: The Ethics of the Commandments." Pages 12–29 in *The Ten Commandments: The Reciprocity of Faithfulness*. Edited by W. P. Brown. LTE. Louisville, KY: John Knox, 2004.

———. *The Ten Commandments*. Interp. Louisville, KY: John Knox, 2009.

Mitchell, M. M. *Paul and the Rhetoric of Reconciliation: An Exegetical Investigation of the Language and Composition of 1 Corinthians*. HUTh 28. Tubingen: Mohr Siebeck, 1991.

Moffatt, J. *Grace in the New Testament*. New York: Richard R. Smith, 1931.

Moore, C. A. *Tobit: A New Translation with Introduction and Commentary*. AB 40A. Garden City, NY: Doubleday, 1996.

Moran, W. L. "The Conclusion of the Decalogue (Ex 20:17 = Deut 5:21)." *CBQ* 29 (1967): 543–54.

Mount, C. *Pauline Christianity: Luke-Acts and the Legacy of Paul*. NTSup 104. Leiden: Brill, 2002.

Munch, P. A. "The Spirits in the Testaments of the Twelve Patriarchs." *AcOr* 13 (1935): 257–63.

Munck, J. "Discours d'adieu dans le Nouveau Testament et dans la Littérature Biblique." Pages 155–70 in *Aux Sources de la Tradition Chrétienne: Mélanges Offerts à M. Maurice Goguel à l'occasion de son soixante-dixième Anniversaire*. BT(N). Neuchatel: Delachaux & Niestle, 1950.

———. *Paulus und die Heilgeschichte*. AJutT 26. København: Universitetsforlaget i Aarhus, 1954.

———. *Paul and the Salvation of the Mankind.* London: SCM Press, 1959.

———. *The Acts of the Apostles*. Revised by William F. Albright and C. S. Mann. AYBC 31. Garden City, NY: Doubleday, 1967.

Neudorfer, H. W. "The Speech of Stephen." Pages 275–94 in *Witness to the Gospel: The Theology of Acts.* Edited by I. H. Marshall and David Peterson. Grand Rapids: Eerdmans, 1998.

Neyrey, J. H. "Josephus' *Vita* and the Encomium: A Native Model of Personality." *JSJ* 25 (1994): 177–206.

Nickle, K. F. *The Collection: A Study in Paul's Strategy*. SBT 48. London: SCM, 1966.

Nolland, J. "Grace as Power." *NT* 28 (1986): 26–31.

———. "Luke's Use of χάρις." *NTS* 32.4 (1986): 614–20.

———. *Luke 1:1–9:20*. WBC 35a. Dallas: Word Books, 1993.

———. *Luke 9:21–18:34*. WBC 35b. Dallas: Word Books, 1993.

von Nordheim, E. *Die Lehre Der Alten. I. Das Testament als Literaturgattung im Judentum der Hellenistisch-Römischen Zeit*. ALGHJ 13. Leiden: Brill, 1980.

Noth, M. *The Deuteronomistic History*. JSOTS 15. Sheffield: Academic Press, 1991.

Novak, M. "The Bias against Democratic Capitalism." Pages 331–39 in *Readings in Moral Theology no. 5: Official Catholic Teaching*. Edited by C. E. Curran and R. A. McCormick. New York: Paulist Press, 1986.

Nowell, I. "The Book of Tobit: Introduction, Commentary, and Reflections." Pages 973–1071 in *1 & 2 Kings, 1 & 2 Chronicles, Ezra, Nehemiah,*

Esther, Tobit, Judith. Vol. 3 of *NIB*. Edited by L. E. Keck. Nashville: Abingdon Press, 1999.

Ogereau, J. M. "The Jerusalem Collection as κοινωνία: Paul's Global Politics of Socio-Economic Equality and Solidarity." *NTS* 58 (2012): 360–78.

O'Toole, R. F. "What Role Does Jesus' Saying in Acts 20:35 Play in Paul's Address to the Ephesian Elders?" *Bib* 75 (1994): 329–49.

Padilla, O. *The Speeches of Outsiders in Acts: Poetics, Theology and Historiography*. Cambridge: Cambridge University Press, 2008.

Paley, W. *Horae Paulinae: or The Truth of the Scripture History of St. Paul Evinced by a Comparison of the Epistles which Bear his Name with the Acts of the Apostles, and with One Another*. London: Longman, 1838.

Parsenios, G. L. *Departure and Consolation: The Johannine Farewell Discourses in Light of Greco-Roman Literature*. NTSup 117. Leiden: Brill, 2005.

Patte, D. *Ethics of Biblical Interpretation: A Reevaluation*. Louisville, KY: John Knox, 1995.

Pepe, C. *The Genres of Rhetorical Speeches in Greek and Roman Antiquity*. Leiden: Brill, 2013.

Pereira, F. *Ephesus: Climax of Universalism in Luke-Acts: A Redaction Critical Study of Paul's Ephesian Ministry (Acts 18:23–20:1)*. Anand: Gujarat Sahitya Prakash, 1983.

Pernot, L. *Rhetoric in Antiquity*, Translated by W. E. Higgins. Washington DC: The Catholic University of America Press, 2005.

Pervo, R. I. *Profit with Delight: The Literary Genre of the Acts of the Apostles*. Philadelphia, PA: Fortress Press, 1987.

———. *Luke's Story of Paul*. Minneapolis: Fortress Press, 1990.

———. *Dating Acts: Between the Evangelists and the Apologists*. Santa Rosa, CA: Polebridge Press, 2006.

———. *Acts: A Commentary*. Edited by H. W. Attridge. Minneapolis: Fortress Press, 2009.

———. "The Paul of Acts *and* the Paul of the Letters: Aspects of Luke as an Interpreter of the *Corpus Paulinum*." Pages 141–55 in *Reception of Paulinism in Acts = Réception du Paulinisme dans les Actes des Apôtres*. Edited by D. L. Marguerat. BEThL 229. Leuven: Peeters, 2009.

Peterson, D. "The Motif of Fulfillment and the Purpose of Luke-Acts." Pages 83–104 in *The Book of Acts in Its Ancient Literary Setting*. Vol. 1 of *BAFCS*. Edited by B. W. Winter and A. D. Clark. Grand Rapids: Eerdmans, 1993.

———. *The Acts of the Apostles*. PNTC. Grand Rapids: Eerdmans, 2009.

Phillips, T. E. Ed. *Acts and Ethics*. Sheffield: Academic Press, 2005.

Phillips, T. E. "Paul as a Role Model in Acts: The "We" Passages in Acts 16 and Beyond." Pages 49–63 in *Acts and Ethics*. Edited by T. E. Fillips. Sheffield: Phoenix Press, 2005.

———. "The Genre of Acts: Moving towards a Consensus?" *CBR* 4 (2006): 365–96.

Pilgrim, W. E. *Good News to the Poor: Wealth and Poverty in Luke-Acts*. Minneapolis: Augsburg Publishing House, 1981.

Platt, E. E. "Jewelry, Ancient Israelite." Pages 823–34 in vol. 3 of *ABD*. Edited by D. N. Freedman. 6 vols. New York: Doubleday, 1992.

Plümacher, E. "Luke as Historian." Pages 398–402 in vol. 4 of *ABD*. Edited by D. N. Freedman. 6 vols. New York: Doubleday, 1992.

Plummer, A. *The Gospel According to St. Luke*. ICC. Edinburgh: T&T Clark, 1913.

Porter, S. E. *The Paul of Acts: Essays in Literary Criticism, Rhetoric and Theology*. WUNT 115. Tübingen: Mohr Siebeck, 1999.

———. "Was Paulinism a Thing when Luke-Acts was Written?" Pages 1–13 in *Reception of Paulinism in Acts = Réception du Paulinisme dans les Actes des Apôtres*. Edited by D. L. Marguerat. BEThL 229. Leuven: Peeters, 2009.

Powell, M. A. *What Are They Saying about Acts?* New York: Paulist Press, 1991.

Praeder, S. M. "Luke-Acts and the Ancient Novel." Pages 169–292 in *SBLSP* of 1981. Chico, CA: Scholars Press, 1981.

Raaflaub, K. A. "Democracy." Pages 386–415 in *A Companion to the Classical Greek World*. Edited by K. H. Kinzl. Malden: Blackwell, 2006.

Raiser, K. "Theological and Ethical Considerations Regarding Wealth and the Call for Establishing a Greed Line." *ER* 63.3 (2011): 278–94.

Randall, F. "The Pauline Collection for the Saints." *Exp* 4th series vol. 8 (1893): 321–36.

Richardson, A. *The Biblical Doctrine of Work*. EBS 1. London: SCM, 1954.

Roberts, R. "The Beatitude of Giving and Receiving." *ET* 48 (1937): 438–441.

Rosenblatt, M. *Paul the Accused: His Portrait in the Acts of the Apostles*. Collegeville: The Liturgical Press, 1995.

Rosner, B. S. "Acts and Biblical History." Pages 65–82 in *The Book of Acts in Its Ancient Literary Setting*. Vol. 1 of *BAFCS*. Edited by B. W. Winter and A. D. Clark. Grand Rapids: Eerdmans, 1993.

———. *Greed as Idolatry: The Origin and Meaning of Pauline Metaphor*. Grand Rapids: Eerdmans, 2007.

Saldanha, A. "Rediscovering Paul: The Indicative and the Imperative." *ITS* 45 (2008): 381–419.

Sampley, J. P., ed. *Paul in the Greco-Roman World: A Handbook*. Harrisburg, PA: Trinity Press International, 2003.

Satterthwaite, P. E. "Acts against the Background of Classical Rhetoric." Pages 337–79 in *The Book of Acts in Its Ancient Literary Setting*. Vol. 1 of *BAFCS*. Edited by B. W. Winter and A. D. Clark. Grand Rapids: Eerdmans, 1993.

Schiappa, E. *The Beginnings of Rhetorical Theory in Classical Greece*. New Haven, CT: Yale University Press, 1999.

Schubert, P. "The Final Cycle of Speeches in the Book of Acts." *JBL* 87 (1968): 1–16.

Schürmann, H. "Das Testament des Paulus für die Kirche: APG 20:18–35." Pages 108–46 in *Unio Christianorum: Festschrift für Erzbischof Dr. Lorenz Jaeger* [. . .]. Herausgegeben von Othmar Schilling und Heinrich Zimmermann. Padeborn: Bonifacius Druckerei, 1962.

Schumacher, H. *Social Message of the New Testament*. RCS. Milwaukee, WI: The Bruce Publishing Company, 1937.

Seccombe, D. P. *Possessions and the Poor in Luke-Actseufel*. SNTU B 6. Linz: Plöchl, 1982.

Seifrid, M. A. *The Second Letter to the Corinthians*. PNTC. Grand Rapids: Eerdmans, 2014.

Seow, C. "The 1 & 2 Book of Kings." Pages 1–295 in *1 & 2 Kings, 1 & 2 Chronicles, Ezra, Nehemiah, Esther, Tobit, Judith*. Vol. 3 of *NIB*. Edited by L. E. Keck. Nashville: Abingdon Press, 1999.

van Seters, J. *In Search of History: Historiography in the Ancient World and the Origins of Biblical History*. New Haven, CT: Yale University Press, 1983.

Shogren, G. S. "Grace, New Testament." Pages 1086–88 in vol. 2 of *ABD*. Edited by D. N. Freedman. 6 vols. New York: Doubleday, 1992.

Smeaton, G. *The Doctrine of the Atonement according to the Apostles*. Peabody: Hendrickson, 1988.

Smith, A. *Comfort One Another: Reconstructing the Rhetoric and Audience of 1 Thessalonians*. Louisville, KY: John Knox, 1995.

Soards, M. L. *The Speeches in Acts: Their Content, Context and Concerns*. Louisville, KY: John Knox, 1994.

Spaemann, R. "Christian Ethics of Responsibility." Pages 133–48 in *Moral Truth and Moral Tradition: Essays in Honor of Peter Geach and Elizabeth Anscombe*. Edited by L. Gormally. Dublin: Four Courts Press, 1994.

Stählin, G. *Die Apostelgeschichte: Übersetzt und Erklärt*. Das Neue Testament Deutsch 5. Göttingen: Vandenhoeck & Ruprecht, 1962.

Stanley, D. M. "'Become Imitators of me': The Pauline Conception of Apostolic Tradition." *Bib* 40 (1959): 859–77.

———. *Pauline Allusions to the Sayings of Jesus*. Roma: Pontificio Istituto Biblico, 1961.

———. "Imitation in Paul's Letters: Its Significance of His Relationship to Jesus and to His Own Christian Foundations." Pages 127–41 in *From Jesus to Paul: Studies in Honor of Francis Wright Beare*. Edited by P. Richardson and J. C. Hurd. Waterloo, Ontario: Wilfrid Laurier University Press, 1984.

Stauffer, E. *Die Theologie des Neuen Testaments*. Genf: Oikumene, 1945.

Sterling, G. E. *Historiography and Self-Definition: Josephus, Luke-Acts and Apologetic Historiography*. NTSup 64. Leiden: Brill, 1992.

———. "Luke as a Reader of the LXX." Pages 161–79 in *The Gospel of Luke*. Vol. 3 of *Biblical Interpretation in Early Christian Gospels*. Edited by T. R. Hatina. LNTS 376. New York: T&T Clark, 2010.

Steyn, G. J. *Septuagint Quotations in the Context of Petrine and Pauline Speeches of the Acta Apostolorum*. Kampen: Kok Pharos, 1995.

Stube, J. C. *A Graeco-Roman Rhetorical Reading of the Farewell Discourse*. LNTS 309. London: T&T Clark, 2006.

Täger, J. W. *Der Mensch und Sein Heil: Studiem zum Bild des Menschen un der Sicht der Bekehrung bei Lukas*. SNT 14. Gütersloh: Mohn, 1982.

Talbert, C. H. *Literary Patterns, Theological Themes, and the Genre of Luke-Acts*. SBLMS 20. Missoula: Scholars Press, 1974.

———. *Reading Acts: A Literary and Theological Commentary on the Acts of the Apostles*. New York: Crossroad, 1997.

Tannehill, R. C. *The Narrative Unity of Luke-Acts: A Literary Interpretation*. Vol. 2. *The Acts of the Apostles*. Philadelphia, PA: Fortress Press, 1986.

Testa, P. I. *Il Lavoro nella Bibbia*. Assisi: Porziuncola, 1959.

Thackeray, H. St. J. *Josephus: The Man and the Historian*. New York: KTAV, 1967.

Tsumura, D. T. *The First Book of Samuel*. NICOT. Grand Rapids: Eerdmans, 2007.

van Unnik, W. C. "Luke-Acts, a Storm Centre in Contemporary Scholarship." Pages 11–32 in *Studies in Luke-Acts*. Edited by L. E. Keck and J. L. Martyn. London: SPCK, 1968.

Varickasseril, J. "Shepherding through Teaching: Pastoral Reflections on the Acts of the Apostles." *MissTod* 8.3 (2006): 214–26.

Verhey, A. *Remembering Jesus: Christian Community, Scripture, and the Moral Life*. Grand Rapids: Eerdmans, 2005.

Veyne, P. *Bread and Circuses: Historical Sociology and Political Pluralism.* London: Penguin, 1990.

Vickers, B. *In Defense of Rhetoric*. Oxford: Clarendon Press, 1988.

Vielhauer, P. "On the "Paulinism" of Acts." Pages 33–50 in *Studies in Luke-Acts*. Edited by L. E. Keck and J. L. Martyn. London: SPCK, 1968.

Wall, R. W. "The Acts of the Apostles: Introduction, Commentary, and Reflections." Pages 1–368 in *Acts, Introduction to Epistolary Literature, Romans, 1 Corinthians*. Vol. 10 of *NIB*. Edited by L. E. Keck. Nashville: Abingdon Press, 2002.

Wallace, R. W. "Law and Rhetoric: Community Justice in Athenian Courts." Pages 416–31 in *A Companion to the Classical Greek World.* Edited by K. H. Kinzl. Malden: Blackwell, 2006.

Walsh, W. J., and J. P. Langan. "Patristic Social Consciousness." Pages 113–51 in *The Faith that Does Justice: Examining the Christian Sources for Social Change*. Edited by J. C. Haughey. New York: Paulist Press, 1977.

Walton, S. *Leadership and Lifestyle: The Portrait of Paul in the Miletus Speech and 1 Thessalonians*. SNTSMS 108; Cambridge: Cambridge University Press, 2000.

Watson, D. F. "Paul's Speech to the Ephesian Elders (Acts 20:17–38): Epideictic Rhetoric of Farewell." Pages 184–208 in *Persuasive Artistry: Studies in New Testament Rhetoric in Honor of George A. Kennedy*. Edited by D. F. Watson. JSNTS 50. Sheffield: Academic Press, 1991.

Wehnert, J. *Die Wir-Passagen der Apostelgeschichte: Ein Lukanisches Stilmittel aus Jüdischer Tradition*. GTA 40. Göttingen: Vandenhoeck & Ruprecht, 1989.

Weiss, B. *Die Apostelgeschichte*. Leipzig: J. C. Hinrichs, 1983.

Weinfeld, M. "The Covenant of Grant in the Old Testament and in the Ancient Near East." *JAOS* 90 (1970): 189–96.

Wenham, D. "Acts and the Pauline Corpus: II. The Evidence of Parallels." Pages 215–58 in *The Book of Acts in Its Ancient Literary Setting*. Vol. 1 of *BAFCS*. Edited by B. W. Winter and A. D. Clark. Grand Rapids: Eerdmans, 1993.

Wenham, G. J. *Genesis 16–50*. WBC 2. Dallas: Word Books, 1994.

Williams, F. E. "Is Almsgiving the Point of the 'Unjust Steward'?" *JBL* 83 (1964): 293–97.

Williams, J. G. *Those who Ponder Proverbs: Aphoristic Thinking and Biblical Literature*. Sheffield: Almond Press, 1981.

Wilson, J. C. "Tithe." Pages 578–80 in vol. 6 of *ABD*. Edited by D. N. Freedman. 6 vols. New York: Doubleday, 1992.

Winter, B. W. "Official Proceedings and the Forensic Speeches in Acts 24–26." Pages 305–36 in *The Book of Acts in Its Ancient Literary Setting*. Vol. 1 of *BAFCS*. Edited by B. W. Winter and A. D. Clark. Grand Rapids: Eerdmans, 1993.

Wright, C. J. H. "Sabbatical Year." Pages 856–61 in vol. 5 of *ABD*. Edited by D. N. Freedman. 6 vols. New York: Doubleday, 1992.

———. "Jubilee Year of." Pages 1025–30 in vol. 3 of *ABD*. Edited by D. N. Freedman. 6 vols. New York: Doubleday, 1992.

Witherington, B. *The Acts of the Apostles: A Socio-Rhetorical Commentary*. Grand Rapids: Eerdmans, 1998.

3. Internet Sources

Cambridge Dictionary. "Greed." Accessed 02 March 2019. https://dictionary.cambridge.org/ dictionary/english/greed.

Cruxnow.com. "Pope vows to fight nun abuse, urges service, not servitude." Accessed 29 May 2019. https://cruxnow.com/vatican/2019/05/10/pope-vows-to-fight-nun-abuse-urges-service-not-servitude/.

Google.com. "Fragment *LI*." Accessed 29 October 2018. https://sites.google.com/site/thestoiclife/the_teachers/musonius-rufus/fragments/51.

Keydifferences.com. "Morals vs Ethics." Accessed 8 February 2019. https://keydifferences. com/difference-between-morals-and-ethics.html.

de Liguori, A. M. *The School of Christian Perfection*. Trans. Cornelius J. Warren. Boston: Mission Church Press, 1910. www.ecatholic 2000.com. Accessed 1 June 2019. https://www.ecatholic2000.com/liguori/school/perfect.shtml.

de Liguori, A. M. *Prayer: The Great Means of Obtaining Salvation and All the Graces which we Desire of God*. Part II. Ch. 2. Catholic Treasury. Accessed 1 June 2019. http://www.catholictreasury.info/books/prayer/pr19.php.

Matters India. "The (almost) free Work of Sisters." Accessed 8 April 2019. http://mattersindia.com/2018/10/the-almost-free-work-of-sisters/.

Vatican News. "Pope at Audience: Life is a time for giving not possessing." Accessed 5 April 2019. https://www.vaticannews.va/en/pope/news/2018-11/pope-francis-generalaudience-7-november-you-shall-not-steal.html.

Wenham, G. "Grace and Law in the Old Testament." *The Highway*. Accessed 20 May 2019. https://www.the-highway.com/law1_Wenham.html.